Being Divine

Ruth Brandon began her career in current-affairs television, then becoming a freelance writer and journalist. She is the author of three books on aspects of nineteenth-century cultural history – *Singer and the Sewing Machine*, *The Dollar Princesses* and *The Spiritualists* – as well as *The Burning Question*, a history of the anti-nuclear movement, the highly acclaimed *The New Women and the Old Men*, and three detective novels.

Also by Ruth Brandon

NON-FICTION

Singer and the Sewing Machine, A Capitalist Romance
The Dollar Princesses
The Spiritualists
The Burning Question
The New Women and the Old Men

FICTION

Left, Right and Centre
Out of Body, Out of Mind

RUTH BRANDON

Being Divine

A Biography of
Sarah Bernhardt

Richard Briers

2002

NORWICH

Mandarin

A Mandarin Paperback
BEING DIVINE

First published in Great Britain 1991
by Martin Secker and Warburg Limited
This edition published 1992
by Mandarin Paperbacks
Michelin House, 81 Fulham Road, London SW3 6RB

Mandarin is an imprint of the Octopus Publishing Group,
a division of Reed International Books Limited

Copyright © Ruth Brandon 1991
The author has asserted her moral rights

A CIP catalogue record for this title
is available from the British Library

ISBN 0 7493 1233 5

Printed and bound in Great Britain
by Cox and Wyman Limited, Reading, Berks

This book is sold subject to the condition
that it shall not, by way of trade or otherwise,
be lent, resold, hired out, or otherwise circulated
without the publisher's prior consent in any form
of binding or cover other than that in which
it is published and without a similar condition
including this condition being imposed
on the subsequent purchaser.

Picture Acknowledgements

The author and the publisher would like to thank the following for
permission to reproduce photographs or paintings held in their collec-
tions: Illustrations 4, 11, 12, 13, 15, 17, 18, 19, 20, 22 (the Mucha and
the *Punch* cartoon), 24, and 32 by courtesy of the Trustees of the Theatre
Museum, Victoria & Albert Museum; 5, 10, 21 and 25 courtesy of the
National Portrait Gallery, London; 23 and 29 courtesy of Hulton-
Deutsch; 8 (*Ophelia* by Millais) courtesy of the Tate Gallery, London;
8 (*La jeune martyre* by Delaroche, the Louvre, Paris) © Photo R.M.N.;
27 courtesy of the Billy Rose Theatre Collection, the New York Public
Library at Lincoln Center, Astor, Lenox and Tilden Foundations; 33
© Harlingue-Viollet, Paris.

For Lily

Acknowledgements

Of the many people who have helped in the writing of this book, I should particularly like to thank: Señora F. M. de la Barra, Nick Humphrey, Jan Marsh, Elaine Showalter, Philip Steadman, Barry Norman of the Theatre Museum, Covent Garden, and Terence Pepper of the National Portrait Gallery. Thanks, too, to my editor, Lesley Bryce, who coped valiantly with unending additions and alterations.

Contents

List of Illustrations

Preface

Sarah Bernhardt's was a peculiarly public life. A good part of it was spent literally in public – acting on stage all over the world. As for her private life – or what other people might have considered a private life – most of that was available to the public as well. From the moment she began to make a name for herself in her early twenties, the press fell over itself to report her smallest activities. Sarah's hairstyles, the cut of her dresses, her large and exotic collection of pets, her forays into sculpture and painting, her quarrels, her lovers – all these were avidly discussed. The treatment she received at the hands of the press brings to mind that accorded to Jackie Kennedy or Marilyn Monroe rather than anything that might be expected of a great classical actress of the nineteenth century.

This being so, the material details of her life were never a matter of great secrecy. They were mulled over minutely as they happened, and have been retold in a number of biographies, written both by those who knew her and by those who treat her as an historical figure. She even wrote a book of memoirs herself, though its relation to fact is, as one commentator delicately put it, strictly 'relative'. But, in considering a woman like Sarah (as she was universally known: 'Can you imagine anyone calling Duse "Eleonora"?' wondered Max Beerbohm), the bald facts of her life are only the beginning – or the end – of the story. An actress's life, after all, is a frustrating thing to pin down. A theatrical performance is gone as soon as it is experienced: for the details of a particular evening, a famous interpretation, we must rely on critics and memoirs – bleak substitutes for the real thing. Details of intrigue and backstage gossip may enliven, but they hardly enlighten the reader as to the real nub of the matter: what was the secret, what was the peculiar magic, of Sarah Bernhardt?

For Sarah was more than an ordinary actress, or even a very good actress. Such was her extraordinary impact, on and off the stage, that she transcended mere personality. The details of her dramatic career are an interesting part of her story, but they are not the reason why she remains a fascinating figure seventy years after her death, a hundred and twenty years after she was to be seen in her early prime. She was interesting, not because she was an actress, but because she was so famous. '*Ci-git Sarah/Qui survivra*' wrote Maurice Rostand after her death: and survive she most assuredly has.

Sarah was so famous that her life takes on a significance beyond its mere events, and on at least two levels. Firstly, Sarah was a phenomenon, and the interest we take in phenomena is generic, and not just particular. What gives rise to them? What combination of circumstances went into the making of Sarah Bernhardt? Why did she choose to be an actress? What made her the kind of actress she was? What made her adopt her extraordinarily public mode of life? Why was she so much greater an international figure than any of the other comparable actresses of the age? Why was she so loved in England, so often reviled in France? What was her relation to the theatrical life of her day? If there had to be a Sarah Bernhardt, why was it *her* – her and nobody else? What was there about her background, her upbringing, her times, her character, that made her the way she was? I think there are very specific answers to these questions – that Sarah's story is rooted in her psychology and in the time and place of her birth.

Secondly, because she was the phenomenon she was – *'la divine'*, *'la grande'* Sarah – her name a byword throughout the world – her life also took on a symbolic significance. She symbolized different things to different people. For those interested in the theatre, she symbolized a certain sort of theatre, a particular approach to acting – an approach whose limitations were shown up in the course of her famous contest with Duse, who embodied the new theatre while Sarah was stuck irretrievably in the old. But those interested in the theatre are a comparatively small group, and Sarah's appeal was much wider than this. She was the first of the goddesses of popular culture. She used the media and was used by them in an entirely new way – a way that was to become a familiar feature of twentieth-century life with the advent of stars such as Charlie Chaplin, Greta Garbo, Marilyn Monroe, and, recently, Madonna, but which in Sarah's day was a peculiarity all her own. And she did this before the days of film (although she did make a few films at the end of her life) – that is to say, when her exposure was all in person. Sarah's fame reached almost as wide a segment of the world's population as Marilyn's, and she appeared in almost as many countries – but *in person*. By the end of her life, millions of people all over the world could say they had seen Sarah – not her shadow on a screen, but the real thing. The amount of travelling this entailed in the age of steam fairly boggles the imagination.

And because she was so very famous she also became a symbol of another sort – a symbol, at a time when women were beginning to rethink their role in the world, of what a woman could achieve, more or less unaided.

1

The autumn of 1844 was a significant season for the French theatre. In September of that year Alexandre Dumas *fils* first met Marie Duplessis: an encounter which was to result in *La Dame aux camélias*, for whose melancholy heroine, Marguerite Gautier, Marie was the model. The next month saw the birth of the little girl who was to be the greatest interpreter of that role – who would, indeed, still be playing Marguerite when she was in her sixties and Marie Duplessis sixty years dead: Sarah Bernhardt.

When Sarah, in her fifties, was being compared with the Italian Eleonora Duse, *La Dame aux camélias* was one of the main points of comparison. Duse, it was agreed, was subtler, more poetically sad. But Sarah was able to do something Duse could not, which was to make herself believable as a cocotte, the tough, pleasure-seeking courtesan of the early part of the play. This, of course, made the subsequent transition into the love-sick, selfless Marguerite of the play's end far more telling.

This affinity with the role of Marguerite on Sarah's part is hardly surprising, for this was a milieu she knew intimately. It was the world into which she was born.

In her book of memoirs, *Ma double vie*, Sarah skates delicately over the question of her birth. When the book opens she is aged three and living with her nurse in Brittany, near Quimperlé, in a little white house with wild pinks growing

1

in the thatch. Her mother Julie, then aged nineteen, 'loved to travel'. She is forever promising to come and visit her daughter in a month's time and then failing to turn up, writing to one or another of her sisters to go and see the child – she will be back in a fortnight. Little Sarah has a number of aunts. The ones called on to do the visiting (but they hardly ever come, either) are seventeen and twenty. Then there are others: one of fifteen and another, older, who is twenty-eight – but she lives in Martinique and already has six children of her own. As for Sarah's father, he has been in China for the past two years – 'Why? I have no idea.' The only hint of her mother's profession is given when, after the child has had a bad accident, falling from her high chair into the fire, Julie rushes over from Brussels accompanied, not by Sarah's father, who is so very absent, but by two other men friends – Baron Larrey, the son of the chief medical officer of Napoleon's armies, and one of his friends, a young doctor. 'They told me later,' remarks Sarah, 'that nothing could have been sadder or more charming than my mother's despair.' Soon afterwards, Sarah and her old foster-parents are whisked over to Paris and installed in a small house at Neuilly. Having got them settled, and reassured that the child has suffered no scarring from her accident, Julie feels free to set out again on her travels, leaving the little household once more to the uncertain care of her sisters.

But, like so many well-laid plans, this one is destined to failure. The nurse's old husband dies, and she remarries. Her new husband is the concierge of an apartment building in town: 65, rue de Provence, near Montmartre. The nurse naturally wants to get in touch with Sarah's mother to discuss what is to be done. But, as always, Julie is out of town and nowhere to be contacted. So, reluctantly, the nurse and her new husband take the child with them.

Sarah hates her new home. The concierge's lodging is one

room above the big carriage-entrance, lit only by a tiny round *oeil-de-boeuf* window, dark and gloomy. The little cupboard where Sarah sleeps has no window at all. Shut up in this horrid place the child pines and fades. Then, one day, playing outside, she sees two fine ladies crossing the court-yard with her nurse's husband, the concierge. They are apparently coming to look at an apartment. One of them seems familiar: and indeed is familiar – is in fact her aunt Rosine, her mother's younger sister. The small girl flings herself upon her aunt and buries her head in the fragrant furs and tears the elegant lace sleeves.

Rosine is astonished, which is hardly surprising. She calms the frantic child, talks to the nurse and all is explained. She gives the nurse such money as she has on her, and promises that she will be back tomorrow. She says nice things to the child. She is 'light, and tender, and coaxing, and without love . . . She brushed my cheek with her gloved hands, flicked a spot of dust from her dress, made a thousand charming, frivolous, cold movements.' Then she leaves. The nurse tries to comfort the weeping child, and takes her up to her room. But Sarah is frantic. She knows her aunt will not be back: she has to go with her now, while she can. So she fights her way free of the nurse and leaps from the window to the street, where she can see Rosine just getting into her carriage. She falls to the pavement at the feet of her horrified aunt. Her arm is broken in two places and so is her kneecap. She loses consciousness and wakes up in a beautiful big bed in the middle of a lovely room with two large windows, where her mother, hastily summoned, is looking after her. It takes her two years to recover from this terrible fall. She gets to know her family, her aunts, her cousins. She can't understand why, all of a sudden, there are so many people concerned with her when, up till now, there has only ever been one.

Thus Sarah on her early childhood: an account which,

3

like the rest of these memoirs, needs to be taken with a good pinch of salt with regard to facts but which is none the less extremely revealing. For one thing, it is full of excellent dramatic detail. On one occasion, after the child has fallen into the fire, she is described as being doused 'still smoking' in a large pail of milk 'fresh from the cow'. As for the leap from the window, it is an act of purest melodrama, such as the grown-up Sarah would perform thousands of times on the stage. In short, from the very beginning it is clear that, for Sarah, life is a drama of which she is the star.

Something else also stands out in this short, vivid interlude with which Sarah begins her life story: and that is the strange, ambivalent nature of her relationship with her mother – a relationship which was to have so decisive an influence on the shape of her life. The pattern of this relationship is set at once, and in telling dramatic form. It is one in which the child Sarah yearns for the love of the mother she adores. But this love is not reciprocated: indeed, it is only at times of the direst crisis that Julie can be induced to take the slightest interest in her small daughter. Julie is distant, both metaphorically and actually: she always has to be called in from a long way away; there is never any sense of certainty about her. Sarah of course perceives this; how could she not? More remarkably, she is able to articulate this perception with no hint of resentment, and without any lessening of her great love for her mother. Describing Julie's descent on Brittany she says: 'Maman, ravishingly pretty, like a madonna with her golden hair and eyelashes so long that they brushed her cheeks when she shut her eyes, handed out gold to everybody. She would have given her golden hair, her white chiselled fingers, her tiny feet, her very life, to save this child to whom she had given not a thought only the week before. She was as sincere in her despair and her love as in her careless forgetfulness.'[1] What

4

is certain is that Sarah's love, at any rate, was never in question.

Sarah Bernhardt's entire life was devoted to the projection of imaginary personae. This is of course true, to a greater or lesser extent, of all actors. But most actors, however famous and successful, have some sort of private life in which they can drop the masks and be simply – or not so simply – themselves. This was not really true of Sarah. She had remarkably little of anything that could truly be described as a private life. Why this should have been the case is a question to which we shall return. But that it certainly was the case is undeniable. She became a legendary personality; and although this would not have happened had she not been an extraordinarily interesting and accomplished woman, she was always happy to help the legend on its way with a little myth-making. Thus, one of her friends records that one day, when the subject of toothpicks came up at table, Sarah asserted that picking one's teeth was one of the great pleasures of life, and furthermore that her mother's table was always provided with a silver revolving toothpick, hung from the ceiling, of which any guest could avail himself at need. As she had happily anticipated, nobody knew quite how to take this. Questioned later by her young friend, she remarked that everybody likes fairy-stories.

If she enjoyed spreading a veil of myth over the least of life's little details, she saw to it that the larger ones were equally thickly covered. Among these was the story of her birth and origins. One day – it was 10 February 1898, when she was at the height of her fame and reputation – she telephoned the journalist Jules Huret to come and see her. She had recently undergone an operation, but was now convalescent, and very bored. She therefore amused herself by telling Huret the story of her life. Her mother, she told

5

him, had fourteen children, including two pairs of twins; Sarah was the eleventh child – a truly amazing feat for a girl of sixteen, which was Julie's age when she had Sarah, if *Ma double vie* is to be believed.[2] Another friend, Maurice Rostand, the son of the playwright Edmond Rostand, spreads yet more uncertainty. He says that the great actor Constant Coquelin, Sarah's contemporary at the Conservatoire where both received their training, always said that Sarah was born in 1841, in the same year as himself and their other contemporary Mounet-Sully, who was to tragedy what Coquelin was to comedy – which would, as Rostand remarks, have made 1841 a great vintage year for the theatre. In fact Sarah's entry-form at the Conservatoire gives her birth date as 22 October 1844. Coquelin dismissed this detail, asserting that she had used her sister Jeanne's birth certificate in order to fall within the age-limits for entry to the Conservatoire – Jeanne being, according to this account, three years younger than Sarah.[3]

Sarah's birth certificate is no longer extant, having been burned when the Hôtel de Ville went up during the Paris Commune. Various lives of Sarah reproduce what they say is her birth certificate, but this is in fact the Conservatoire entry-form just referred to. This says that Rosine Benardt was born on 22 October 1844, the daughter of Julie Benardt, modiste, native of Berlin, now domiciled in Paris at 22, rue de la Michodière. Another source of details is Sarah's certificate of baptism, also reproduced in lieu of a birth certificate. She was baptized at the age of twelve, at the convent of Grand-Champs, Versailles, where she was at school. This gives her baptismal names as Sarah Marie Henriette, and states that she is the daughter of Edouard Bernhardt and Julie van Hardt, and gives the date of birth as 25 September 1844.

Where, amid all this welter of information – if anywhere – are the true facts?

Let us start with her mother's nationality. Sarah told Jules Huret that 'My mother, as you know, was a Dutch Jewess.'[4] After the Franco-Prussian war she conceived a real hatred of Germany, and would have nothing to do with the notion that she was in any way German herself. 'I am Jewish, certainly, but German – absolutely not!'[5] she declared. What, then, of her mother's description of herself as a native of Berlin?

The answer seems to be that European Jews at that time were indeed the cosmopolitans so reviled in anti-Semitic literature half a century later. They moved between Jewish communities, unmindful of national boundaries. This had been the family history of two of the greatest ornaments of the French theatre during Sarah's lifetime: the actress Rachel's father and the playwright Ludovic Halévy's grandfather had both made their way to Paris from the Jewish communities of Germany (though at very different levels: Rachel's father was a peddler, Halévy's grandfather, a distinguished rabbi). In the same way Julie Benardt, or van Hard's, family seems to have moved to Holland.

Sarah's mother Judith – generally known as Youle or, in French, Julie – was the third of five daughters of an oculist named Maurice Bernhardt who settled in Rotterdam. His first wife was called Jeanne van Hard; and in addition to their daughters, they had a son, Edouard. Edouard Bernhardt, then, is Sarah's uncle, not – as the certificate of baptism assumes – her father. When the eldest girls were in their mid-teens Jeanne van Hard died and their father married again, whereupon the two eldest girls, Julie and Henriette, ran away. They went first to Basel, then to London, where Maurice Bernhardt tried to trace them; but before he could catch up with them they crossed to Le Havre. Here the civil register records that on Saturday, 22 April 1843, twin girls, Lucie and Rosalie, were born to Julie Bernardt (the spelling of Julie's surname varied, sometimes she called herself Bernardt, sometimes Benardt. It was Sarah who definitively changed the spelling to Bernhardt.) The twins died, Lucie on 2 May, Rosalie six days later. Julie, their mother, was described as an *'artiste musicienne'*, the daughter of Maurice Bernardt, oculist, and the late Jeanne Hard. There is no mention of the babies' father, but he was probably a Havrais naval officer called Morel, the son of a rich arms-dealer[6]. Sarah says her father's family came from Le Havre: the lawyer representing his family, who came to discuss the money he left in trust for her, came from there. And it was a place of which she was fond. When she could first afford to take a country house it was at Ste Adresse, close by; and when her troupe returned from the United States after their first grand tour, they gave a special celebration performance for the citizens of Le Havre before leaving for Paris. But there is no mention of Sarah's birth in Le Havre, so it seems probable that she was born in Paris, where Julie lived at 5, rue de L'Ecole de Médecine, on 22 October 1844, the date most usually given for her birth.

Since the rue to L'Ecole de Médecine is in the heart of the Latin Quarter, the traditional haunt of students in Paris, it is likely that young Morel installed Julie there while he himself pursued his studies. Then the romance came to an end, as such romances do, and Julie had to fend for herself. Morel, however, did not abandon her completely: he certainly recognized his daughter, kept up with her progress while he was alive and left her one hundred thousand francs in trust when he died – which she was to receive as a dowry when she married. Meanwhile she was placed with his old nurse near Quimperlé, which is where we came in.

As for Julie, her immediate future, at any rate, was clear. Living as she did, and where she did, she was clearly destined to be a *grisette*.

La vie galante was a notable feature of Parisian life at this time, and indeed for the rest of the century. Thousands of people made their living from it. Most of those who enjoyed it when Julie was young were neither very vicious nor very rich. Its mainstays were the students who teemed in the narrow streets of the Latin Quarter, and the *grisettes*: the Larousse definition of *grisette* being 'flirtatious young working girl'. Boys and girls would meet and enjoy themselves at the *bals*, of which there were literally hundreds. Dancing was the rage: it was estimated that during carnival time, 380 establishments were open for dancing. 'You must take her dancing as often as you possibly can or you'll never get anywhere,' counselled the author of the *Physiologie de la grisette* in 1841[7]. You could dance the *galoppe*, the *chahut*, the quadrille, the can-can, the waltz; in 1843, the polka was introduced and took Paris by storm. And when the dancing was finished, your girl might invite you to her room, perhaps in the hope of a modest supplement to her earnings as a milliner or modiste, perhaps through sheer force of intoxication – of the waltz and of whatever champagne you had been able to afford. But even such an uncommercial transaction might lead to something: marriage, possibly; or perhaps elevation to the ranks of the higher gallantry. That was what happened to Esther Guimond, who dressed herself up as a taffeta pierrot to spend carnival night dancing at the rue du Bac. By the time morning came it was pouring with rain: she had spent all her money on her pierrot's dress and satin slippers, and there was none left for a cab. So there was nothing for it but to walk back home to the rue Saint-Lazare. Then what should happen but that a great man – a rich, bored man – passes her on the Pont-Royal, stops his carriage and asks why a girl like her is walking in the rain in satin slippers on a day like this? To which, quick as a flash, Esther replies, 'Because I knew perfectly well you'd tell me to get into your carriage.' Which he did; he took her home, set her up, and Esther Guimond was soon one of the richest and best-known courtesans of the day.[8]

The story of Esther Guimond must have been known to all the hopeful young *grisettes*. Julie could hardly expect to contract much of a marriage: she was penniless and a mother besides. And while it was unlikely that she would have quite such luck as Esther – not many did, and, to judge from her photographs, Julie was no great beauty, nor particularly vivacious – nevertheless she was very young, and pretty enough, and soon made it on to the next rung in the ladder of gallantry: she became a *lorette*, defined by Larousse as 'an elegant young woman of easy virtue', under the special protection of Baron Larrey (who, it will be remembered, accompanied her on her mission of mercy to Quimperlé). After which she wrote to her sisters telling them of her good luck and urging them to join her in Paris. Two were already married; but the other two, Rosine and Henriette, soon arrived and did even better than their sister. Henriette got herself married to a rich *rentier*, Félix Faure, and became a pillar of respectability, while Rosine, who was much prettier and more dashing than her sister, was soon established at 6, rue de la Chaussée d'Antin.

This meant that Rosine was doing very well in her profession. It was reckoned that a girl in the rue de la Chaussée d'Antin cost a minimum of 500 francs a month, and required a horse and carriage.[9] In fact Rosine lived in the same house as Anna Deslions, the queen of the *haute bicherie* of Paris. Julie, however, was not quite so classy. *Lorettes* were so called after Notre Dame de Lorette, the parish in which most of them lived: and this was Julie's district, as may be seen from the birth certificate of her second daughter Jeanne, which survived the Commune. It records that in 1851, on 22 May, Jeanne-Rosine, daughter of Julie Benardt, was born. Julie is described as a *rentière* of 64, rue de Provence[10] – the building next door to that from

10

which little Sarah supposedly made her death-defying leap from the window to her Aunt Rosine's carriage.

What are we to make of this? It is of course possible that Sarah's account is strictly true, that Rosine was indeed visiting the building to inspect an apartment, and that Julie decided to take it after Sarah was restored to her bosom. Another possibility is that Julie always lived in this building – maybe it was she who found the concierge's position for the nurse's new husband. This would mean that, even if Sarah lived nominally in her mother's apartment, she would spend her time, as before, with her nurse in the concierge's lodge. Certainly it seems likely that the central proposition of Sarah's account is true – that, physically or metaphorically, she felt her mother was lost to her and that, physically or metaphorically, she had to jump from a window and break her bones in order to gain her attention and that of her flighty aunt. It is also clear that Sarah was all too keenly familiar with the interior of the concierge's squalid lodging. In a later chapter, we shall discuss the full significance of this dramatic tale in the development of the complex character who was to be Sarah Bernhardt.

2

Whatever its real or metaphorical significance – whether Julie had really vanished from Sarah's life, to be recovered by the extraordinary coincidence of Rosine's chance reappearance, or whether, as her address of two years later seems to indicate, the distance was merely emotional and the little girl was simply expressing her despair in the most dramatic way she could imagine – the incident of the jump from the window had its material effect. For the next two years Sarah lived with her mother, and not in the concierge's lodge. It seems likely that, during this time, she made frequent visits to her Dutch grandparents – a convenient solution for Julie: if Sarah could no longer be left with the concierge then some other arrangements had to be made, since Julie's life was no more geared to the care of a small child than it had ever been.[1] Then, just before the birth of the baby who was to be Sarah's sister Jeanne, Julie announced that Sarah was to be sent to boarding school.

Sarah recounts that she was filled with joy at this news. She could neither read, write nor do her sums; she had spent five years with her nurse and the next two recovering from the effects of her leap from the window. Now she was to end her long, bored isolation and meet and live with other children. She describes, with her usual loyalty, how her pleasure at this prospect was marred only by the sight of her mother's tear-filled eyes. But it seems unlikely – if these tears ever existed anywhere but in Sarah's fond imagination – that they were induced by the prospect of

12

losing her daughter's company, a pleasure of which she had been only too eager to deprive herself hitherto and for which she was never to manifest any great desire. Perhaps she was piqued by Sarah's too-evident joy. At any rate the arrival of the new baby would doubtless console her in her loneliness. Sarah learned that Julie was pregnant again at the same time as she was told of the plans for her own future, the two, of course, being intimately connected. One invalid child might perhaps be coped with, but an increasingly lively small girl *and* a new baby are a handful for any mother, let alone one in Julie's line of business. Sarah's departure, then, probably occurred early in 1851, since the new baby was born on 22 May of that year.

Sarah's description of her journey to Madame Fressard's pension in Auteuil provides one of the few glimpses of her bizarre home life as a child – though there is no evidence that she considered it particularly strange: indeed, it is most unlikely that she did so. Children's capacity to take their surroundings for granted and accept them with all their peculiarities is, after all, the salvation of most parents, and Sarah had had little opportunity for comparison. But anything less like the normal sedate and respectable convoy which might customarily transport a child to her first school can hardly be imagined.

Sarah was done up for the departure in her best blue velvet dress, and she and her mother, ready an hour too early, anxiously awaited the carriage which was to transport them to Versailles. This turned out to be the magnificent equipage belonging to Aunt Rosine. The concierge and various neighbouring shopkeepers watched while Sarah's small trunk was loaded on, followed by Julie, 'calm and slow', Sarah, and, lastly, Rosine, 'flighty and unsettling', as Sarah describes her. This carriage was followed by another containing three gentlemen. Neither Sarah's father nor Baron Larrey figured among them, the former having of course disappeared from the scene years ago, the latter now having been relegated to the status of family friend. The gentlemen were Régis Lavolie, a man about town whom Sarah describes as a friend of her father, and who was to be her godfather when she was baptized; Général de Polhes; and a fashionable painter of horses and hunting scenes called Fleury. These were, it may be presumed, the current special friends of Julie and Rosine; one of them was perhaps the father of the coming baby. It turned out that they were going on to book dinner at a fashionable restaurant on the outskirts of Auteuil, to which everyone would repair when Sarah had been disposed of.

Sarah, accustomed to a life of piercing monotony, avidly enjoyed the journey, even though the road was dull and muddy. Julie and Rosine talked to each other in German while she kept her nose glued to the window. Finally they arrived at Madame Fressard's, 18, rue Boileau. Sarah took to Madame Fressard at once. She was evidently a comforting figure, used to frightened little girls. She was, Sarah remembered, dark, with very white teeth, large eyes and plump, long-fingered hands, and she smelt good. She knelt down and tried to talk to the child, but Sarah refused to say a word, and all the noisy encouragement and scolding of her mother and aunt failed to unseal her lips. They went on the customary tour of the dormitories. Then Julie took Madame Fressard to one side and presented her with a long list of Sarah's medical requirements. Madame Fressard evidently received her instructions with a pinch of salt. She remarked, looking at Sarah's mop of curls, that it wouldn't be possible to curl her hair at school, but Julie replied that, on the contrary, it would be impossible to straighten it. (Dealing with this frizzy thicket was to be a constant source of trouble to the young Sarah.) Then the question of provisions arose. Like many a neglectful parent, Julie evidently quieted her conscience with bouts of extravagant present-giving. Sarah

14

was provided with twelve different pots of jam and six pounds of the very best chocolate. She also, to Madame Fressard's astonishment, had a large pot of cold cream, which was to be applied every night to the child's hands and face: an absolute essential, insisted Julie. She would pay for the extra laundry. (In fact, Sarah recalled, her sheets were changed once a month like everyone else's.) Then it was time to go.

Now that the moment had arrived, the child clung to her mother. Sarah recalls, apparently without irony, that everyone was at pains to console, not the little girl about to be abandoned, but Julie: assuring her that the child needed to go to school, that it would do her good, and so forth. Général de Polhes, who had a soft spot for the little girl, lifted her in his arms and said, 'Well, my girl, you're entering barracks! You'll have to keep in step now!' And when Sarah pulled his long moustache, 'Better not do that to the lady!' – for Madame Fressard, it appears, had a slight moustache. Then they all disappeared in a whirl of skirts and words and Rosine's loud laughter, and Sarah was left to her new prison.[2] What Madame Fressard made of it all is not recorded.

Arbitrariness is a feature of most children's lives. A child's life is controlled from outside, and explanations are not necessarily to be expected. Nevertheless, Sarah's life since the hurried departure from Quimperlé had been more than usually subject to adult whim and largely devoid of the consistency and reassurance she so desperately sought – and, against all logic, always hoped to find – in the unstable figure of her mother. The comparative normality and happiness of her earliest childhood is perhaps reflected in her continuing affection for the countryside in which she spent it. Belle-Isle, where she was to spend all her summers for more than thirty years (whenever she was not on tour), is off the Breton coast not very far from Quimperlé. But for the rest, life had been a fight. Later, she was to adopt the motto '*Quand-même*' – 'Against the odds' – as her device. It reflects a view of life which must have been hers for as long as she could remember. Sarah grew up to be an exceptionally intelligent and observant woman. It therefore seems fair to suppose that she was an exceptionally intelligent and observant child. This child's efforts to compose a life for herself '*quand-même*' – in spite of the emotionally gruelling and disorienting circumstances of her childhood – had important long-term consequences for Sarah's adult life. But they also had immediate consequences: not surprisingly, Sarah was a very disturbed child. The visible form this disturbance took was temper-tantrums of awesome violence and severity, which left the child so shaken that she would have to spend two or three days in the infirmary. Even in adult life she always had a violent temper, but by then she also had other means of expressing herself and achieving her ends. As a child, it must sometimes have seemed that there was no other recourse open to her. 'My rages were almost like bouts of madness,' she said.[3]

Nevertheless, she spent two relatively peaceful years at Madame Fressard's, and was resigned to staying there until she was grown up. She learned reading, writing, and polite accomplishments such as embroidery and singing. A young actress at the Comédie-Française, the sister of one of the boarders, came to recite verse on Thursdays. On Thursdays and Sundays the girls were allowed out for a walk, which in a small way compensated for their imprisonment during the rest of the week. And, on the instruction of her uncle by marriage, the rich financier Félix Faure, there were frequent visits to her aunt Henriette, Julie's sister. The Faures had a big house at Neuilly with a stream running through the grounds, and Sarah used to spend hours fishing there with her two cousins. Henriette did not like Sarah, whom she considered a bad influence on her own daughter – after all,

16

no one knew better than she how easily she might have been living Julie's life instead of that of a rich, respectable matron in her suburban mansion; it was something she wished to forget, and Sarah was a constant, unwelcome reminder of it. But Faure was a pious and dutiful man, and took an avuncular interest in his wife's niece, who was, after all, not yet lost.

So life went on uneventfully. And then, out of the blue, Tante Rosine turned up to take her away. Sarah's father wanted to place her elsewhere, and since he was footing the bill, there was to be no arguing. Julie was away travelling, as usual, so Rosine had come 'between two waltzes' to pick Sarah up.

Once again her life was being disrupted without warning, in the most arbitrary manner, and Sarah responded with a temper-tantrum which outdid anything she had yet achieved. For two hours she screamed and shouted, abused her aunt and her mother for taking her away, Madame Fressard for letting her be taken; rolled on the floor, rushed outside, climbed trees where no one could reach her, threw herself into a pond in the garden, and was finally fished out, exhausted. Rosine, with what enthusiasm it may be imagined, took her back to the rue de la Chaussée d'Antin, where for three days she lay in bed with a high fever. And here she records one of her rare sightings of that legendary figure, her father.

'As handsome as a god', was how he seemed to Sarah. He came to see her often, accompanied by his friend Rossini, who lived next door. 'I looked at him proudly,' Sarah recounts. 'I didn't know him very well, as I hardly ever saw him. But I loved his charming voice and his soft, slow movements. He was rather an imposing figure. I noticed that even my giddy aunt calmed down when he was there.' After a while Sarah, too, calmed down, and the doctor declared that she was fit to be delivered to her next destination, the fashionable convent school of Grand-Champs at Versailles.

But by whom? Julie was still away: she had been taken ill in Haarlem. Rosine offered to take her, but Sarah's father was having none of that: perhaps he was concerned at the impression this might create. Julie might be no more respectable than Rosine, but she gave a less flighty impression, and she was, after all, Sarah's mother. So she must be awaited. Meanwhile Sarah would live at Tante Henriette's, where her aunt bore her like a burden and tried to keep her away from her cousins, and her uncle was kind to her behind his wife's back. Finally Julie announced her imminent arrival. Sarah's uniform was marked with red embroidered S.B.s, her uncle gave her a set of silver cutlery and a drinking glass, the kind maid who had been her friend gave her a purple scarf and Tante Henriette gave her a scapular and her blessing. Thus equipped in body and soul the little girl – she was now aged ten – set out for Grand-Champs. Before she left she had a serious talk with her father who explained to her the circumstances of her life. It was the first time anyone had talked to Sarah in this way. It made her cry. She sat on his knee, she recalls, and leaned her head against his chest. He told her that if she was good, he would come to fetch her from the convent in four years and they would go travelling together – a rosy promise which was not to be fulfilled. Then, next morning, they set off for Grand-Champs: the only occasion on which Sarah was ever taken anywhere by her father and mother together. It was the last time she ever saw her father. Nearly seventy years later Sarah, who by then was a legendary figure, beguiled her time during a spell of enforced idleness by writing a novel called *Petite Idole*, about a beautiful young girl who becomes a famous actress. It is naturally based largely upon her own experiences, but in some significant details the life of her heroine, Espérance Darbois, is quite

18

different from Sarah's own. For in her old age Sarah was evidently still dreaming of the ideal father and family she would so much have liked to have had. Espérance's father is no shadowy unknown quantity: he is a famous philosopher, a teacher at the Sorbonne, calm, dignified and respected by all; her mother is sweet, gentle, domestic and proper. As everyone in the book never tires of saying, it is almost inconceivable that such a respectable bourgeois pair should ever have given birth to such a ravishing genius as their irresistible daughter. But luckily for the world – and, as she would probably have agreed later, luckily, too, for Sarah – her family was not like that; not like that at all.

Grand-Champs was a convent much in vogue, and among the pupils were several girls whom Sarah was to know later in life – notably Sophie Croizette, who was later to become a colleague at the Comédie-Française. It was here that she had her first experience of theatricals, in a playlet about Tobias and the Angel which the pupils put on for Monseigneur Sibour, the Archbishop of Paris, who, when it transpired that Sarah was not baptized, but that this ceremony was planned for the spring, promised to baptize her himself, if he could. But he was assassinated before this could happen. And there was another death which affected the small girl more nearly: she heard that her father, who had been planning to come back to see her baptized, was also dead. So that was the end of that particular dream.

Nevertheless, Sarah was happier during her years at Grand-Champs than she had ever been. For the first time in her life she was settled and secure, and the prospect of a life with solid foundations opened out before her.

Life with Julie was lived from day to day. The future, if it was thought about at all, existed as a time to be dreaded rather than looked forward to, when the attractions which earned Julie and Rosine their living would have faded, and when, if they had not managed to contract some advantageous marriage or make some wise investments, the black pit of poverty lay before them. Julie, always tired (at least in Sarah's presence), suffering, or so she said, from a bad heart, had neither the physical nor the psychological resilience of such as Caroline 'La Belle' Otéro, who, at forty-five, after disposing of the greater part of a *puchero* – 'beef, bacon and pork-rind, boiled chicken, *longanizas* and *chorizos*, all the usual stew vegetables, a mountain of chick-peas and ears of corn, a dish for people who really like to eat' – would leap to her feet, snatch up her castanets, and, shouting, 'To the piano, Maria!' would dance her Spanish dances from ten in the evening until two in the morning. However, Julie would no doubt have appreciated Otéro's *mot*: ' "Remember that there's always a time when even a miser will open his hands wide." – "The moment of passion?" – "No, the moment when you twist his wrist." '[4] It seems more likely that she would have shared the views of Liane de Pougy: 'Oh, how bored I am! What an arid life! Always the same – going out, shopping, trying on, then, at the end of an insipid day, dinner! And what dinner! Shut up in a stuffy, fashionable restaurant suffocated by cooking smells and tobacco . . . with friends, and what friends! If you can call them friends . . . And why? So that we can do exactly the same thing tomorrow . . .'[5] Such a view of life seems more in accord with the expressionless, rather unhappy face which looks out from Julie's photographs. And of course Liane was at the top of her profession, loaded with worldly goodies, in a position to retire gracefully should she wish to do so (which she eventually did, becoming Princess Ghika) while Julie was only in its middle ranks. When Sarah first played *La Dame aux camélias*, the critic Francisque Sarcey wrote: 'I didn't think there was anything more I could learn about this character, but Mlle Sarah Bernhardt shed new light on her. This is not a courtesan who is dying of consumption, which is touching but really rather vulgar. What we have

20

here is a courtesan who is dying because she holds her profession in contempt and can see no way out of it . . .'[6] Julie, if we are to judge by Sarah's portrait of her, was not a sensitive woman, but this was, no doubt, her situation, and it was a situation her daughter Sarah was only too aware of.

Now, however, another way presented itself. Sarah loved the convent. She loved the kindly nuns, and she knew they loved her; she especially adored the Mother Superior, mère Sainte-Sophie, with her short, round figure, her laughing face and big blue eyes, her charm, her smile which 'lit up the whole convent', and her great kindness and understanding. This was the kind of mother she had dreamed of but never had: she idolized mère Sainte-Sophie and never forgot her.

As the moment of her baptism approached, Sarah buried herself in her catechism and church history. She felt mystically withdrawn. The requiem mass for Monseigneur Sibour reduced her to tears. 'I was enveloped in a mystic and ardent love, which was nourished by the religious practices, the setting of the services, and the persuasive, fervent encouragement of my teachers . . . The charming and peaceful memory still makes my heart bound,' she recalled.[7] It was not surprising that she decided that she would like to become a nun.

All her family – her mother, her aunts, her uncle Faure, her godfather Régis, her sister Jeanne's godfather M. Meydieu, her little sister Régine's godfather Général Polhes (Régine was four, nine years younger than Sarah) – and a crowd of others: godmothers, cousins – crowded to the convent for the baptism: it had been agreed that all Julie's girls should be baptized at the same time. They were got up in elegant mourning for Sarah's father; Rosine wore a sprig of lilac in her hat 'to liven up the mourning', a concept which seemed strange to Sarah. But the centre of all this attention felt detached, concerned with another world.

All this did not mean that Sarah had changed character. She was known as a tomboy and a collector of strange pets – spiders were particularly preferred – and this passion for animals was strengthened when she was allowed to bring back two little goats from a holiday at Cauterets in the Pyrenees where she went with Julie after her first communion. She was now nearly fourteen, though still frail and childish; when she asked Julie if she could become a goatherd her mother replied, 'Better that than a nun!'

During the ten months she spent at the convent after her baptism she did little work, lost as she was in a mystical dream. She spent the holidays largely in the company of Sophie Croizette, who lived not far from the country house Julie had taken. The girls' chief pleasure was playing in the antique shop owned by the father of another of their friends, Pauline Masson. They liked to change round all the price-tickets and then hide and enjoy the chagrin of M. Masson when he came in with some rich client.

It was this mischievous strain which ended Sarah's peaceful convent days. The fatal incident concerned a shako belonging to a soldier in the Satory barracks, which was situated next door to Grand-Champs. In the course of some horseplay in the barracks, this shako was thrown over the wall separating Satory from the convent garden, and landed at the feet of Sarah and a group of her friends. The girls heard alarmed voices on the other side of the wall, and then a soldier appeared. The nuns hid themselves behind some trees (this was an enclosed order) and the giggling girls all denied having seen any shako. Sarah, always given to showing off, now saw her opportunity. She seized the shako and, quick as a flash, scaled the big gymnastic apparatus which stood nearby, unhooking the wooden ladder by which she had climbed on to the beam and pulling the rope ladder up after her. Then she stood up and taunted the soldier. She had his shako, but she wasn't going to give it back.

Now she was the centre of everyone's frustrated attention, a delightful position. Mère Sainte-Sophie begged her to come down and give the shako back. The soldier swore, jumped off the wall and ran towards the apparatus. Nothing could be done: there was no way of reaching the miscreant. A sister rang the alarm bell, and the barracks, thinking there was some emergency, sent a group of soldiers post-haste to offer help. When the story was told to the officer who had brought them, he sent his men and the shako-less soldier back to barracks. The latter obeyed, shaking his fist; then, seeing how ridiculous Sarah looked wearing the shako, which was balanced on her ears, he burst out laughing. Infuriated by this she threw it at him: 'Take your rotten shako back!' Meanwhile mère Sainte-Sophie knelt at the foot of the apparatus, crying with shame and frustration.

Sarah still would not come down: not till everyone had gone. They went. She was alone. The sun went down. It started to get cold. She was now very frightened, and began to cry. She had just begun to think of climbing down by the rope ladder when she heard César, the gardener's dog, barking and growling beneath her. He had seen this unknown person on the apparatus and had come to guard his territory. Nothing Sarah could do would pacify him: he would recognize neither his name nor her voice, but kept on barking and growling. There was no coming down now even if she wanted to – which she did.

Sarah was trapped, and was now getting hungry into the bargain. She lay on her stomach on the beam and sobbed. She was abandoned. Then she heard her name: it was mère Sainte-Sophie, who helped her down and stayed with her throughout the three weeks of pleurisy which followed.

Julie, of course, was travelling: she was in Scotland, and was coming back by slow stages. Rosine was in Baden-Baden, Paris's favourite spa. Tante Henriette visited often, and so did Baron Larrey, who was fond of Sarah. Finally Julie arrived, stayed with Sarah while she convalesced, and then took her back to Paris. She promised that Sarah would return to the convent when she was better, but Sarah soon learned that this was not to be. She begged to be allowed to return; the dowry her father had left her was enough for a nun's dowry, she wanted to take the veil. Her godfather forbade it. In two years' time, maybe: not now. Now she had to learn all the things she didn't know, which was to say, just about everything, with the governess her mother had hired for her. This was a sweet-voiced, middle-aged old maid with red moustaches and a big nose, but the manners and bearing of a perfect lady – indeed, she had been governess to three archdukes. Her name was Mademoiselle de Brabender. Sarah took to her at once, and threw herself into her studies. She dreamed of returning to the convent, not as a pupil, but as a teacher.

3

'When I heard that I wasn't going back to the convent,' wrote Sarah, 'it seemed to me that I had been thrown into the sea, and I didn't know how to swim.'[1] And yet, on the face of it, there seemed to be no real reason for such terror. Mlle de Brabender was a kindly guide, and if holiness was what Sarah wanted, she was holy enough: she lived in a convent in rue Notre Dame des Champs, and declined all Julie's invitations to install herself in the apartment at 22, rue de la Michodière, where the Benardts were now living. But the girl's instincts were not mistaken.

There is a famous drawing by Toulouse-Lautrec which shows an old tart, fat and coarse, bringing a tray of breakfast in bed to her daughter who is just starting out in the profession. A fair exchange: the mother has kept her daughter all these years, and now it is the daughter's turn to earn the money. It is hard to imagine that such ideas never passed through Julie's head, though Sarah, at fourteen and fifteen, must have seemed very unpromising material: skinny, childish and intractable to the point of neurosis. Nevertheless, it must have been made clear to her that she would soon have to start pulling her weight, if not in this way then in another.

Sarah repeatedly remarks on her mother's tears whenever the question of her taking the veil was raised. The assumption was that Julie was upset at the prospect of losing her daughter to the religious life. There was probably something in that: no mother – and especially no Jewish mother –

could fail to blench at such a prospect unless she was completely devoid of feeling, and there is no evidence for that in Julie's case – it was just that her feelings did not last very long or go very deep. And there were other upsetting aspects to such a decision. It was hard to imagine any more definite comment upon, and rejection of, Julie's way of life – and, so far as that went, of Julie herself – though Sarah would have been the first to deny any such thing. But there was also a more material aspect to be considered, which was that if Sarah entered the convent this would also mean that she was completely lost to Julie as a means of possible future support – and that was something that really did cut deep. Sarah's future duties in this respect must have been the subject of frequent discussion between them after her return from Grand-Champs, and the discussions must have been unpleasant ones. Otherwise why should Sarah have felt such foreboding when, one fine September day when she was nearly fifteen – not long, that is to say, after her return from Grand-Champs – her mother announced that, after lunch, there was to be a family council? Doubtless the convening of this council, to discuss the thorny question of Sarah's future, had frequently been threatened.

The guests at lunch were Tante Rosine, Régis Lavolie, Sarah's godfather – who, as he often made clear, thought very little of the way she was shaping up – and the duc de Morny, whom Sarah describes as 'a great friend of my mother and father'. The nature of this friendship is unclear, but it is not hard to guess at its probable basis. This is unlikely to have been that of a meeting of true minds or social equals, for the duc de Morny was a very great man indeed in the France of 1859. He was the half-brother of the Emperor, Louis-Napoléon, on the 'wrong side of the blanket': both of them were sons of Queen Hortense, Napoleon Bonaparte's daughter-in-law, but she was a notoriously amorous lady, and Morny was not the son of her husband,

Bonaparte's son, the King of Holland. Nor, if it came to that, was Louis-Napoléon. Even while he occupied the imperial throne, the guide who showed visitors through the Royal Picture Gallery at The Hague would point to the portrait of a Dutch Admiral and declare: 'And this, ladies and gentlemen, is a portrait of the father of the present French Emperor, Napoléon III.'[2] But while this might be an open secret it was one never to be discussed in polite society, while Morny made no secret of the circumstances of *his* birth – in fact he was very proud of it, and sported *armes parlantes*: hortensias on his coat of arms, indicating that he traced his lineage through his mother.

Morny was the architect of the *coup d'état* which brought his half-brother to power in 1851, and in which he himself was catapulted to wealth and prominence. He was, as this might suggest, a very able politician, and was at this time President of the *Corps législatif*. He was also a devotee of the arts, particularly the theatre, a competent amateur dramatist – he wrote a farce entitled *M. Choufleury restera chez lui* – and a Maecenas to aspiring young writers and playwrights. When the young Alphonse Daudet first came to Paris, Morny kindly attached him to his household as a sort of supernumerary secretary, a job, it was understood, without any real duties, but which existed in order to give him a foothold in society from which he might construct a career. Daudet would go and see him when he was dressing in the morning – the only time he could ever be sure of catching his patron – and they would discuss plots: Morny's idea of the denouement of a farce was always the same – 'But, my dear boy, it's very easy: all you have to do is to introduce *un médecin: homme du monde: ami de famille . . .*'[3] A year after Sarah's family conference he was to extend a similar helping hand to the young Ludovic Halévy, whose success as a librettist for Offenbach's disreputable *opéras bouffes* distressed his high-minded family, who wanted him to be a serious

27

civil servant. Morny, delighted at the thought of getting to know a talented dramatist who could help him with his own writing, gave Halévy the post of secretary to the *Corps législatif*.

As though all this were not enough, Morny was also a leading member of that company of rakes and high-livers known as the 'Lions', whose box at the Opera was known as the *fosse aux lions*, or lions' den. He was married to a Russian lady, Princess Troubetzkoy, but everyone knew that his mistress was the Comtesse Le Hon, whose husband was credited with the bitter *mot*: 'It is not amusing to be a *père de famille* without having any children.'[4] But this was far from exhausting Morny's amorous energies. He was also a well-known frequenter of fashionable courtesans. He was an *ami* of Cora Pearl, the English girl who became one of the *grandes cocottes* of Paris, whom he met out skating on the lake in the Bois de Boulogne: '"Cora on ice?" he said . . . "What an antithesis!" "Well," I replied, "since the ice is broken, give me a drink." "I could ask no more."'[5] Cora, then, was at the height of her renown; but that did not save her, later on, from the fate which must always have been at the back of Julie's mind. In his *Confessions* Arsène Houssaye, who had been director of the Comédie-Française in Rachel's time (and had been one of the great actress's many lovers), recalls meeting Cora Pearl, whom he had known at her zenith, when, middle-aged and lonely, she had fallen on hard times. She, who had lived so sumptuously, was now staying in a seedy room above a carriage-shop. 'What, my dear Cora, what about all your friends, doesn't even one come to see you these days?' 'The fact is,' replied Cora, 'the Republic's done for them like it has for me, but I can't bring myself to charge less. I'm like those bric-à-brac dealers who won't lower their prices even when they're bankrupt.' Houssaye remarks: 'She didn't want to admit to herself any more than to me that her face had lost most of its wicked charm . . .'[6]

Given all these different aspects of Morny's character, it seems probable that it was the rake, rather than the politician or theatrical enthusiast, who had formed the friendship with Julie's family. If he had (as Sarah implies) known Julie when she was still with Sarah's father, then this must have been years before, because, as we know, after Sarah was born the two split up; in which case it is possible that he shared Julie's youthful charms and had, in his good-natured way, kept up with her through the years. But other possible explanations are given of his presence at the family council. One account says that Julie was his latest passion, and that he provided for her in his will when, in 1864, he died, like so many of his contemporaries, of syphilis. But this, too, seems improbable: he was a connoisseur of women, and the Julie of this period, plump, fair, rather pudding-faced, had long passed her peak. Another possibility is that he was a friend of Rosine's, and that she brought him to Julie's. This seems more likely: Sarah describes them flirting throughout the lunch which was to precede the council of war. (Alphonse Daudet, who was in a position to know, provides a sidelight both on Morny's sex-life and on the kind of service Rosine might have been expected to provide. Daudet told Edmond de Goncourt that Morny 'never slept with a woman but . . . every morning, on a corner of one of the official divans on the first floor of the Parliament buildings, did homage to Venus with a caller dressed in all her petticoats and pantaloons, delighted and satisfied with this one and only indulgence in sensual pleasure.'[7]) During this lunch Sarah's sister Jeanne teased her for crying, and Julie avowed that 'there are moments when she drives me to despair.'[8] Then coffee was brought and they all moved into the salon, where they were joined by uncle Félix Faure; M. Meydieu, who was Jeanne's godfather, and who, like Julie, openly preferred Jeanne to Sarah ('So we're all here on your account are we, dearie? All these busy people who've got something better to do than bother themselves with what's going to happen to a little show-off. Now if it was your sister there wouldn't be any problem.'⁹) and whom Sarah, not surprisingly, disliked in return – so much that she remembered her dislike all her life, and resuscitated M. Meydieu as the nasty, egotistical, moralizing old bachelor godfather in *Petite Idole*, loathed by the heroine; and, the last member of the party and the one Sarah hated most of all, Maître Clément, a lawyer from le Havre representing the family of her dead father.

The coffee was finished, the cups taken away. Jeanne left the room. Morny made to leave as well, but Julie begged him to stay and give his advice on the problem. Then the door opened and Sarah's greatest friend came in. This was Madame Guérard, who lived in the apartment above. Pale, dark-haired, slender and serious, Sarah's name for her was '*mon petit'dame*', and she was to be Sarah's inseparable companion for the rest of her life. Various social pleasantries ensued. Then Régis Lavolie stood up and said, 'Well, we're here to discuss the child; let's get on with it.'

The possibilities – or lack of possibilities – in a case like Sarah's must have been clear to everyone in the room. The best thing she could do, or so it must have seemed, was to make a decent marriage. This was certainly what her father had thought: he had left her a hundred thousand francs which she was to receive on that auspicious occasion, money which until then was to be held in trust by Maître Clément.

But in order to operate satisfactorily within this social framework a person needed certain qualities that Sarah patently did not possess, such as discretion, self-control and a certain amount of cynicism. These were all exemplified in her aunt Henriette Faure, who had achieved the very position Sarah might hope for if she was lucky. But it was clear from all her posturing, weeping and fervent religious declarations that the girl was, on the contrary, a pig-headed little romantic. Her hundred thousand francs of *dot*, even combined with her stick-like thinness and unpredictable temper, would probably buy her a respectable and prosperous tradesman – she had, after all, youth on her side – but it was most unlikely she would be prepared to accept such a person, or be anything but miserable if she was prevailed upon to do so. Julie naturally found such an attitude incomprehensible, and selfish with it. But to Sarah there must have seemed little to choose between buying a man's support and protection by the provision of certain services, as Julie did, and buying the same with her hundred thousand francs: she would still have to provide the services, and she would have bartered away her freedom into the bargain.

There was, of course, always the possibility of love. The English expected to find this even within marriage. Some twenty years earlier the famous actress Marie Dorval had written an indignant letter to a friend regarding her lover, the poet Alfred de Vigny, who was visiting his in-laws with his English wife: 'My jealousy at knowing he is with her is real, and I swear to you that he is obliged to sleep with her. It's literally true, yes, sleep with her, as they do in England. All the English sleep with their wives, they won't even have been given two rooms, he'll have wanted to show himself a good husband to his father-in-law.'[10] It was of course possible to find loving marriages even in France, but in the milieu Sarah inhabited they were the exception rather than the rule. They were a bonus when they occurred but they were not to be expected; and the whole world in which Julie and Rosine lived – the *demi-monde*, as Dumas *fils*, its assiduous chronicler, so aptly called it – was a function of the French view of marriage, a view not often stated in so many words but everywhere recognized. From this view stemmed the equivocal but by no means abject position of women like Julie. They were an essential function of the equation. Men such as Morny, Baron Larrey, General Polhes and the rest were prepared to fulfil their social obligations so long as it was clearly accepted that they could, if they wished, lead the best part of their lives outside the marital home.

The life of a *femme entretenue* like Julie was, in many ways, not so very different from that of any other middle-class housewife. She looked the same, she had the same interests and concerns. She did not have the legal security of marriage, so she had to take what she could while she was able to get it. But she had the satisfaction of knowing that her customers spent their time with her because they preferred to, not out of obligation. Indeed, it was a frequent grumble of moralists at this period that there was no longer any very visible distinction between a respectable lady of fashion and a courtesan. They dressed in the same way, went to the same places – knew the same people. And if Julie had to earn her own living, so did a great many other women whose husbands had died or otherwise departed, leaving them with children to support as best they could. The difference, of course, was in the social framework. If the courtesan was on her own, so were her children. Even those members of her own family who had achieved respectability – namely, Tante Henriette and her children – were not eager to associate themselves with Julie, Sarah, Jeanne and Régine. It was Félix Faure – who had cared little enough for social position to marry Henriette in the first place, and whom Sarah describes as being very kind and pious – who concerned himself with Sarah, not his wife.

One thing was clear: if Sarah was not prepared to go along with the kind of marriage which might be arranged for her, she was going to have to support herself. Julie, as she must have told Sarah often enough, and now informed everyone else, had only a *rente viagère* – i.e. the capital which provided her income was one in which she had only a life interest: she could neither touch it nor leave it to her children. Sarah, if she did not marry, would have no money of her own, and this would be true even if she took the veil, as she kept telling everyone she wanted to do. Maître Clément was happy – only too happy, in Sarah's jaundiced view – to confirm this. The money had been left to provide a temporal, not a spiritual dowry. Of course, it was not essential to have money in order to become a nun, but Grand-Champs, at least, was not entirely detached from the financial realities of the temporal world. If Sarah brought no *dot* with her, she would have to enter the convent as a servant. Julie remarked that she would never allow this; and indeed, it is very doubtful if this notion had ever entered Sarah's calculations. Her position at the convent had been that of a paying pupil, i.e. a young lady. What she wanted was to regain what she had had there during those happy years – a loving, secure, predictable world with a ready-made family. Uncle Faure, a perceptive man who was fond of Sarah, observed that as far as he could see her faith was based upon a need to love and be loved – a remark which did not please Julie, who reaffirmed that she would be very upset if Sarah persisted in this course. Sarah, she declared, must have a career.

But what career? Not her mother's career – that went without saying. And yet, in some ways, Julie's world was not the worst possible place for an intelligent and ambitious woman to find herself. Just because it was not bound by the iron rules of society, the *demi-monde* offered opportunities for manoeuvre and influence not otherwise available to any except the wealthiest and best-connected. At the very top, there was the possibility of great wealth; and, once one had achieved that, there was really no reason to end up penniless like poor Cora Pearl. 'When you're *chic*, when you have your lackeys, carriages, etc., don't gaily throw your money out of the window, lay by something for a rainy day,' advised Léonide Leblanc, 'Mademoiselle Maximum', who was in a position to know. '... Buy shares, speculate, speculate ... Women are terribly lucky on the Bourse. And when you are no longer twenty, you will at last be able to console yourself for your vanished charms with a handsome income, thanks to which you will marry Monsieur Some-one-or-other ... who will give you his name, and his youth, ... and that's enough! ... When we have been easy women, we shall be honest women. We shall end as we should have begun.'[11] (That, indeed, was the story of Sarah's Tante Rosine, who at the age of forty married a M. Richard, director of the Agence Havas.)

And, as Léonide's own career showed, the perquisites of the successful courtesan were by no means limited to money. A successful *biche* might – like Léonide herself – have been born a simple peasant, but she could end up knowing and influencing the most celebrated men of her day. Men like Morny, Meydieu, Faure, Lavolie – the men who attended Julie's council of war, the kind of men who frequented expensive cocottes – would, if they had been English, have been clubmen. In England as in France, men took their serious pleasures outside the home, but whereas in England these were often conducted in the all-male setting of the club, this was not so in France. Those activities which in England took place in the men's clubs – the convivial meetings, the political and literary discussions, the escapes from the humdrum duties of the family hearth – in France took place in the mixed company of the salons, political, literary and artistic, which were run by those formidable ladies the *salonnières*. Here serious life was con-ducted in a setting which celebrated brilliant conversation in mixed company. There were, of course, some all-male clubs, such as the famous Jockey, which were modelled on

English gentlemen's clubs. The duc de Morny belonged to the Jockey. But, in a neat inversion of the English relation between club and drawing-room, these were essentially frivolous and social. The real business of life went on in the salons. It was therefore naturally accepted that women should be taken seriously, that they might influence events, that their opinions should be sought and considered; and the most successful courtesans of this age – Esther Guimond, Apollonie Sabatier – were those who were best able to please their clients, who were also their friends, on every level. After the fall of the Second Empire, when Gambetta was the most powerful man in France, there was speculation that he might marry his close friend and ally Juliette Adam, the celebrated political *salonnière*, whose husband had just died. But Mme Adam knew there was no chance of this: Gambetta was hopelessly attached to Mlle Leblanc. Everyone knew that; just as everyone knew that the witty Esther Guimond – whom we met in her muddy white satin slippers at the very start of her career – held court for Emile de Girardin, the hugely influential editor of *La Presse*, and knew, too, that he had virtually abandoned his wife, the beautiful and cultivated Delphine Gay, for her, and that all Girardin's friends met in her salon. In the same way the salon of the luscious 'Présidente', Apollonie Sabatier, Baudelaire's white muse, was a literary mecca, and that of the rapacious Paiva a centre of brilliant conversation. One didn't meet respectable women at these places – one didn't meet many women there at all – but one met all the most interesting and influential men.

It was even known for courtesans to make grand marriages – though rarely into the French *gratin*: they seemed rather to favour, or be favoured by, Russians, Romanians and Teutons. Thus 'La Madone' became Princess Soltikoff; Rosalie Léon became Princess von Wittgenstein; Adèle Rémy actually turned down Prince Bagration; 'La Paiva' married, first, a weak Portuguese count Paiva from whom she sucked the juice and then, grandly annulling her first marriage, became Countess Henckel von Donnersmarck; and Liane de Pougy became Princess Ghika.

But all these successes required qualities in which, even at such a young age, it was already clear that Sarah was completely lacking; the most important of these being the capacity to put expediency before personal preference. As Léonide Leblanc put it: 'The heart, you know, is an extra you must dispense with if you're going to be happy in this world . . . But alas! We aren't made of wood. You may fall in love. If you do, just remember this: if it's a poor young man, take care that you always put usefulness before pleasure.'[12]

Not that Sarah had yet shown any propensity to fall in love, suitably or unsuitably – the very opposite: she took no interest whatever in men. This was possibly a reaction against her mother's enforced preoccupation with them. Not that that mattered: a courtesan need not like men – indeed, it was well-known that many of the most famous preferred women. But she must be able to dissimulate her aversion. Putting other people's preferences first was the courtesan's business. That was what she was paid to do (and as a rule of thumb, she could reckon that the more bizarre the preferences, the higher the pay). But this was not Sarah's way, then or ever.

Part of the attraction of the convent for Sarah was that it was entirely removed from this world of material needs and distasteful decisions. 'The cloistered life is the same for everyone . . . The noise of the outside world breaks on the heavy door of the cloister. Ambition consists of trying to sing louder than the others at Vespers, of trying to get a bit more room on the bench, of sitting at the head of the table, of taking part in the tableau of honour.'[13]

But there was also a certain dramatic attraction in the

thought of becoming a Bride of Christ. 'I already saw myself as the novice sister just admitted. I saw myself lying on the ground, covered by the heavy black cloth with the white cross, the four heavy candles placed at the four corners. I planned to die under that cloth, I've no idea how.'[14] In the continuing series of dramas of which Sarah's life consisted, her vision of the nun's life focused on – and terminated with – that brief moment in which she would play the starring role. There seems little reason to doubt the whole-hearted nature of her desire to take the veil. But, equally, one can hardly doubt that the roots of this desire were psychological rather than religious. They had to do with the way she felt the convent life would fulfil her emotional needs. Her religious faith, though probably genuine enough, played little part in her life once she had entered the theatre, which equally satisfied those needs, surrounding her with its own self-sufficient world, and providing her with the possibility of emotional fulfilment within that world, just as the convent would have done.

So the discussion went, in a most unsatisfactory way, with everyone getting upset and nobody having any very helpful suggestion to make. The duc de Morny soon got bored. He got up and said, 'You know what you should do with this child? Send her to the Conservatoire.' Upon which he took his leave.

Perhaps Morny simply said the first thing that came into his head in order to escape from a boring and embarrassing occasion with good grace. But he was a man of excellent judgment, used to summing up a situation and deciding on the appropriate course of action. He knew Sarah, and in terms of psychology it must have been clear that his sugges-tion was an excellent one. Sarah was self-centred and insubordinate, qualities which deeply unsuited her for the life of a religious. The convent's real attractions for her were, firstly as a way of escape from a world she knew and hated, the sordid world (sordid emotionally, if not materially) inhabited by her mother; secondly, as a self-contained source of emotional security; thirdly, because it was dramatically satisfying to imagine; and, lastly, because this was one of the few things which was socially possible for her.

But the theatre, too, had all – or most – of these advantages. It was, like the convent, like the *demi-monde*, a world apart, where antecedents were of no importance and all that mattered was the business in hand and the participants' ability to perform it satisfactorily. It was also, like the convent, a place where a person might abandon her own personality – was indeed encouraged to do so – in order the better to submerge herself in the role in hand: a matter, as we shall see, of no little importance in Sarah's case. The only question was whether she would prove to have any aptitude for it.

When the duc de Morny became Minister for the Interior after the 1851 *coup d'état*, one of his first acts was to license *La Dame aux camélias*, the new play by Alexandre Dumas *fils*. It was Dumas' first play, it was to be his best and most enduring, and it had previously been refused a license by Faucher, the interior minister Morny had replaced. Morny was thus instrumental in launching the young man on his dramatic career (the play is, appropriately, dedicated to him). And now he had launched another career: that of the actress who was to become the greatest interpreter of Dumas' greatest role.

4

The duc de Morny's suggestion was far from being greeted
with general enthusiasm. Sarah describes the scene in her
memoirs with her usual flair for dramatic detail. Morny,
having made his effect, disappeared smartly before anyone
could comment, remonstrate or ask him questions. The
pious Mlle de Brabender was shocked and pursed her lips as
if someone had made a joke in bad taste. Tante Rosine made
little excited exclamations. M. Meydieu shook his head.
Nobody, Sarah remarks, seemed particularly pleased. Then
her godfather remarked, 'She's too thin to be an actress,'
and Sarah declared passionately that she didn't want to be
one; she had seen the great Rachel once at Grand-Champs,
dying, in the last stages of consumption, it was a fate she
had no desire to share. (Another version, given in an earlier
attempt at memoirs which never got completed, has Julie
leaping indignantly to her daughter's defence – or rather
her own, for she takes Régis' criticisms of Sarah as a slur
upon herself. 'An actress!' cries Régis. 'Why, she's as ugly as
a louse!' ' "Ugly!" shrieked my mother, bounding under the
outrage, "ugly, my daughter ugly! You're all insane, she is
charming; she has a wild air; only look at those eyes and
tell me if they aren't superb! And that curly hair," she
added, passing her hand through my unkempt locks . . .
"She's thin, undersized, always sick," persisted my brutal
godfather, "apprentice her to a milliner! She's too insignificant to go to the bad; that's what she should do." But the
old gentleman [in this version Morny remains for the

discussion] insisted upon it that the stage offered chances of success . . . Finally we decided that I should be presented to M. Auber. M. de Girardin, who was to visit my aunt next day, would arrange everything about that.'[1] And for a start, it was decided to take her to the theatre that very night.

Sarah left two accounts, too, of that first visit to the theatre, one in her memoirs, the other as told to her granddaughter Lysiane in her old age. In the second of these Julie and Sarah are accompanied by Dumas *père*, who points out everyone and explains everything to the dazzled girl. Even the adoring Lysiane finds it strange that such a detail should have been forgotten the first time round, for in her memoirs, Sarah is accompanied by Julie, Mlle de Brabender and her odious godfather, while Dumas *père* is mentioned only in connection with her first serious success, as Anna Damby in his *Kean* nine years later. Sarah explains that, before Dumas died, 'he had a bitter quarrel with my family, and I promised mama that I would never talk about all that. But now! It's so far away now!'[2]

Whoever her companions were, the two accounts concur on the important details. The theatre was the Théâtre Français, home of the Comédie-Française, the company which all the pupils of the Conservatoire aspired to join. The evening's programme was Racine's *Britannicus* to be followed by a second play, *Amphitryon*. And, despite her initial horror at the prospect opened up by the duc de Morny, by the time the evening came Sarah felt much better. The day's events had sweetly massaged her sense of self-importance. 'When I got up in the morning I was still a child, and in the space of a few hours, events had turned me into a young girl. I had been discussed and argued over. I had been able to say what I wanted, admittedly not to any great effect, but I'd said it nevertheless. And now people were going to have to be nice to me, to persuade me to do what they wanted. They couldn't force me: I had to agree. And I felt so pleased and proud about that that I was almost inclined to give them what they wanted.'[3] Indeed, Sarah had correctly identified the first step out of the arbitrary world of childhood. For the first time she was, to some extent, in charge of her own fate.

The actual evening's entertainment, however, was almost too much for her. She was completely overcome during *Britannicus*, so much so that when the curtain fell at the end she was, to her godfather's disgust, crying hopelessly and quite incoherent. For *Amphitryon* she made an effort to pull herself together and concentrate, but that was no better: she found the fate of Alcmène so sad that she burst into noisy sobs, to the great amusement of the rest of the audience, and had to be taken away by her mother and Mlle de Brabender.

However, despite this, or perhaps because of it – for too much emotion is better than none at all – preparations for the Conservatoire now took over Sarah's life. Copies of Racine, Corneille, Molière, flooded in from all sides. Her godfather and M. Meydieu, her mother's 'erudite and unbearable' friend, coached her in the clear delivery of tongue-twisters (another role assigned, by the time Lysiane got to tell the story, to Dumas *père*). Then word came from Tante Rosine that an interview had been arranged with M. Auber, the composer who was then Director of the Conservatoire – which seems to support the theory that Morny was Rosine's friend rather than Julie's, for this was certainly his doing: in Lysiane's account, this news came in a letter sent by Morny himself. Auber would see Sarah at nine the next morning. It was arranged that Sarah would go with Mme Guérard, her '*petit'dame*'.

The interview was an unsatisfactory occasion, its purpose clear to nobody. Presumably Morny wanted to introduce his protégée to Auber, and Auber felt he must humour such a powerful patron.

Sarah was overawed by M. Auber: 'His fine head, with its white hair, ivory complexion and wonderful burning black eyes, his slender, distinguished figure, his melodious voice, his distinguished name.'[4] She was not used to meeting people like this, and hardly dared reply to his questions. Finally he said to her, 'And do you like the theatre very much?' 'Oh, no, monsieur,' she answered; a reply which naturally amazed him. Mme Guérard stepped into the breach. She explained the position: how Sarah did not want to get married, how she had no money of her own and would not inherit any from her mother, how she therefore had to do something (but really wanted to enter a convent) . . . So here they were, in spite of the fact that Sarah did not care for the theatre.

M. Auber, with perfect politeness, agreed that the convent was hardly an independent career. How old was Sarah? he enquired. Fourteen and a half, replied Mme Guérard. Nearly fifteen, interjected Sarah. Auber laughed, and remarked truthfully that in twenty years' time she would be less punctilious. Then he got up, indicating that the interview was at an end. Was it true, he asked Mme Guérard, that Sarah's mother was an extremely pretty woman? Oh, extremely, replied '*mon petit'dame*'. Auber opened the door and told Sarah not to worry. She would be grateful to her mother one day for having forced her hand now. Meanwhile she should cheer up: 'Life's worth taking seriously, but gaily too.' A fat singer passed, knocking into Sarah, and Auber whispered in her ear that she should take care not to get fat like that: 'Fat is the enemy of women and art.' As they went down the stairs Sarah heard him murmur a saw about the most beautiful women having the plainest daughters.

Certainly she was no conventional beauty, with her frizzy reddish hair and stick-thin angularity, in those days of sleek *bandeaux* and feminine curves. But the duc de Morny had said she should be an actress so an actress she must be. She noticed that even the propsect of her being an actress lent her a sort of glamour in her godfather's eyes – though the kind of actress he had in mind was not, as she noted later, the classical variety. He, like all the rest of the household, was now occupied in helping her select a passage for her Conservatoire audition.

The day arrived. Sarah was got up with the greatest elaboration. Julie had had a dress specially made for this occasion from some black silk supplied by a family friend, a young Dutch Jew just starting out in business. The dress had a tight bodice and a low neck, with a gathered collar and a fichu; beneath the skirt her white pantalettes peeked out over golden slippers. On her head, although the summer was drawing on to autumn, she wore a big straw hat. When Mme Guérard appeared, Sarah ran forward to greet her – and her dress ripped at the shoulder. Julie turned angrily to the young Dutchman, who had just come in, but he briskly disclaimed responsibility: 'I told you it was a little scorched, that was why I let you have it cheap.' Finally the tear was mended and Sarah, Mlle Brabender and Mme Guérard set off, squashed into a two-seater *fiacre*, for the Conservatoire, 15, Faubourg Poissonnière.

By the time they arrived, the waiting-room outside the audition room was already full of hopeful boys and girls, each with his or her retinue of mothers, aunts, cousins, brothers and sisters. In *Petite Idole* Sarah draws a picture of the boys whispering together in a group in the corner, eyeing the girls as they huddled on the benches with their mothers. A boy and girl came out of the audition, red in the face and quarrelling; another girl was called in, taking with her a boy and another little girl who were to give her her cues. Sarah gave her name to old Léautaud, who was in charge of the hopefuls. She would give a passage from *L'Ecole des femmes*. And who was to give her cues? he enquired. She was nonplussed: this was a detail she had not considered. He pointed out some boys who might do, but she didn't know them and wouldn't ask them. So what was she proposing to do? In that case, she told him, she would recite a fable from La Fontaine – *Les Deux Pigeons*. He shrugged and went to note down this eccentric choice, while Sarah retired to wait, feeling sick.

The story of Sarah's audition for the Conservatoire has passed into theatrical history.

Her name was called, and for the first time in her life she found herself entirely alone, in a large room with a stage at one end and a table in the middle. At the table sat the auditioning committee; Auber, Beauvallet the tragedian, Provost and Samson, both famous actors, and Augustine Brohan, a leading actress, all, of course, members of the Comédie-Française. Léautaud pushed her onto the stage, hissed 'Curtsy, then start, and stop when the president rings his bell.'

Sarah curtsied and began:

> Deux pigeons s'aimaient d'un amour tendre.
> L'un d'eux s'ennuyant au logis . . .

At this point someone – Beauvallet – groaned: 'This isn't a classroom! What a grotesque idea, to recite a fable!' And Sarah stopped, her heart beating. A silver-haired gentleman, Provost, then said, 'Go on, child,' and Brohan said, 'Well, it'll be shorter than a scene, anyway.' Louis Verneuil, who was for a short time Lysiane's husband and so heard the story either from her or from the aged Sarah herself, has a slightly different version of this incident. He says that when the *Deux Pigeons* was announced Beauvallet began to protest. Auber wrote Morny's name on a scrap of paper and passed it to him, at which point the judges became well-disposed and attentive. But even if this version is correct there was no way that Sarah could have known about it at the time, which suggests either that one of the committee told her about it later, when they had become colleagues, or that it was a piece of gossip that she picked up.

Sarah began again:

> Deux pigeons s'aimaient d'un amour tendre.
> L'un d'eux s'ennuyant au logis
> Fut assez . . .

'Speak up,' said a little white-haired man – Samson. 'We can't hear you.' Terrified, Sarah stopped. 'We're not ogres,' said Samson. 'We shan't eat you.' He whispered something to Auber who said, 'Start from the beginning, and louder.' Brohan groaned: 'Oh, God, at this rate it'll take longer than a scene!' This made everyone laugh. Sarah pulled herself together. She was furious. 'I've often thought about that day,' she reflected later, 'and I've realized that perfectly good, intelligent, compassionate people lose their good qualities when they become part of a group. They aren't personally responsible and all their worst instincts are awakened.' Obviously she did not formulate this to herself at the time; nevertheless, she no longer felt intimidated by these people who were behaving so badly. She started again, and no longer cared what anyone thought. Her voice had warmed up, and speaking more loudly improved her diction. At the end, Auber rang his bell. She descended from the platform, suddenly exhausted. Auber stopped her on her way out. 'Well, little girl, that was very good,' he said. 'M. Provost and M. Beauvallet both want you in their class.' Beauvallet, Sarah realized, was the actor with the booming voice who had been so rude to her at the start. 'Who do you want to be with?' asked Auber.

Sarah pointed at Provost.

'Perfect,' said Auber. 'Better get your handkerchief out, Beauvallet, you poor fellow. The child's all yours, Provost.'

Sarah suddenly understood and cried joyfully, 'Then I'm in!'

And Auber said, 'Yes, you're in, and I've only one regret, that such a pretty voice isn't destined for music.' For Auber, of course, was a musician.

So runs the story; and doubtless it is, more or less, true. In later years, Sarah used sometimes to recite *Les Deux Pigeons* as an encore to her adoring audiences. The only doubtful detail is whether there was ever any real suspense about the outcome. If she had recited the opening paragraphs of that day's newspaper, would it have been any different? Sarah was Morny's protégée, for what reasons one didn't enquire, and it was important that the duc de Morny should remain well-disposed towards the Conservatoire and the Comédie-Française. If Morny wanted her to attend the Conservatoire, was there ever any possibility that she would be turned down?

Be that as it may, she was not turned down, but rushed out in high excitement to announce her good news to Mlle de Brabender and Mme Guérard. She was immediately surrounded by other hopefuls who wanted to know what it had been like, what she had recited . . . she told them; they were astonished, and Sarah, she recounts, 'could have died of joy.'[5]

Her two kind friends offered to take her to a confectioner's to buy some celebratory cakes, but no, Julie must be told. So they piled into a cab and rolled post-haste back to the apartment where everyone was waiting to hear what had happened. Julie was leaning out of the window when they arrived. Mme Guérard waved and shouted, 'She's in! she's in!' and Sarah could have cried with rage, for she had the scene all prepared in her mind – how she would look very sad, and how Julie would say, Well, I'm not surprised, you're really so stupid, poor darling, and how she would fling her arms round her neck and surprise them all! But for the rest of their lives together, Sarah would never be able to break Mme Guérard of her terrible habit of ruining all Sarah's best stories.

Still, nothing could really spoil that day. When Julie opened the door, Sarah begged her to pretend she didn't know what had happened. So she shut the door again, and Sarah rang, and Marguerite the cook opened, and there were Julie, Régis, Jeanne, Régine and Tante Rosine, and when Sarah hugged her mother and cried 'I'm in!' everyone was astonished and delighted, and even little Régine, that sad child who never laughed, danced a bourrée and gave a small smile.

5

Sarah, even now, did not especially want to be an actress. In fact, left to herself, she would have studied painting – she had, and was always to retain, a great facility for the visual arts. Whether or not she was a serious student she had at this point begun to do a little painting and even to exhibit – in October, 1860, there was a favourable notice in the *Mercure de Paris* of her painting 'The Champs Elysées in Winter', which won the first prize in an exhibition at the Académie Colombier. But whatever she did she wanted to be *somebody* – an independent person. The importance of this was brought home to her only a few months later, when her godfather, Régis, took her aside in order to put a proposition to her. The proposition was very simple. A friend of his wanted to marry Sarah, but Sarah couldn't bear him and had turned him down – 'he was so dark, so hairy, so covered with beard that he revolted me.' Régis now explained to Sarah how foolish this was. The friend was not only rich already, but he had expectations . . . Nevertheless, Sarah did not want to marry him. Why not? 'I don't love him!' Régis, the man of the world, explained that one never did love – before. That came after. After what? Pushing all this to one side, Régis broached the essentials of the affair. Julie was not well-off. Her income came from a factory owned by Sarah's grandmother, who could not abide her. Her income would be cut off, and what would she do then, with three children to support? Sarah's father had arranged things very badly. Now, if she married Monsieur B., he would settle three hundred thousand francs on her, she could give her own hundred thousand to her mother, and everyone would be happy. The only solution was for Sarah to marry.

She would not do so, however, even though the gentleman himself promised her that in that case he would die of misery (he did not, but became very rich and, Sarah affirmed, much better-looking once he had white hair). And although the effort involved in resisting this piece of emotional blackmail was very great, the fact that she was at the Conservatoire gave her strength she would not otherwise have found. She reasoned that, if she became a successful actress, she would be able to support her family in an infinitely preferable way.

The Conservatoire, at the time Sarah entered it, was a curious and unique place. It was, as the name suggested, primarily a school of music: the drama section had been set up only in 1786, when the collapse of the provincial theatres which had been the traditional training-ground for the French stage meant that, if the French theatrical tradition was not to disappear, some more formal way of transmitting it had to be devised. This sense of tradition was very strong within the school and the Comédie-Française, the theatre to which its best students might expect to graduate. (Another theatre, the Odéon, was also attached to it, but its repertoire and traditions were broader and less rigidly classical.) Samson, who had been one of the judges at Sarah's audition and who was to be one of her tutors, was himself a pupil of Talma, who had been the first great actor to emerge from the Conservatoire; and Talma had been a pupil of Molé, one of the school's original founders. Talma and Samson, as well as being professors at the Conservatoire, had both been *sociétaires* of the Comédie-Française, as had Samson's pupil, the incomparable tragedian Rachel, who had died before she could take up the professorship which had been created for her; her place had been taken by Augustine Brohan.

The students were continually reminded of this distinguished and direct lineage. The Comédie-Française, and with it the Conservatoire, were part of the state; they represented a significant strand of its cultural heritage. The distinguished critic Jules Lemaître (who was to become one of Sarah's staunchest supporters) wrote a slightly, but not very, exaggerated spoof on this grave and respectable aspect of these establishments, in the form of a letter to a young lady recently graduated:

Mademoiselle,

When your father, a civil servant at the ministry of education, died three years ago, leaving you alone with your mother, it was you who had the idea that you might go to the Conservatoire. How right you were to choose the peaceful, bourgeois profession of acting rather than other more difficult and adventurous possibilities! You are the daughter of a civil servant, and you wanted to be a civil servant. And that is what you are.

Educated in a State establishment, you will take an engagement at the Odéon, which is a State theatre. There, you will play the classics; and, on Thursdays, you will fulfil your pedagogic function by reciting Racine and Molière to schoolchildren. When you show some talent you will enter the Comédie-Française, the premier State theatre. You will enter it with respect. You will play plays by academicians and you will soon be elected a junior member . . .

None of the violent passions which you simulate every evening, in correct conformity with the 'traditions' of each role, will trouble your private life for an instant. You will by then be twenty-five. A distinguished lawyer and a rich financier will ask for your hand. But you will choose one of your colleagues, an infinitely more serious figure, a full member, a professor at the Conservatoire and a Chevalier of

50

the Legion of Honour . . . The dissolute bourgeois at whose houses you will occasionally consent to give recitations (but only as a couple) will marvel at your domestic virtues. You will have children . . . and, your retirement pensions fully in order, you will age gracefully, plump and dignified, loaded with honours, in your little house in the Avenue de Villiers . . .[1]

Such was the establishment Sarah was now entering; and such, if she played her cards right, might be her expectations. Every morning Julie gave her money for bus fares one way for herself and Mlle de Brabender – they were expected to come home on foot – plus eight sous for cakes. But as neither of them could bear buses, on alternate days they walked; the other days, they treated themselves to a cab.

The Conservatoire, like most acting schools, taught voice production, deportment, mime, and the classical repertory. It laid particular emphasis on declamation, of which there were several competing traditions, the two main ones being based on *chant*, which emphasized poetical recitation concentrating on cadence, rhyme, caesura; and *vérité*, concentrating on content and reducing verse to prose. Allied to *chant* was the recitative technique known as *mélopée* which so astonished some of Sarah's foreign audiences. In her own treatise, *L'Art du Théâtre*, Sarah lays great emphasis on the differentiating details of these two systems. She says: 'Declamation is the art of speaking, or declaiming, beautiful verse with precision, tenderness or fury.'[2] This is a sentence of great technical precision. '*Dire* stresses content, *déclamer*, music. *Tenderness* and *fury* are opposed to *precision*, for *precision*, an attribute of technique, is representative of the *chant* system, while *tenderness* and *fury*, emotional attributes, represent *vérité*.'[3]

Sarah was not a model pupil, but she worked hard. Her favourite teacher was Régnier, who taught the *vérité* style of speaking; he was mild-mannered and charming. Beauvallet

51

the tragedian, who had been so boorish at her audition, she detested; he had a beautiful deep voice, but he could not give that to anyone else, and it was not, in Sarah's opinion, any substitute for talent. Samson, by contrast, had a delicate, piercing voice and was very distinguished. He taught simplicity of approach. Provost, Sarah's main teacher, was more pompous; he liked ample gestures, a broad and sustained style. He did not like Sarah. She was noisy and always late; she annoyed him, but he could not help being interested in her, and he was very hard on her. For two hours at a time he would make her go over every doubtful gesture, every badly-produced cry, every wrong inflection, keeping her standing on stage all the time. 'He was pitiless and extremely interesting,' recalls Paul Porel, a contemporary of Sarah's at that time. When, at the end of all this, Sarah fell, exhausted, Provost simply picked up his wide-brimmed hat and stumped off muttering 'Well, that's a role you'll remember if you ever get to play it!'⁴ Sarah even attended the deportment classes given by M. Elie, an old beau, frizzed, made-up, wearing a lace jabot, at which the few who bothered to turn up were relentlessly schooled in the different ways of sitting down, walking nobly, indicating 'Leave me, sir!' without speaking a word . . . 'Everything,' he would say, 'is in the look, the gesture, the attitude.' His class did not take him very seriously. 'We walked about as nobly and solemnly as camels,' recalled Sarah of one of his exercises – but he taught her one of her most fundamental principles: that appropriate gesture *precedes* speech, something she never forgot.

Sarah took it all very seriously. For her, it was the key to the door of freedom. The incident of the rich suitor whom she had summarily rejected had brought all those alternatives which had been so painfully discussed at the family council out of the realms of hypothesis into the world of facts. On grounds of sheer irresponsible prejudice she had chosen to condemn her family to financial insecurity. The only way for her to redeem herself (in her own eyes as well as theirs) would be to prove that she could earn her living – and, preferably, theirs as well – on her own terms. Sarah's attitude to her family is a subject to which we shall return; but it should be noted that she never displays any resentment at Julie's mercenary expectations of her – which is not to say that she did not recognize them for what they were. On the contrary: she did recognize this, recognized and described it, just as she recognized and described her mother's coldness, shallowness and inadequacy, and these things caused her a great deal of pain. After she turned down the rich suitor, she tells us, she wept on her mother's shoulder, and then shut herself in her room and, for the first time in many weeks, regretted the convent. But this did not affect her feeling for her mother: it simply sharpened her desire to do well by her and gain her approbation. And there was only one way in which Sarah would ever gain Julie's approbation – by making a good living and supporting her. As long as she did not do this she would never be able to escape the knowledge that she had, in Julie's eyes, wronged her family by declining to become the rich and, incidentally, unhappy Madame B.

By now she was growing out of gawky childhood into young womanhood. Paul Porel speaks of her 'distinction, originality and grace' at this time – the qualities, no doubt, which had enslaved poor, hairy Monsieur B. Another contemporary, Marie Colombier, of whom we shall hear more, gives a description of her at this time which, although it is part of a work deeply malicious in intent, is probably fairly accurate. Sarah, says Colombier, was tall and slim – in fact she was not particularly tall, but her extreme slenderness and erect carriage gave that impression. 'Her features were regular and pure, resembling her mother's Jewish features but more refined, but you wouldn't have called her pretty any more than you would have called her ugly. There was something fleeting and unformed about her, which recalled an unfinished statue in a sculptor's studio. She lacked the finishing touch . . . under the grace of that vague adolescent face could be sensed . . . the imminent bloom of womanhood. But there was an unforgettable strangeness about her, especially in her eyes which were wonderful and very long. They changed colour with the light and the movements of her face, gold when she was a dreaming child, cat's-eye green when she was angry, dark blue when she smiled.'[5]

The Conservatoire course lasted for two years. At the end of each year there were competitive examinations, one in tragedy, one in comedy. On the outcome of these examinations depended the immediate future careers of the students. Those who did best would be admitted to the companies at the Comédie-Française or the Odéon; the rest would take their chances in the theatre of the boulevards. In her first year, Sarah did extremely well in these competitions. For her tragic scene she took Voltaire's *Zaïre*, against the will of her tutor, Provost – and played it, what was more, according to her own ideas, not his: he wanted her to declaim the scene's climax violently, while she thought it would be much more effective done softly and tenderly (which was much more in keeping with the light timbre of her voice). In the event she played the scene her way and won great applause and a second prize, to the indignation of the audience, which felt she should have won; but Sarah herself felt this decision was correct; 'I was very young and I hadn't been studying long.' In comedy she was first runner-up with *La Fausse Agnès*. In her second year she did not do so well; she was expected to win the tragedy, but failed to do so, while the comedy prize was won by Marie Lloyd, with Sarah in second place.

54

Marie Colombier gives a vivid picture of the excitement at the Conservatoire on the days of these competitions: all the streets around it choked with carriages belonging to the families of the competing students, the great court crowded and buzzing with spectators all pushing to try to get near the door leading to the room where the competition was taking place. Then the sudden 'Ah!' which heralds the appearance of the Minister of Beaux-Arts, indicating that the competition has ended; he is followed by the Director of the school, important civil servants, critics, hangers-on, all making for the gate and piling into their carriages. Then a free-for-all as everyone tries to get as near as possible to the door from which the students now emerge, the boys either very pale or very red, the girls more finished and coquettish; the air filled with the sound of mothers calling their off-spring, eager to know how they have done.[6]

Sarah had not been at her best on the day of her final competition. Julie had insisted that she should have her hair done by Julie's own coiffeur and he, at the sight of Sarah's frizzy mop, had thrown up his hands, suggesting that the best thing would be for the girl to shave her head and then try to train the hair, as it grew again, to something more like civilization. After more than an hour and a half in the hands of this despairing gentleman, who had brushed her, combed her, pinned her, and tried to straighten her hair with curling-tongs, Sarah emerged with her hair pulled back from her temples, her ears showing incongruously naked, and a pile of little sausages on top of her head; her forehead, usually veiled in a froth of blond curls, bare and implacable. This construction was held in place by a liberal application of beef marrow and pins.

To make matters worse, her old tutor, Provost, had recently been taken ill and had been replaced by Samson, with whom Sarah could not get on. He had insisted that she play two pieces by Casimir Delavigne for the competition;

55

she thought they were both rubbish; he still insisted. Now she turned up to play her miserable parts, late, crying and hideous. Her sympathetic friends took out the pins, but all the head-shaking in the world could not make things much better. Sarah's turn was announced. She could hardly remember what she was going to say, and when she began, could not recognize her voice at all, it was so drowned in tears. She heard a sympathetic lady in the audience say, 'Poor little thing, they shouldn't have let her compete with such a cold!' She finished, made her bow, left the stage and fainted.

When she came to herself she found that she looked a little better. Her hair had recovered some of its life; her face was less swollen. There was no hope for the tragedy: she resolved, therefore, to win the comedy prize. Comedy was not generally her forte. But today she would win it – that, she told herself, or back to the convent!

And indeed she thought she had won it. Her part was a stupid part, a conventional, sensible married woman, while she was a child who looked even younger than her age. But she played it brilliantly. Then she stood back to await her glory.

But it was not to be.

The boys' prizes were called first. There was no first prize this year; Paul Porel won the second prize.

Now the girls' prizes. Sarah took a step forward from the doorway in which she was standing.

The announcement was of a unanimous choice: Mlle Marie Lloyd – not to be confused with the British music-hall artist of the same name, but a beautiful tall, dark girl, a great friend of Sarah's. She had played Célimène; and although she had played it without any particular brilliance, such was her physical perfection for the part that there could have been no other choice. She *was* Célimène. 'She had entered laughing and radiant . . . the personification of

Célimène, that twenty-year-old flirt, so unconsciously cruel.'[7] So, at least, says the Sarah of the memoirs; and adds that she has never forgotten the lesson she learned that day about the importance of completely realizing a role one is to play. 'Every time I create a part the character is before me in every detail, dressed, hairdressed, walking, waving, sitting down, getting up.' Another version of the same encounter has it that the reason Marie Lloyd took first place that day was because she was under the protection of M. le Ministre himself, so that there could be no other possible result.[8] If this is true, it could be said that there was a certain justice about it: Sarah, after all, was only in the Conservatoire at all for very similar reasons. At any rate, Sarah was devastated. She felt faint, and remained sitting on her bench long after most of the other students had left the room. Marie Lloyd came and sat down beside her. 'Are you sad?' she asked.

'Yes, I wanted to win the first prize, and it was you instead. It isn't fair!'

'I don't know whether it's fair or not,' replied Marie Lloyd, 'but I promise you, I didn't do it on purpose!'

'I couldn't help laughing,' Sarah recalled. And then Marie, who was an orphan and not very happy at home, suggested that she should come home with Sarah. Which they did: all four, Marie, Sarah, Mme Guérard and Mlle de Brabender piling into a carriage together to return to 265, rue St Honoré, where Julie now lived.

6

However much better she may have felt in the carriage, trundling home with Marie and her two faithful supporters, Sarah knew as soon as they arrived that her second prize was not enough. If she was to be permitted a respite from nagging about marriage, she had to win the first prize and become successful. Consequently, the nagging began at once. Her godfather, congratulating Marie on her prize and her beauty, took the opportunity to point out once again to Sarah that she was too thin to be an actress, that she was not pretty enough, that her voice was too weak . . . in short, that she should give it all up and marry the rich miller who kept proposing to her, or the Spanish tanner who was crazy about her. In despair, she hid herself in her room and took refuge in sleep.

There was no question of resigning herself. That was never on the cards. Sarah had already adopted the motto 'Quand-même' – which was to be hers throughout her life. 'Quand-même' encapsulates a view of life which postulates the reverse of resignation. In resignation, Sarah knew, darkness lay. Any happiness or success she had enjoyed had been achieved in spite of circumstances. In her memoirs she tells how she first consciously adopted this device during one of those unsatisfactory interludes spent at her aunt Henriette's house, when she had bet her cousin that she would be able to jump a particularly wide ditch, and had done so *in spite of* getting soaked to the skin and torn by brambles in the process. According to Lysiane, it was a little later, after her débuts at the Français, that she acquired her first notepaper printed with '*Quand-même*' – courtesy, like so much else, of Morny. This detail may or may not be true, though if she ever needed all the defiance she could muster, it was then. Just now it seemed improbable that she would ever achieve these débuts.

But she need not have despaired. The duc de Morny had not abandoned her. When she awoke, she found a note from Mme Guérard awaiting her: 'While you were asleep, the duc de Morny sent word to your mother to tell her that Camille Doucet had just assured him that your engagement with the Comédie-Française is all agreed on. So don't worry, my dear child, you can face the future with confidence. – Your petit'Dame.'[1]

Morny had seen Doucet, who was Director of Beaux-Arts, and Doucet had arranged an interview with M. Thierry, director of the Comédie-Française, which was to take place next day. This, Sarah's first entrance on to the stage of adult life, was managed by her aunt Rosine with just that knack for the flashily inappropriate most horrendous to the tender seventeen-year-old ego. It was decided that none of Sarah's dresses would do for the interview: they were all too little-girlish. One was therefore lent by Rosine, a dress which Sarah remembered with horror years later, cabbage-green, trimmed with black velvet. This was surmounted by a sky-blue bonnet with long ribbons. Thus attired, Sarah set off in her aunt's smart carriage, complete with lackey. This showy arrival did not make a good impression, but happily Sarah did not yet realize this. The interview with Thierry was brief. He handed her a contract, which would have to be signed by her mother. Leaving his office she met Coquelin, her old comrade from the Conservatoire, who was waiting for her in his usual good-natured way. He shook her hand cheerfully: 'Well, that's that, then!' She descended the stairs, she recalls, four at a time, and ran into a group standing in front of the door. This consisted of Doucet, Régnier and Beauvallet. She thanked Doucet profusely, but he insisted her engagement was nothing to do with him; she hadn't done well in the examination, but . . . 'We've still got faith in you,' said kindly Régnier. 'Haven't we, Excellency?' Doucet affirmed that he thought Sarah would be a great artist. Beauvallet said coarsely, 'That's quite a carriage you've got!' but Doucet, who knew Rosine, said, 'It's her aunt's,' and Sarah was forgiven. Such was her first day at the Comédie-Française.

Various other initiation ceremonies also took place. Rosine gave a grown-up dinner-party for her niece. She invited Morny, Doucet, Rossini, M. de Walewski the Minister of Beaux-Arts, Julie, Mlle de Brabender and Sarah, who wore her first evening-dress. After dinner more guests arrived, and Sarah recited with Rossini playing an appropriate accompaniment. Among the guests that night was the young Comte de Kératry, who was probably Sarah's first lover, a handsome hussar who paid her a great deal of attention, thus putting Rosine's nose distinctly out of joint. No woman approaching thirty – especially not one who makes her living from her attractions – likes to be upstaged by her seventeen-year-old niece; and, to judge from the photos Nadar took of her at this time, Sarah was now ravishing, with her cloud of hair, her pure, delicate features, her long, dreamy eyes. Kératry was one of the high-living *lions*, a young man very much à la mode. In a few years he would become *Préfet* of Paris. By that time he was married to a beautiful creole; now, he was still a bachelor and a connoisseur of women. No doubt Rosine felt that such a catch was wasted on her unworldly, inexperienced niece.

The next thing was the notice to attend her first rehearsals at the Comédie. The system there was brutal. Newcomers to the company were given three débuts, in which they took the leading role in different plays. What they made of these was up to them. Sarah's débuts were to be in Racine's *Iphigénie*, a play called *Valérie* by Scribe, and Molière's *Les Femmes savantes*, to take place in August and September. When her first rehearsal for *Iphigénie* was called, Sarah arrived an hour early, feeling very nervous. She was met by the company manager, Davenne, a kind man who took her in hand and showed her round.

The Comédie-Française – the *maison de Molière*, as it is known – had, and still has, a weight of tradition heavy upon it – burdening it, some might say. The full force of this was concentrated in the actors' green-room, the *foyer des acteurs*. This very particular place, with its very particular atmosphere, figures in all the many novels of this period which take a young actress as their central figure – and not just a young actress, but a young actress of Jewish extraction: Edmond de Goncourt's *La Faustin*, Félicien Champsaur's *Dinah Samuel*, Henry James' *The Tragic Muse* . . . Goncourt describes it as 'a curious and intimate museum . . . where all the old dramatic triumphs, painted or sculpted, still live on the walls, and seem to lean smilingly over the actor or actress who rests there today during an interval . . . In this little museum, to sit down under the gaze of the dead, the living have big armchairs, ample sofas with beautiful curves, eighteenth-century furnishings which were given by King Louis-Philippe in exchange for a chandelier which he remembered having seen in his father's house when he was a child, and whose crystal drops Beauvallet had a habit of breaking with his cane whenever he entered the foyer in one of his bad tempers.'[2] James' Miriam Rooth is tremendously excited by this place. She says: 'Oh, it's enough to see *this*; it makes my heart beat . . . It's full of the vanished past, it makes me cry. I feel them here, the great artists I shall never see. Think of Rachel (look at her grand portrait there!) and how she stood on these very boards and trailed over them the robes of Hermione and Phèdre!' Sarah, however, felt altogether overwhelmed by the crowd of ghosts, and was not calmed by the other artists when they finally appeared, indifferent and somewhat loud-mouthed. She tried on her costume; it looked awful; the costumier told her that if she wanted another she would have to pay for it herself.

She would also need a make-up box. These were made by a M. Massin, the father of one of her friends at the Conservatoire, Léontine Massin, whose workshop she visited under the supervision of the mother of another friend, Mme Dica-Petit, who was Dutch and so had got to know Julie. The Massins lived on the sixth floor of a house in rue Réaumur: the door was opened to them by Léontine's little hunchbacked sister, and soon Sarah was hugging her friend, to the great disapproval of Mme Dica-Petit. Léontine had seen the announcement of Sarah's débuts in the papers; she herself was just about to start rehearsals at the Variétés. She was to become a famous *demi-mondaine*. Had she already begun to acquire this reputation? Was this why Mme Dica-Petit was so disapproving? At any rate, M. Massin, Léontine's father, gave them a cold welcome. The little hunchback sister apologized and explained that it was because he was cross that Léontine wasn't going to the Français . . . Sarah began to realize that there were dramas and troubles in other households besides her own.

Sarah's first début was set for the first of September. That morning, she stood staring at the theatrical posters displayed at the corner of the rue Duphot and the rue St Honoré, and there it was: *Débuts de Mlle Sarah Bernhardt*. She got to the theatre around five o'clock and climbed up to the little dressing-room she shared with another girl in a house on the other side of the rue de Richelieu, opposite the theatre and rented by it. A little closed-in bridge led over the road from one building to the other. Dressing took a long time, and so did making-up. Mme Guérard and Mlle de Brabender were both there offering conflicting advice. Julie was to go straight to the theatre. Rosine was on holiday.

By the time Sarah got down to the stage, the curtain was already rising. She was in a state of complete terror: stage-fright was something which was to torment her for the rest of her life. She heard a familiar voice behind her. It was Provost, her old teacher, and beside him was Samson, who was playing that night in a Molière comedy which was to follow Sarah's play. She flung her arms round Provost's neck, and he tried to calm her: vainly, however. The blood sang in her ears, she was oblivious of everything. Then Provost heard her cue and pushed her onstage. She clung on to her father, Agamemnon, then threw herself into the arms of her mother, Clytemnestra: she could not stand unaided. Finally the act ended and she rushed up to her dressing-room and began to tear off her costume. Mme Guérard wanted to know if she had gone mad? There were four more acts to come. Finally, she took command of herself and managed to finish the piece. 'I was insignificant,' she says of herself. Francisque Sarcey, the most powerful critic in Paris, was a little kinder. 'Mlle Bernhardt, who made her début yesterday in *Iphigénie*, is a tall, pretty girl, with a good carriage and a lovely face; the top part of the face in particular is remarkably beautiful,' he wrote. 'She holds herself well and speaks with perfect clarity, and that is all that it is possible to say at the moment'. But by the end of her third début, *Les Femmes savantes*, twelve days later, he was being less kind. 'Mlle Bernhardt . . . was as pretty and as unremarkable as in the roles of Valérie and Junie' [he meant Iphigénie] . . . The performance was very poor and does not bode well. It is unimportant that Mlle Bernhardt is not up to the part. She is a beginner, and it's inevitable that most of the beginners we see will not succeed – that only happens with very few. But the sad thing is that most of the actors around her did little better. And they are full members! But all they had to differentiate them from their young colleague was a greater familiarity with the stage; they are what Mlle Bernhardt will be in twenty years if she stays with the Comédie-Française.'[3]

She was not, however, to stay with the Comédie-Française.

This is not because she never intended to do so. On the contrary: her career was marked out for her, just as Jules Lemaître had described it to his imaginary young correspondent, though it did not look as if Sarah would be as successful as that. After the anticlimax of her débuts, it seemed more likely that she would be one of those who never makes it to the leading roles, but stays with a company playing serving maidens and then character roles, until her career ends in the oblivion whence it never emerged. For it was generally true that if an actress was to succeed, she gave at least some hint of her potential at her débuts. In the case of Rachel this had taken some time – she had started out as Camille in Corneille's *Horace* on 12 June 1838, when Paris was emptying for the summer, and it was not until the critics returned at the beginning of September that the then most important critic, Jules Janin, gave her the notice that started her career: 'Now at last we have the most stunning and marvellous young girl whom the present generation has seen on the stage. That child (learn her name!) is Mlle Rachel . . .' But Rachel had been good enough for the then director of the Comédie, Védel, to maintain her in her roles against the indifference of empty summer houses; and Janin had picked her out at the Gymnase a year earlier. And they had been right. Rachel lifted the Comédie from the trough into which the craze for the new romantic drama had sent it in 1830, and remained its star attraction until her early and tragic death. That, of course, had left a terrible gap; and now once again the *maison de Molière* was in the doldrums. Racine and Molière are to the French drama what Shakespeare is to the English: a staple diet which can pall through sheer surfeit if constantly presented in mediocre productions. Earlier in that year, 1862, another actress, Agar, had made her début as Phèdre at the Français, and had done well enough, but Théophile Gautier, commenting on her performance, remarked that 'tragedy, these days, seems to have lost its drawing power for the public'; he thought that, unless the presentation was something special, people preferred to read a part that they had already seen acted a thousand times. Agar, at any rate, did not stay with the Français but left for the modern plays of the popular boulevard theatre, possibly helped on her way by the jealousy and bad feeling of her erstwhile comrades. She was to be Sarah's partner in the latter's first great success seven years later. Meanwhile it was clear that there was still no prospect of a new Rachel.

How was it possible that the actress who would be so triumphantly acclaimed should show not the slightest vestige of this talent in her early roles? The answer must be that Sarah, whatever she was, was not what one might term a born actress. There was nothing instinctive about her art. She was not one of those who, like Rachel, knows almost without being taught (though not, let it be emphasized, without thinking) – exactly what she should do on stage, exactly how to approach a role. Neither was she, like her great English contemporary Ellen Terry, or Eleonora Duse, who was later almost to eclipse her in critical esteem, a child of the theatre, born in the wings and carried around with the props. On the contrary; 'Theatrical life was uninteresting to me,' she said of herself at this time. 'I never went inside a theatre except to act.'[4] She had great gifts, but she had to learn how to use them and herself. When, many years later, she told her pupil May Agate that 'the way to learn to act was to start doing it' and that 'if you had the makings of an actor in you, the rest would come'[5], she had perhaps forgotten her own beginnings and how nearly the rest had *not* come. And she was also without doubt glossing over the immense intellectual effort, the technique so mastered and assimilated that it no longer felt like technique, which was such a fundamental aspect of her art. It is worth noting that she had already acquired some of the most characteristic aspects of this technique by the time she left the Conservatoire, both in terms of what she learned from her teachers there and what she worked out for herself as suiting her particular style and limitations. She records at least two arguments over such technical points. One was with her favourite teacher, Régnier, who insisted that an actor should never turn his back on the audience, while Sarah insisted that this was sometimes inevitable. How could she escort an old woman offstage without turning her back? Could Régnier leave the room without turning his back on Sarah? He tried, lost his temper and left, slamming the door behind him.[6] (This, at least, is the way she tells it in her book on acting, *L'Art du Théâtre*. In her memoirs, this incident involves not Régnier but an old professor at the Sorbonne, an habitué of the Odéon at the time Sarah was starring there, who takes it upon himself to supply the criticism absent from her reception by the adoring student Saradoteurs. But although the cast of this two-hander changes slightly, the action remains exactly the same.) Later, some of her most striking effects were to be achieved by the deliberate turning of her back to the audience. There was also the argument over her delivery of the closing speech in *Zaïre*, when she insisted upon the tenderness which suited her voice and character rather than the fury Provost considered appropriate – and tenderness and subtlety rather than bravura were always to be the hallmarks of her best performances.

But technical mastery, of course, can never be the whole story – and especially not when one is very young, as Sarah still was when she first conquered Paris in 1867. An actress must have something more to offer, or her performance will be nothing more than an empty shell; and a shell, even a very beautiful one, does not engage the audience, as Sarah so evidently and rivetingly did. But what, apart from technique, can an actress offer who does not have an inborn theatrical gift? The answer, of course, is herself. Sarah Bernhardt, Arthur Symons once remarked, was an 'extraordinarily interesting woman', and as a result of this, her performances on stage were also extraordinarily interesting. 'Everything in her is ruled by thought,' said another critic, Yetta Blaze de Bury. 'You see Sarah: you see a *'fantaisiste'*, an exquisitely well-appointed brain, thirsting for assertion and blossoming.'[7] It could be said – it often was said – that Sarah Bernhardt was her own greatest creation. It was she whom people came to see in their droves and across continents – this fascinating and brilliant woman interpreting her roles as no one else could interpret them. Whether Sarah was ever anyone other than Sarah onstage was an argument which raged throughout her career.

But if this was the foundation of her art, then it is easy to see why as a young *débutante* she could not succeed. In September, 1862, Sarah was just about to turn eighteen – and no eighteen-year-old can be said to be an 'extraordinarily interesting woman', whatever her potential and whatever other attributes she may already possess. She rarely yet knows who she is. This was particularly true of Sarah, who despite the unorthodox circumstances of her family life, was not at all sophisticated. After her aunt Rosine's party had given her her first taste of life in the great world, she records that 'I came back home quite changed . . . The only knowledge I had of life was what I had gained in my studies and in the family. But I had just had a glimpse of the real world, with its hypocrisies and inanities. I asked myself anxiously how I would make out in it: I was so shy and so straightforward.'[8]

In other words, she was as yet a blank sheet. But the next few years were to leave their mark.

7

Sarah's exit from the Comédie-Française came not many months after her débuts there; and if there is a certain inevitability about the story, this is not just because of hindsight but because it resulted from that gut insubordination – a kind of barely-suppressed fury above which she seemed always, at this time, precariously to be skating – which had ended her days at Grand-Champs, which made her the despair of her mother and her aunt Henriette, which had exasperated her professors at the Conservatoire and which made it inconceivable that she should stay long with an institution as riddled with hierarchy and authoritarianism as the Théâtre Français. There is an inevitability, too, about the immediate cause of the disruption – Sarah's little sister Régine.

Sarah loved Régine with an indulgent love – that love which she was to vouchsafe to all members of her family, but especially to her mother, her son Maurice, and this sister. Whether they liked it or not – and there is no evidence that Julie did like it – they were the centre of her emotions. In the arbitrary, shifting world in which she had grown up and was in many ways always to live, there was a wonderful inevitability about blood relatives to which she clung. She was not blind to their deficiencies – indeed, she recorded them in her memoirs with that bizarre objectivity which we have already noted: Julie's cold selfishness and inability to love anyone but her middle daughter, Jeanne; the impossible, hoydenish, foul-mouthed behaviour of little

Régine. But this did not affect her love for them, which sprang from her own deepest needs and which she could not control.

It is easy to see why she felt so close to Régine: the little girl was like her in so many ways – it must have been like seeing a little ghost of herself. Sarah must have understood so completely how Régine was feeling. Unlike their sister Jeanne, neither of them was loved by their mother. The reasons for this are unclear but may be guessed at. Possibly Sarah and Régine had both occurred at inconvenient moments in their mother's life; perhaps she had been more attached to Jeanne's father than to either of theirs. Whatever the reason, the result was inescapable. Julie could not bring herself to extend any affection to her eldest or her youngest daughter. In Sarah's case this had led to the years spent with the nurse, which had only been brought to an end by desperate measures, followed by banishment to Mme Fressard's and Grand-Champs, and her present sad awareness that, whatever she did, she could never really please her mother. Régine was still a small child, but already she was showing many of the traits that Sarah must have recognized from her own childhood. She was attention-seeking and ungovernable; and because she was always left in the charge of the cook, Marguerite, she acquired neither education nor manners. At least Sarah, thanks to her father, had received as much education as girls might expect in those days; added to which the convent had given her security and taught her manners. Régine had received none of these advantages, nor did it seem likely she would do so. Julie had wanted to send her to Grand-Champs, and at first the nuns had agreed, even though she was much younger than most of their pupils; but they had not been able to control her and she had been sent home. She was extremely pretty, with blonde hair and big blue eyes, but the face that stares out from the photograph is rebellious and mistrustful.

The incongruity of this angelic-looking creature uttering the coarse and knowing obscenities which were inevitably to be picked up in the company of the servant in a household such as Julie's was deeply shocking. Sarah was aware of this, but she loved Régine and sympathized with her boredom and feelings of rejection. So when Régine asked to be taken out for a treat, she was inclined to indulge her: her life, after all, was so much more amusing than the little girl's.

This had already led to trouble, or potential trouble. At the end of her first year at the Conservatoire, Régnier came to ask Julie if she would permit Sarah to perform in a play of his at the Vaudeville. She would be paid twenty-five francs a performance, seven hundred and fifty a month. Sarah was overjoyed, and begged Julie to allow her to do this: Julie, with her customary indifference, said she must do as she wanted. So Sarah asked to see Camille Doucet, director of the Beaux-Arts, in order that the arrangements might be made. She would go with Mme Guérard, since Julie would not stir herself; and Régine begged to come with them.

Régine was then five, and began as many naughty five-year-olds would, by climbing on the furniture and overturning the waste-paper basket. M. Doucet remarked that she was not a very good little girl, to which Régine promptly replied: 'You're a silly old man and if you make me cross I shall tell everyone that you put vinegar in the holy water. — That's what my aunt says!' And when Sarah, appalled, tried to smooth over the situation, Régine jumped up with clenched fists and began to hit Sarah: 'Are you saying Tante Rosine didn't say that? Then you're a liar. She did, and M. de Morny replied . . .' – but Sarah was not waiting to hear what M. de Morny had replied: she clapped her hand over Régine's mouth and dragged her away, howling, through the waiting-room full of people, before she could say more

71

terrible things. She did not get the part, and naturally attributed this to her sister's outburst, which was all the worse because she had a great regard for the sweet-natured Doucet (it turned out that he had refused Rosine some favour, an unaccustomed state of affairs which had put her in a bad temper with him). But Régnier explained that, on the contrary, he had been her warmest advocate: simply the Ministry had wanted to keep Sarah at the Conservatoire for her second year, and not to spoil her débuts by exposing her too soon in an inferior theatre. So all was well that ended well. 'I felt like jumping on her, the dreadful little girl,' said Sarah.[1]

But the next time things were not to be so easily mended.

The occasion was Molière's birthday, January 15, which was always celebrated at the Théâtre Français by all the actors paying homage onstage to the bust of the great playwright. This was Sarah's first experience of one of these ceremonies, and Régine begged to be allowed to come along. Julie said she could, and sent old Marguerite along as well.

All the actors, wearing their appointed costumes, were assembled in the foyer, and when the call-boy came to announce that the ceremony was to begin, everyone crowded into the long corridor lined with busts which led to the stage. Régine, for once, was behaving properly. Sarah held her by the hand. In front of them was one of the senior *sociétaires* (full members of the Comédie, who helped to run it and shared in the profits), a fat, elderly actress, Mme Nathalie, who (as Henry James put it) 'did the mothers and aunts and elderly wives . . . A perfect mistress of laughter and tears.'[2] On this occasion, however, the laughter was not in evidence: all was tears. Nathalie was very quick-tempered and self-important. Régine, trying to avoid stepping on the train of another actress, stepped on Nathalie's, who abruptly turned round and pushed her off with so much force that the child was sent flying against the pedestal of one of the busts, and cut her head open. Régine screamed and ran to Sarah, who shouted, 'You horrid creature!' and slapped Nathalie twice on the face. Uproar ensued: Nathalie fainted, some were indignant, some were approving . . . someone threw water at Nathalie's head, at which she suddenly revived and scolded, 'You'll ruin my make-up!' while Régine explained, 'It was all a mistake, big sister, I didn't mean to do it, the silly old cow's mooing for nothing!' – at which sympathizers laughed while Nathalie's friends shrugged their shoulders and shook their heads. Meanwhile the ceremony was twenty minutes late and the public was getting impatient. The line re-formed, and the procession started forward again.

Sarah felt no compunction at what she had done, but her instinct told her she would have to pay for it. Bressant, a charming actor who was popular with everybody, had only expressed what she knew when he said, 'This little affair will have to be cleared up, *chère* Mademoiselle. Nathalie's short arms are very long. You were a bit hasty, but I like that, and anyhow, the child is such a scream, and so pretty – but – '

Sarah spent that night crying, more from nerves than anything else; and next day, sure enough, there was a letter from the Administration requesting her presence at one o'clock for an interview 'concerning you personally'. She did not show this to Julie: since she had entered the theatre she was free to manage her own affairs, and came and went unchaperoned.

At one o'clock precisely she presented herself in the director's office. It was M. Thierry, whom she disliked, with his limp handshake and bunged-up nose. He read her a sermon on her general indiscipline and want of respect, and advised her to apologize to Mme Nathalie. He had asked Nathalie if she would come in; Sarah would make her apologies in front of three members of the committee (the

Comédie-Française was run by a committee of the *sociétaires*); the committee would decide whether or not a fine should be imposed or whether Sarah's engagement should be terminated.

Sarah said nothing. She thought, she says, of everyone at home: her mother would be so disappointed, her godfather would burst out laughing, her aunt Faure would be triumphant, Brabender would cry, Mme Guérard would defend her ... Thierry said, 'Well?' and Sarah said, 'I shan't apologize, so don't call Mme Nathalie. I'm resigning at once.'

At this Thierry softened. He was shocked at such rashness. He sat down and explained what a silly idea this was, what a wonderful place the Comédie was to work, and that Sarah should think again. Then, seeing Sarah softening, he offered once more to call Mme Nathalie. Sarah begged him not to: 'I should only slap her again.' 'Then I shall call your mother.' 'No, that's no good, my mother would never put herself out for me' [another of Sarah's bleak little *aperçus* of reality]. 'Well then, I'll go and see her.' 'No,' said Sarah, 'she's put me in charge of my own affairs.'³

The upshot was that Thierry said he would think about things, and Sarah returned home, having decided that she would say nothing about all this to her mother. But, too late! Régine had told the whole story and everyone was cross with her. Sarah locked herself in her room, and for some days nothing more was heard from the theatre. Then, one morning, came a rehearsal notice: she was to come for the reading of *Dolores*, a new play – the first new play she had been involved in. Amazingly, when she got to the theatre, she found she was to take the lead. This would normally have gone to one of the leading actresses, Mlle Favart, but she was indisposed. Sarah said nothing and read the part. Then, five days later, she met Nathalie – the inevitable moment she had been dreading. Nathalie said, 'Don't worry, Mademoiselle, I've forgiven you – I've just made sure you won't keep that role you like so much!' And, sure enough, a few days later, Sarah heard that Favart was feeling better after all – and she was so young – and the role was a heavy one . . . It was too much. She stormed into Thierry's office, told him what she thought, and insisted on handing in her resignation then and there.

The effect of this rash move on the atmosphere at home was all that Sarah had dreaded. The only place where she felt at peace and safe from reproachful looks and half-overheard whispers was upstairs at Mme Guérard's, where she spent increasing amounts of time and learned a few basic domestic skills, such as how to scramble eggs and prepare chocolate. Then, one day, she noticed that Julie was looking mysterious and seemed to be waiting for someone. The someone turned out to be Régis, Sarah's godfather, who arrived with a letter bearing the crest of the Gymnase theatre. The letter was from Montigny, the theatre's director, and a friend of Régis.

Régis could simply have told Sarah what was in the letter, but with his usual want of tact – or, which amounted to the same thing, of any regard for his goddaughter's feelings – he showed it to her. She read: 'As a favour to you I'll give your protégée an engagement, even though she sounds perfectly impossible.' But, whatever the form of the offer, it was an offer, and it made Julie happy. And this, as we have seen, was a matter of great importance to Sarah. So she thanked Régis and went with relief to receive her mother's kiss of forgiveness.

Sarah was not much taken with Montigny, whom she thought very self-important, and he, it seems, thought just as little of her. When the moment came to sign the contract he assumed that it would need Julie's signature as well, and when she explained that she was now her own mistress he remarked, 'That seems a foolish idea, to emancipate a bad girl like you. What can your parents have been thinking

75

of?' Sarah bit back her reply, signed, and returned happily home.

The Gymnase was a very different place from the Comédie-Française. It was a 'boulevard' theatre, presenting mostly light modern plays. Its stars at that time were Blanche Pierson, a beautiful blonde actress of some reputation, and Céline Montalant, who was just as beautiful but dark. Sarah was to understudy another young actress, Victoria Lafontaine. At first she did well enough, and was soon playing roles in her own right; but this peaceful interlude was not to last.

The occasion of her break with the Gymnase was, or so she says in her memoirs, a play by Raymond Deslandes called *Un Mari qui lance sa femme*, in which Sarah was to create the role of a flighty Russian princess. She says she thought it a rubbishy role and the Princess Dunchinka a rubbishy character, and one which suited her not at all. She was (she says) in despair, and thought about giving up the theatre altogether and opening a shop. She talked about this to old Meydieu, who encouraged her. What he had in mind was a sweet-shop – he had a very sweet tooth and knew lots of good recipes. But when they went to look at a shop and when she saw the little flat above it where she would have to live, this idea suddenly seemed not so attractive after all. So, crossly, she rehearsed Dunchinka; and the role turned out to be as bad as she had feared. After the first night Julie said, 'You poor child, you were so ridiculous as your Russian princess! I was really ashamed of you.' Perhaps she did not know how hurtful this would be to Sarah, but this seems improbable: more likely, she didn't care. At any rate, says Sarah, 'I really felt like killing myself.'[4] As usual, she rushed for comfort to Mme Guérard, who dissuaded her from this extreme course. What she now did, however, was only marginally less extreme.

At six the next morning Sarah returned to Mme Guérard

with an idea. She was going to Spain, now, at once. She would live on her savings and she would be accompanied by – *'mon petit'dame'*. Mme Guérard was understandably horrified. How could Sarah expect her to do such a thing? What about her husband and her own children? – her daughter was only just two years old! But Sarah was not to be dissuaded. She went downstairs to pack a suitcase, and returned. If Mme Guérard would not go with her, had she anyone else to suggest? She had, or Sarah thought of someone – a young woman named Caroline, who did a little dressmaking for the Guérards, and who had offered her services as a maid to Sarah. Caroline was rudely awakened from her slumbers (it was still very early in the morning) and finally agreed. Sarah had nine hundred francs saved up; Mme Guérard agreed to lend her six hundred more. 'I felt ready to conquer the world,' says Sarah. Caroline repacked Sarah's trunk and got together a suitcase of her own.

In Julie's apartment, everyone was still asleep. But not for long: it was nearly eight o'clock. Marguerite would soon be preparing breakfast – coffee for Julie, chocolate for Sarah, bread-and-milk for the little girls. It was time to go. Sarah wrote a tender letter to her mother, imploring her forgiveness. There was also a letter for Montigny at the Gymnase.

It so happened that, when this was delivered, Montigny was talking to Victorien Sardou, then just beginning his phenomenally successful career as a playwright – the latter part of which would be almost exclusively taken up with plays written for Sarah Bernhardt. The Gymnase was just then presenting Sardou's first plays, *La Perle noire* and *Les Gouaches*. Sarah's letter arrived at about four o'clock. Montigny read it, swore, and called the manager, to make sure that the understudy would be ready for the evening's performance. Then he sat down again, obviously angry. Sardou enquired what had happened. Montigny said, 'It's that girl who's already walked out of the Comédie-Française. I engaged her, I can't imagine why, and now she's walked out on the Gymnase as well.'

'Ah, yes,' says Sardou, 'that girl with curly blonde hair. What's her name, now? Sarah something – ' 'Bernhardt, not that it matters,' responded Montigny. 'After two exhibitions like that, I'm damned if she'll ever get another engagement in Paris . . .' Sardou read the letter, which, he says, was absurd and disconnected, furious and despairing by turns, raging at the role Montigny had forced her to play and at the same time begging him to forgive her. 'What a funny girl!' he said.

'Not for directors,' growled Montigny.[5]

But by then Sarah was past caring about Paris or the theatre: she was on the train bound for Marseille and the boat to Spain.

On the face of it this behaviour, as recounted in Sarah's memoirs, seems both inexplicable and extreme. However, these memoirs, although they are entitled *Ma double vie*, presumably referring to her professional and her private life (and, as we shall see, with other, deeper resonances as well), in fact omit the most important event ever to occur in Sarah Bernhardt's life. This was the birth of her son Maurice. The precipitate flight to Spain took place at the end of April, 1864; Maurice was born on 22 December of the same year. The moment when Sarah lost her head and ran away was therefore just the time when she would first have suspected she was pregnant – a far likelier explanation of her panic and disorientation than her discontent with a role, however bad. That would not be everlasting – far from it, if the play was that bad – and could be faced out, while Julie's scorn was nothing to the anger she would feel at the mad escape to Spain. But the bad role and her mother's unpleasant reaction to it coming on top of the confusion caused by the sudden realization of her probable condition – that is something different. It would explain the suicidal feelings, and makes the decision to run away both pathetic and understandable.

There is also, of course, the question of Sarah's relations with the baby's father at this juncture to be considered. Clearly the affair must have been going on concurrently with her engagement at the Gymnase. Did he know about the baby? Sarah's reactions at this time – first to kill herself, then to run away – indicate that either she did not dare tell him, and wanted to hide her condition from the world, or else that she had told him and he had declined to take any responsibility for the child. The approach to Meydieu – the desire, however fleeting, for a more settled income and way of life – are also more satisfactorily explained in the light of her awareness that she would now have a baby to support.

Who was the baby's father? Sarah always let it be assumed that it was the Prince de Ligne, the scion of a great Belgian family. This may have been wishful thinking – given the choice, one would rather father one's child on a prince: apart from anything else it makes for a better story, a detail to which Sarah was never indifferent; and then princes are generally well-off – another potentially relevant detail when it comes to bringing up a child. Another possibility, she once hinted, was the Duke of Clarence (a versatile fellow: one of the other roles wished on him was that of Jack the Ripper.) But Ligne was certainly a likely candidate. It was always asserted (with Ligne in mind) that Maurice looked like his father.

According to her granddaughter Lysiane, Sarah met Ligne in Brussels in June, 1863. Lysiane, who was very close to her grandmother, but was necessarily writing many years after these events, places this *after* the débâcle at the Gymnase. But in fact Sarah went to the Gymnase in 1864. There is no indication in her memoirs of the length of time that elapsed between her leaving the Comédie-Française in

January, 1863 and her engagement by Montigny, but if we assume that this was early in 1864, then she spent a whole year 'resting', in which case a trip to Brussels – if it took place in the summer of 1863 – must have come as a welcome relief.

In Lysiane's account, the moving spirit behind this trip was Alexandre Dumas *père*, who plays a large part in her version of Sarah's early life. He figures not at all in Bernhardt's own memoirs, and neither do these mention the trip to Brussels. This does not mean that the trip did not take place, nor (as we have seen) that she did not know the elder Dumas. For one thing, Sarah is not a reliable witness as to facts; for another, *Ma double vie* never makes any mention of her love-life, so that if this was all that occurred during the Brussels trip then she would not mention it. As to her knowing Dumas, it seems quite probable that he would have been acquainted with Julie or Rosine. He, like his son, was a renowned ladies' man – at one time they were *both* in pursuit of Marie Duplessis, the original *Dame aux camélias* – and Lysiane's story is supported by a number of letters to Dumas from a friend of his named Jean Bruce, to whose care Dumas had confided Sarah.

Dumas seems to have arranged for Sarah's trip to Brussels in the aftermath of a particularly acrimonious row between Sarah and her mother. She travelled with Mme Guérard, who settled her into the Hôtel de Hainaut et Flandres, recommended by Dumas, and travelled back to Paris next day, by which time Sarah was under the wing of the Bruce family.

Sarah, says Lysiane, met the Prince de Ligne at a masked costume ball given by Bruce a few days after her arrival in Brussels. Bruce wrote to Dumas:

So, my dear Dumas, your young friend, Sarah Bernhardt, has taken Brussels by storm. At our ball she made a conquest of the Prince de Ligne. I think they have met since. Are you angry with me for having given this young lady too much to distract her mind, or are you going to congratulate me for having helped an actress to shed her prejudices? Everything depends upon the point of view from which you look at your protégée: from the respectability of her present or from the greatness of her future. Ever yours, J. Bruce.

P.S. I have just returned from the Hôtel de Hainaut et Flandres. Sarah has not put in an appearance there for a week. She is said to be travelling 'with friends'. I am rather afraid that these friends, reduced to a single person, have limited the extent of her travels to the Boulevard de la Toison d'Or [where the Ligne family mansion was]. That is what happens when one lets a dragon-fly loose with a butterfly. You have been warned. Like Pontius Pilate I salve my conscience with the sentence in your letter: 'It is time this child spread her wings. Her vocation is entirely out of line with the careful maxims with which her mother loads her. I would rather see her do something foolish than just fritter away her life.'

   I believe, my friend, that your prayers have been answered. J.B.[6]

8

Bruce's last sentence, with its implications regarding Sarah's innocence and the prudishness of her upbringing, seems to conflict both with what we know of Julie and with the public perception of Sarah's attitude to the opposite sex. For Sarah's relations with men, like so much else in her life, are a matter of legend. 'I have been one of the great lovers of my time,' she told her young friend Suze Rueff from the eminence of her glittering sixties – a time of life which, in any other woman, would mean that she was discussing history, not just past but long past: but Sarah, then, was still a honeypot for stage-struck young men who fell hopelessly in love with her. And if she was still, even then, a formidable contender in the sexual lists, what had she not been in her prime? There was Pierre Loti the novelist, so desperate to get himself admitted to her intimate company that he had himself delivered to her, rolled up in a costly Persian rug . . . There was her famed affair with her leading man at the Comédie-Française in the 1870s, Mounet-Sully, the handsomest actor in France, when the audience's pleasure at watching the duo play love scenes onstage was titillated by the knowledge that this was merely a continuation of what went on offstage . . . If gossip was to be believed – and there seems no reason why, in this case, one should not believe it: exaggeration there might have been, but not very much – Sarah slept with all her leading men, her playwrights and her critics, not to speak of a great many of the artists, politicians and other interesting men of her day. Is it possible that such an enthusiast for the amorous life should not have shown her inclinations from the very first?

The question is, did inclination come into it? Promiscuity is one thing; inclination, quite another. It is a commonplace that promiscuity and inclination do not necessarily go hand in hand. Quite the reverse – especially in the case of women, like Julie, for whom sex is simply a matter of business.

If all parents influence their children's attitudes towards sex, both by what they say and – more importantly – by the way they behave, since it is through actions rather than words that people's real attitudes are perceived, then in Julie's case these two sets of instructions – the conscious and the unconscious – were full of contradictions. On the one hand, her own attitude to sex, like that of the sister to whom she was closest, was governed entirely by the question of money. Desire did not come into it, any more than did love or conventional morality. On the other hand, the upbringing she gave Sarah – or bought for her at Mme Fressard's and then Grand-Champs – emphasized both morality and that romantic view of life prevalent among schoolgirls.

Part of Sarah's desire to become a nun may have stemmed from the fact that this course would have resolved these contradictions in the most final way possible. Julie's preferred form of resolution – to make an advantageous marriage – was much less satisfactory. Advantage in this case, as we have seen, was judged in financial rather than social terms: no great name was going to marry Julie's daughter. In effect, Sarah was to sell herself to the highest bidder, an arrangement which, in all but the number of men involved, would virtually replicate her mother's own way of life.

Dumas *fils*, in his preface to *La Dame aux camélias*, points out how little difference there is morally between a marriage contracted for purely financial reasons and the life of a woman such as Marguerite Gautier (or Julie van Hard). This

83

was abundantly clear to Sarah, who, while she passionately loved her mother, clearly rejected her way of life, with its humiliating dependence on handouts from men. It is noticeable that, from the moment she started to earn her own living in the theatre, Sarah insisted on financial independence. She might go into debt: if she did, she would sell her jewels, her clothes, her house. But she would not be financially beholden to anyone, especially not to any man. The number of those who sponged on her, beginning with her son, was often remarked, but that was the way she wanted it. However, when Sarah declared that she would not marry for money, only love, Julie dismissed this as the stupidity which, in Sarah's situation, it was. It was, after all, not only in Julie's circles that marriage was viewed as a business transaction. Anyhow, what did Sarah know about love?

The answer, of course, was nothing at all. Love, in that sense, was something she had never experienced. She had never seen a loving marriage – for, clearly, Aunt Henriette did not *love* her husband, whatever he might once have felt about her – and she did not know what it was to be a beloved child – although, of course, she could see that other parents loved their children: her aunt Henriette loved *her* children, although she certainly did not love Sarah. And from Sarah's point of view, Aunt Henriette was no advertisement for marriage. It had brought her material prosperity, certainly, but she was hardly an example upon which her niece would wish to model herself.

All this amply accounts for the fierce quality of *family* love in Sarah. It was the only source of love available to her. If she loved Julie enough, perhaps Julie might be induced to love her; as for Régine, and, later, Maurice – even Jeanne – they did love her, and depended upon her, and she would never fail them as she had been failed. So they could do no wrong as far as she was concerned. In her usual clear-eyed way, Sarah was perfectly aware of this. Later on, when people remonstrated with her about the effect her infinite indulgence was having on Maurice – the advantage he took of her, his hopeless irresponsibility in business affairs – she would say, 'You mustn't blame him, it's the way he's been brought up.'

But this – which constituted Sarah's real emotional life – had nothing to do with men, and could not have anything to do with men, because in her experience men had nothing to do with it. At the point she had now reached, her one experience of a satisfactory and secure life – that of the convent – was, of course, completely without men. Her father was an unreal, ideal figure whom she had met perhaps three times. Her godfather disliked her; Meydieu bored her; these were the male fixtures in her mother's life. Her uncle by marriage, Félix Faure, was kind to her and cared about her; she was grateful for this, but she was not his primary concern.

If the relationships with men of which Sarah had first-hand knowledge had nothing to do with love, then neither did they have anything to do with self-respect. They were demeaning relations of dependence. What was more, they were not even fun. The picture we have of Sarah's home life at this time evokes the most drearily bourgeois milieu. Sarah's enemy Marie Colombier painted a picture of Julie's apartment as a slovenly, whorish sort of place; but nothing could have been further from the reality as Sarah remembered it. Julie's drawing-room was green and yellow, ugly but bright, she recalled. It was spotlessly clean, as one would expect from a Dutchwoman, whatever her calling. There were lots of potted plants, some real, some artificial. The chairs were covered with embroidered linen, trimmed with green ribbons.[1] In this brightly-coloured, uncomfortable place Julie spent her evenings playing whist with Régis, Meydieu and other old friends.

Sarah did not want this kind of life, with or without a husband. What, then, did she want? She wanted, as she said, to be 'somebody', by which she meant, not to be dependent on anybody. This, not the sexual morals, was the aspect of Julie's life she could not bear, and it was this aspect of Julie's plans for herself that she could not bear. This being so, it follows that, despite her convent education and the strict rules set (but not followed) by her mother, she would set no great store by chastity. Virginity was nothing but a bargaining-point in a transaction in which she took no interest – that of buying a suitable husband. As for men, she liked flirting with them – she was, indeed, a compulsive flirt – and Sarah was never one to deny herself something she liked.

After their first meeting at the masked ball Ligne, dressed as Hamlet, gave Sarah, dressed as Queen Elizabeth of England, a rose wrapped in a handkerchief so that the thorns would not prick her. 'When she got back to her room, Sarah removed the handkerchief from the rose. In one corner of the fine linen she discovered a closed crown with a small "L" embroidered inside it,' runs Lysiane's account.[2] All that remained was for the Prince to gather her up in his arms and whisk her off to his turretted castle, where he would make her his Princess.

That, of course, was not how Julie saw it. Looked at from her point of view it was quite clear what was happening. Sarah was starting down the slippery slope with which she was only too personally familiar, and from which she knew only too well how hard it was to turn aside. So when she realized what was happening, she did the one thing that she knew would bring her errant daughter running back to Paris: she fell ill and sent urgent summonses to return, as she was at death's door. According to Lysiane, this happened while Sarah was in Brussels; according to Sarah's own memoirs, it was this, in the form of a frenzied telegram sent by Mme Guérard, which brought her back from Madrid, where, as usual, she had fallen on her feet, made friends, and was being entertained and fêted and taken to all the bullfights. In either case the motivation was clear and the effect as desired. 'I softly opened the door of the bedroom, which was hung with pale blue silk. Maman was lying in bed, pale, her face thinner, but wonderfully beautiful. She opened her arms like two wings [note the instinctive use of dramatic gesture] and I threw myself into this nest, so white and so full of love.'[3] Everyone cried and embraced, except Régine, who turned stonily away, furious because Sarah had not included her in the great adventure of running away.

But it was (from Julie's point of view) too late: for Sarah, as we know, was now pregnant, and seemed well set to follow in her mother's unsatisfactory footsteps. Certainly her theatrical career seemed to be in abeyance – for reasons unstated by Sarah, but which are not hard to divine: a heavily pregnant young woman is not easy to cast, and the birth of a first baby takes some adjusting to. And meanwhile Sarah – not to mention her baby, who was born in December 1864 – had to live. But how?

Sarah's financial position was in fact slightly better than it had been. Julie had prevailed upon Sarah's grandmother to release half the money due to her on her marriage – fifty thousand francs; and the old lady had added that, while she would continue to take the interest upon the remaining fifty thousand, she would hold the sum aside, in case Sarah should ever change her mind and decide to get married after all. This had all been decided before Sarah returned home to resume the life of an unmarried daughter.

But it soon became clear that this life could not, anyway, continue. Too much had changed – and was, of course, about to change even more drastically. Sarah would have to find a place of her own – which she did, round the corner in the rue Duphot, where she installed herself with Caroline, the young *femme de chambre* she had taken to Madrid, with a cook, with the baby, and with her sister Régine.

It is evident that the atmosphere in which this departure took place was far removed from that (possibly fanciful) scene of loving reconciliation to which the prodigal daughter had first returned home. It is at this point in Sarah's memoirs that she describes her mother's occasional accesses of apo- plectic, choking, goggle-eyed rage – which she understood so well because she herself suffered from similar rages. It is therefore fair to assume that at least one such outburst took place at this time, and that it became clear that the two women could no longer share the same roof. That this happened almost at once seems likely, since Sarah recounts how she arranged that Meydieu would look for an apart- ment for her when he came to see her the day after her return from Spain. Lysiane recounts that Sarah, when she went to her room after leaving her mother, found her cupboards filled with Jeanne's clothes and toys. Perhaps this was the precipitating factor; perhaps it was the news of Sarah's pregnancy. At any rate, Meydieu found the apart- ment; Mme Guérard helped to furnish it. When everything was ready, Sarah invited Julie to see it, and (she says) soon persuaded her that everyone would be better off if she lived independently.

And then occurred yet another of those appalling family occasions which Sarah recounts so coolly. The apartment was ready: an amicable conversation was taking place between Sarah and Julie as to the arrangements for Sarah's move. Jeanne and Régine were listening. Suddenly Régine, who had not spoken to Sarah since her return from Spain, jumped on to her lap and cried, 'Take me too, and I'll love you again!' 'I looked at my mother, rather embarrassed,'

Sarah continues. 'She said, "Oh, take her, she's unbearable." And Régine, jumping down, began to dance a bourrée . . . Then she hugged me tightly, jumped on to maman's chair, kissed her cheeks, her hair, her eyes – "Are you happy I'm going, then? You'll be able to give everything to your Jeannot now!"' Julie blushed slightly, but could not help giving a loving glance at Jeanne. 'She pushed Régine away gently, rested her head on Jeanne's shoulder, and said, "There'll just be the two of us, then." And there was such a complete lack of realisation of what she was saying and doing,' Sarah continues, 'that I was stupefied. I shut my eyes so that I wouldn't have to see any more and all I could hear was my youngest sister's bourrée. She was singing, with every step she took "Us two, the two of us, the two of us!"'[4] Evidently life for Régine without Sarah in the house was as unbearable as her own behaviour – as unbearable as Sarah's own life had been at her age, when there was no one to love her and she wanted so much to love and be loved.

So Sarah set up house in the rue Duphot with the two beings upon whom she would lavish that love which had always been denied her, and who would love her unreservedly in return for the rest of their lives: her sister Régine and her son Maurice. And they all returned to Julie's for dinner every evening.

9

In 1864 Sarah played seven roles before she left the Gymnase; in 1865, after Maurice's birth, she was employed only once. She had very little money of her own. The Prince de Ligne failed, as might have been expected, to marry her. According to Lysiane Bernhardt this was not for want of trying. Lysiane's version (and that of her husband Louis Verneuil) is that, having lost sight of Sarah, Ligne spotted her in her solitary theatrical engagement that year (in a musical fantasy called *La Biche au bois* at the Porte-Saint-Martin), got her address from the theatre, and moved in with her and the baby. Delighted by this domestic bliss he begged her to marry him and give up the theatre. But the wedding plans were upset by a secret visit paid to Sarah by Ligne's uncle, Général de Ligne, who pointed out the terrible distress and embarrassment that this marriage would cause the rest of the princely family and begged her not to marry his nephew, who would in any case hate her after a short time for having ruined his life and cut him off from his family. The uncle, according to this version, won her over; she declared she could not give up her art and would therefore be unable to marry the Prince; at which, sadly, Ligne took his leave. A rather more brutal version is offered by the egregious Marie Colombier. According to this, Sarah, on finding she was pregnant, sought out Ligne, who happened to be enjoying himself at a party. He came out and greeted her cheerfully enough, but when she told him why she had come to see him, his good humour vanished at once and he dismissed her with the brutal sally that 'When you sit on a bunch of thorns, it's hard to know which is the one that pricked you!'[1]

It is impossible to know which, if either, of these versions is nearer the truth: they both bear the mark of fantasy, either of the adoring, romanticizing granddaughter or of the foul-mouthed and jealous (but undoubtedly intelligent) Marie Colombier. Both might have some element of truth: Ligne might have dismissed her brutally, then, when he ran across her again, have been stricken with remorse and smitten by the old attraction. The essential point remains: Sarah found herself alone with a baby and had, somehow, to support him.

Given that this is a situation as old as human society, the interesting point here is how remarkably well-placed Sarah was to cope with it. Indeed, it is not much of an exaggeration to say that hers was almost the only milieu at that time in which she might confront such a life as now faced her with comparative equanimity. Had her family been more respectable, an illegitimate baby would literally have been considered a fate worse than death. One need only read the letters of Marthe de Montbourg, the aristocratic daughter of a pious Norman family who became pregnant in 1892 at the age of twenty, to see what might happen in such a case: the girl, unable to imagine any life or career outside marriage, forced to accept any man who would take her and agree to give her child a name, however unpleasant and money-grubbing a rogue he might be; the mother and sister, unable to face the village gossips, forced to sell up the family home and move to the other end of France; finally, the whole family broken and destroyed – a tragedy entirely self-induced, and all on account of the need to keep up appearances.[2] At the other extreme, the extra-marital adventures of the avant-garde young women of the left in England at this time show that, even in those self-consciously advanced circles, an illegitimate child was – in spite of all the brave words – something to be hushed up and hidden, an enormous and barely surmountable problem for all concerned.[3] But in the Parisian *demi-monde* these social problems did not arise. A person was on her own there, and must cope with any situation as best she could. If she coped successfully, she would be accepted on her own terms.

The existence of this stratum whose denizens might know everybody, go anywhere, which included some of the most brilliant and amusing coteries in town but which nevertheless remained officially invisible to respectable society, was a wonderfully cynical and sophisticated construct unique to Paris. The phrase *demi-monde* was coined by Alexandre Dumas *fils* in 1853 as the title of a play. It was intended by him to apply to once respectable ladies who had been socially undone by giving their all unwisely rather than selling it indiscriminately, but the felicitous phrase was soon extended to cover the whole of that until then indefinable area for which a catch-all description had been so much needed. Its broad tolerance provided a framework not only for cocottes such as Julie and Rosine, but also for groups and personalities who were able to flourish within it and produce their own strange blossoms out of an individuality untrammelled by convention – poets such as Baudelaire and Verlaine, delightful *salonnières* such as Apollonie Sabatier, 'La Présidente', bohemian men of letters such as Théophile Gautier, who was in love with the ballerina Carlotta Grisi, had two daughters by her sister, a son by yet a third lady, and remained on (more or less) excellent terms with all of them. It could accept the disgraced Oscar Wilde, always intellectually far more at home in Paris than London, and the lesbian coterie centred around the American Nathalie Barney, immortalized by Radclyffe Hall in *The Well of Loneliness* – which, of course, was banned in England. And it was a refuge at difficult times of their life for talented women who fled thankfully from the straitjacket of respectable married life to its capacious, all-embracing arms – women such as George Sand, who was to be a friend of Sarah's when her career took off again only two years later, and Colette, who would admire her so much at the end of it. This, however much Julie might yearn for the respectability of her sister Henriette, was her world and Sarah's; and in it, if Sarah could survive financially, she would at least be able to raise her baby unburdened by the strictures of conventional morality. In this respect, she had her own mother's example before her. Clearly, in the same predicament Julie had coped. Sarah might not want to lead the same kind of life as her mother: but what lay before her was quite obviously not a fate worse than death.

And in another way, too, Julie's example was a help to her daughter. For while in detail she might not be much of a model, being by her daughter's account lazy, unloving, casually cruel, parasitical – nevertheless she was in her way a self-supporting woman, and her assumption was that Sarah, too, would support herself: 'I want her to have a career,' Julie had said, thus giving the duc de Morny the cue for his momentous suggestion: 'Send her to the Conservatoire!' The fact that the choice of career was still so limited – schoolmistressing, shopkeeping, the stage, the bed – was less important than the fact that Sarah had an example before her of the possibility of a woman sustaining a comfortable independent existence with a fair amount of self-respect. She remarks in her memoirs that if Julie did not marry Régis, this was by her choice, not his: she preferred, at her time of life, to maintain her independent existence rather than submit to a man as head of her household.

The importance of such an example to an aspiring, intelligent young woman can hardly be overstated. In England, such brilliant and talented young women as Eleanor Marx

93

(daughter of Karl) and May Morris (daughter of William) were handicapped because their models of achievement were all men – fathers, lovers, mentors. They wanted to do the same things as the men did, and at the same level, but they could not; not because they did not have the capacity, but because they were not men. Society – even the most progressive society – did not know how to cope with women like them and was not very eager to find out how it might do so. 'I'm a remarkable woman – always was, though none of you seemed to think so,' wrote May Morris at the end of her unappreciated life.[4] There was, too, the awful case of Alice James, the brilliant sister of brilliant brothers (William and Henry James), children of a talented father and domestic, self-effacing mother. Alice was always conscious of her capacities, and only too aware of their under-use: unlike her brothers, she never had any occupation, and was never well enough to marry, even had she met a man who might have fulfilled her exacting criteria. Like so many women of her generation she took refuge in invalidism – never well, but without any definable symptoms, until in 1890 cancer of the breast was detected. Only then, in the face of death, did she come to life: *something was happening*! 'It is the most supremely interesting moment in life, the only one in fact when living seems life, and I count it the greatest good fortune to have these few months so full of interest and instruction in the knowledge of my approaching death,' she wrote to her psychologist brother William. 'It is as simple in one's own person as any fact of nature ... and I have a delicious consciousness, ever present, of wide spaces close at hand, and whisperings of release in the air.'[5] It is hard to think of a more terrible epitaph for a wasted life.

But the three most famous women in France during Sarah's lifetime – Bernhardt herself, Colette and Marie Curie – all had strong women upon whom to model themselves. Curie's was her elder sister Bronya, who left their home in

Warsaw for Paris in order to study medicine. Colette's was her mother, who had herself led a bohemian life in Brussels with her brothers when she was young and who was the strong support of the family: it was from this adored mother that she took her cue and her example: 'From the earliest age I have wanted to shine in the eyes of my family. It wasn't enough to love them. And that is still my ambition.'[6] Like Sarah, Colette wanted her mother's approval more than that of anyone else in the world. Unlike Sarah, she could always, so long as she was true to herself, feel that she had that approval. But the essential thing for both was that their model, in a life outside the merely domestic, was female, not male. Sarah, of course, had several such models – Julie, Rosine, mère Sainte-Sophie: what she signally lacked was any equivalent male figure.

Nevertheless, however accommodating the moral atmosphere, it was necessary to live, to dress, to eat, to clothe and feed the baby, to pay the wages of Caroline and the cook and the rental of the apartment; and in the absence of theatrical engagements there was no alternative but to take lovers. How far Sarah was able to follow her preferences at this stage and how far she had to bow to necessity it is impossible to tell. 'Ma chère Marie, I am not rich enough to love you as I should like to nor poor enough to let myself be loved as you would like to,' wrote Alexandre Dumas to Marie Duplessis in the letter which ended their affair[7]; a letter which (having bought it back at a sale of autographs) he later presented to Sarah, his Dame aux camélias, with the words, 'This letter is the only remaining relic of this story. I think it now belongs to you by right, since it is you who have returned youth and life to the dead past.'[8] (This was in January, 1884, when Sarah was already thirty-nine; but, as we shall see, calendar years were of little relevance to Sarah's stage personalities.)

Among her protectors at this point in her life were Robert de Brimont, a rich industrialist; the Marquis de Caux, who later married Adelina Patti; and the banker Jacques Stern. At least two of these remained her friends: when her flat was burned out without insurance some years later, Caux persuaded Patti to sing at the money-raising benefit held for her, while Stern allowed her to use his mansion in the rue Taitbout for her field hospital in the 1870 war when its original quarters in the Odéon became too dangerous. Morny, her original helper, was no longer there: he died of syphilis, the universal scourge, in 1864. His death deprived many artists of a powerful protector, and also removed the last vestige of liberalism from the inner councils of the Second Empire, which slipped into that habit of ever more rigid repression which would eventually seal its fate.

Did Sarah at this point abandon the idea of a theatrical career? Not necessarily: there was anyway not much of a gap in some instances between the courtesan's career and that of some actresses (though these were not usually the kind of actresses that Sarah aspired to be). Among the actresses at the Gymnase while Sarah was there were Léontine Massin and Nathalie Manvoy, both of whom had been Sarah's contemporaries at the Conservatoire and both of whom were now noted *biches*.

At any rate, despite all the changes in her life Sarah had kept up with her theatrical acquaintances. Among these was Josse, an actor at the Porte-Saint-Martin who had now become the manager of that theatre, and who often let Sarah have seats there. Turning up at five o'clock one day to claim these seats – for a production called *La Biche au bois*, starring an actress from the Odéon, Mlle Debay, the singer Ugalde and the famous dancer Mariquita – Sarah was astounded to hear Josse cry, 'Here's the princess, here's our

Biche au bois, it's the god of theatres who's sent her along!'[9] It transpired that Debay was indisposed, there was no understudy, everyone was at their wits' end. *La Biche au bois* was the great success of the season – during the seven or eight months it ran while the 1865 Exposition was on its receipts amounted to more than eight hundred thousand francs.[10] For the production to close prematurely would be a disaster. Sarah allowed herself to be persuaded, despite the fact that her Conservatoire training had hardly fitted her to take the lead in a musical. Hurriedly she learned Debay's lines, was fitted into her dress, and was onstage when the curtain went up.

Sarah was back in the theatre. Marc Fournier, who was then the director of the Porte-Saint-Martin, offered her a three-year engagement. He was at that time the most successful director in Paris, and an offer from him was not to be turned down lightly. On the other hand, the ambiance of the Porte-Saint-Martin was not exactly that of the kind of theatre in which Sarah wished to make her name. It was one of the huddle of theatres stretching from the Gymnase along the boulevard Saint-Martin to the boulevard du Temple – a stretch familiarly known as the boulevard du Crime – and which included the Ambigu, the Porte-Saint-Martin, the Gaîté, the Folies Dramatiques, the Funambules, the Cirque Olympique, the Petit Lazari, the Délassements Comiques, the Théâtre Historique. These featured popular entertainments varying from light comedy and melodrama to a sort of cabaret with interaction between actors and audience, where the performance might begin as early as six o'clock, and which was the speciality of the Petit Lazari; a theatrical fare which ranged from comparatively respectable pieces such as *The Lyons Mail* (Ménier's *Le Courrier de Lyon*) which travelled over the Channel to arrive in London in a sanitized form – borrowings such as this constituted a large part of the English popular theatre – to unregenerate

97

and untranslatable offerings which had no equivalent anywhere else, though parts of the English music-hall might
approach them. The boulevard du Crime was the regular
haunt of the young high-livers of the Jockey Club, the
jeunesse dorée, who came in search of the *grandes demoiselles*,
who might be actresses or *demi-mondaines* or (as we have
seen) both, with whom they might expect to finish the
evening at the Café Anglais or the Maison Dorée. This clique
included Princes Charles and Edouard de Ligne; so that it is
more than probable that Sarah's Ligne did re-encounter her
during her brief appearance in *La Biche au bois*.

Each of the theatres in the boulevard had its own speciality; so that to accept Fournier's offer, tempting though it
might be, meant that Sarah knew she would be committing
herself to three years at a theatre whose highest ambition
was light entertainment. And before she did this (which
would be a great deal better than doing nothing) she decided
to try possible alternatives. One was a new play, *La Bergère
d'Ivry*, by Lambert Thiboust, a friend of Josse's. Sarah found
him charming and he thought she would be ideal for his
heroine. But there was a problem. Thiboust's play was to be
put on at the Ambigu, whose new director, Faille, was very
much under the thumb of Robert de Chilly. Chilly had been
an actor but had married a rich woman, had retired from
acting and taken up management. He was currently the
protector of a very pretty girl, Laurence Gérard, whom he
intended for the leading role in Thiboust's play. However,
nothing was yet settled. Faille agreed that the author's
wishes should come first: but he could do nothing without
hearing Sarah at an audition.

The audition was arranged: Sarah stood on stage at the
Ambigu, dimly lit, and recited from *On ne badine pas avec
l'amour*, discouraged by the sight of Faille sitting in the front
row picking his nose. 'I thought I was quite charming, and
so did Lambert Thiboust. But when I had finished, poor

Faille stood up heavily, talked to the author in a low voice, and summoned me to his office: "My dear child, you have nothing to offer the theatre!" I was thunderstruck. "Nothing at all." The door opened. "Look," he said, indicating the new arrival, "here's M. de Chilly who was listening to you, he'll say the same thing." M. de Chilly nodded, shrugged, and murmured, "Lambert Thiboust is mad, no one's ever seen such a skinny shepherdess!" Then he rang the bell and said to the messenger, "Bring in Mlle Laurence Gérard."'[11]

Sarah understood at once. Everything had been fixed from the start. She passed Laurence Gérard in the foyer, and caught a glimpse of the two of them reflected side by side in one of the mirrors: 'She was plump, with a wide face, magnificent black eyes, a rather common nose, thick lips and something – *ordinary* – about her; I was blonde, slim and frail as a reed, with a long pale face, blue eyes, mouth a little sad, and with an air of distinction.'[12] She was momentarily consoled. But however distinguished her air, there was no doubt that Chilly would never employ her.

Five days after this débâcle Debay returned to her role in *La Biche au bois*. Sarah would either have to sign up with Fournier or risk unemployment again. In desperation she wrote to her old friend Camille Doucet, and next day received a letter giving her an appointment at the ministry.

He was waiting for her when the messenger showed her in, standing with his hands stretched out towards her. 'You impossible child,' he said. 'Now, now, you must calm down. You mustn't waste all those wonderful gifts rushing about and running away and slapping people . . .' Sarah says she was reduced to tears, as well she might have been. 'Now,' she records Doucet as saying, 'how are we going to set all these stupidities right?' He thought a minute, then brought a letter out from his desk. 'This might be the thing,' he said.

The letter was from Félix Duquesnel, who had just been appointed associate director of the Odéon – the other associate being Sarah's enemy Chilly. He was asking for young artists to inject new life into the Odéon company. Doucet would write to him, and they would see what they could do.

Sarah went home and waited nervously, taking the opportunity to polish her Racine roles while Mme Guérard tried to calm her and give her some confidence. Finally the note she had been hoping for arrived and she rushed round to Doucet's office. She found him beaming with smiles. 'It's all arranged,' he said, 'though not without difficulty. You may be young but you're famous already for being quite impossible. But I've given my word that you'll be as meek as a lamb.' Sarah promised that she would be meek, if only out of gratitude. 'All right,' he said, 'here's a letter for Félix Duquesnel: he's waiting for you.'

10

Twenty-eight years later, Duquesnel recalled that interview. 'There before me,' he wrote, 'stood the most ideally charming creature it is possible to imagine – Sarah Bernhardt aged twenty – what more can one say? She wasn't pretty, she was better than that.

'She was dressed à la chinoise, a blouse in pale crepe de chine, embroidered with bright colours, of a Chinese cut; her stockings and her shoulders half-uncovered; a feather fan at her belt; and on her head, a little roof of fine straw with little tinkling beads all round which shook at the least movement. She had with her a maid who was carrying a beautiful pink and white baby in her arms, Maurice Bernhardt. Our interview was very quick, we understood each other without needing to say very much. I could see that I was faced with a wonderfully gifted creature, with enormous energy hidden beneath that frail, delicate appearance, and extremely self-willed. As a woman, she was all that was charming and seductive; as for the artist, you would feel her quivering there inside the woman; all she needed was to be shown the way, to be put in the spotlight. – And I need hardly add that there was that voice, crystal-pure, which grabbed your heart with its heavenly music. I knew at that first interview that I'd seen the fiery cross, just like St Hubert.'[1]

It was half past ten in the morning. Sarah had had time to go home and make herself beautiful: she herself found the effect 'deliciously crazy'. What she saw before her in

Duquesnel's 'artistically furnished' little salon was a young man, elegant, smiling and charming. Sarah could not believe that such a lovely blond, laughing young man could seriously be director of a theatre like the Odéon. Of course – and here was the snag – he was not the *only* director. He told Sarah to come to the Odéon at two o'clock and he would introduce her to his associate.

At two o'clock Sarah was at the Odéon, where she had to wait for more than an hour. 'Only the promise I'd made to Doucet stopped me from walking out,' she recalled. Then Duquesnel appeared and said, 'Come and meet the other ogre.' And there was Chilly – 'that ugly little man'.

Chilly had little time for Sarah. He looked her up and down, pretended not to recognize her, pushed a piece of paper across the desk and indicated where she should sign. Mme Guérard said Sarah should read it first; Chilly said, 'Quite right, read it quickly, then sign or don't sign, but hurry up.' When she had signed, he remarked: 'Let me tell you that he's responsible for you, not me, because I wouldn't have engaged you for anything in the world.'

Sarah snapped back, 'Well, if there'd only been you, I wouldn't have signed, so we're quits.'[2] But she had signed, and was now employed for 150 francs a month.

Sarah did not make an auspicious début at the Odéon any more than she had at the Comédie-Française. Her first role was in Marivaux's *Jeu de l'amour et de l'hasard*, and as she herself remarked, 'I wasn't right for Marivaux, who needs qualities of coquetry and preciosity which I didn't have then – and still don't.' After the performance Chilly took the opportunity to make a coarse joke about her thinness; she felt herself losing her temper, and once again was only saved by shutting her eyes and conjuring up the vision of Doucet. Then she realized that this was no vision but the man himself. As usual he was charming and encouraging but strictly truthful. He congratulated her on her lovely voice, and added, 'And how much we shall enjoy your second début!'³ Sarah's miseries were compounded by the distressing circumstances surrounding the death of her old and faithful friend Mlle de Brabender. She had died at the convent where she had lived ever since Sarah had known her, and the young nuns who laid her out had been appalled to find that, overnight, the corpse had sustained a strong growth of red beard and moustache. This, in combination with the flowing locks of her hair and the mouth, now fallen in without its false teeth to support it, so that the nose nestled into the moustache, made a terrifying sight, and although the sister who had dressed the corpse assured everyone that it was indeed that of a woman, the whole affair made a sad end to what had been a dignified and self-effacing life.

But things could only improve. Sarah had her supporters – and not only Doucet and Duquesnel. The leading man at the Odéon at this time was Pierre Berton, whom she had known at the Gymnase. Sarah does not mention him in her memoirs, but Berton was not only her leading man, he was also much in love with her at this time. It was he who had helped Doucet to arrange that first interview with Duquesnel; and after her failure in *Jeu de l'amour et de l'hasard* he, as well as Duquesnel, interceded for her with Chilly. So she stayed on at the Odéon, understudying and playing a few roles, and began to pick up a following – the young students, soon nicknamed the '*Saradoteurs*,' who were always to be her chief supporters during this first period in Paris. And by 1867 it began to look as though all this support might be justified, for in that year Sarah at last had some success – in Racine's *Athalie*, in which she played the role of Zacharie. Duquesnel had had the idea of staging this with Mendelssohn's musical setting, using pupils from the Conservatoire for the choruses; but rehearsal after rehearsal showed that this would never work. What was to be done? It was Chilly, of all people, who suggested that Sarah, with her lovely voice, should speak the choruses – which she did. It was a success: the choruses were encored, and Sarah took three curtain calls. Her first triumph! It was not enormous: but, she recalled, 'so full of light for my future!' Afterwards Chilly, *tutoying* her for the first time, said, 'You're adorable!' Sarah was somewhat taken aback by this unaccustomed familiarity from her old enemy, but replied gamely, 'You think I've fattened up a bit, then?' He went off giggling, and after that the two of them were friends and always called each other *tu*.[4]

Sarah always remembered her days at the Odéon with affection. 'How I loved it – I only left it with regret. We were all friends, we were all happy.' And they were almost all young.

The Odéon, like the Théâtre Français, was a state company, but it was the junior company and altogether more carefree and less regimented. Situated just opposite the Luxembourg gardens, the young actors often went across for a game of ball when they were not needed at rehearsals. They lived and breathed theatre. Sarah compared it with her unhappy few months at the Comédie-Française, 'that artificial, malicious, jealous little world!' and with the Gymnase, where nobody talked about anything but dresses, hats – anything so long as it had nothing to do with art. The Odéon engagement had the added advantage that it was (apart from her unforeseen sally into vaudeville at the Porte-Saint-Martin) the first job she had landed entirely on her own. The duc de Morny had got her into the Conservatoire, and the knowledge that she was his protégée had helped to squeeze her into the Comédie-Française even though she had not won a prize. The job at the Gymnase had been a favour to M. Régis. But at the Odéon she was beholden to nobody; she was there, if not on her merits (for it was as yet unclear whether these really existed) at least on account of her charm, which was a quality entirely her own and no negligible theatrical asset. The Odéon became her world. She could never wait to get back to it, to leave the boring summer sunshine for its cold, damp staircases, for the dark stage barely lit for rehearsals by the *servante* (a single hanging light), for her little dressing-room. She brought Julie to see 'behind the scenes' one day, but her mother, predictably, was quite unable to divine the nature of the mysterious attraction this stuffy, dark place had for her perverse daughter. 'You poor child! How can you spend your life in a place like that?' she inquired, returning with relief to the bright daylight outside. But Sarah, on the contrary, felt she was only really alive when she was in the theatre. That first summer she had taken a little villa in Auteuil, from which delightful place she drove herself in to rehearsals in a *'petit-duc'* drawn by two lively ponies donated by Rosine, who had found them unmanageable. Rehearsals took place morning, noon and night, and Sarah could ask for nothing more.

The Odéon was the poets' theatre. The old and the young romantics congregated there: Flaubert, Louis Bouilhet, George Sand, François Coppée. Sand in particular was associated with the theatre, and was another important female role-model for the young Sarah. She had three plays produced there at this period, all adaptations from her novels: *L'Autre*, *Le Marquis de Villemer*, and *François le Champi*. They were great successes, for her anti-clerical stance endeared Sand to the students who formed such an important part of the Odéon's public. Sarah loved her. She remembered her rehearsals with Sand as 'exquisite hours' and Sand herself as 'a gentle, charming creature, very shy. She talked very little and smoked all the time. She had big, dreamy eyes. Her mouth was rather heavy and vulgar, but

105

very kind. She had perhaps been medium height, but she seemed as though she'd grown shorter.'[5]

Sarah idolized George Sand, who had been the heroine of such a beautiful real-life romance, and Sand was kind to the young actress. When Sarah cried at having such a small part in the *Marquis de Villemer*, Sand promised her something more substantial in *François le Champi*, and kept her promise: Sarah played the role of Mariette, and had a great success.

Sarah thought highly of Duquesnel as a director – she found him 'full of wit and gallantry and youth' – but Sand did not share this enthusiasm. In fact she found both Duquesnel and Chilly incompetent as directors and thought they commanded no respect from the actors. 'The direction is so hesitant, so incapable, that no one works when I turn my back,' she reported to her son when rehearsals of *L'Autre* began. She had to think of everything – props, lights, furniture, costumes. Someone was always absent or sick at rehearsals. Mlle Page, who played the supporting female role, was 'furious' because she did not get the lead: Sand described her as someone you would not want to touch with pincers. Sarah Bernhardt, the leading lady, was 'silly' but 'a charming character'.[6]

George Sand at this time was in her sixties, nearing the end of a long and illustrious career, while Sarah Bernhardt, in her early twenties, had hardly started on hers. There is a pleasing symmetry in the fact that these two extraordinary women met, worked together, and liked each other, just as there is about the meeting between Colette and Sarah at the end of Bernhardt's career. For each of them achieved something unique in her generation. Each took on the world on her own terms; each scandalized it in the most thoroughgoing and outrageous way; and each, by the end of her life, had become a legendary figure, an embodiment of French culture.

Sand had been part of the Romantic upheaval of 1830

when, simultaneously with the overthrow of Charles X, Victor Hugo, Théophile Gautier and the rest had marked a violent break with the traditions of French literature up to that date. With her man's dress and her many lovers, she had been a notorious figure. Now she was respectably received in the best society. The Emperor and Empress attended the premieres of her plays; the Emperor's cousin Prince Napoléon, 'Plon-Plon' as he was popularly known, was a close friend. Sand introduced him to Sarah, who was not, at first, much taken with him. His manners were brusque; he paid her compliments which she found impertinent. Sarah edged towards Sand, and Plon-Plon laughed, 'She's in love with you!' To which Sand replied, 'She's my little Madonna, leave her alone!'[7] But later Sarah got to like Plon-Plon extremely; he was a man of great wit and learning, and was very good-looking, although too fat: he bore a remarkable resemblance to his famous ancestor, who was a hero of Sarah's.

It was in a play by another of the Old Romantics – *Kean*, by Dumas *père* – that Sarah scored her first significant success. This was in 1868, when she was beginning to become known and to gather her vociferous following of *Saradoteurs*. The role was that of Anna Damby, Kean's mistress; Kean himself was played by Pierre Berton, who was then her lover.

This was by no means an easy success. Dumas was no longer particularly highly regarded as a playwright; he was an establishment figure, while his comrade and fellow-Romantic of the heady days of 1830, Victor Hugo, was proscribed by Louis-Napoléon's increasingly unpopular Empire and was living in exile. A group of Hugo's supporters chose the night of *Kean's* premiere to make a loud protest about this state of affairs: the theatre was filled with calls of '*Ruy Blas! Ruy Blas! Victor Hugo! Victor Hugo!*' Hugo's supporters were infuriated still further by Dumas' appearing in his box in the company of his latest mistress, Ada Montrin, who was not popular and whose appearance was greeted with sustained catcalls. Sarah, staring through the peephole in the curtains was terrified. She said to Duquesnel, who was standing beside her, 'I'm frightened, I think I'm going to faint . . . What can we do if I'm too frightened?'

'Nothing,' replied Duquesnel. 'Be frightened. Play. And whatever you do, don't faint.'

The curtain rose, and the storm did not abate. The theatre was filled with catcalls, whistles, and rhythmic chants of '*Ruy Blas! Victor Hugo!*' Berton was already onstage, and had not been well received. Sarah was dressed, she thought very strangely, as an English girl of the 1820s, and was petrified by a gale of laughter which greeted her as she appeared. Then the *Saradoteurs* came to the rescue, applauding her so loudly that the laughter was no longer heard. Sarah took courage and felt ready for the fray. But there was no need to fight, for by the time she reached the end of her second long speech, in which she betrays her love for Kean, the audience was won over and she received a loud ovation. Even then she was unsure of what had happened. There had been the noise at the end of her speech, and then sixty students, their hands locked together, rushed round and threatened to invade the stage. Sarah was terrified by what appeared to be a demonstration against her, and when her cue came to leave the stage she rushed up to her dressing-room, where she stood shaking, dimly hearing the roar from the auditorium. Duquesnel found her there, and with difficulty persuaded her that this was no threat but sheer enthusiasm. The show would not be allowed to go on until she came back on stage and spoke to her devoted audience. So she took his arm and allowed him to lead her onstage, still wearing the kimono wrap which she used between scenes. Next day, the *Figaro* saluted her: 'Mlle Sarah Bernhardt appeared in an eccentric costume which only heightened the storm, but her warm voice, that astonishing voice, moved the public. She conquered it, like a little Orpheus.'[8]

Sarah was now on the brink of real fame. This was to be hers the next year, 1869, when she took Paris and the critics by storm playing the part of Zanetto, an Italian Renaissance boy minstrel, opposite Mlle Agar in François Coppée's two-hander, *Le Passant*.

Coppée was very young at the time – twenty-three or four, a little younger than Sarah. He was then the lover of Mlle Agar, the Odéon's leading tragedienne, who, it will be remembered, had débuted at the Comédie Française in the same year as Sarah. This, so gossip had it, had been the doing of the Emperor, with whom Agar had had a passionate affair. Doucet had warned her against taking up the post under such conditions, but Agar replied, 'I'm not worried. If it were ever said I'd gone to bed with the Emperor, they'd have begged me to come to the Français years ago!'[9] But she had not lasted in that solemn atmosphere any more than Sarah had. Agar was then about thirty-five, a statuesque beauty, tall and pale with thick dark hair; Coppée was small and slim, and somewhat resembled Sarah's hero Napoleon Bonaparte. It was common knowledge that Sarah, as well as Agar, was very taken with Coppée. She always had a weakness for men who looked like Napoleon. But for once she met with no success, and was naturally nettled by Coppée's preoccupation with Agar, that 'young matron' – as Sarah describes her in her memoirs. (She does not mention Coppée's other amorous preoccupation at this time, which was with Mlle Doche, the actress who had created the part of Dumas' Marguerite Gautier. Doche had been very pretty, and had, as well as being an actress, been known as a successful courtesan; but now, sixteen years later, her looks were fading and she was getting 'really quite old' – observed Robert de Montesquiou (a good friend of Sarah's) in his catty way.[10] Coppée was very nervous; this was his first play; if it was put on, Agar would play the woman's role, and he hoped that Sarah would take that of the boy. Agar handed her the manuscript and Sarah agreed to read it in her carriage on the way home after rehearsal.

Halfway there, she was so enchanted by the play that she turned the carriage round and rushed up to Duquesnel's office. She met him on the stairs, and he was somewhat taken aback by her excitement. 'You look as if you'd won first prize in the lottery,' he said, and she replied. 'Yes, something like that!' and persuaded him to read the play then and there. He, too, was delighted with it, and it was agreed that it should be performed at a benefit which was to take place a fortnight later. They could use the scenery from a production which had recently been taken off, and Agar and Sarah would provide their own costumes. That way the new production would cost hardly anything, and Chilly would have no reasonable grounds for refusing them.

Le Passant was a wonderful success. Coppée had hit a charming and sentimental poetic vein which perfectly embodied the romantic fantasies of its time. On the night of the premiere the theatre was packed with 'le Tout-Paris of the Empire: there was a noise of jangling spurs, waxed moustaches met other moustaches, the women were plastered with glistening diamonds ... there was a scent of violent and vulgar luxury, of bribes, police and splendid indigestion ... All the old masters were there, too, to inspect the work of their pupil – Gautier, Banville, Augier, Leconte de Lisle ... all except Hugo, who was elsewhere' (he spent the last part of Napoléon III's reign exiled in Guernsey). And for this materialistic, over-sophisticated crowd Coppée's charming versification of the encounter between a ripe, dreamy courtesan and the tender young minstrel Zanetto who offers her his naive and chaste love proved irresistible. 'The low-cut ladies wriggled their buttocks in their seats; *sous-préfets* ... rolled damp eyes. Princesse Mathilde in her box passed out from sheer pleasure.'[11] Francisque Sarcey, the most powerful critic in Paris (the same Sarcey who had been so dismissive of Sarah's débuts at the Français), wrote: 'It's nothing but a dream, but what a charming dream! idealized shadows slipping through the poetic blue . . . Mlle Sarah Bernhardt's costume recalls the sculptor Dubois' Florentine minstrel. Unfortunately, her person is not ideally adapted to men's clothes. But how delicately and tenderly she spoke those delicious lines! . . . She was fêted, called back, acclaimed by a delighted public . . . The performance was a triumph from beginning to end.'

Everyone wanted to see *Le Passant* and meet its stars. Aspiring poets and playwrights tried in vain to repeat its success (something not even Coppée himself managed to do). As for Sarah, she was fêted not only in the theatre, but in society. Comte Robert de Montesquiou, one of the leaders of literary fashion (and a model for some of the most famous characters in literature, including Huysmans' Des Esseintes and Proust's Baron de Charlus), had himself photographed with Sarah, wearing identical *Passant* costumes. Agar and Sarah were invited to give private performances for Princess Mathilde, Plon-Plon's talented sister, and at the Tuileries before the imperial family. On this latter occasion Sarah took Mme Guérard along with her, and when the two of them were left alone for a moment, took the opportunity to practise her curtsey. She was engaged in this when she heard a stifled laugh, and looked up to find the Emperor himself, laughing and clapping his hands. How long had he been there? How many incorrect attempts had he witnessed? . . . Confused, Sarah sketched – a curtsy: but the Emperor was having nothing of it. 'Save it for the Empress,' he said. 'You can't do anything that will compare with what you were doing before.'[12] The performance at the Tuileries was a great success. The Prince Imperial, then aged thirteen, helped Sarah and Agar arrange plants up the staircase on which the action took place, and Sarah was able to admire his long eyelashes. The Empress disappointed her on account of the extreme ugliness of the voice which issued from her lovely face; Sarah much preferred the Winterhalter portrait, which resembled her closely but was unable to speak. But she was very taken with the imperial family – she, and she alone, credits the Emperor Louis-Napoléon with a keen wit – and was saddened when, in the following year, they were ousted from power and the Republic declared.

Sarah, then, had made it. She was the toast of Paris. She was not yet at the height of her early fame – that would come in the 1870s, when she was in her thirties – but it was beckoning. She could see her way forward. She was no longer a person one could neglect. She had 'become someone'.

She had made it – but it had been a struggle, and a near thing. It seems more than likely that, had it not been for that chance illness of Mlle Debay on the day Sarah turned up at the Porte-Saint-Martin, she would never have returned to the theatre, but would have sunk back into that world of shadowy protectors and unsatisfactory liaisons into which she was born, and from which, like Marie Duplessis, she might well have taken an early leave. For Sarah, the theatre was necessary, not just because she had the potential to be a great actress but, perhaps, for her very survival.

One of the most curious characteristics of Sarah's memoir *Ma double vie* is the oddly incomplete picture it gives of her private life. Of course, there are scenes from childhood – if childhood is to be included at all, this is unavoidable. But they are disconnected, short sequences from a movie whose script is unfinished or which has not been properly cut together. Then, as she grows up, the story becomes some-

112

what more connected, but it is notable for the fact that personal relationships play no part in it. The birth of her son Maurice is not mentioned. After she returns from Spain and leaves her mother's house, her life (according to this book) consists exclusively of roles and adventures. So that if one is to take the book at face value (a singularly unwise thing to do!) Sarah Bernhardt's personal life seems to have had no importance for her whatever.

In addition to these curious omissions, the book does nothing to dispel a sense of arbitrariness which pervades all accounts of Sarah's life, and which was (it would seem) characteristic of it when viewed from the inside as well as from the outside. Personages come and go; life continues with no apparent motivation, its course decided, as often as not, by uncontrollable temper-tantrums which bring a particular phase to an end: life in the concierge's lodge, at the convent, at the Comédie-Française. The impression is of an equilibrium barely maintained, of fury constantly struggling to break through, sometimes contained but sometimes no longer containable. But no one's life is arbitrary in that way. People act in a particular way for a particular reason. Sarah's memoirs read as if they were written in a code to which neither she nor we possess the key.

As we have already seen, they are not even factually very reliable. Sarah was notorious for her capacity to reinvent the truth. She was well known for the pleasure she took in giving strange and increasingly wonderful new accounts of any event in which she had been involved. But the doubtful relation of *Ma double vie* to actual fact does not affect its revelatory qualities as a document about Sarah's life.

First of all, it is the highly conscious creation of an exceptional intelligence. One must assume that the picture it gives of Sarah's life is, at least to some extent, the picture she wanted and intended to give. Thus, it may be that she considered her private life was no concern of her public; it

113

may be that this was intended as a purely professional memoir, and she did not want to slow the story down with irrelevant details. Certainly, by contrast with most actresses' memoirs, the book is beautifully paced, vividly written, full of good stories, lively and witty. (Max Beerbohm remarked on its unexpected excellence in this respect.) Here is the public Sarah, with selected sidelights on her childhood to lend verisimilitude. But if anyone wants to find the private Sarah, she is not here.

Who was the 'real' Sarah? Did such a person exist? Suze Rueff tells a story about one of the great actress's innumerable trips to England. In the morning she was rehearsing, she met friends for lunch, there was a performance in the evening, and to fill in the afternoon she had agreed to give a recital in some far-off suburb. On their way to the afternoon engagement Suze asked Maurice Bernhardt if it was really necessary for his mother to work so hard? Maurice replied, 'And what else would Mother do in the afternoons?'

Talking about *Ma double vie*, Maurice Rostand remarks, 'Through the life which Sarah Bernhardt invents for herself and whose story she tells herself, we soon see her real life appear – not her 'double life' as she too modestly terms it, but her multiple life, her innumerable life.'[13] Commenting on her Hamlet (yes, Sarah, at the age of fifty-four, played Hamlet) a critic remarked that 'she is to dramatic art what Baudelaire is to poetry. A fantastical, intelligent and new expression; . . . a troubled and unrestful mind, the explorer of her art . . . trying to give life to different figures which attract her, receiving, however (I insist on this), so much more than she gives, that in her last creation, Hamlet, she has become the young Prince of Denmark, much more than Hamlet has become Sarah Bernhardt.'[14]

What all this seems to suggest is that Sarah Bernhardt, to an unusual extent, lived in and through her roles. And in this sense it may be that the theatre was literally a lifeline for her. In being able to be, one after another, so many different people, Sarah had no need to decide who she was – who was the 'real Sarah' – and it was this which enabled her to survive her disastrous childhood, which would have made such a decision so difficult.

How does a person cope with a childhood such as Sarah's, so devoid of love and security and any opportunity to develop self-esteem? One stratagem is, of course, to deny the experience and to try and proceed as though everything were normal. But this stratagem, as Freud discovered, is prone to fail; when it does, breakdown may ensue.

Another possibility is to pretend that these things happened *to a different person*. In such a situation there may exist within an individual, as well as a 'host' personality who is usually dominant, a number of different personalities, or 'alters', each of whom is able to cope with a particular set of social circumstances for which the 'host' is inadequate. When one of these sets of circumstances presents itself – when what is required is, for example, flirtatiousness, or the ability to deal with unwanted sexual advances, or submissiveness, or aggressiveness – one of the 'alters' takes over from the host. This condition is known as multiple personality disorder. Here is a recent description of a typical case history:

'Mary's father died when she was two years old, and her mother almost immediately remarried. Her stepfather, she says, was kind to her, although "he sometimes went too far". Through childhood she suffered from sick headaches. She had a poor appetite and she remembers frequently being punished for not finishing her food. [One of Sarah's memories of convent life is of being unable to eat the food and passing it on to hungrier fellow-pupils; another is of swallowing the contents of an ink-well in order to kill herself and punish her mother for forcing her to drink a *panade*, a sort of bread and butter soup, one of several occasions when, as a child, she contemplated suicide.[15]] Her teenage years were stormy, with dramatic swings in mood. She vaguely recalls being suspended from her high school for a misdemeanor, but her memory for her school years is patchy . . . She is well informed in many areas, is artistically creative, and can play the guitar; but when asked where she learned it, she says she does not know and deflects attention to something else . . . She claims to have strong moral values; but other people, she admits, call her a hypocrite and liar.'[16]

This fits astonishingly closely with Sarah's own history. Was she, then, a multiple? It seems to me very possible that she was. If so, was there (as there usually is) a particular incident or series of incidents which sparked off the disorder?

There is usually, though not always, an element of child sexual abuse in histories of multiple personality disorder and while there is no way of knowing whether or not this occurred with Sarah it seems not improbable. The most usual aggressor in such abuse is a stepfather, and of course there was no shortage of stepfather figures in Sarah's childhood. It is possible that one of Julie's more vicious lovers might have taken a sexual interest in the little girl as well as her mother; another highly plausible candidate would be her nurse's second husband, the concierge. Sexual interference might well account for the panic-stricken horror she felt at being left in the concierge's lodgings before she made her spectacular cry for help by jumping out of the window. The situation there must have been pretty extreme to make a small child behave in this way.

The best-known examination of the phenomenon of multiple personality is probably the film *Three Faces of Eve*. Interestingly, one of the most perceptive critics to have dealt with Bernhardt, Muriel Bradbrook, mentions this film in connection with her, citing the violent contrast between her turbulent, flamboyant, publicity-seeking offstage personality, punctuated with those alarming rages, with her plaintive, elegant and mellifluous stage persona. But there has recently appeared a much closer parallel than this.

In her book *My Father's House* the Canadian writer Sylvia Fraser describes the way in which she dealt with a childhood in which, from the age of five until she was well into her teens, she was persistently raped by her father. Her stratagem was the one just described. She developed an 'alter' to whom all these things happened, while her 'host' self blocked out the experience altogether and remained completely unaware of it – so that until, in her late forties, she was able painfully to reconstruct the events of her childhood, Fraser was quite unable to account for the fear and despair she felt whenever she entered 'her father's house'.

While she was a child, Fraser appeared to be perfectly normal, exceptionally pretty and bright. One of the few indications that all was not well was her proneness to lapse into terrible, uncontrollable temper-tantrums over some apparently trivial incident. At first it was thought that these were fits, and the doctor was called; later, they were dismissed as bad behaviour rather than illness. The parallel with Sarah as a child is obvious. Fraser, as an adult, was able to account for these frightful accesses of rage in a way quite impossible to her younger, unselfconscious self, and in a way that it never occurred to Sarah Bernhardt to attempt. Partly, they were a result of her 'alter's' rage becoming uncontrollable: the tantrums were its outlet. Partly, 'anger feels better than anguish. To be angry is to be powerful like Daddy, not helpless, like . . . like . . .'[17]

As she grew into her teens, Fraser developed yet another alter – one she calls 'Appearances'. She was what Fraser terms a 'glamor-puppet' and her job was 'to demonstrate that everything was super keen while I was most despairing

. . . She did not react to real circumstances out of real emotion. She was programmed like a computer and, like a computer, she played to rule . . . Appearances began as my servant and then I became hers. Her strings were live wires that burned my hands. Increasingly, I danced as fast as I could . . . while she pulled her strings, always upping the stakes whenever she grew bored or became frightened.' Fraser adds, 'Though I frequently lost control of her, I never lost conscious contact with her, as I did with my other self. I always knew − painfully − what she was up to because I always had to pick up the pieces from her disasters. If my other self was my shadow, then she was 'our' billboard − one that increasingly advertised the wrong things.'[18] It is hard to imagine a more exact description of the kind of quasi-hysterical, compulsive, self-destructive behaviour which constantly recurs in Sarah's life. Fraser describes the public perception of her 'Appearances' self: 'There is in our midst, gentlemen, a strange and deadly character, a woman of towering arrogance and ambition which she hides behind a cloak of desirability and seduction.'[19] And as a description of how most of the world saw Sarah, that is hard to better.

If Sarah was a multiple this would explain several of the bizarreries we have already noted in connection with her accounts of her early life, such as the odd impersonality with which she is able to describe her mother's cruelty: the person writing this description being, not Sarah herself, but an alter, the one who deals with situations of that sort. It would account for the omission of personal details such as the birth of her son. If the person writing the book was the professional actress while the person who fell in love with the Prince de Ligne and got pregnant was someone else, then such episodes − which did not happen to the writer − might be not so much forgotten as simply blanked out. Similarly, her mother's profession is not part of this story, where the somewhat transparent pretence is one of normal

118

family life. This of course may simply be a reflection of the attitude automatically assumed by the young Sarah, both in school and at the Conservatoire. Neither at a respectable *pensionnat*, nor even in the relatively lax atmosphere of the Conservatoire, could she actually have wanted her fellow-pupils to know what her mother did for a living (though, inevitably, they must have found out sooner or later). Here was yet another fact which must if possible be blocked out.

Multiplicity would also account for the salient fact about Sarah's subsequent relations with men – that is, her complete failure to become deeply involved with any of them. The 'alter' conducting Sarah's sex life would have no access to her emotional life. This would enable her to separate episodes such as her descent into courtesanship after Maurice's birth from her 'host' persona.

In this context – that is to say, in the context of a character so uncannily like Sarah in so many of her reactions and experiences – it is interesting to see how Fraser dealt with the problem of relations with men. She records that all men found her extremely sexy, all assumed she was 'asking for it' and assumed, too, that she would be what was then termed an 'easy lay'. This was in sharp contrast to her actual feelings, which were generally of revulsion. But even when she was with a man who attracted her and whom she liked, Fraser could not feel easy – could not, indeed, experience any feelings at all: 'He kisses me. My lips are cold, like plastic. I can't do anything about that. They aren't under my conscious control . . . But I have been adding up the gasoline and the corsage, my guilt about my withdrawal against his legitimate expectations, and I feel something owing which, being an honest tradeswoman, I feel obliged to deliver.'[20] Since Sarah never spoke about her own sex life except, as we have seen, to say, in a romantic but inexact phrase, that she had been one of the 'great lovers of her time' there is no way of knowing whether this is how she, too, felt about men. But if it is posited that she suffered some sort of sexual abuse in childhood, then her early desire to become a nun takes on another dimension. The idea of celibacy, under those circumstances, may have seemed very positively desirable to her. Failing that, it is not hard to believe that she did what was expected or necessary in any given context, fulfilling, as well as she could, her side of the bargain. That would chime with what we know of Sarah's character: she was nothing if not a pragmatist. Marie Colombier, who, although ill-disposed and malicious, was very perceptive about these things (she, too, suffered from many of the disabilities she attributes to Sarah) describes her as being 'one of those women who can never love'[21] – love, in this context, referring to sexual relationships with men: Colombier had little interest in other applications of the word. It seems quite likely that this was true. The ability to love implies trust and the willingness to submerge yourself in the beloved. This is simply not a position in which it is possible to imagine Sarah. Trust was not part of her nature. She needed to be in control, in a position to dictate events. Any situation in which this was not the case rapidly became intolerable to her. The development of her career, which is to say the development of her life, hinged on the realization of this. Colombier also asserts that Sarah's promiscuity masked a vain search for the man who would be able to arouse her sexually – and this too carries conviction. This is, after all, often the case with compulsive promiscuity – although the 'great lover' image Sarah later cultivated of course implied just the opposite: that sex was an unending source of sensual delight for her, of which she could never have enough.

There are various other characteristics which are common in multiples and which were certainly part of Sarah's make up. Anorexia is one of these. Sarah's extreme thinness was such that it made her a butt during the whole of the first part of her career. When she appeared as Iphigénie in her first début with the Comédie-Française, the house laughed instead of crying when, during her big speech, she held out her arms and a wag called out, 'Watch out, you'll stick yourself on her toothpicks!' After she became famous this thinness was the subject of countless cartoons and jokes; and throughout her life, although she prided herself on the excellence of her table, people always noticed that she herself hardly ate anything at all.

Anorexia is often a reaction when girls are raped by fellatio, and in this context it is hardly necessary to point out that the *panade* Sarah could not bear to take might seem particularly repellent – and the fact that she remembered it so clearly is perhaps indicative that it held some particular horror for her. But anorexia has other connotations as well, all of them apposite in Sarah's case. It is a way of exercising power, of asserting control over one's own life where one is otherwise unable to do this. And it is also generally connected with self-hatred and self-destructive urges – both also very common reactions to incidents of incestuous or quasi-incestuous child rape.

Throughout the whole of Sarah's career, on the surface so glittering and so fulfilling, the death-wish constantly hovers in the wings. There was the famous coffin which she had specially made and lined with satin, and which she kept in her bedroom – an action generally explained as a vulgar seeking for sensation and effect. It certainly seems more than likely that this was part of its attraction; it also had other meanings which will be discussed later. But that it was a constant reminder of beckoning and perhaps not unwelcome death can hardly be denied. There was at least one suicide attempt, briefly reported in 1867 (Sarah was not yet well-known: she was 'an actress engaged at the Odéon Theatre'), in which she took an overdose of laudanum, and was only saved by a friend who persuaded her to drink a

121

quantity of strong coffee as an antidote.[22] Then there were, on her first American tour, at least two episodes when she deliberately, and with all the compulsive, hysterical style of 'Appearances', put herself into great physical danger: once when she climbed far out on an icicle high over the Niagara Falls – so far that she could not get back; and once when (accompanied by her sister Jeanne) she let herself get stranded on an ice-floe in the St Lawrence. On the level of emotional self-destruction, there was the business of her bizarre and short-lived marriage. And in the theatre one of her hallmarks was the number, realism and gruesome variety of her death-scenes.

Multiplicity might also explain part of her fascination with *travesti* roles. Cross-dressing often appeals to multiples, and Sarah was always fascinated by male roles, of which *Le Passant* was not her first: that being the role of the duc de Richelieu in a Conservatoire production. In all Sarah acted twenty-five male roles in the course of her career, and they included some of her most famous parts: L'Aiglon, Lorenzaccio, Pelléas, and of course Hamlet.

For such a person, it is obvious that the stage may be a form of natural therapy. All sorts of different situations may be acted out, great numbers of different personalities assumed, simply in the course of the working life. It is often remarked that well-known actors may seem, offstage, rather devoid of personality, as if they can only achieve definition within the characters of their onstage roles. The late Jill Bennett, for example, was quoted as saying that she only felt really happy in rehearsal.[23] And to act out one's death on stage may relieve the compulsion to try it out for real.

Charcot, the great neurologist who was practising in Paris at this time, saw things somewhat the other way about: he thought that in all hysterical phenomena, such as he demonstrated in his patients during his weekly public lectures, emotion, imagination, suggestion, fabulation and lies played a part. He insisted on the phenomenal acting abilities of hysterics. Conversely, might not great acting ability itself be a pathological symptom, marking out the potential hysteric? The stage, as we have seen, was not Sarah's choice; but once it had been so fortuitously foisted upon her, and once she had acquired the maturity and self-control to school herself into the use of her natural gifts – her intelligence, her voice, her capacity for absorbing herself in a role – those gifts, as Camille Doucet had perceived, were very great.

Thus it may literally be said that the stage was the saving of Sarah Bernhardt. How literally may be seen if her fate is compared with that of her two younger sisters. Both died young, Jeanne in 1900 when she was forty-nine, by which time she had been a morphine addict for many years, as was her daughter Saryta, who died soon after her; Régine at the age of only nineteen in 1874.

Morphine addiction as a form of self-annihilation is today such a commonplace that it hardly needs enlarging upon. Sarah had done all she could to give Jeanne the benefit of her own experience in the theatre. She presented her to the director of the Odéon with the words, 'I'm bringing my sister to see you; she's no better than I was when I failed to get my first prize; but she'll do what I did: she'll work and get better.'[24] Jeanne, however, was not a good actress. Although she was pretty in a fair, Flemish, regular way, she could not make the grade; she had little talent and lisped slightly. If she was a morphine addict, we may assume that the one thing she most signally lacked was Sarah's will-power and determination. When Sarah formed her own troupe she gave Jeanne more than one acting opportunity, taking her with her on tour to America, while Saryta played in *Léna* and *L'Aiglon*. But neither was able to find salvation from the hopelessness of her life in the theatre as Sarah had done.

Régine's case was an even sadder one. She had grown

123

into an extremely beautiful young woman: 'What a ravishing family the Bernhardts are!' someone remarked in the Goncourts' hearing one night at a party in 1875. 'Did you ever see little Régine? Charming – but she died . . .' Sarah modelled her bust shortly before her death and describes her 'lion's eyes, with long, long, savage eyelashes . . . a slender nose with mobile nostrils, a tiny mouth, a firm chin in a pearly face surmounted by a helmet of moonrays – I have never seen hair so pale, so brilliant, so silky.' But the sulky, foul-mouthed, raging child had not grown out of her misery. 'That beautiful face was without charm,' Sarah continues. 'Her look was hard, that mouth never smiled.'[25] For Régine there had never been much to live for. Sylvia Fraser describes her other self, the one she suppressed, as 'wary, bitter, case-hardened, vengeful, jealous, frightened, furious, egocentric, inventive and sly.'[26] Perhaps this is a description of the self that Sarah, too, was able to suppress; it is certainly a description of Régine. She died in Sarah's big bamboo bed while her sister slept in the famous coffin, which she had recently had installed. 'She didn't mind about the coffin at all – she was used to it,' Sarah commented; but by then Régine was past caring about anything, if she ever had. She died of consumption, like so many hopeless girls of her time.

But Sarah did not die in this way, although – and here is the interesting point – she easily might have done. She certainly appeared to have had consumption as a girl. When she was fifteen, a doctor gave her only a few months to live. More than once (a subject to which we shall return) she coughed blood onstage. Her physique was famously frail and thin. And just as, when she was a child, she had promised herself that she was going to die in order to spite her mother, so at the ripe age of thirty – in fact, not long before the death of Régine – she promised herself that she would die onstage 'vomiting blood' in order to spite Perrin, the administrator of the Comédie-Française, which she had recently rejoined, and who was making her play when she felt neither ready nor fit. It was August 16, a crushingly hot day. The play, as it happened, was Voltaire's *Zaïre*, the piece in which Provost had so ruthlessly coached her at the Conservatoire, and in which she had insisted on her own, rather than his, interpretation of the finale. 'Because I wanted to faint, wanted to cough blood, wanted to die in order to enrage Perrin, I had given the whole of myself: I had sobbed, loved, suffered, and I had genuinely been struck by Orosmane's genuine dagger, giving a genuine cry of genuine pain; for I had felt the blade penetrate my breast and . . . had really thought I was dying; for the whole of the last part of the act I hardly dared move my arm, I was so convinced I was in my last agony. I was a bit frightened, I must admit, to realize what an unpleasant game I was playing on Perrin. Imagine my surprise when, after the curtain fell, I jumped up for the curtain-call and took my bows, all ready to start again . . . That day I realized that my body was under the control of my intellect.'[27] The theatre had allowed Sarah to take control of her life. By giving her both something to live for, and a way of exorcizing the spectres of her childhood, it enabled her, unlike either of her sisters, to survive that childhood and even to make use of it.

11

Sarah had now begun to make a pleasant little niche for herself in both her profession and in the social world. *Le Passant* (which was to be not only Coppée's first, but also his greatest success) established her as the Odéon's leading attraction. She and Agar were much in demand at society parties; when Agar was unavailable her place was taken by Marie Colombier, who had been one of Sarah's contemporaries at the Conservatoire. Her student fan-club showered her with flowers, wrote her interminable odes and sonnets, and applauded her every appearance in whatever capacity, much to the annoyance of older habitués whose approach to the theatre was more discriminating.

She had for some time been living in a large apartment on the corner of the rue Auber and the boulevard Haussmann. The household here included Régine (from time to time), Sarah's maid, Maurice, Maurice's nurse, Sarah's old grandmother from Holland (Julie's stepmother), and *her* nurse. Neither Sarah nor Julie liked the old lady, who was blind and exigent and who had never got on with her husband's children. She had been driven out of her previous lodgings by smallpox, which had ravaged her host's family, and Sarah, with her habitual recognition of family duty, had agreed to take her. Perhaps on account of this, the old lady had given her a lot of antique Dutch furniture which had belonged to her and which was very valuable (or perhaps the furniture had come first and the offer of lodging as a consequence). This did not mean, however, that the grandmother was happy with her lot. She was an observant Jewess, cold and self-centred, very tall, generally dressed in grey; at the top of this long, thin, grey body was a small head with protuberant blue eyes which never closed even in sleep. She did not much like living at Sarah's. She found Maurice too noisy, and no doubt other aspects of the household were not to her taste, either. For Sarah's household was not orderly. Pierre Berton remembered with horror his only visit to the apartment in the rue Auber. 'It was a Saturday afternoon; we were going over a part together, and I had promised to finish the recital at Sarah's home. I arrived about three o'clock, and was met at the door by a tumble-haired whirlwind in an old chemise and skirt, whom I with difficulty recognised as Régine, Sarah's little sister. Régine looked as if she had not had a wash for a week, and perhaps she hadn't . . . She dragged me into the salon, and here I got another shock, for the room was in the most frightful mess you can imagine. Empty wine bottles rolled about on the carpet; the remains of a meal stood partly on the mantelshelf and partly on the table, all mixed up with sheets of manuscript, which I saw were books of the plays which Sarah had appeared in. Photographs in gilt frames were here and there, most of them tumbled on their faces, and over all was a thick layer of dust. I had to dirty two of my handkerchiefs before one of the chairs could be trusted not to soil my trousers. From another room a baby kept up a wail . . . When Sarah finally appeared, it was in a long smock covered with paint and grease. Her hair was done anyhow, and her wide-set eyes sparkled with fun as she viewed my distaste for her surroundings.'[1]

This happy, slapdash life was, however, soon to be brought to an end.

It was, Sarah recounts, a day when she was not acting. The Odéon, like the Comédie, was a repertory theatre, and Sarah did not appear in all the plays. Writing after the event she recalled that she had dreaded some misfortune all day, but this seems improbable, a shadow cast backwards in retrospect. What she had done was finally to arrange, or get Madame Guérard to arrange, for some fire insurance for the apartment. The letter setting out the terms of the policy had arrived that day, and she arranged to sign it the day following. In the evening some friends came to dinner: Rose Baretta, an actress, Arthur Meyer, a young journalist who was making a name for himself (and who was to remain one of Sarah's intimate friends until her death), and Charles Haas, a Jockey Club dandy, who is famous for having been Proust's principal model for Charles Swann in *À la recherche du temps perdu*. The fact of Haas' presence shows that Sarah was now considered an extremely desirable and interesting young woman, for Haas (who never married) was known as one of the most discriminating womanizers in town.

At about nine o'clock dinner ended, and the four settled down to enjoy themselves. Sarah left the room for a moment to check that everything was all right in the rest of the house and found her maid complaining of a terrible headache. So she told her to get everything ready for the night and then to go to bed herself. Sarah then returned to the salon, where, after a short while, cries of 'Fire! Fire!' were to be heard from the street. Charles Haas stuck his head out of the window and said, 'It looks as if it's your flat that's on fire!' And sure enough, the flames were coming from the two windows of Sarah's bedroom. She had already had occasion to reprimand her maid a couple of times for being careless about setting a candle where a draught might catch it from the open window, but evidently to no avail: the flame had caught the lace curtains of the bed.

Sarah's first thought was for Maurice. She rushed to the room he shared with his nurse and his governess, woke them and snatched him up. Soon all three were deposited with a kindly confectioner who kept a shop opposite. Then she returned to rescue her grandmother. This was not so easy: smoke had made the main staircase impassable, and the door leading to the kitchen from the service stairs was triple locked and had to be broken down – a task for which Haas's elegant but slight shoulder was not sufficient: a brawnier substitute had to be brought in. Meanwhile smoke was filling the apartment.

The old woman, once awoken, was not grateful to have her life saved, but insisted on her trunk being brought out from the big cupboard where it was kept and would not budge without it. Finally she was bundled out on the back of a helper. At this point Sarah fainted, and came to in her mother's bed, with her grandmother installed in the salon still grumbling about her trunk while Julie scolded her in Dutch for her selfishness.

Sarah found herself ruined. Her apartment and everything in it was completely destroyed; the insurance policy had not been signed; and, worse, the fire had damaged the whole building, and the insurance company was holding Sarah responsible for the expenses of repair. And she had not a sou. She had invested nothing in securities: everything she owned had been in her flat. She could never resist surrounding herself with knick-knacks and pretty things; dealers knew her as easy game, she was to be seen in all the antique shops, she would bring home truckloads of trophies from all her tours. She particularly mourned a tortoise called Chrysargère whose shell she had had inlaid with precious stones. A hotel offered to house her for free if she would consent to dine in its dining-room every night for a month, but she scornfully declined this offer. On the other hand she could not stay at her mother's. What, then, was to be done?

Duquesnel offered her a benefit – the one at which the Marquis de Caux persuaded his new wife, the singer Adelina Patti, to perform, with the result that it was sold out and the insurance company's claims could be met in full. But this by no means solved Sarah's problems. She took a small furnished flat, but it was gloomy and dark. Her wages were small; her relatives were disinclined to help. Some disapproved of her being an actress, although that had hardly been her own choice. Her aunt Henriette Faure wanted nothing more to do with her, though she still saw her uncle. Her rich friends thought her extravagent to the point of madness, and could not believe that she had nothing at all invested in shares which might have survived the fire . . .

Salvation took the entirely unexpected form of Maître Clément, the notary from Le Havre whom Sarah had so much disliked at the family council when he had refused to release her hundred thousand francs. She had, of course, already received half of this, now gone up in smoke with everything else. Maître Clément arrived out of the blue. He had read about the fire and wanted to know about the circumstances. Sarah told him everything, including the sad details of her lack of insurance. This seemed to reassure him. He had understood that she had set the fire herself because she was short of cash, so that she could touch the insurance money – an item of gossip which was presently going the rounds. But things being what they were he thought he could help her. It turned out that her father had left her better off than anyone had expected, money which her grandmother was holding for her in the form of an annuity, and if she would agree to insure her life for forty years for the benefit of the buyer, he would see to the selling of that annuity for a good price (he probably bought it himself). Within a few days Sarah was in receipt of a hundred and twenty thousand francs. She took a sunny apartment in the rue de Rome and prepared to take up her life again.

But before she could properly do so, there was to be a longer and more important interruption.

The prosperity and self-confidence of the Second Empire

1. Sarah and Julie   **2.** *below left* Régine
3. First *travesti* part: as the duc de Richelieu at the Conservatoire

4. Portrait of Sarah by Félix Nadar, taken at the time of her débuts. She is about eighteen. This wonderful picture marks the start of Sarah's life-long love-affair with the camera, which was to make her face familiar throughout the world

5. As Duquesnel put it: 'Sarah Bernhardt aged twenty – what more can one say?'

6. Robert de Montesquiou and Sarah, both dressed in *Le Passant* costumes

7. The famous coffin photograph
8. The inspiration for the coffin photograph is obvious when it is placed beside Millais' *Ophelia* and *right* Delaroche's *La jeune martyre*, both popular pictures in Paris at this time, and both exhibiting the fashionable decadent view of the ideal woman: passive, submissive and preferrably dead

9. Sarah in her white silk artist's suit by Worth

10. The toast of London and Paris: as Mistress Clarckson in *L'Etrangère*, 1879

11. Early days at the
Comédie-Française.
The spiral-line
seductress sits in the
Queen of Spain's chair

12. Jean Mounet-Sully
as Hernani – portrait
by Paul Nadar

13. The Vamp: Théodora

14. Marie Colombier

15. As Fédora, by Paul Nadar

16. Family group: Saryta, Damala and Sarah, with Terka and Maurice (*sitting*), taken shortly before Damala's death and Maurice's marriage

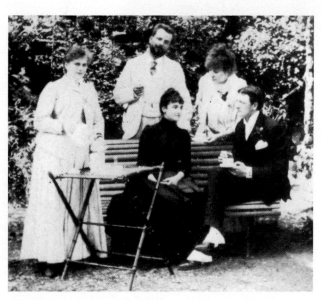

was such that, to many, it must have felt both solid and permanent. But of course neither solidity nor permanence had been a feature of French life during the past century, which had seen the upheavals of the Revolution, the glorious days of Napoleon, his disgrace and the restoration of the monarchy in the person of Charles X, *his* removal in 1830 to be replaced by the 'bourgeois monarch' Louis-Philippe, the inception of the Second Republic in 1848 with Louis-Napoléon as President, to be transmogrified into Emperor in the 1851 coup d'état. With such a history it was clear that not all Frenchmen would support the Empire; and as the years had gone on Napoléon III had become increasingly intolerant of dissent, which had grown stronger the more it was suppressed. By the late 1860s support for the republicans was so strong that new outbreaks of civil unrest were feared. Sarah herself had had occasion to experience this tension in 1868 when she went to perform *Le Passant* at the Tuileries. On her way to the palace she and the Comte de Laferrière, who was to present her, had met an old friend, Général Fleury, who had passed the time of day and then left them, calling out: 'Good luck!' at which a passer-by growled, 'Maybe, but not for long, you load of good-for-nothings!'[2]

These potential disturbances were feared even by those who did not much care for the Emperor; for civil war was not the only cloud on the horizon. There was also Bismarck, lurking in Prussia with his eyes covetously fixed on the Rhineland provinces of Alsace and Lorraine. All he was waiting for was an opportunity – the kind of opportunity which might be provided if France were now to tear herself apart. When that failed to happen, he manufactured his own opportunity; and, by the summer of 1870, it became increasingly clear that there was going to be a war with Prussia.

War was declared on July 19, and the announcement was

greeted with patriotic fervour and enthusiasm. Parisians thronged the streets, singing the 'Marseillaise' and shouting 'To Berlin! To Berlin!' It was not, however, the Parisians who were to enter Berlin, but the Berliners who would take Paris. Inexorably, the news of defeat after defeat dissipated the triumphant mood of the war's beginning, until, in the first days of September, the news of Sedan reached the capital – Sedan, in which the Emperor had insisted on taking command himself, which he had survived when so many thousands had been killed, and at the end of which he had surrendered his sword.

It was the moment the Republicans had been waiting for. Huge crowds gathered in the streets of Paris searching for the chant which would express their feelings. Down with the Corps législatif? No. Vive la République? Too soon for that! Vive la France? Nothing new in that. Death to the Prussians? Not quite yet. At last they hit on the word: *Déchéance – dé-ché-ance*, they chanted – downfall – signifying, as it had signified in 1830 and in 1848, the end of the existing state of affairs.[3] The next day, 4 September, the crowds massed outside the Tuileries, where the Empress was (it was supposed) still in residence. But she had fled in the carriage of her American dentist; the Imperial Guard surrendered; and the Republic was declared without a shot being fired. Republican politicians considered this a triumph, though there were many in the crowd who felt unsatisfied, lusting for a bloody vengeance on the aristos and bonapartists who had deprived them of their revolution – a lust which would find its expression next year during the Commune

Meanwhile even the loftiest republicans could not conceal their curiosity about what the private apartments of the Tuileries – now exposed to public gaze – had *really been like*. In the Empress's rooms they found countless bottles of rosewater, *flacons* of cologne and perfume, boxes of rice powder. At the foot of her bed stood another bed, thickly curtained with muslin – why? For whom? Was she afraid of sleeping alone, or was she under surveillance? In her bookshelves, a strange mixture of holy books and pictures and risqué semi-pornography. About two hundred hats, a perfect railway-station of dresses: the dressmakers' workshops were directly over the empress's apartments. So reported Juliette Adam, who was to be one of the *grandes dames* of the Republic, in breathless detail.[4]

Sarah was not among those who welcomed the declaration of war. On the contrary: the very prospect made her ill. In July of 1870 she began to cough blood. Her doctor declared that the prognosis was grave, and sent her to take the cure at Eaux-Bonnes, near Bordeaux. Here she stayed, anxiously scanning the news bulletins as they were posted up, until by the end of August it became clear that the enemy was closing in and she must get back to Paris, whence she would send her family to safety, although she herself intended to remain come what may. As usual, the prospect of action brought about a miraculous improvement in her health. All thought of dying was abandoned for the present.

At Bordeaux, the Paris train was full to bursting. Sarah and Maurice finally pushed their way into a compartment designed for eight, and already containing nine, of whom one was a very fat lady who complained bitterly about the new arrivals. Sarah riposted cruelly that in that case the fat lady could get out: she took up enough space for three, so that would mean only seven remained. The fat lady was not mollified, and got even crosser when three young men insisted on standing and giving their seats to the newcomers. Finally a compromise was arrived at: the six thinnest passengers would sit on one side, the four plumper, on the other. Maurice sat on the knee of one of the young men, who introduced himself as Félix Faure – the namesake of

Sarah's uncle: but this Félix Faure was later to become deputy for Le Havre (like Sarah's Havrais relatives, his family were arms dealers), President of the Republic, and was to die ignobly in the arms of his clandestine mistress in the Presidential palace. Sarah's description of him – 'a tall, handsome boy with a fair face, blue eyes, white-blonde hair which gave his face a pleasant youth and freshness' – makes him sound very young indeed; but in fact he was at this time already a married man with a daughter, Lucie, almost the same age as Maurice. Sarah was recognized, and one of the lady passengers introduced herself as a relation by marriage, so that all in all the uncomfortable journey was finally accomplished in good spirits. When they got to Paris Sarah had the mortification of seeing the fat lady, to whom she had been so cruel, met by her husband, who held out a telegram in silence: on reading it, she fell sobbing into his arms.

Sarah's first thought was to get her family – her mother, her aunt Annette, another of Julie's sisters who had been looking after her apartment, Régine, Jeanne and her little daughter Saryta, Maurice and his nurse – out of Paris and into safety. She was not the only person thinking in those terms. The Gare du Nord was a seething melée of would-be travellers fighting for tickets. Sarah's party consisted of nine persons; she had to enlist the aid of four brawny helpers (including a curé, which helped) to secure their tickets and see her group safely into their reserved compartment. When the train drew out she found Madame Guérard at her elbow. How, wondered her faithful friend, would she bear life without her little boy? And indeed, like so many Parisians who deprived themselves of their children at this time in order to ensure their safety, Sarah returned to her apartment 'stupefied by the absence of life around me, and by the absence of love'.[5]

But there was no time to brood. It was clear Paris was

going to be besieged, and there was work to be done. Provisions must be laid in and preparations made, both privately and publicly. 'I rush about getting my provisions together,' recorded Juliette Adam. 'There are so many things to think of. Everything is liable to run out, even salt, pepper and mustard ... All I think about is Australian mutton, Liebig ham, canned vegetables, groceries! I always come home loaded down with stuff. If I find some new conserve I dream about the amazement of my friends when I offer it to them in three months' time! When the conquering heroes return I shan't garland them with laurels, but offer them a bottle of young carrots or a bag of curly kale. My hero will have had to accomplish the most outstanding feats before I offer him a Dutch cheese.'[6]

Sarah, too, was laying in provisions, but not for herself alone. She might disapprove of the new Republic – she regretted the pretty Empress, the Prince Imperial's long eyelashes, the Emperor who had been so charming to her, the elegance of the court – but she was a fervent patriot, and she was determined to do her bit. Many large public buildings, including the Conservatoire, the Théâtre Français, the Masonic temple, were being converted into military hospitals. Sarah obtained permission to open another such in the Odéon, and set about provisioning it, starting with a flock of forty hens and six geese which she quartered in her apartment. Because her hospital was for the military, not civilians, she was excluded from sharing the municipal stores; but she had old friends in high places.

Chief of these was the Préfet of Paris, M. de Kératry. At first, Sarah could hardly believe that this was the same young man she had met at Rosine's not so very many years ago, and who had courted her so assiduously. But so it was, and when Sarah came into his office in the Tuileries (so different, she reflected sadly, from the last time she had been there!) the fortuitous meeting put them both in the best of humour. Sarah reeled off a list of everything she needed, from potatoes and coffee to firewood; Kératry promised her she should receive it all and gave her helpful hints about procedure. As a finishing touch she demanded his beautiful fur-lined overcoat for her convalescents; laughing regretfully, he emptied its pockets and handed it over. (Next time she came to see him he made a great show of locking his overcoat away in a cupboard and hiding the key.) Kératry was as good as his word. He sent her ten barrels of red wine and two of eau-de-vie, thirty thousand eggs packed in chalk and bran, a hundred bags of coffee, twenty cases of tea, forty cases of Albert biscuits, a thousand tins of conserves and a great many other necessaries. Then she turned to her other friends. Menier, the chocolate manufacturer, sent five hundred pounds of his product. The rich miller who had wanted to marry her all those years ago contributed twenty sacks of flour, including six of cornflour. Félix Potin the high-class provisions merchant, who had been a neighbour of hers, sent two cases of raisins, a hundred cans of sardines, three sacks of rice and twenty loaves of sugar. M. de Rothschild sent two barrels of eau-de-vie and a hundred bottles of his own wine for the convalescents. And an old fellow-pupil from her days at Grand-Champs, who had married a rich country gentleman, sent a hundred tins of salted butter. For the rest, all Sarah's acquaintance had been stripped of top-coats; she had bought two hundred flannel waistcoats; and her aunt Betzy, the grim grandmother's sister, who lived in Holland, sent three hundred nightshirts and a hundred pairs of sheets. Sarah was set up, for the moment at least. Later, when the Prussians began to bombard the city and the Odéon became dangerous – it was actually hit, although the shell did not explode – she moved her entire establishment to the enormous apartment of her banker friend, Jacques Stern, in the rue Taitbout.

Sarah's hospital was run with very few staff. She had

bought an enormous stove for her cook, who set herself up in the foyer of the theatre, and whose husband became chief nurse. Then there was Sarah herself and (mentioned in her memoirs) two additional helpers: Mme Guérard and the Odéon's character actress, Mme Lambquin. There was also, although Sarah does not mention her, Marie Colombier, her erstwhile partner in *Le Passant*, who was at this time still her friend. Paul Porel, who had been at the Conservatoire with the two of them and had played opposite Sarah in her last play at the Odéon, records that he re-met her at this time in a new role – that of a wounded soldier – and that Marie Colombier was one of his nurses. But by the time Sarah came to write her memoirs Colombier's malicious and wounding skit, *Les Mémoires de Sarah Barnum*, had put paid to such friendship as there had been.

Colombier was motivated with regard to Sarah by a vindictive and unassuageable jealousy. Her book, in which Sarah is portrayed as a sluttish whore motivated entirely and solely by rapacity and a desire for adulation, was a great success, running into many editions. Its effectiveness derives from the fact that Colombier did know a great deal about Sarah's life. Names are barely disguised and instantly recognizable; the situations described are never very far from the truth. But the gloss put upon them is always extremely distasteful.

At this distance it is easy to see, and to say, that this tells us more about Colombier than it does about Sarah. If the underlying motivations Colombier attributes to her subject are always those of a whore with money and personal advantage in mind, if Sarah's acting talent is seen as strictly secondary to her talent for getting powerful men into bed and her success a consequence of the latter rather than the former, then it is fair to say that this was Marie Colombier's view of the theatre as borne out by her own personal experience. Colombier was much more successful as a whore than an actress, and eventually entirely abandoned the stage for the bed. But Colombier was not only nasty but also intelligent and perceptive (one of the reasons her book was such a success was that she was a good writer with a racy style and an excellent eye for detail), and some of the remarks she makes about Sarah ring perfectly true. With regard to the hospital she observes that 'as always, [Bernhardt] took her role more than seriously and entered into the skin of her new character'. This sounds (and was!) malicious, but, given the importance of role-playing in Sarah's psychological life, it was also probably quite true. Colombier also speaks of 'the confused pleasure she found in the exercise of her new duties and in exercising her authority'.[7] And this too it is very easy to believe. For here, for the first time in her life, Sarah was at nobody's beck and call but was running her own show – something she found so satisfactory that, from this moment on, no other life would really do for her.

The siege began in the middle of September, 1870, and went on for three and a half months. That winter was the coldest for twenty years. Everything was in short supply. Even the rich found it hard to manage – Mme de Rothschild held a charity auction at the Gare d'Austerlitz at which cabbages fetched unimaginable sums – while the sufferings of the poor beggared description. It was necessary to queue for hours in the freezing cold in order to get any bread, meat or milk, or any hand-out from the soup kitchens. Sarah saw these shivering queues from the windows of the theatre. Sometimes she would send Guillaume the nurse out with a little eau-de-vie to keep them going; more than once she took in women suffering from frostbite. By January there was no more firewood: rich and poor shivered alike. Pigeons and other small birds, snared on the rooftops, became a gastronomic prize. The siege, wrote Edmond de Goncourt, had been 'a joke for two months. In the third month the joke went sour. Now nobody finds it funny any more.'[8] Half a pound of horsemeat, including the bones, was two people's ration for three days. A small turnip cost eight sous and a pound of onions, seven francs. There was no butter, or indeed any fat except candle-fat and axle-grease. The poor traditionally lived on potatoes and cheese, but cheese was 'just a memory', said Goncourt, and potatoes could only be got by those who knew the right people; even then they cost twenty francs a bushel. A working man might earn three francs a day. 'The greater part of Paris is living on coffee, wine and bread,' Goncourt concluded.

Only food and warmth mattered; only money – in increasing amounts – would buy those. Shopkeepers who dealt in other commodities resigned themselves to taking all manner of IOUs and sureties. 'It doesn't mean a thing so long as France wins,' remarked Juliette Adam's haberdasher. 'But if we have to see her defeated and find ourselves bankrupted at the end of the siege into the bargain – that will be too much!'[9] To add to their discomforts, nobody could really be sure what was happening outside. Paris was cut off from news as well as everything else. The only post was by carrier pigeon; the only way to reach the outside world was by balloon. Gambetta was ballooned out; so was Kératry; nobody knew what had happened to them, or if they were safe, until they managed somehow to smuggle a message back in to the besieged city. There were rumours of victories in the provinces, but these were soon overtaken by other rumours, of defeats. Everyone who could had sent their children to safety: nobody knew what had become of those children. Sarah had supposed her family was at Le Havre, but a couple of notes from Julie – mere sentences on the thinnest of paper, brought in who knew how – told her, first, that they were at the Hague, and then, to her horror, at Bad Homburg, in the land of the enemy.

In fact nothing can have seemed more natural for Julie than to go to Homburg. The fashionable German watering-places – Ems, Baden-Baden, Homburg – were the traditional summer resorts of the entire *haute bicherie* of Paris. The end of the summer season was marked by their return from these spas, when they would once again be seen driving in the Bois de Boulogne. Rosine, in particular, was an habituée of these places; Julie knew people in Homburg, it was the natural place to go. And of course she personally was not French. But for Sarah, who emphatically *was*, the thought that her mother and son were in Germany filled her with fury. However, there was nothing she could do about it, and it was a relief to know they were safe and well.

Meanwhile the hospitals, harried by shortages, took in increasing numbers of wounded. As firewood ran out Sarah burned the theatre benches, the seats, Gothic armchairs used in the productions . . . She, like everyone else, cultivated pretty Mlle Hocquigny, who was in charge of supplies; and just when it seemed they must all freeze, this *dea ex machina* let her have another ten thousand kilos of wood. Someone had found a new way of preserving meat: all the hospitals were given some. But when the container was opened, the stink was so terrible that Sarah was for throwing the whole lot out. Mme Lambquin advised her against this: better, she said, to put the meat back in its container and return it to the Mairie: these were not days for throwing anything out, however rotten. It was good advice: another hospital which had thrown out its consignment of the rotten meat was attacked by the mob and the staff had to flee for their lives. But the Parisians did not lose heart. Even when the Prussian bombardment began, Sardou recorded, 'people [went] to see the shells fall in the St Jacques district just as they used to go and watch the skaters at the rink. You meet a friend. Where are you off to? I'm going to the bombardment.'[10] A German soldier who was brought to Sarah's hospital was cheerful despite his wounds and the taunts of his French fellow-patients because, he told Sarah, he was convinced the Parisians could only hold out for another two days; he knew there was nothing left in the city. Seventeen days later, when he was convalescent, she triumphantly served him a wing of chicken. His face fell. She did not tell him it was one of the forty she had laid in at the start of the siege.

The privations were terrible, and life at the hospital was continually harrowing and exhausting. Yet it is clear, both from the length of her account of these dreadful months and from its tone, that Colombier was right: she enjoyed her life then as much as she ever enjoyed anything. Of course she was not unique in this reaction. It is well attested that war gives people a sense of purpose and usefulness, frees them from nagging social constraints, imbues the present moment with extraordinary vividness. Sarah, running her hospital, was tireless and valiant. Everyone acknowledged it: it added enormously to her popularity during the following years. And it in no way diminishes the stature of what she did if we perceive, in that inexhaustible energy, those unexpected reserves of strength, the first emergence of characteristics which were, as her life went on, to become almost her hallmarks. When she was running her own show – her own troupe, her own theatre, her own hospital – Sarah could always be relied on. In the most adverse circumstances, she would soldier on. Invariably, she worked harder than anyone else. It was only when she was an employee – i.e. when she was not in control of her own life – that she became capricious, unreasonable and unreliable.

The siege ended; Bismarck imposed his terms. They included an indemnity of two hundred million francs to be paid at once. Finances were so bad that it was touch and go whether these could be found; eventually Baron Alphonse de Rothschild personally guaranteed the sum. But the sufferings of the Parisians were by no means over. First there were the bloody months of the Commune; and even when that was over – at what cost in bitterness and destruction! – there was the intolerable invasion.

Who can imagine what invasion means, who has not experienced it? 'For two months [wrote Ludovic Halévy] I have had in my home a very decent, well-educated and courteous Prussian officer, who gave me bonbons on New Year's Day. I dared not refuse them, but I put the bag at the bottom of the cupboard, and, please believe me, I would not eat this Prussian's bonbons for love or money. He will not be happy if peace if declared. "It is too soon," he told me last night, "much too soon. France has not suffered enough. She is not destroyed enough. We shall be forced to return sometime in the future . . . We shall be upset if we have to start another war; we shall be more wicked, more angry. The French are rebuilding very quickly. When you have reconstructed your homes, and that will not take long, you will have only one idea in mind, and that will be to come and destroy our homes." As for me, I could not help saying, "Oh, that is quite true!" And then, taking no offence, he told me, "You see, this war is going to end too soon." '[11] People found their homes commandeered, their possessions looted or destroyed, their daily lives dictated by the Prussians. Even when these demands were reasonable it was intolerable; when they were not, there was nothing to do but grit one's teeth and carry on silently. One effect of all this was the emergence of a strain of xenophobic ultra-nationalism which crossed all political boundaries, uniting republicans with monarchists, and whose most notorious consequence would be the Dreyfus affair twenty years later. Meanwhile, life must go on.

12

Paris was reopened on 31 January, 1871. As soon as possible after that, Sarah decided to set out in search of her family.

Leaving Paris was no easy matter. Quite apart from the possible dangers and difficulties of the journey – railway lines were cut, horses were scarce, the country was infested with Prussian soldiers for whom women travelling alone might seem easy targets – travel permits and visas had first to be obtained. Once again Sarah pulled strings. One of her friends, Paul de Rémusat, arranged for her to see M. Thiers, President of the new Republic, who let her have a safe-conduct, while impressing on her, as did Rémusat, the dangers of what she was undertaking. Nevertheless she determined to go – but only with a companion. When she asked Mlle Chesneau, Maurice's young governess, if she would like to come on the journey, she 'jumped for joy' – so, at least, says Sarah – and the two young women prepared to leave Paris at once.

They set out on February 4, and found it passably difficult to surmount the very first hurdle. In order to leave Paris one's permit had to be stamped by the German authorities, and Sarah was turned back twice before she managed to find an officer who would let her through. He did so not without reluctance: to contemplate any journey was madness. Sarah persisted. Finally he summoned a carriage which he said would take her to Gonesse, where the provisions train was due to leave in an hour. He gave her an introduction to the station-master there – 'and after that, God help you!'

God did help her, of course. After many adventures, rough passages and inconveniences the pair reached Homburg without being either raped or robbed and found Julie and her party safe and sound. Then all that was needed was to get back to Paris, which they finally achieved, arriving at St Denis at four in the morning to find no trains moving into the city. The railways in Paris, like everything else, were controlled by the Germans, and trains moved only when it suited them. After an hour of looking and arguing a sympathetic officer was found who arranged for a locomotive to take the party to the Gare St Lazare. The journey took two hours: they finally arrived at seven o'clock to find more trouble. Revolutionary stirrings were in the air. The driver, with whom Sarah had got into conversation, advised her to leave: 'You'll be better off anywhere but Paris. They'll soon be fighting here.' Nevertheless, having come so far, now was not the moment to leave. They got down to find a complete lack of transport. Sarah lived in the rue de Rome, not very far away, but Julie never walked anywhere and the two children, Maurice and Saryta, were terribly tired and incapable of putting one foot in front of the other. In despair, Sarah hailed a passing milkman. For twenty francs he agreed to take Julie, Sarah and the children to her apartment at number 4, and for another twenty to come back and pick up the rest of the party.

The ride was not a comfortable one, nor dignified, and Sarah saw that Julie was furious at this last indignity. She would probably have preferred to have been left in peace at Homburg. When they arrived she scolded Sarah for an hour. 'Poor pretty maman. It wasn't my fault,' was Sarah's only comment.

For a while they remained in Paris. Paris was now above all a political city, and Sarah, with her unique double reputation as glamorous actress and patriotic heroine, knew all the men at the centre of affairs. She was a frequent guest

144

at Emile de Girardin's – Girardin was publisher of *La Presse* and the most influential journalist of his day, and a great friend of Sarah's – and here she met Gambetta, the white hope of the republicans, Henry de Rochefort, whose vicious lampoons had done so much to discredit the Emperor, and Paul de Rémusat, who although he was a monarchist was a favourite of Thiers, the President. These were the men of the new Republic. Their dinners with Sarah afforded some break in the grim daily reality, when it was possible to turn for a while to jokes and literature and even to perform some amateur theatricals – Sarah mentions an evening when the company played the entire first act of Hugo's *Hernani*, with Gambetta successfully taking the part in which Mounet-Sully was later to have such a great triumph.

But these were not Sarah's only political acquaintances. She also knew some of the leading figures on the other side – the Communards whose aim was to upset the Republic for their own revolutionary utopia. She was a friend of Flourens, one of their leading theorists, whom she describes as a good and charming man whose aims were happiness and prosperity for all, but who had failed to resolve the perpetual revolutionary contradiction – of how happiness is to be obtained at the point of a gun. She also knew a more sinister figure, Raoul Rigault, who for a short while held the post of Préfet of police. He, in addition to his political interests, was an amateur playwright whose mediocre work Sarah refused to take seriously – as a result of which he used his position of power to make life unpleasant for her and for Mme Guérard until, not long afterwards, he was shot.

The upheavals of the Commune were now gathering force – upheavals encouraged, naturally, by the Germans, who relished the prospect of what remained of France tearing herself apart. But Sarah saw these new events in a more positive light. Her journey had taken her away from Paris for eleven days. She had left a city cowed, miserable and apathetic; when she came back, life had returned. The walls were covered with multicoloured posters full of political extremism; and where the war and the siege had reduced women to tatters, children to depression, men to discouragement, now the renewal of political life had awakened them from their bad dream. Even if the sentiments were of the most basic – 'Down with monarchies! Down with Republics! Down with the rich! Down with the priests! Down with Jews! Down with the army! Down with the bosses! Down with the workers! Down with everything!' – at least the life they signalled was better than stupefaction.

But despite this return of interest, life in Paris soon became extremely dangerous, and Sarah, along with everyone else who was able to do so, left for the suburbs – in her case, the pretty town of St Germain-en-Laye. For despite all her new political acquaintances and despite the pleasure she expressed in the reawakening of political life, this was never one of Sarah's main interests. Although it was flattering and exciting to know all these men who were at the centre of everything, and thus in a way to feel that she was at the centre of everything herself, this was not really the kind of life she enjoyed, ever or – especially – then. As she later said to Reynaldo Hahn, one of the many young men who worshipped her in her legendary fifties and sixties, 'I was silly, like all young women are . . . I was stupid enough to prefer the company of a whole lot of elegant cretins to the extraordinary men who surrounded me. When I think that one day I left Victor Hugo in the middle of a conversation to go and meet some people from the Jockey Club!'[1] And if she could do that to Victor Hugo, how much more expendable must have seemed all these politicians – never, after all, a race noted for their glamour – when compared to the elegant life offered by such discriminating bons viveurs as her old friend Charles Haas.

And, despite all the ravages of war, such a life was still available at St Germain. The crowd gathered on the great terrace overlooking Paris and watched the city burn; but every day Sarah went horse-riding through the forest with her new beau, Captain O'Connor – presumably the descendant of one of those Irish soldiers who fled to France after Napoleon's army came too late to help them in their uprising against the English. According to Marie Colombier, O'Connor had originally been Régine's young man – she would now have been about seventeen – but was seduced by the glamour of her elder sister, to Régine's mortification: a not impossible scenario. At any rate, O'Connor – blond, handsome, elegant, rather snobbish, but charming – was Sarah's constant companion, and together they rode all the paths through the great forests which encircle St Germain. But a number of sharpshooters were hiding in the forest and shooting at any soldier who seemed to be on the government side. One of these shot at Sarah and O'Connor and then ran off, even though he must have been hit by O'Connor's answering shot. The Captain insisted on setting off in pursuit, and, when they caught up with the culprit (who had fallen and could move no further), bent over him, evidently with the intention of finishing him off. Sarah was appalled: suddenly she saw the mask of a brute superimposed upon the elegant dandy she knew. She begged him not to kill the man and they returned to St Germain in silence. She remained friendly with O'Connor, but could never see him afterwards without being reminded of that horrifying metamorphosis.

But all this was no more than an interlude. During that spring the Commune was defeated. It was time to go back to Paris and pick up the threads of as normal a life as could be constructed.

The wife of Octave Feuillet the playwright recorded her sad impressions as she returned to Paris from Jersey, where she had been living with her children:

At the end of an avenue burgeoning with spring one saw the shell of a chateau. Further on, mutilated woods, dead branches blocking the road. And the nearer we got to Paris the worse the ruination. There was not a house left standing in Asnières . . . The river banks where the *grisettes* and the students used to enjoy themselves were as deserted as the banks of the Dead Sea . . . Where there had been little inns and benches wreathed with vines there was a heap of ruins and around the ruins a few thin horses grazing on the grass which had grown since the disasters.

When we got to Paris . . . there were no cabs. Not a vehicle in the place. We had to walk to our hotel, followed by a porter carrying the cases. Going through the place Vendôme I had to shut my eyes so as not to see the great gap left by the broken-down column. There was desolation everywhere. Silence and darkness everywhere. There was no gaslight. Everyone carried their own little lantern, as they used to do in provincial towns, and all these pale little lights criss-crossing each other in the great black spaces made a very unreal effect.[2]

Nevertheless, as the Prussian officer had predicted, rebuilding was soon under way. After so many months of concentration on the basic necessities of staying alive, of killing and destruction, people began to turn with relief to the reconstruction of civilization, with all its amenities and frivolities. Women began to think about pretty dresses again; theatres started to open their doors. One morning Sarah received a rehearsal notice from the Odéon. 'I shook out my hair,' she recalled, 'and pawed the ground like a young horse eager to get going.'

They started with a new piece, *Jean-Marie* by André Theuriet, with Paul Porel playing the lead opposite Sarah. It

148

was a great success. But it was nothing out of the way. What was needed now, Sarah felt, was something outstanding – something that would make her a big star.

That something now appeared in the person of Victor Hugo.

13

Victor Hugo, who in his youth had been a royalist and supporter of Charles X, had been disillusioned by that illiberal and unrealistic monarch and had celebrated his fall in 1830 with the ode 'A la jeune France'. Since then he had moved steadily leftwards. His writings had been banned by the Imperial censorship, and he had left France, settled in Guernsey, and refused the proffered amnesty: he had vowed not to set foot in France while the Second Empire lasted. It fell on 4 September 1870; the next day, Victor Hugo returned to Paris. He arrived at nine thirty-five in the evening, accompanied by his mistress Juliette Drouet, his son Charles Hugo and daughter-in-law Alice. A huge, excited mob was there to welcome him, and 'rushed towards him with such fervour that they nearly suffocated him'.[1] Some friends managed to manoeuvre him into a small café opposite the station and up to a room on the first floor. Paul Meurice, one of his most faithful supporters, managed to push his way into the café and told Hugo he absolutely must address the crowd. Hugo opened the window, and a vast clamour was heard. 'You have repaid me in an hour,' Hugo told them, 'for nineteen years of exile.'

Hugo went first of all to stay with Meurice. Paris had changed greatly since he was last there. He liked it, he said; 'I wouldn't have liked to see the Bois de Boulogne in the days when it was crowded with carriages, barouches and laudaus. But now that it's a quagmire, a ruin, it appeals to me ... It's beautiful, it's grandiose!' As for Haussmann's great new avenues, he said, 'Yes, the Empire did nothing to provide a defence against foreigners; everything it did was designed to provide a defence against the populace.'[2]

Now the populace – or at any rate the Communards – had been duly crushed. But the Republic was still in place and Hugo remained.

A year later, not long after the theatres had reopened, it was announced to the Odéon actors 'rather mysteriously and solemnly' that they would be putting on one of Hugo's plays, *Ruy Blas*. This, like all his plays, is a verse drama. It is the story of Don Cesar de Bazan, who wishes to avenge himself on the Queen of Spain, who has turned him down. Another possible suitor is Don Sallust; Don Cesar's revenge is to send his valet, Ruy Blas, to impersonate the absent Don Sallust, a ruse which works only too well, as the two fall hopelessly in love. Naturally, all ends in melodramatic disaster.

Sarah's feelings at this were, she says, rather mixed. She had not been brought up in Republican circles, nor were her own instincts Republican. As she somewhat coyly put it, her family was 'rather bourgeois' and its friends and connections cosmopolitan and upper-class. Since she was a child she had heard Hugo spoken of in denigrating terms, as a rebel and a renegade; and although she had read and loved his works, she felt little sympathy for the man. On the other hand, she was dying to play the Queen, and said as much to Duquesnel, who said he had been thinking the same thing himself. However, it was by no means certain that she would be able to do so, because Jane Essler, an actress then much in fashion, was the *petite amie* of Paul Meurice, Hugo's great friend, who would doubtless press her cause with the Master.

So Sarah began politicking to secure the role she wanted so much. A friend introduced her to Auguste Vacquerie, the brother of Hugo's son-in-law, who promised to put in a word for her. Two days later he came back with the news that her chances were good. It seemed that even Meurice felt she should have the role, and so did Geoffroy, an old actor, much respected, who had been called back from retirement to play Don Sallust. Sarah (she says) was astonished that these people, whom she did not know, should know her, but this assumed innocence is not very convincing. In fact she had made a point of meeting and charming both Meurice and Geoffroy, and they had persuaded Hugo, who had seen her in *Jean-Marie* and thought she would probably do. Soon she got the notice for the read-through of the play, which was to be at two o'clock on 6 December at Victor Hugo's apartment.

Sarah, the spoilt darling of her public, felt thoroughly affronted at this news. Why should she (not to speak of everyone else) have to put themselves out for Hugo while he didn't so much as budge? What was the theatre there for if not to provide a place where plays could be read on neutral ground? She said as much to the little 'court' of friends who had taken to visiting her at five o'clock in the afternoon – Arthur Meyer the critic, Georges Clairin, a young painter who was one of Sarah's great friends, the inevitable Mme Guérard, the lover of the moment – and they, of course, threw up their hands and exploded in indignant agreement. A number of replies were drafted in rebuttal of Hugo's impertinent proposal, any one of which, had it been sent, would undoubtedly have lost her the part. Then, in the nick of time, another friend turned up. This was Marshal Canrobert, one of the heroes of the recent war, who was very fond of Sarah. He, too, threw up his hands – at the stupidity of what had been going on. He agreed that Sarah should probably not go to Hugo's – there was no reason why the usual practices should not be followed on this occasion, and the play read through at the theatre. But she should be a little tactful and remember that Hugo was a

152

great genius, and worthy of respect on that account! So the following letter was sent:

> Monsieur, The Queen has caught a cold, and her lady in waiting forbids her to go out. You, better than anyone, know the etiquette of this Spanish court. Pity your Queen, Monsieur!

The letter was sent by hand, and elicited the reply: 'I am your servant, Madame. – Victor Hugo.'

Next day, the reading was begun on the stage of the theatre, and Sarah, at last, met Hugo. She was bowled over by him. Even at seventy, Hugo was a fine-looking man. 'In his hair,' recorded Goncourt, 'there were some rebellious white locks reminiscent of Michelangelo's prophets, and on his face a strange, almost ecstatic tranquillity. Yes, a sort of ecstasy, but in which now and then his dark bright eyes, so it seemed to me, lit up with an indefinable expression of evil cunning.'[3]

Sarah, however, saw no evil cunning, but wit, goodness, gaiety and gallantry, and great dignity and nobility. She immensely enjoyed the *Ruy Blas* rehearsals, which were taken either by Hugo himself, or, in his absence, by Meurice or Vacquerie. There were one or two problems: Lafontaine, who was playing Ruy Blas, had great presence but his delivery was poor on account of his false teeth, while Tallien, who played Don Guritan, though a delightful fellow popular with everyone, was not a great brain and could not adapt himself to Hugo's concept of his part. Hugo, at rehearsal, enjoyed chivying the actors with improvised rhyming couplets. On one famous occasion Sarah, bored by some long hiatus which did not concern her, perched on a table where she sat watching and swinging her legs. It was the point in the play where the Camarera Mayor is setting out the do's and don'ts of how a Queen of Spain ought to behave:

153

> *. . . Une reine d'Espagne*
> *Ne doit pas regarder à la fenêtre . . .*
> *Quand le roi n'est pas là, la reine mange seule . . .*

Hugo, catching sight of Sarah, spontaneously reproached her:

> *Une reine d'Espagne, honnête et respectable*
> *Ne devrait pas ainsi s'asseoir sur une table.*

Sarah leapt off the table, but found herself unable to think of a suitably witty reply, and was in a bad temper for the rest of the day. Nevertheless, the more she knew Hugo, the more she loved him. The two became close friends. The question everyone asked, and to which no one knew the answer, was – how close? There is, of course, no telling from Sarah's memoirs. She writes that she often used to visit him in the morning, when they would have long and delightful conversations; after one of these sessions she was so excited that, feeling she must speak to someone who admired Hugo as much as she did, she rushed round to Marshal Canrobert's house, and providentially met him just going out – to lunch with her: an invitation which had entirely slipped her mind. She makes a point of saying how ordinary-looking and badly-dressed she found Hugo, but that his great domed forehead and majestic bearing set him apart as an unmistakable grandee. There was, of course, an age difference of almost fifty years between them. But Hugo's sexual appetite, once legendary, was still keen: he was at this time conducting a passionate affair with Judith Gautier, Théophile Gautier's beautiful daughter. And for Sarah, to admire a man was, as often as not, to sleep with him. It therefore seems more probable than not that the two were lovers for a time.

The premiere of *Ruy Blas* was on 26 January 1872. It was a great occasion. Everyone who was anyone was there: the place was crammed, from the fashionable first-nighters in the stalls to the enthusiastic students in the gallery.

For Sarah the evening was a great triumph – perhaps the greatest and most important in her career of so many triumphs. That night, she said, 'tore away the last thin veil which still obscured my future, and I knew that I was going to be famous'. The audience went wild. Afterwards, mobbed by enthusiastic admirers, she was in a daze, through which she hazily made out Hugo and Emile de Girardin coming towards her, the crowd parting before them like the Red Sea. All the idiotic reservations she had had about working with this great genius flooded through her mind, but before she could apologize for her stupidities she found him kneeling before her, kissing her hands and murmuring, 'Thank you, thank you.'

'How small, ashamed and happy I felt!' she wrote.[4] She felt like falling into his arms, but did not quite dare to do so; instead, she contented herself with the arms of Girardin, an old and faithful friend, who led her aside and kindly warned her against getting carried away by this success into more antisocial stupidities and risky self-indulgences of the kind which had endangered her career before. But it was a promise she could not give, for these acts of defiance were, she knew, an ineradicable part of her nature.

Later that night the triumphant *Saradoteurs* unharnessed the horses from her carriage and insisted on pulling her home themselves. By then she was so keyed up that there could be no question of going to bed. She kept Mme Guérard talking till dawn, and then, after seeing her home, still felt too wound up to sleep, and walked around Paris for an hour. There are few moments of perfect happiness in the life of any individual. This was one of Sarah's.

Ruy Blas, largely on account of Sarah's performance, became the hit of the season at the Odéon, and its young star, at long last, a national celebrity. Those were happy days. Sarah was happy at home with Maurice and Mme Guérard, who more and more took the place of her mother and her secretary, happy in her friends, and happy in her work. But, like all good things, this could not last for ever. There were two reasons for this. One was that the greater the acclaim for Sarah the actress, the more it began to be whispered that, by rights, she ought to be, not at the Odéon, but at the Comédie-Française. The Français was the senior company, and the natural home for the best actors and actresses, of whom Sarah was now undoubtedly one.

The second was, that she had to earn more money.

Sarah was not very highly paid at the Odéon. Her salary until May 1872 was seven hundred francs a month; from August 1872 until June 1873, eight hundred; and, had she stayed that long, it would have risen to a thousand from June 1873. This was not a lot – and it was by no means enough to sustain the style of life Sarah now favoured, maintaining a luxurious and open-handed household full of servants and animals, not to speak of Maurice and any other members of her family who might need a helping hand, her horses and carriage, her legendary extravagance when it came to clothes and furnishings . . . The excess came out of the money she had received from her father via Maître Clément but that was now almost finished. So when the expected letter arrived from the Comédie-Française – as, inevitably, it did – Sarah tried to use the leverage to get Chilly to raise her salary.

The tale, as Sarah tells it, is a small dramatic masterpiece. The letter arrives from Emile Perrin, the recently-appointed director of the Comédie. She agrees to go and see him at three the next afternoon. Then she goes to find her friend Duquesnel, and shows him the letter. What should she do? 'Stay at the Odéon,' he inevitably advises. 'Anyway, your engagement's still got a year to run and I shan't let you go.' All right, says Sarah: raise my salary. The Comédie has

156

offered twelve thousand a year: how about fifteen? Duquesnel promises to put the proposition to Chilly, but advises her to stay even if they can't find more money.

However, when Sarah sees Chilly, it is clear that Duquesnel has mentioned only that she has been offered more money elsewhere – not where the offer came from. Chilly dismisses the idea with his accustomed brutality. 'Don't be silly! This is where you belong. Where could you go? At the Gymnase there's nothing but modern dressy pieces, that's no good for you. Vaudeville, the same thing. You'd break your voice at the Gaîté, and you're too good for the Ambigu . . . You can see that, can't you?'

'And what about the Comédie?' says Sarah, at which Chilly falls about laughing. Out of the question, he assures her. Her dreadful behaviour is a legend at the Comédie. None of the leading actors can stand her, they won't admit she's got an ounce of talent, it's out of the question. The long and short of it is, the Odéon is the only place for her, and no, he won't give her a rise. 'Do you take me for an idiot?'

'Yes,' replies Sarah, 'for a triple idiot,' and runs out of his room and out of the theatre, where she bumps into Paul Meurice, who tells her he has just come from her apartment where he had left a message from Victor Hugo inviting her to a celebration dinner for the hundredth performance of *Ruy Blas*; the same message that he is just about to deliver to Duquesnel and Chilly. 'Fine,' says Sarah, and leaps into her carriage. 'To the Comédie-Française!' And she drives off, leaving Meurice gaping on the pavement under the Odéon arcades. End of Act One.

Act Two opens in Perrin's office. He is not especially welcoming: he has created a carapace for himself, cold, biting, silent, within which the real Perrin – a likeable, witty, rather shy fellow – hides himself. Sarah is met by the

157

carapace. He holds out a chair for her with affected politeness. 'Well, Mademoiselle, have you thought about it?'

'Yes, Monsieur, and I've come to sign.' And without more ado she takes up a pen, from which a large blot drops onto the clean sheet of white paper on the desk. The carapace makes as if to remove the offending sheet, but Sarah stops him. 'Wait, fold it over, if it makes a butterfly I'll know I should sign; if it's something else, then I shan't!' And she folds the paper. They both lean over it to see what will emerge; Perrin begins to laugh; the carapace is broken. A beautiful butterfly is revealed. Sarah signs, both are delighted, and they chat away like old friends.

Sarah returns to the Odéon, where Duquesnel reproaches her justifiably for having been so hard on Chilly. Sarah holds out the engagement she has just signed. Duquesnel reads it; he is, naturally, upset. 'You shouldn't have done that without warning me,' he says, reasonably enough. 'I didn't deserve that.' And indeed Sarah knows he did not. Now Chilly arrives, panting and furious. It's a base act, she has betrayed them all, and what's more, he will hold her to her engagement, he will exact the maximum possible fine ... Furious in her turn, Sarah tries to excuse herself to Duquesnel, her faithful friend, and goes off to prepare for the evening's performance. End of Act Two.

Act Three is set some weeks later, at Victor Hugo's celebration dinner. It is the first time Sarah has been present at an occasion of this sort, and she is very excited. She is seated between Chilly and Victor Hugo and although she and Chilly have scarcely spoken since the contretemps over the pay-rise and the broken contract, they make it up now. On Hugo's other side is Mme Lambquin, Sarah's old ally from the hospital, who is playing the Camerera Mayor, and opposite, Théophile Gautier, Hugo's old comrade-in-arms from the great days of the Romantics. Beside Gautier is

158

Paul de Saint-Victor, a writer and critic who hates Sarah, and whom she hates in return.

The dinner progresses genially. At the end Hugo rises to toast the company. When he turns towards Sarah, Saint-Victor bangs his glass down so violently on the table that he breaks it. 'Have mine,' says Sarah, sweetly offering him her own glass. If looks could kill, Sarah would be dead on the instant as Saint-Victor takes her glass. Then Duquesnel leans over to tell Sarah to remind Chilly that he must reply. She does so, but he looks at her heavily and says, 'They're holding my legs.' She looks more closely while Duquesnel prays silence for Chilly's speech. He is clutching his fork desperately; she notices that the tips of his fingers are white, while the rest of his hand is purple. Silence falls. Everyone looks at Chilly. 'Get up,' hisses Sarah, who is now really perturbed. He makes a movement, then his head falls forward over his plate. Pandemonium! Someone sends for Chilly's son. Two waiters arrive and carry him into a small salon next door. Duquesnel and Sarah go with him; Duquesnel stays with his colleague but tells Sarah to go back and rejoin the rest of the guests. Everyone tries to tell themselves that Chilly will be all right, except Victor Hugo, who says simply: 'It's a fine death.' Then Duquesnel appears. They have taken Chilly home; a few days' rest . . . Everybody chatters with relief. Duquesnel takes Sarah aside: Chilly is dying.

Sarah turns to go and find her cloak. Old Mme Lambquin bumps into her – she is a little drunk, and is waltzing with Tallien. She apologizes; Sarah whispers in her ear, 'Don't dance, mother Lambquin: Chilly is dying!' Her face changes abruptly from purple to white; her teeth chatter. Sarah apologizes now, for having given her such an awful shock, and offers to take her home. On the way, Lambquin confesses that she is terribly superstitious, and that last Friday a card-reader told her that she would die eight days after a dark, middle-aged man who is 'mixed up with your life'. At first she laughed at this, as she is a widow and has no liaisons. But the card-reader was furious and said, 'It's no good shouting at me, I'm telling you the truth. This is a man who gives you your living! And there are two of them – one dark, one fair! It's true!' – at which Lambquin slapped her face and left. But she recognized the two men right enough – Duquesnel and Chilly . . .

Chilly dies three days later, without recovering consciousness. And twelve days after that, Mme Lambquin dies, saying to the priest who is giving her the last rites, 'I'm dying because I believed in the devil!'[5]

14

Sarah's new engagement with the Comédie-Française was thus a triumph of perversity. Neither side was enthusiastic about the new arrangement; part of the reason Chilly had made Sarah so angry with his summing-up of the view of her prevalent at the Comédie was that it was perfectly true. Both parties had preferred things as they were before. But in a very real way events were not entirely in their control. The Comédie was an organ of the State; the State was answerable to its citizens; and so many of those citizens now thought Sarah was the best young actress in France, and saw in her, moreover – partly on account of her gallantry during the recent war – a kind of ideal apotheosis of the Frenchwoman, whose rightful place could only be in the appropriate national institution, that the pressure for her to join the Comédie had become irresistible. Sarah took nothing with her from the Odéon – she left all her costumes and dressing-room furniture – and in addition had to pay a fine of six thousand francs for her broken contract. Disencumbered, she embarked on her new life.

The Comédie-Française embodied the French theatrical tradition in a quite unique way. It had no equivalent in any other country. 'The *traditions* of the Comédie-Française – that is the sovereign word, and that is the charm of the place – the charm that one never ceases to feel, however often one may sit beneath the classic, dusky dome,' wrote Henry James. 'The Théâtre Français has had the good fortune to be able to allow its traditions to accumulate. They have been preserved, transmitted, cherished, until at last they form the very atmosphere, the vital air, of the establishment.'[1]

For most of the members of the company at the Comédie, this tradition was their very lifeblood, an enormous inspiration and privilege to be nurtured and handed on. Sarah, however, felt it like a dead hand. 'I'm fed up,' she yawned one day in the august foyer. Mlle Favart, the leading tragedienne, happened to be present, and snapped, 'Please remember you're not at the Odéon now, Mademoiselle.' Sarah crossed the room and, curtsying deeply, murmured in her most bell-like tones, 'No, at the Odéon I would have said, I'm pissed off!' (*Je m'emmerde*.)[2]

Favart, needless to say, was not a friend of Sarah's. She had a few: Marie Lloyd and Sophie Croizette, the two *jeunes premières*, whom she had known as a schoolgirl and student; Coquelin and Laroche, who had been her contemporaries at the Conservatoire; and Mounet-Sully, who had been her colleague at the Odéon, although they had rarely met there, since they tended to play in quite different pieces. There was also Madeleine Brohan, 'so good she touched your soul, so witty she delighted your intellect, so indifferent that she desolated her adorers'.[3] For the rest, Sarah felt as if she was stepping into a cage of wild animals.

Her spirits were not lifted by the news that rehearsals for her first play would take place in the foyer. One can understand her depression. When the Goncourts attended the reading of their play *La Faustin* there, they sat 'on a red plush sofa, at a table covered with a green baize cloth on which there stood a reading desk and something to drink. There were ten people there, silent and solemn, and on the wall facing us hung a picture representing the death of Talma.'[4] The play now under rehearsal in this gloomy hall was Dumas *père's Mademoiselle de Belle-Isle*; this was the special request of the powerful critic Francisque Sarcey, who had been so dismissive of the young Sarah at her first débuts but who was now one of her great admirers. The rehearsals did not get off to a good start. In the play, the marquise de Prie loves the duc de Richelieu, who is himself in love with Mlle de Belle-Isle; and the action hinges on a scene where Richelieu mistakes the marquise for his beloved, having agreed to a nocturnal rendezvous set up, as he thinks, by Mlle de Belle-Isle but in reality by the marquise. But Madeleine Brohan, playing the marquise, was at this period enormously fat, while Sarah was positively skeletal, so that the notion that the one could under any circumstances be mistaken for the other was clearly absurd. Finally it was agreed that Sophie Croizette (herself no mean weight) should replace Brohan.

The first night was 6 November 1872. The house had been sold out for weeks: everyone was eager to see the Comédie's newest recruit. A great success was confidently forecast. But the performance did not go well. Sarah was appalled to notice, five minutes into the piece, that Julie had left her seat in the balcony. She had been struck when she first came on by her mother's unusual pallor, and was now in a state of terror, knowing that Julie suffered from a weak heart, and was quite unable to concentrate. Somehow she got through the first act, which seemed endless. As soon as she reached the wings she tried to find out what had happened, but nobody knew. Finally a messenger brought her the news that her mother had had a slight heart attack, and had been taken home. Croizette helped Sarah to her dressing-room; Mme Guérard was despatched to find out how Julie was. Meanwhile the play must go on. The audience, naturally, knew nothing of all this and began to get angry, assuming that this lacklustre performance was yet another of Sarah's well-known caprices. Sarah, meanwhile, spoke her lines and kept her eye on a door in the wings which Mme Guérard was to open as soon as she returned; she was to nod her head if all was well, shake it if the news was bad. The door opened; Guérard nodded. Sarah was overwhelmed by relief. It was the middle of her big scene, where she reproaches the duc de Richelieu for destroying their chance of happiness. Bressant, who was playing Richelieu, asked, 'And why didn't you say that someone was listening to us, that someone was hidden?' To which Sarah replied, 'There's Guérard with my news!' Bressant managed to get through the scene; and by the last act, Sarah was herself again. Sarcey, in his review, assumed that her early disastrous performance was due to stage-fright, from which she famously suffered, and drew attention to the beauties of the last act and the potentialities revealed therein. But Paul de Saint-Victor, her old enemy, stuck the knife in as far as it would go. He wrote: 'The artificial reputation she made at the Odéon and brought with her to the Comédie-Française does not stand examination . . . What good work can Mlle Sarah Bernhardt do at the Théâtre Français? The idea of giving her a leading part in a modern drama is out of the question.'[5] Naturally Sarah's performance picked up on succeeding nights, and in the end the play became a great success – but by then it was being put about that she had imported a claque.

The timing of Julie's heart-attack is too pat to pass unremarked. What she told Sarah was that she had thought her so unattractive on her first entry that she felt quite appalled, and then enraged when she heard the woman beside her giggle and say, 'That little Bernhardt girl's nothing but bones!' So much emotion was too much for her, and brought on the attack which forced her to leave. The theatre doctor, who had been the first to attend her, said: 'Your mother has an extremely nervous heart.' To which Sarah replied, 'I know, she's very ill,' and burst into tears. (This was at the end of the first act.) And her final comment on Julie's attack was the usual, 'Poor maman!' But one might with more justification say, Poor Sarah. Julie had succeeded in ruining Sarah's first night, one of the most important of her career, when it seemed as if the daughter she had never liked was finally going to succeed at the very top of the profession she had never wanted her to take up. Her conflicting emotions when faced with this spectacle were simply too much for her.

For the next few months, Sarah had very little success. She appeared, in addition to Mademoiselle de Belle-Isle, as Junie in *Britannicus* and Cherubin in *The Marriage of Figaro*, yet another cross-dressing role. She remembered both these as great successes, but with the exception of Sarcey, the critics took little notice of her. These were followed by a resounding failure – *Dalila* by Octave Feuillet, in which blonde, frail Sarah was cast as the dark, ferocious princess while the strapping Croizette played the blonde, ethereal, dying young girl. Sarah had to pad herself out with cotton-wool and try to appear voluptuous, while Croizette confined her ample bosom as best she could under tight bands. Sarah, at least, did not carry conviction in her new figure; *Le Figaro* observed that all she possessed of the enchantress was her wand (*baguette*, also the word for a long, thin French loaf) – that wand being her own long, thin person. After that, even Sarcey – who had a personal stake in this, as he had been one of the loudest advocates of Sarah's move to the Comédie – seemed to lose confidence in his protégée; while her enemies stepped up their attacks.

Sarah never had any difficulty making enemies. On the contrary, she seemed to court them. Her tantrums, her propensity for self-advertisement, her compulsion to push a situation just too far, were the reverse side of that capacity and need to absorb herself in her roles which made her such a compelling actress. But her bad behaviour could only be justified by great and continuous success. There were only too many people waiting for Sarah to make a fool of herself and delighted to decry her when she did so. There were obvious reasons for this: they disliked her on account of her behaviour and, when she became successful, they were jealous into the bargain. But there were also other, less apparent reasons why Sarah was a figure people liked to decry.

One of these was anti-Semitism. The Franco-Prussian war had destroyed the Second Empire and established the Third Republic. But one of its other legacies was an extreme nationalism and xenophobia, which was not (as might have been expected) confined to right-wing Catholic monarchists but was also shared by a great many progressive anti-clerical republicans (such as the political *salonnière* Juliette Adam). One consequence of this was an inclination to distrust and attack anyone whose roots or loyalties might be perceived as being less than wholly French and (especially) in any way linked with Germany. The Jews, with their international connections and their often Germanic-sounding names, were an obvious target in this respect. They had been emancipated during the Revolution and as a result now held a powerful position within the community, particularly (as usual) in financial and cultural circles. The Dreyfus affair was to show just how many leading figures in French life had Jewish connections, and how deeply aware everyone was of them. Of course, anti-semitism has more complex roots than this. Freud traced it to a northern European guilt at abandoning ancient gods for Christianity, which could be blamed on the Jews who must therefore, paradoxically, expiate it; others attribute it to the perennial suspicion of the outsider and the position of the Jews 'outside history', condemned, after the expulsion from Palestine, to be perpetual outsiders. But that it was given new life by the Franco-Prussian war is undeniable. In 1873, for example, a novel was published entitled *Le Docteur Judassohn*, which was about a German spy, the eponymous Judassohn, installed in Paris by Bismarck long before the war, who becomes a great banker in France, gets to know everyone, and sends valuable information back to his masters. During the war he is in charge of the Paris *ambulances* and so is able to relay the latest military news to the Germans . . .

To attack Sarah, who was so presumptuously setting herself up as the new star of that cultural holy of holies, the Comédie-Française, for her Jewish and possibly even German ancestry, thus seemed perfectly natural to many people. This was the occasion when Sarah felt compelled to write the letter in which she disclaimed any suggestion of German ancestry. 'I should be really very much obliged,' she wrote, 'if you would include in your next *feuilleton* a few words to correct the mistake you made in your article on the revival of *Dalila* at the Comédie-Française. Since that day I have received a perfect avalanche of insulting and threatening letters. Nothing less than this could have induced me to write to you. I am French, absolutely French. I proved it during the siege of Paris, and the Society for the Encouragement of Good Works awarded me a medal. Would it have done so had I been a German? All my family come from Holland . . . If I have a foreign accent – which I much regret – it is cosmopolitan, but not Teutonic. I am a daughter of the great Jewish race, and my somewhat uncultivated language is the outcome of our enforced wanderings.'[6] Then and always, great play was made (especially by the cartoonists) of her Jewishly hooked nose – a feature noticeable only to the eyes of prejudice. As it happened, Sarah was and remained exaggeratedly anti-German – she would not tour there for many years, and caused a great scandal when, at a dinner in Copenhagen, she gratuitously insulted the German ambassador. It seems likely that this prejudice was not unconnected with the prejudice she herself encountered. She could never do enough to prove that she was the most patriotic of Frenchwomen.

Of course, Sarah was not the first Jewish actress to make her mark upon the Comédie. There had been the incomparable Rachel, who had become an icon of French cultural life, whose family background had been as base as Sarah's – and whose disregard for convention about as complete. How ineradicably both Rachel and Sarah were perceived as being, first of all, Jewish, may be seen from the two novels which were written about them at this time. *La Faustin*, by Edmond de Goncourt, has more of Rachel in her; *Dinah Samuel*, by Félicien Champsaur, is based upon Sarah. In both of them stress is laid upon the heroines' Jewishness. It renders them at once alien and powerful, with the power of the not-quite-knowable, but it is also inseparable from the vulgarity of their families, and from their own materialism, personified by their reluctance to give up the unattractive but rich Jewish bankers who subsidize them. In *Dinah Samuel* (a more unpleasant and less interesting book than *La Faustin*) this moral dilemma is personified in the character of Montclar, a noble but poor young man who has been in love with Dinah since his first impoverished youth, and whom she likes but will not entertain on account of his poverty, preferring her crass banker. Finally, many years later, they meet again; he is now rich and powerful and she agrees to go to bed with him. In the final scene, Champsaur shows his real hatred for his leading character. Montclar and Dinah are in bed; Dinah is asleep. As she sleeps beside him, he watches her disintegrate before his eyes: her hair is dyed and he can see the undyed roots, her complexion is painted on and the paint is running. It is a truly horrific scene, and deeply expressive of the author's view of women such as Dinah Samuel – or Sarah Bernhardt. Not least among its undertones is that of a kind of exorcism, as though Dinah/Sarah has used some kind of witchcraft to ensnare the

168

upright Aryan Montclar, a witchcraft that disintegrates with her make-up and sets him free. (Certainly descriptions of Dinah earlier in the book show that Champsaur, who clearly identifies himself with Montclar, was as susceptible as most other men to Sarah's charm.) Throughout her early career, Sarah had to contend with the racist and misogynist venom of such as Champsaur.

So the summer months of 1873 passed without success. But Sarah persisted, and so, to give him credit, did Emile Perrin. After her disastrous performance in *Dalila* Sarcey had written: 'I fear that the management has made a mistake in already giving Mlle Sarah Bernhardt leading parts. I do not know whether she will ever be able to fill them, but she certainly cannot do so at present.' In August, however, she played yet another leading role: that of Andromaque in Racine's play of the same name, opposite Mounet-Sully as Oreste.

Mounet-Sully was the dashing *jeune premier* of the Comédie, the leading young tragedian, just as Coquelin was the leading comedy actor. Sarah had known them both before, but she had not really noticed Mounet-Sully. Now, however, she certainly did notice him.

Henry James remarked upon the fact that the actors (and actresses) of the Comédie-Française at this time were not a beautiful lot. He was making the point that, such was their wonderful style and ability, this was of no importance: they were able to represent beauty when it was needed, and that was enough. Mounet-Sully, however, was an exception to this rule. He was, remarked James, 'from the scenic point of view, an Adonis of the first magnitude'.[7] He was also a magnificent actor. When Sarah arrived, he was the lover of Mlle Favart, the tragédienne, who was, however, beginning to pass her prime. Sarah, perhaps inevitably, determined to supplant Favart on both fronts, and, so far as Mounet-Sully was concerned, she soon succeeded in doing so.

Mounet-Sully was no Parisian townee. He came from Bergerac in the south-west, from a Huguenot family which had endowed him with great seriousness and sincerity. He and his brother Jean-Paul Mounet, who, after studying medicine, decided instead to join his famous brother at the Comédie-Française, were both big, brawny fellows. 'He will dare anything,' said the critic Jules Lemaître of Mounet-Sully, 'he has not the slightest fear of seeming ridiculous. After roaring like a lion he will whimper like a new-born baby because that is what he feels he should do. His sincerity and, therefore, his security are complete. He genuinely displays his soul in his art.'[8]

Now, with all his splendid soul, he fell in love with Sarah, and she, in so far as she was capable of such a thing, with him. Their affair lasted a long time – so long that everyone who knew Sarah was astonished. It was understood that he would have liked to marry her, but marriage was not for her. She had Maurice: what could marriage give her that she did not already possess? Happily unmarried, they spent their days together in his bachelor apartment in the rue Gay-Lussac, and their evenings acting opposite each other at the Théâtre Français. In *Andromaque* the intensity of their feeling perhaps spilt on to the stage: at any rate, their success together was enormous. 'Mlle Sarah Bernhardt,' wrote Sarcey, no doubt with relief as well as pleasure at this vindication of his judgment, 'was tender, bewitching, coquettish, and above all feminine. Her performance was like an air, sad and passionate by turns, played by a master hand on a violoncello.'[9] As for Mounet-Sully, 'How handsome he was as Oreste!' Sarah recalled. 'His entries, his rages, his madness, and the wonderful plastic quality of that marvellous artist, how beautiful it all was!'[10] A fortnight later she played Aricie in *Phèdre*, and, although this is a secondary part, she was a great success in it. 'There can be no doubt about it now,' Sarcey wrote. 'All the opposition excited by Mlle Sarah Bernhardt's success must yield to facts. She simply delighted the public ... Her voice is genuine music. There was a continuous thrill of pleasure among the entire audience.'[11]

15

It seemed that Sarah was at last set comfortably upon the road outlined by Jules Lemaître. She had taken her place in the Comédie, allied herself with the leading actor (even if she had not been able to bring herself to marry him), and nothing, it would appear, now lay between her and a lifetime's delightful and respectable celebrity. Nothing – but Sarah's own character and the nature of the Comédie-Française, which were, of course, perfectly designed to grate upon one another.

From the company's point of view, it is hard to see that Sarah could have been received with anything but resentment. What distinguished the Comédie-Française from all other theatrical companies was, as Henry James had noted, its vivid sense of continuing tradition. Sarah had already showed what she thought of that tradition and the respect for hierarchy associated with it when she was barely out of the Conservatoire, and she had had her richly deserved come-uppance. Now here she was, become some sort of sensation, being lured back into the *Maison de Molière* for which she had shown so little regard, and expecting to step without more ado into the front rank. There must have been a good deal of *schadenfreude* at her signal lack of early success, and her ensuing triumphs cannot have made her more popular. For Sarah's style was wholly at odds with that of the Comédie-Française. The Comédie did not have stars. It had leading actors, of course, but its successes were successes of the ensemble. That was part of its tradition.

Rachel had been a star. But Rachel had also been an unsurpassed genius, and what was more, her loyalty to the *Maison de Molière*, her devotion to its traditions, had never been in question. But Sarah, as far as anyone could yet see, was no Rachel; neither was she interested in anything outside the furthering of her own career. Later, this individualism would become marked to the point of caricature: the plays she chose to act in, and particularly those written especially for her, tended to feature one dominant heroine (or, if she was playing a male role, hero) beside whom the rest of the cast paled into insignificance. Ensemble playing was never her forte. From her point of view, a production was only a success if she dominated it. When, for example, she played Aricie in the production of *Phèdre* which finally re-established her in Sarcey's eyes, she says, revealingly, that although hers was only a secondary role, 'I was really the success of the evening.'[1]

Sarah's real problem vis-à-vis an institution like the Comédie-Française was that it required its members to approach life in a way which, for Sarah, was constitutionally impossible. It was a government department, hierarchical and authoritarian, and she was incapable of accepting authority, however benign. All her brushes with authority had ended in tears: at the convent, during her first engagement with the Comédie, in her relations with Chilly. The happiest times of her life had been either when she was in charge, as with her hospital, or in the informal comradely atmosphere which prevailed at the Conservatoire and the Odéon. Her compulsive desires to make herself conspicuous, to avoid boredom by pushing any situation just a little too far, were precisely those guaranteed to make life impossible in the Comédie-Française.

So now, having got nicely settled, she started needling authority in the person of Emile Perrin. She began by teasing him, which amused her and drove him to fury, which she

enjoyed watching; and then she began to play more dangerous games.

At the Comédie you took the roles which were allocated
to you. Sarah, however, found that all the roles she now
wanted to play seemed to have been allocated to Sophie
Croizette. Perrin and Croizette were said to be 'very close
friends'. Sophie explained that she played Perrin along and
got just what she wanted. Why, she wanted to know, did
Sarah not do the same? But Sarah was not capable of
diplomatic dissimulation; and neither was she Perrin's *petite
amie*. So she decided to take the bull by the horns. One of
the roles she wanted was that of Camille in Musset's *On ne
badine pas avec l'amour*, which had been given to Croizette.
So she went to Perrin and asked for it – putting on her
prettiest voice, it is true; but that was hardly the same as
letting him think it had all been his idea. Naturally he
refused. Sarah's voice lost its docile charm, Perrin became
angry, and the incident ended with Sarah storming out and
slamming the door behind her.

Not having got her own way, and feeling herself under-
used and unappreciated at the Comédie, Sarah began osten-
tatiously to put her energies to other uses. She went riding
first thing every morning, and, when she got home, she
went to a studio she had taken at 11, boulevard de Clichy,
where she had started to sculpt. She showed a certain
aptitude for sculpture, and it soon became her ruling
passion; she showed up at the theatre only when she had to
rehearse or perform. Perrin, predictably, was extremely
annoyed at this new departure. 'I wouldn't mind,' he
grumbled to Francisque Sarcey, 'if it was a question of an
actress who did a bit of sculpture in her spare time. What
worries me is that I seem to be employing a sculptress who
does a little acting when she happens to have a moment.'[2]
But despite all this show of defiance Sarah was not happy –
rather, the defiance was itself an indication of her unhappi-

ness — and, as always when she was unhappy, her health seemed to suffer. She would start to cough blood in an alarming way; she often fainted. Sarah's friends began to get worried, and Perrin decided to give her another chance in a new play by Octave Feuillet, *Le Sphinx*. There were two *jeunes premières* roles in this play, of which Croizette had the more important. But at the read-through Sarah found the role she had been allocated interesting enough, 'and I decided,' as she revealingly remarks, 'that there would be two leading roles — that was all there was to it.'[3]

At first the rehearsals went well enough. Feuillet was both puzzled and dazzled by Sarah. 'What a strange girl,' he wrote to his wife:

'It's the first time in my whole career that I've come across the real actress that all the novels are written about, the eighteenth-century courtesan actress, an elegant, made-up, eccentric, insolent young thing . . . Unlike any of the other actresses she comes to rehearsals all dressed up, or at least very well-dressed, in her own way: velvet from head to foot. Velvet dress, velvet jacket, a black lace scarf draped over her shoulders, and a little high collar. In this get-up, with her hair all frizzed out and usually holding a few bunches of flowers, she goes through her role carefully, gravely, just as she should. She sometimes strikes beautiful attitudes, à la Rachel. Then at the end of the act she suddenly does a dance step, jumps off the stage, sits down at the piano and accompanies herself in a strange negro melody, which she sings in a very pretty voice. Then she gets up, starts striding around like a clown, crunches her chocolates — she always has a bag full of chocolates — pulls a lipstick from her bag and reddens her lips, shows a set of teeth as white as fresh almonds and starts on the chocolates again. There's nothing so funny as to see her and Croizette going off together after rehearsals, with their mothers following behind. [Sarah's 'mother' was of course not Julie but Mme Guérard.] They go off like two startled goddesses, noses in the air, with their little hats balanced on the back

175

of their enormous blonde hairdos, twirling their parasols, talking and laughing at the tops of their voices, making all the passers-by turn round, and then they go into Chiboust's patisserie and stuff themselves with cakes.'[4]

What seems to have struck Feuillet was the unreality of this figure. Real actresses, of whom he had met a great many during his long career, were not like that. They reserved their role-playing for the stage. Actresses like Sarah, who when not playing their roles never stopped playing the role of an actress, existed only in books. But of course what Feuillet was seeing was, precisely, Sarah in her role of the coming young actress, the Sarah appropriate to her conception of this part. Life was a series of roles, each to be dressed appropriately and given the correct setting. As the sculptress in her studio she wore an exquisite white silk pyjama suit made by Worth. As to what happened when it got spotted with clay, one did not enquire. In each of her roles, Sarah was a finished creation.

Rehearsals of *Le Sphinx* went well until it became clear that Sarah was trying to give her role just as much import-ance as Croizette's. That led to trouble. Sophie Croizette, although she was genuinely a good friend of Sarah's – Lysiane Bernhardt says she was one of Sarah's *'petit cour'* at this time – was not such a good friend that she was happy to see her position as the company's leading *jeune première* undermined. One day she fell flat on her face during rehearsals – no small matter, since she was tall and statu-esque – and was furious with Sarah because, she alleged, she had slipped on some petals which had dropped on the stage from Sarah's eternal posies. Two factions began to form, Croizettists and the Bernhardtists: in Sophie's corner all the bankers and the rich old men, who appreciated her luxuriant curves, in Sarah's, the students, the artists, the failures and the dying (or at least that was how Sarah put it). The conflict took concrete form in a scene where Croizette, playing Blanche, kissed Delaunay, who was playing Savigny, the husband of Berthe, played by Sarah. The kiss took place in a moonlit glade. Croizette's kiss had been more daring than was usual for the Comédie-Française at that time, and was greeted with applause – for the final rehearsals were, by tradition, open. Then, to the surprise of Croizette and Perrin, there was a renewed outbreak of applause. Sarah had entered, crossing a little bridge, her wrap trailing disconsolately from one hand; she, too, was bathed in moonlight – a delightful effect. Perrin, infuriated, cried out, 'One moonlight effect is enough! No moonlight for Mlle Bernhardt!' To which Sarah, quick as a flash, pointed out that Perrin had no right to deny her her moonlight – for did the script not read 'Berthe moves forward, pale and sobbing, in the moonlight'? 'I'm pale, I'm sobbing, I want my moonlight!' cried Sarah. Impossible, said Perrin; Croizette had the principal role, therefore she must have the principal effects. Feuillet was appealed to. He decreed that Croizette was beautiful in her moonlight, and Sarah enchanting lit by her little moonbeam. Sarah declared that she would not play without her moon and the rehearsal was suspended. For two days Sarah received no notice of rehearsal. Later, she learned that Perrin was trying to get someone to replace her – a girl she and Croizette had nicknamed 'the Crocodile' because she was always lurking around the theatre waiting for someone to fall ill so that she could snap up their role. Then Feuillet intervened. Sarah would return 'and the moonlight will bathe both of you', he declared.[5] It did; *Le Sphinx* was a triumphant success, though not until some tense moments had passed. At the *répétition générale*, the dress rehearsal which was traditionally open to invited members of the public, Croizette suddenly declared that she was unwell, and the audience was kept waiting on the pavement while attempts were made to cure her indis-

177

position. Finally, an hour and a half late, the doors were opened. At the end of the third act there was another slight hitch, when the artists did not appear to take a curtain call: it seemed that Croizette had gone straight to her dressing-room, and Sarah and Delaunay, in a spirit of loyalty and camaraderie, refused to appear without her. After this, however, all went swimmingly.

Nevertheless, relations with Perrin were still tense, and Sarah's health got worse. Feuillet was appalled to see her coughing blood; the effect was particularly shocking when superimposed, an inescapable reminder of illness and reality, upon the charming, vivacious and wholly artificial creation that was Sarah's performance as an actress in rehearsal.

It was now August 1874, the time, as it happened, of Régine's last, harrowing illness. The weather had turned very hot and steamy. Sarah begged Perrin to give her some leave, but he refused, and insisted on casting her as Zaïre. And this was when the performance took place that we have already alluded to, when Sarah, to pay Perrin out, literally tried to play herself to death and realized, when she jumped up at the end of the performance, that she was not at the mercy of her body; on the contrary, it was at her disposal – and all she had to do was impose her will upon it.

Not long after this Régine died, and Sarah became so ill that even Perrin took pity and gave her two months' leave. She was supposed to spend it in the Midi but in fact took the opportunity to revisit her beloved Brittany, spending most of the time in Finistère at the Pointe du Raz and the Baie des Trépassés, the land and seascape whose fierce, bleak beauty always soothed her.

Then it was back to Paris and the theatre, although it was November before she was fit enough to play again. Perrin came to visit her in her studio one day. Did she, he enquired, know the role of Phèdre? Sarah was taken aback. Yes, she knew it – she had studied it for herself, even though she had only played Aricie. But as for playing it . . . 'Work it up,' said Perrin. 'I have a feeling you'll be playing it.'

Sarah's opportunity to play Phèdre arose as a side-effect of one of the interminable political games which went on between actors and management at the Comédie. The leading tragédienne, Rosélia Fargueuil, was as yet not a *sociétaire*, that is a full member of the company, helping to run it and sharing in the profits. She was trying to persuade Perrin and the committee to promote her, and had threatened not to play Phèdre in the next production, which was scheduled for 21 December, less than a week later, if the committee did not promise to make her a *sociétaire* at its next meeting. Perrin called Sarah to his office and offered her the role. Fargueuil, he said, would almost certainly get her promotion, but the committee was not prepared to give in to threats. The posters would go up that very day.

Sarah was in a state of terror. If she failed in the role – *the* French tragic role – her enemies would be delighted; but how could she succeed at such short notice? Coming out of Perrin's office she ran into her old teacher, Régnier, and begged him to go through the role with her. Sarah knew that, quite literally, she could never compete with the ghost of her illustrious predecessor in that interpretation. For Rachel's equipment as an actress was very different from Sarah's. Rachel had had a powerful, resonating voice and a commanding presence of overwhelming tragic dignity. But Sarah was cast in an altogether lighter mould, and could not manage big, passionate vocal effects. She had always recognized this; it had been the reason why she had insisted on playing the last scene in *Zaïre* for pathos rather than tragic fury when she was at he Conservatoire. This lightness of voice and presence was the feature that gave critics most pause when it came to assessing the possibilities open to her. After her failure in *Dalila*, Sarcey wrote: 'She imperson-

179

ates soft and gentle characters admirably, but her failings become manifest when the whole burden of the piece rests on her frail shoulders.'[6] That was the view of a friend; Paul de Saint-Victor, who decidedly was not a friend, wrote, 'She displays nothing but a subdued plaintiveness, and when she tries to intensify her tone she merely strikes a jarring note. She seeks to be imperious and is merely violent; her disdain is without hauteur and her allurements are vulgar.'[7] If that had been true in *Dalila*, a comparatively minor play, what could she make of Phèdre, the peak of the Racinian repertory?

It was not that Sarah was particularly young or inexperienced for this role. On the contrary, she was now thirty, and it was more than twelve years since her first débuts at the Comédie. But because of the lightness of her voice and her physical frailty – which also meant that she looked and sounded much younger than she was – she had tended to avoid the classical repertory's most grandly passionate roles. Corneille, whose heroines make grandiose declamations concerned with such abstract notions as *gloire* (a barely translatable concept combining honour, reputation, personal standing) and whose psychology is only with difficulty encompassed by any modern woman, was an author she always avoided. In *Petite Idole*, the novel she wrote when she was in her seventies, she gives her young heroine Espérance the same dramatic tastes as herself. Espérance won't think of playing Corneille. 'But he's superhuman,' remonstrates her friend Geneviève.

'That's just what I don't like,' replies Espérance. 'Racine's human, that's what I like about him. I can't feel with any of Corneille's heroines, and I suffer so terribly with Phèdre's pain!'[8]

Phèdre could be seen – as Rachel had seen her – as the embodiment of tragic passion. But there are also other ways of reading her. Phèdre, it will be remembered, falls hopelessly and tragically in love with her stepson, Hippolyte,

180

who does not return her guilty passion but loves the young princess Aricie. Phèdre is unable to conquer her passion, blurts it out to the horrified Hippolyte, and finally kills herself. The role can be played on the symbolic level, as grand tragedy, but it can also (in Sarah's view unlike any of Corneille's heroines, but like almost all of Racine's) be read on a human level. Phèdre is the tragic figure of legend, but she is also a sad and tender woman in the agonizing throes of unrequited love. That is not how Rachel played her; but it was the only way possible for Sarah. Régnier (according to Sarah's memoirs) recognized this at once. 'Don't be afraid,' he advised her. 'I can see exactly what you can do with this role. The great thing is not to force your voice. Play it for sadness and tenderness, not fury, and everyone will be the better for it, even Racine.' (On the other hand, in the account she gave her friend Reynaldo Hahn a few years before she wrote the memoirs, Régnier advised Sarah not on any account to play Phèdre with so little preparation: she would strain her voice in vain, it was an impossible idea.[9])

When Sarah had first rejoined the Comédie-Française the previous year, Théodore de Banville, the poet and critic, wrote: 'Make no mistake; the engagement of Mlle Sarah Bernhardt at the Comédie-Française is a serious and revolutionary fact. Poetry has entered into the house of dramatic art; or, in other words, the wolf into the sheep-fold.'[10]

That night, for the first time, Sarah showed the public exactly what he had meant. She brought to the tragic repertory a uniquely Romantic and poetic reading which infused it with a life and excitement it had not known since the great days of Rachel – who had approached it so very differently. 'Rachel,' said Sarah, 'approached it academically. But from the very beginning I put into that role everything that a woman could feel who has been driven to madness by love.'[11] Critics and public were overwhelmed. For Sarah's great achievement was quite original. Her chosen roles – the ones in which she had already made her name, the ones she was to prefer for the rest of her career – were for the most part melodramas played in the high Romantic style. Eventually this left her beached high and dry, a sort of cultural fossil. But now, in the greatest of all *classical* roles, she abandoned the stylized gamut of classical attitudes and did 'what nobody has dared to do before: she plays with her whole body. This is something quite new. The most emancipated girl, playing a love-scene on stage, only plays with a part of herself. She doesn't let herself go completely, partly because she doesn't dare, partly because she's thinking about her part . . . The woman is on the stage, but that isn't who's playing: the actress is the one playing the role. But with Mme Sarah Bernhardt, on the contrary, it is the *woman* who is playing . . . Even in scenes where she is concerned with passions other than love, she is not afraid to bring forward, if I may put it this way, the most intimate and secret parts of her feminine personality. There, I think, lies the most astonishing novelty of her style: she puts into her roles, not just all her soul and wit and physical grace, but all her sex as well. Such daring would be shocking in anybody else; but . . . her light and ideal grace offsets all her audacities and makes them exquisite.'[12] 'Before the one [Rachel],' wrote one critic contrasting Sarah and Rachel in this role, 'we turned cold with a thrill that seemed to travel through the nerve-centres; for the other [Sarah] we feel an intense and tender pity.'[13] Sarah liked to recount that Offenbach, who was leader of the orchestra at the Comédie at that time, immediately saw what she was aiming for and said, 'Yes! That's the way to do it!'[14]

It is hard to believe that this was altogether a conscious piece of technique on Sarah's part. She did have very definite techniques, and she thought about them long and hard. But, on stage as in any other aspect of artistic creation, one can only do what one's self allows one to do; and the

182

requirement of Sarah's self was that she be enabled to play out to the limit all the roles which Sarah Bernhardt might otherwise have found it impossible to confront. What Bernhardt's audiences saw was not just Sarah Bernhardt playing Phèdre and speaking Racine's sublime poetry (though they saw that as well). But they also saw the very incarnation of Phèdre herself; and the effect was something extraordinary. Francisque Sarcey said that 'Mme Sarah Bernhardt . . . has always taken instinct for her guide . . . [She] is a woman before she is an actress. She feels, she talks, she lives as a woman on the stage.'[15] Now at last the personality – or personalities – imposed upon her by her childhood experiences combined with the experience she had acquired during the past years on and off the stage, and Sarah Bernhardt came into her own. 'Go and see her!' was Sarcey's recommendation a few years later to all those young people who had never yet realized to what extent Racine was a great dramatist, and not just a turgid schoolroom set-book. '[You will] see just how living and contemporary our old classics really are. Strip them of their tragic jargon, and they are modern dramas, the most moving it is possible to imagine. And yet, if you only knew how much penetrating intelligence and force of character are needed to throw off the yoke of tradition, in even the smallest respect! I think that in [Sarah Bernhardt's] case, it is more a question of the intuition of genius.'[16]

In January 1875, Sarah was finally accepted: she was made a *sociétaire* (member – though as yet not a full member) of the Comédie-Française. Her youthful ambitions seemed to have been fulfilled. She had joined her old classmate Coquelin (who had been elected almost as soon as he had joined the company, in 1864) and her friendly rival Croizette, among the select few; and, as if finally to wipe out the memory of her first, unhappy spell there, her old enemy Mlle Nathalie retired the following April, 1876.

183

16

Although Sarah would no doubt have been angered had her *sociétariat* been refused, receiving it did not make her happy, since for her part she had had to sign a long contract with the Comédie which meant that she now felt trapped and tied down. As a distraction, she began to construct a suitable setting for the celebrity she was fast becoming. Until now, her life had been shaped by circumstances – the character and milieu imposed by her childhood, the profession into which she had been thrust, the buffeting of random events such as her friendship with Maurice's father, the chance re-entry into the theatre at the Porte-Saint-Martin, the gift of *Le Passant*. But now that her talent was recognized, she was no longer at the mercy of chance. And although she remained locked within certain inescapable compulsions, within these parameters she was now able to set about constructing the life and persona she preferred.

She began by building herself a house. A sister of the Dutch grandmother she so much disliked – perhaps the Aunt Betzy who had supplied nightshirts and sheets for her hospital – had left her a sizeable sum of money, which she used to buy a piece of land on the corner of the rue Fortuny and the avenue de Villiers. The house was designed by the fashionable architect Escalier, who happened also to be the son-in-law of her old teacher and colleague Régnier. (Not long after this Mme Escalier left her husband to become the mistress, and later the second wife, of Alexandre Dumas *fils*.)

The house cost five hundred thousand francs; and that was without any of the elaborate furnishings with which Sarah stuffed it. Where did the money come from? She was now earning twenty thousand francs a year – a substantial sum, but not enough. Marie Colombier, inevitably, hints at generous subventions from her old friend Jacques Stern the banker. Thérèse Berton, the wife of Pierre Berton, says that part of the secret was that she never paid for anything. She was so famous that furniture dealers, among whom her taste for elaborate pieces quickly became known, were glad to let her have an item and take their money as and when she could pay them, because the fact that Sarah Bernhardt had bought a particular article was certain to start a fad for it. If she did not pay them, they took it back, something that never worried her in the least. Throughout her life she paid her debts, when all else failed, by selling her possessions, and then went out, earned more money and bought a new lot. Meanwhile she haunted the dealers' showrooms and took what she wanted, regardless of cost. The Goncourts saw her one day at Bing's, a dealer in Japanese curios, 'turning everything over, moving everything around, and every now and then putting something on the floor, saying, "That's for my sister."'[1] In the same way, says Thérèse Berton, she never paid for any of her clothes, any more than she followed the mode; it was enough for Bernhardt to wear something for it to become the mode. People copied her little high collars, her undulating dresses with their unmistakable line. When, ten years later, her arms grew so thin that she had to conceal them even when she wore evening dress, she invented shoulder-length gloves, which immediately became the rage.

The house was finished: now it had to be decorated. Sarah had by this stage acquired a great many painter friends, mostly decorative artists of the second rank – it was at this time that she first met Louise Abbéma, who was twenty and

185

having her first show, and who was to be a life-long member of the little court – who, perhaps regrettably, reflected her taste. Paris at this time was remarkable for the number of great painters working there, but these were not the ones Sarah preferred. The only exception to this rule of mediocrity was Gustave Doré, with whom she sometimes used to go off on sketching trips, accompanied by Georges Clairin, who was at this time her lover and who remained her friend for life, and Victor Hugo, whom she insisted on teaching to paint: he showed an unexpected aptitude for pen-and-ink drawings. Clairin painted his famous portrait of her at this time: she sits with narrowed eyes, staring out of the canvas, draped spirally along a sumptuously cushioned divan, a wolfhound at her feet. It was Clairin, known to all his intimates – he had a large acquaintance among society ladies – as 'Jojotte', who appointed himself the chief decorator of her house and the arbiter of her taste. His own inclinations ran to rich hangings, rare flowers, an undulating line – all of which were to be Sarah's hallmarks for the rest of her life. Clairin and Sarah assembled a team of friends to paint murals and ceilings: Sarah mentions Escalier, who was a painter as well as an architect, and four or five others. Sarah herself much enjoyed climbing the scaffolding to join in the work, wearing her sculpting trousers to do so. Her aunt Rosine, catching her thus one day, was terribly shocked – the more so when, at midday, Sarah descended, ran to the piano, and played a loud ditty summoning the rest of the crew – whom her aunt took for ordinary house-painters – to a hearty lunch. '*Oh! peintres de la Dam' jolie,*' ran the first line of this song; and for the rest of their lives Clairin addressed Sarah as 'Dame Jolie'.[2]

In this appropriate setting, Sarah now set about leading a life reminiscent (as more than one observer remarked) of those improbable Feuillet and Dumas heroines she so often portrayed onstage. Her life was unreal and outrageous, and every detail of it was followed and recounted by the popular press. Her penchant for sculpting from the life, her love of exotic pets (she was particularly fond of large cats, pumas and lion cubs, and had a whim at one point to have a tiger's tail grafted onto the base of her spine – she actually found a surgeon to undertake the operation before friends dissuaded her), her habit of joining her 'workmen' for lunch – all these things were perfectly genuine parts of her life, but, along with her thinness, her love of horse-riding, her ever-changing lovers, and every other tiny particular of her habits, these foibles provided endless fodder for journalists which she was very far from discouraging. As Henry James put it, 'She has in a supreme degree what the French call the *génie de la réclame* – the advertising genius; she may, indeed, be called the muse of the newspaper ... She is a celebrity because, apparently, she desires with an intensity that has rarely been equalled to be one, and because for this end all means are alike to her.'[3] James, with his acute eye for character and motivation, was absolutely right: there was (as we have seen) much that was compulsive about Sarah's behaviour in this respect.

Was this what so worried people about this aspect of Sarah's character? For undoubtedly they *did* find such an avidity for publicity in a great artist unsettling; and compulsive behaviour is worrying precisely on account of the lack of control underlying it. But there was another facet of Sarah's new way of life which was equally disturbing. This was the way in which she now took on board various current social fashions and, in her own way, stood them on their heads, so that in her hands they came to signify just the opposite of what they were meant to signify.

Perhaps the most notorious of these displacements was her handling of the nineteenth century's Romantic image of sickness and death in young women. Ask anyone today what they know about Sarah Bernhardt and they will probably reply that she had only one leg and that she slept in a coffin: two claims to notoriety dating from opposite ends of her life. The loss of her leg, which happened in 1915, was certainly not willed by Sarah; but the coffin, with its surrounding publicity, certainly was.

We have already encountered the famous coffin-bed: she slept in it during Régine's last illness. It was one of the outward expressions of that suicidal self-hatred which was a legacy of her childhood. She, who pushed death away by dint of unceasing activity until her eightieth year, perversely courted it when she was young. She told her granddaughter Lysiane that she had first wanted a coffin when, after the disappointment of her first débuts at the Comédie-Française, she had become very ill and had been told by the doctor that she was in danger of dying of galloping consumption. At that point, 'I begged mama to buy me a pretty coffin. She refused, naturally. But I did not want to be put on a bier in something ugly.'[4] If this is really true, then once again Sarah sketches, in a few detached sentences, what must have been a mother-and-daughter conversation of truly gothic horror. At any rate, she finally prevailed upon the 'little court' to club together and buy her the coffin of her dreams.

After Régine's death in the summer of 1874, stories about Sarah and her coffin became common currency. It was generally assumed that her very public fascination with the paraphernalia of death was yet another example of her publicity-seeking mania. The sailor-novelist Pierre Loti, who became obsessed with Sarah during this period, recounts a visit he paid to her at her house. 'Sarah Bernhardt is ill; she is not receiving company. Nevertheless, an exception is made for me . . . An old woman, very witty and talkative, doubtless an old actress [almost certainly Mme Guérard] is sent to keep me company. About three quarters of an hour later I'm allowed to go up to the sumptuous, funereal bedroom, hung with black silk. Deep in her big four-poster bed, Sarah is huddled under her white satin quilt bordered with swansdown; she looks like someone pretending to be ill; I've never seen her with such lively eyes. With an exquisitely graceful gesture she holds out her hand for me to kiss, just like in the second act of *Ruy Blas*. Lazarus the skeleton is there, seated beside her; the talkative old woman sits down on her other side, which is altogether more of an embarrassment.'[5]

The coffin and other deathly trimmings, then, simultaneously satisfied two compulsions: the death-wish and the need to seek notoriety. But they also had other, subtler resonances. For in a very marked and unique way, the second half of the nineteenth century saw sickness and death as aesthetic attributes where women were concerned. The consumptive heroine was a familiar and popular figure in its literature. From Little Nell to Marguerite Gautier, she caught the popular imagination. *La Dame aux camélias* was far and away the most eagerly-welcomed play in Sarah's repertoire: when all else failed, she was a reliable winner and moneyspinner. Dumas' play was also the basis for two operas – *La Traviata* and *La Bohème*. And when they were not reading about consumptive ladies or watching them on stage, nineteenth-century burghers liked to hang them on the walls. The pre-Raphaelite trend epitomized in Millais' *Ophelia* was merely one aspect of a fashion for cadaverous ladies which swept Europe and America. (Sarah herself sculpted an Ophelia in bas-relief for the great Columbian Exposition in Chicago.) The beautiful female corpse became an object of decadent admiration. Photographs of Sarah in her coffin were distributed among her admirers. When the English painter W. Graham Robertson visited Count Robert de Montesquiou, he came upon the photograph of a beautiful young girl tastefully laid out in her coffin, with candles on either side and strewn with flowers and palms. 'You know her, don't you?' asked Montesquiou, who was the acknowledged (by himself, but also by others) leader of taste in Paris.

' "No," I whispered. Did I ever see her? Could I have known her when she was alive?

' "She isn't dead," he said smiling. "That is Sarah Bernhardt." '⁶

We need not go quite so far as to assume that the late nineteenth century preferred its women dead, but there were certainly some attributes of the dead and dangerously ill which people at that time found very appealing: their weakness, their fragility, their passivity. Not only were dead and dying women supremely unchallenging, but there was also a perverse aura of sado-masochistic unattainabililty about them which made the image an extremely titillating one.⁷

It was made very clear that a middle-class woman in the nineteenth century was required to complement, not supplement, her mate. She was not wanted in the bank, the office, or wherever it was he made his living. It was not that these occupations required brute strength; nor – one had only to look at the extensive managerial responsibilities required of chatelaines in earlier epochs, or at the qualities of those intelligent and companionable women often found beside their men in the seventeenth and eighteenth centuries – that women did not have the intelligence and capacities to deal with them. Rather, if the social boat was to be kept on an even keel, a pretence must be made by both parties that she did not have these capacities. Her sensibilities were to be deemed such that the rough and tumble of business would be too much for them. What, then, *should* she do? She should allow herself to be kept in that luxurious idleness permitted by the increasing amenity of life and the availability of a pool of cheap servants. She should be his angel in the house. That way, she would both proclaim his status (and therefore her own) and feed his fantasies. And when a woman was too intelligent, too strong-minded, too energetic to support this role, then, rather than upset everybody by challenging the status quo, she was encouraged to be ill. 'One day,' wrote Alice James, 'when my shawls were falling off to the left, my cushions falling out to the right and the duvet off my knees, one of those crises of misery in short, which are all in the day's work for an invalid Kath [her companion] exclaimed, "What an awful pity it is that you can't say *damn*." I agreed with her from my heart. It is an immense loss to have all robust and sustaining expletives refined away from one! At such moments of trial refinement is a feeble reed to lean upon. I wonder, whether, if I had had any education, I should have been more, or less, of a fool than I am?'[8] Clever, clear-sighted Alice, as we have seen, took refuge in welcome death. Sarah, though possibly afflicted with the fashionable disease, refused to succumb because she had a real occupation, and a real will to live. Nevertheless, she played with (probably subconscious) cunning upon decadent notions of the ideal woman.

This was, of course, a deeply equivocal – and therefore worrying – position to take up. And her stance was just as equivocal in other ways. For example, there was the whole question of being an actress, and just what that entailed.

It was generally accepted that being an actress was not something you did if you were a girl of good family. There were exceptions – Aimée Desclée, who died tragically young in 1874, was one – but they were exceptions: respectable French girls did not expect to earn their living, and especially not in the theatre. When the duc de Morny made his momentous suggestion, one of the assumptions behind it was that Sarah, in spite of her convent education, was not respectable. Sarah herself, in her novel *Petite Idole*, makes this very clear. Her heroine's family are all quite appalled by her wish to go on the stage. Her mother is a typically under-occupied housewife, concerned entirely with entertaining

191

and with bringing up her daughter to be a nice girl. As far as her father is concerned, agreeing to Espérance's wish, as he is eventually persuaded to do, is a supreme sacrifice. When Espérance and her mother go to the Conservatoire to see about entry formalities, all the other girls there are daughters of either the respectable or unrespectable poor: their mothers are a piano teacher, a cocotte's chambermaid, a dressmaker, a shopkeeper. Among her own contemporaries we know that Croizette's mother was a poor widow, Marie Lloyd was an orphan, Léontine Massin's father made make-up boxes, Marie Colombier was the illegitimate daughter of a Spanish Carlist soldier and a country girl from the Creuse whose mother came up to Paris and treated her so badly that she ran away from home when she was fifteen. So Sarah's own background carried no particular stigma in the Conservatoire.

Many cocottes also found themselves on the stage from time to time. Dumas *fils*, in his introduction to *La Dame aux camélias*, points out that the variety theatres were frequently used to display available wares in the most complete and inviting fashion. Cora Pearl once appeared on such a stage costumed (insofar as she was costumed at all) entirely in diamonds. Liane de Pougy and Caroline 'La Belle' Otéro were dancers. Blanche d'Antigny, one of the *grandes horizontales* of the end of the Second Empire, took lessons in singing and declamation and took the stage at the Palais-Royal in 1868 to a general chorus of approbation from her men friends on the various papers, which was broken only by Barbey d'Aurevilly, who took her to pieces in *Le Nain Jaune*, remarking, among other things, that one 'must take into account . . . the part played by this lady's diamonds. They certainly perform better than she does.'[9]

Did this, conversely, mean that all actresses were members, too, of that other profession? The assumption certainly was that they would not be insulted to be invited to bed in suitable circumstances. Very few of them contracted lasting marriages and most were fairly promiscuous. Even if not financial, the rewards for favours rendered could, in the right cases, be substantial. Sleeping with Emile Perrin did no harm at all to the career of Sophie Croizette; and it was quite simply taken for granted that actresses would sleep with influential critics in order to court good reviews. It was constantly said that Sarah slept with Francisque Sarcey. 'Where? When? How much?' the duc de Joinville famously wrote to Rachel, to receive the equally famous reply: 'My place. Tonight. Free.' No particular stigma attached to actresses on account of this behaviour. In that section of the *demi-monde* known as *la vie de bohème*, it was accepted that the rules were not those governing the bourgeoisie. Arsène Houssaye tells a story about Mlle Georges, one of the great actresses of the early years of the century, who lived on into her eighties. A retirement benefit was being given for her, and she wanted to go onstage: Houssaye begged her to stay in the wings. She said, 'with a bitter smile, "Ah, if I were ten years younger, you'd be singing a different song, because I'd give you one of those hours a man remembers all his life!" She was,' adds Houssaye, 'eighty years old at the time.'[10] It was certainly quite the usual thing for an actress to have a protector, or a series of protectors, who would either provide her with money or favours. Sometimes this meant that she was competing with the cocottes on their own ground – it was well-known, for example, that Marie Duplessis, the original of Marguerite Gautier, was madly jealous of Mlle Doche, the actress who created the part after Marie's death. (Osgood Field, who tells this story, adds a detail that presents Marie in a more human light than Dumas' sempiternal Tart with the Heart of Gold. She was apparently renowned, among other things, for being quite unable to speak the truth, and when asked why this was so, she replied, 'I like telling lies because they keep the teeth white.'[11])

193

For a large number of highly intelligent men in France at this time, the courtesan was, quite simply, the ideal woman. A large number of novels featured cocottes as their heroines. Edmond de Goncourt recorded a very typical opinion when he described the visit of a playwright friend, Borelli: 'After telling me all sorts of stories, he ended up by saying that the only women he liked were tarts. He praised them to the skies, declaring that these creatures, born in the humblest circumstances, managed to become the arbiters of taste and fashion in Paris, thanks to their wonderful diplomacy and *savoir-vivre*, for they knew that they would lose their position if they were seen with a pimp on their arm or a vulgar dress on their back. And comparing them with society women, who start with so many advantages, he observed that the latter only lowered themselves if they tried to be at all striking.'[12]

The great attraction of the successful courtesan was, of course, that she was as unthreatening to a man's view of his rightful position in the world as one of those idealized female corpses whose images might grace her walls. By a supreme irony, no one could personify the pure ideal of the angel in the house, of the weak and dependent woman whose only aim was to make a place of beauty and luxury in which to refresh and entertain her man, better than a courtesan, because her job consisted of just that: the nourishing of those fantasies which keep men happy. The fact of her frequent contempt for her clients, a distaste often extending – as in the well-known case of Liane de Pougy – to a sexual preference for women, did not necessarily diminish her attractions.

In the world of courtesans, it was the men who called the shots. Perhaps the supreme example of this was the story of Victor Hugo and his mistress of half a lifetime, Juliette Drouet. She had been a beautiful and flirtatious young actress with many admirers and more than one protector,

194

leading a gay life filled with pretty dresses and parties. Then came Hugo and the *coup de foudre*. This being France there was no need for Hugo to hide Juliette away and pretend she did not exist, as Charles Dickens did with his *inamorata* Nelly Ternan. But there were to be no more parties for her. At Hugo's insistence, and to please him, she gave everything up – the protectors, the stage, the pretty dresses – and retired to a life of scrimping, saving, paying off her debts and living only for the moments she could spend with her lover. Hugo was notoriously and habitually unfaithful to her, as he had been to his wife; this continued to cause her great pain even when he was in his seventies and courting Judith Gautier, and she was little younger; she bore it then as she had always borne it. In a sense Juliette Drouet's life is a complete nineteenth-century morality; the whore who gives up everything for the love of a great man, and spends the rest of her life atoning for the sins of her fleeting youth. As the Goncourts' friend Borelli put it, 'The great cocottes are all women born in the provinces, who have something of the servant about them and are quite prepared to say *Monsieur le comte* to the man they are sleeping with.'[13]

The actress, on the other hand, was not subordinate in this way, because even if she was to some extent materially dependent on men, they did not constitute her primary source of income or interest. This independence, allied to sexual freedom – of which Rachel had been the supreme example, the most successful actress of her time, the most sexually free and the most richly courted – made actresses at once more interesting and more worrying to the men who frequented them – which was to a large extent the same men who frequented the courtesans. The Goncourts record a conversation with Flaubert on this subject in which the great novelist 'gives us his recipe for possessing [actresses]: you have to be sentimental and take them seriously. Then we discuss the question whether they make

195

love as often as men say they do, or whether care for their health and the strain and fatigue of acting force them to confine themselves to skirmishes. We talk about the extra-ordinary influence they have on the criticism written by their lovers.'[14] Flaubert, that is to say, is trying to diminish the threat of the sexually independent woman by question-ing both her sexuality and her motives. On another occasion, Flaubert and Dumas *fils* conducted much the same argument with George Sand apropos women writers. Dumas said to Sand: 'You – why, you have never loved anything but the prefigurings of the heroes of your future novels, just like the marionettes whom you dress up to perform your plays. [Sand had a famous puppet theatre at her château, Nohant.] Can that be called loving?' To which Sand retorted that 'What remains to be proved is the possibility of a pretty woman writer, who is really gifted, continuing a simple, loving, faithful wife like any other woman.'[15] But whatever she might say, her companions preferred to think of women like her – that is to say, women who led their own intellectual and professional lives, and who were more interested in these than in men (except from time to time) or domesticity (ever) – as being fundamentally unnatural. In *La Faustin* Goncourt shows quite clearly what he thinks. La Faustin is rehearsing, and when the director makes some observation replies, 'with an astonishing condescension, "Oh, if that's what you feel, then of course I must be wrong!" – But the obsequious phrase was said in the most sarcastic voice . . . There is something very particular about actresses during this time when they are incubating a role, and especially during the annoying and vexatious work of rehearsing: it is as if they were enveloped in austerity, coldness, *asexuality*. They seem to have abandoned all their natural gracefulness, they never smile any more, in fact they seem as serious as men when they are thinking about business.'[16] Less directly, but more dramatically, Goncourt reveals his deeply equivocal feelings about this aspect of the actress – her professionalism taking precedence over womanly feelings and wiles – in the last scene of the novel. In this, La Faustin is watching by the death-bed of her lover Lord Annandale. He has been unconscious; but he regains consciousness to see his mistress practising the rictus of the death-bed agony she has been observing in the dressing-table mirror. Goncourt tried to laugh this off as being, firstly, based upon a story told him by Rachel's maid (which she denied), and, secondly, as a description of the inevitable professional detachment of the artist. And this was not so far-fetched: in the 1880s, Sarah was an avid attender at the famous weekly presentations of the great neurologist Charcot at the Salpêtrière, the asylum where he worked, in which he demonstrated various forms of hysteria as manifested by his patients. But for all this there is no mistaking the emotion with which the scene is filled – a feeling of distaste, almost of fear.

It may be imagined that Sarah, with her horror of being dependent upon any man, her refusal to behave as etiquette dictated either in her private life or within the Comédie-Française, and her apparent success in living entirely upon her own terms, reinforced such worries to an extreme degree; and this perhaps accounts for the virulent nature of some of the emotions she aroused, as expressed by the cartoonists of the day.

However, unperturbed by these as by all other external manifestations, she continued gaily upon her new life, supported – as she was to be for the rest of her life – by the group of friends she referred to as her 'little court'. Some of these – Clairin, Abbéma, Geoffroy, Arthur Meyer, and of course her son Maurice – would stay with her until they died; others were the good friends of the moment. But from now onwards, the 'little court' was always there to give her unconditional support in battle, sometimes in the most literal way. In Paris of the 1870s and 80s, duelling was by no means unusual. Maurice Bernhardt in particular was a fine swordsman and a most persistent duellist on his mother's behalf; he made his first attempt to fight for her – on account of an obscene caricature – in 1880 when he was only sixteen, but his challenge was insultingly refused on that occasion because of his extreme youth. Other gentlemen – probably lovers of the moment – took up similar challenges: once two duels were fought over an unpleasant piece which appeared in the humorous journal *Le Triboulet*. Ernest Pronier, one of Bernhardt's biographers, sees this rather melodramatic aspect of her life as being part of Sarah's tendency at this time to live out in real life the somewhat absurd parts she had to play on the stage. Certainly it seems that she was rather tickled to be duelled over. The loser in one such contest wrote, 'Madame, I throw myself at your feet and humbly ask your pardon.' To which she replied, 'I forgive you. Please get up!'[17] And in *Petite Idole* the novel ends with the heroine's two lovers, a duke and a count, both of whom want to marry her, duelling over her to the death. (The duke wins; Espérance, the young actress, conveniently dies soon after.)

If Sarah's preoccupation with death was one of the cultural signs of her time, so too was her 'little court'. In many ways it was simply another Paris salon.

Almost anyone might open a salon. You did not need to be respectable: some of the most brilliant salons were those of chic courtesans such as La Paiva, 'La Présidente', Laure Hayman. It was generally observed that the only difference between these and respectable salons was that there were no wives present. But in fact wives were never a great feature of salons, one of whose most notable characteristics was that they were run *by* women *for* men. 'Twenty men friends and five women will suffice to found a salon'[18] was Madame d'Agoult's advice to Juliette Adam (as an experienced *salonnière* to a young woman just starting out on that career), but habitués noticed that Madame Adam was often the only woman present at her own soirées.

One of the leading salons of this period was that run by the Comtesse de Loynes. Now elevated to a kind of respectability by a marriage so brief as to be virtually non-existent, she was an ex-courtesan whose *nom de guerre* (bestowed by Dumas *fils* when, at the start of her career, she was briefly on the stage) had been *La Dame aux Violettes*. She had, however, no ambitions to be received by the *salonnières* of the *grand monde*, where she would always have been a parvenu, but preferred to preserve her own place in the world of which she was a leading attraction. The habitués of this beautiful and intelligent woman included several of Sarah's most devoted friends, such as Prince Napoléon ('Plon-Plon'), Emile de Girardin, and Arthur Meyer, who wrote a book about Mme de Loynes and her salon. In the course of this, Meyer sets out the qualities of a successful salon. 'If you want to conduct a choir, you must not take part yourself,' he observes. (He thought Mme Straus, one of the most brilliant of the respectable *salonnières*, had 'the misfortune to be too witty and didn't bother to hide it'.) The lady desirous of founding a salon must possess 'the supreme art of stimulating conversation without dominating it; she must know how to listen and to make others listen to those whose talk is worth hearing ... A true mistress of the art will know how to offer the racquet, but will stop herself from throwing the ball. She must flirt a little, but equally with all her friends, so that each, when he is with her, feels that he is the one she likes best, without ever feeling inferior to the others when all are together ... It is the work of a magician: it needs the wiles and tact of a woman. Famous men have had their salon, but it was the salon of a lady friend ... No man that I know of has had a salon of his own

... What man could preserve such delicacy or would tolerate such subservience?'[19]

Not Sarah — that much was sure. Yet her 'little court' followed some of these rules. The talk was good and free, the hostess was a delightful flirt (although the company was invariably mixed — Sarah never surrounded herself with men to the exclusion of women.) But just as, by being an actress, and an exceptionally assertive actress, Sarah violated the code which enabled the more traditionally-inclined men to relax and enjoy themselves with women — which made them feel worried and resentful — so the 'little court' broke the most fundamental unspoken rule of the salon, which was that it centred around the guests — the male guests. At Sarah's the centre of the salon was quite clearly the hostess herself; and this in spite of the fact that the most brilliant men of her day — men like Victor Hugo, Gustave Moreau, Pierre Loti, Marshal Canrobert, and many other playwrights, critics and actors — were all happy to participate. Raconteurs liked to evoke a scene of this period: Sarah in her studio at the Avenue de Villiers with all her court around her, avidly watching while she sculpted in her delightful sculpting outfit. Suddenly Marshal Canrobert said, 'I've thought of your epitaph! All you'll need on your tomb is: Resting at last!' To which Sarah replied, pointing to the circle of admirers, 'Not exactly, Marshal! They'd do better to put, *They* can rest at last!'[20]

As for those who did not love her, as often as not they hated her, or were always ready to do so; and not only, or even mainly, for those reasons which they were so quick to adduce — because she was too loud, too self-centred, too all-pervasive, too thin, too Jewish, too outrageous — but on account of those deeper feelings of unease and disturbance which she aroused in them, but which were so hard to express except in these more superficial terms.

17

From 1876 to 1879, Sarah was at the height of her equivocal success at the Comédie-Française. She was renowned and acclaimed to an unprecedented degree; to an equally unprecedented degree she was resented and lampooned. 'A woman needs more talent than a man if she is to become famous,' remarked Arsène Houssaye, adding that public opinion, like Molière himself – that masterly reflector of opinion – was always distrustful of *Précieuses ridicules* and *Femmes savantes.*[1]

It was during this period that Sarah created some of the roles for which she was to become best known throughout her career. One of the salient facts about that career was the extent to which it remained set in the mould of her early successes – even (as we shall see) when she was playing in pieces which had been newly written for her. But *Phèdre, L'Etrangère, La Dame aux camélias, Frou-Frou, Adrienne Lecouvreur,* all to become seasoned war-horses of her repertoire, were either pieces she played at this time with the Comédie or else ones she tried out during her 1880 season in London, undertaken to raise money before she set out for her first tour of America.

The rivalry with Sophie Croizette continued, and in a way embodied all that most infuriated Sarah's many detractors. Croizette possessed many of the virtues Sarah (according to her critics) lacked: she was charming, vigorous, plump, and although perfectly modern, she was modern without flouting tradition. And yet, she did not have Sarah's drawing power. Henry James, who was never one of Sarah's greatest fans, and who was a great enthusiast for everything that was most traditional at the Comédie, recorded in 1876 that Bernhardt and Croizette, then the coming young actresses at the Français, 'are children of an . . . eminently contemporary type, according to which an actress undertakes not to interest but to fascinate. They are charming – "awfully" charming; strange, eccentric, imaginative. It would be needless to speak specifically of Mlle Croizette,' he went on, 'for although she has very great attractions I think she may (by the cold impartiality of science) be classified as a secondary, a less inspired, and (to use the great word of the day) a more "brutal" Sarah Bernhardt. (Mlle Croizette's "brutality" is her great card.) As for Mlle Sarah Bernhardt, she is simply, at present, in Paris, one of the great figures of the day. It would be hard to imagine a more brilliant embodiment of feminine success.'[2] Nevertheless, Perrin and Sarah's other detractors at the Comédie persisted in trying to behave as if this were not the case.

For a long time the public had been waiting for another play from Dumas *fils*; and one day he and it announced themselves at Sarah's house. It was called *L'Etrangère*. The plot concerns an impoverished duke, the duc de Septmonts, who has sold himself and his title to the daughter of a wealthy retired tradesman, and who is deceiving her with an even wealthier but socially untouchable American, Mistress Clarkson, the daughter of a woman who has been abandoned, pregnant, by her faithless lover, and who has vowed revenge on all men. The action turns on Mistress Clarkson's efforts to get herself accepted, even for a cup of tea, by the duchesse de Septmonts, the duc's efforts to achieve this for her without betraying his own relations with her (she has also ensnared the duchesse's father and lover, whose relations with the duchesse are as yet only platonic) and the machinations and betrayals thus ensuing.

As often with Dumas it was rubbish, but highly workman-like and slightly risqué rubbish, and the first read-through went excellently.

According to Dumas, Sarah was to play the duchesse and Croizette the vamp; but at the read-through Sarah was handed the role of Mistress Clarkson, which she passed to Croizette, saying, 'Look, they've mixed up the roles,' to which Croizette replied sharply, 'No they haven't, I'm playing the duchesse de Septmonts.' Then fell an ominous silence during which Sarah started to giggle; it was quite obvious that this was a plot to give Croizette the best role, and they were all waiting apprehensively to see how she would react. But they need not have worried: Sarah was delighted to play Mistress Clarkson.

About a week before the play's opening Sarah received an anonymous letter to the effect that Perrin was trying to get Dumas to change the play's title to *La Duchesse de Septmonts*. She rushed to the theatre and confronted Perrin with the letter; he looked embarrassed, muttered that he recognized the handwriting, and tried to go off with it, but Sarah snatched it away and dashed off again, this time to see Dumas. She caught him just going out; they went back into his house, and, once in the salon, Sarah let herself go in one of her terrible rages, of the kind she used to have when she was a child, but which now overcame her only rarely. Dumas sat while the torrent of words washed over him – how he had broken all his promises to her, how he and Perrin had plotted against her, how he should be ashamed of himself, and so on and on. When she had finished he told her that he had thought she wouldn't really mind – that her heart wasn't in the theatre any more but in her painting and sculpture. 'I haven't seen very much of you,' he said, 'and people let me think whatever I liked. This fury of yours interests me very much!' And he promised that the title would not be changed, and demanded a big kiss to prove they were friends. So that was settled; Sarah and Coquelin, who played the Duke, had a great success; and from then on she always played the part of the Etrangère. No one thought the piece was very good; everyone agreed that, while Dumas could carry this one off on the strength of his former reputation, that would not survive if his next play was as indifferent as this one; meanwhile, the usual crowds packed the theatre to see Sarah vamp Coquelin in her amazing black and yellow creation as Mistress Clarkson. After this Sarah had another great success in another indifferent play, *Rome vaincue* by Parodi, in which she played not, as might have been expected, the virtuous vestal virgin granddaughter, but the wise grandmother, and gave a virtuoso impersonation of blindness. Many agreed with the critic who commented that her talents seemed to be wasted. 'Already she has saved from merited failure the odious and hazardous role of Mrs Clarkson . . . and she is now saving from the fate it deserves M Parodi's tragedy.'[3]

But all this was leading up to the grand climax of Sarah's career with the Comédie: Victor Hugo's *Hernani*.

Hernani had been the theatrical flagship of the Romantics. Its premiere at the Français in 1830, when Hugo's following of students, led by Théo Gautier in his famous red waistcoat, had carried the day for the new Romanticism over the husk of Classicism, had been one of the most famous occasions in the history of French literature. The revival of *Ruy Blas* in the first days of the Third Republic had showed that, whether on account of the resonance of his name and reputation, political as well as literary, or because of the glamour and power of the acting, or because Hugo's early verse still spoke to people's hearts in spite of the operatic simplicity (some might say crudity) of his plot and characters – or perhaps because of a combination of all these – he was still a mighty box-office draw. In 1867, when the political climate was different, the Comédie had in fact put *Hernani* on with some success, although it was miscast, with the urbane, smiling Delaunay as Hernani and Bressant, a comic actor whose big feet stole the show when Sarah saw the production, as Charles V. But with Mounet-Sully as Hernani, the outlaw chief who is really Don Juan of Aragon, and Sarah Bernhardt as Doña Sol, it was unthinkable that the piece could fail.

When it had first been put on Mlle Mars, the Doña Sol, an actress in the grand classical tradition, had literally been unable to bring herself to speak the line '*Vous êtes mon lion! superbe et généreux!*' After weeks of arguing with Hugo in rehearsals she had substituted '*mon seigneur*' for '*mon lion*'. But her talent, professionalism and beauty had nevertheless triumphed in the part, so that she had looked like a dazzling girl of eighteen in the wedding scene of the last act, even though she was then over forty. Sarah, in 1877, was still only thirty-three; she had, like Mlle Mars, a girlish figure, a wonderful voice and a classical training; but, unlike that stern classicist, she was a Romantic by temperament and melodrama was her preferred form.

Sarah had not seen Hugo since, after she complained she could never find him alone at his house to talk to – there was always some man in a red tie declaiming about politics, or some tattered woman looking for a favour – he invited her to lunch, with the promise that they would be alone afterwards to talk as much as they wished. During lunch, however, a terrible draught froze her feet, the food was bad, and an unwashed German guest sitting next to her was unutterably boring. All this combined to send her into a dead faint, after which she crept away in shame without taking leave of her host.

Now, however, they met at rehearsals, which everyone enjoyed. Worms, who played Charles V, was admirable and imposing, Mounet-Sully was the embodiment of the beautiful and gifted Romantic hero, and Sarah as Doña Sol was

205

exquisite and bewitching. However, on the first night not all the audience was able to concentrate exclusively on the play. The premiere took place in the middle of a political crisis, and the many politicians present were as concerned with their own drama, making and unmaking cabinets in the foyers during the interval, as with the action taking place onstage. Victor Hugo himself left the theatre with Gambetta, and the two great figures of the Republic were warmly cheered. But in the poet's heart, Sarah had triumphed over politics. That night Victor Hugo sent Sarah a letter:

> Madame,
> You were great and you were charming; you moved me greatly, old soldier that I am, and at one point, while the public, enchanted by you, applauded, I found myself crying. That tear is yours. I am at your feet. – Victor Hugo.[4]

With this letter came a little box with a chain from which hung a diamond teardrop. Later Sarah lost it at Alfred Sassoon's house; he, one of the richest men in the world, offered to replace it, but she refused. Who could replace Victor Hugo's tear?

Inevitably, this success was not followed by peace. On one side there was jealousy within the company; on the other, Sarah, having achieved what she had set out to achieve – a dazzling success on her own terms, without benefit of patronage such as Croizette received from Perrin – immediately began to feel restive. Having extended the limits of tolerance and carved out her own niche within the company, albeit at the expense of some bad feeling, she began, as always, to push those limits still further. And as if she had not enough to do, with Maurice, her unending social life, her sculpture and (as Perrin saw it) the added detail of rehearsals and performances, she now took up painting under the guidance of Alfred Stevens, another of the then members of her 'little court'. The subject she chose, again inevitably, given her own tendencies and the preferences of the time, was *La Jeune fille et la Mort*, a large canvas nearly two metres long. (In *Petite Idole* she remembers Stevens in a not very complimentary way, using a variant of his name, Albert Styvens, for the bizarre Belgian count who determines to marry the heroine.)

Perrin saw this as yet another time-wasting and energy-consuming publicity stunt and came to remonstrate. Why did she do it? Why kill herself with all this sculpture and painting? Was it to prove to herself that she could do it? 'No!' cried Sarah, adding revealingly, 'it's to tie myself down, to make it necessary for me to stay here!'[5] She explained that she felt a desperate desire to travel, to see other scenes, to breathe other airs, to see bigger trees and wider skies, and if she did not fill her life with tasks and commitments she was afraid she would not be able to resist. Perrin no doubt thought this, like the coffin, like the morbid subject of the huge painting, was so much posturing; but the whole of her future career was to prove that she was, at that moment, speaking no more than the honest truth. That endless, compulsive rush from place to place, performance to performance showed, if it showed anything, that the effort required to stay still was literally impossible for her. There was something attendant upon staying in one place which she could not, or did not wish, to confront: possibly herself.

Meanwhile she made sure that, in Paris, no such dangerous void would remain. Her life was full to bursting – as it was henceforth to remain. Literally, she had not a moment to herself. The novelist Pierre Loti tried in every way he could to engineer a private meeting during one of his shore-leaves (he was an officer in the French navy). He was no stranger to dressing-up and posturing himself; his journal reveals his passion for assuming the *outré* dress of the different peoples with whom he became familiar during the course of his voyages and about whom he wrote so beguilingly in his novels, while in Paris he himself was an equally exotic figure, dressed up and as often as not made-up, with built-up shoes to increase his diminutive height. Perhaps a certain fellow-feeling was part of Sarah's attraction for him; but in her house he made no attempt to compete in point of exoticism, preferring to wear his blue sailor suit – itself, as he was well aware, a bizarre enough garment in those circles. Revisiting her after a year's absence, he found her salon 'even more crammed with strange and precious objects from all the corners of the Orient, with sprays of rare flowers everywhere. An entire court of literary personages and artists, and my blue collar makes quite an effect.

Sarah is in a black dress, with a bunch of fresh roses on the bodice . . . Her welcome immediately puts me on an equal footing with everyone there . . . I ask for a private meeting the next day, and she counts up the hours on her fingers, mentally going through the day, which is already so full; finally I have an appointment for one-thirty in the afternoon.

At one-thirty precisely I ring at the door. A smiling maid shows in 'sailor Pierre' and says 'Madame is coming'. In a moment there indeed is 'Madame', looking dreamy, dressed in black as she was yesterday, and the roses she wears perfume the air sweetly.

She sits me down next to her on a divan embroidered with Chinese dragons with gold claws; hothouse plants spread their wide leaves over our heads. There is a vague melancholy in Sarah's eyes, a strange contrast with yesterday's animation before her court of admirers; her voice is fresh and pure, and what she says sends me into I don't know what delicious dream . . .

208

Suddenly there is a knock on the door and the spell is broken. People come in, tradesmen, fitters, dressmakers, bringing in wonderful clothes – 'This evening at six,' says Sarah, putting her hand on my arm like she does in *Hernani*, 'I'll get rid of all these people and we'll be alone.'

I get to her house exactly on the hour, hurrying my cabman along. In front of the house a dozen carriages are standing; distracted servants are running about the courtyard, everything is upside down.

'So this is our tête-à-tête!' she says to me, smiling. 'Come in, monsieur Pierre, I'll be with you in a moment!' ... I can still see the scene in the big salon: M. Bastien Lepage, mademoiselle Louise Abbéma, mademoiselle Samary, the old lady companion, the maids, the big wolfhound from the Clairin picture, the Danish bitch, everyone milling around in indescribable disorder.[6]

The muddle on that particular day was caused by the fact that the Comédie-Française was going to London and the day of departure had just been brought forward; but other descriptions of Sarah at home give a very similar picture.

The last straw as far as Perrin was concerned came when Sarah took a ride in a hot-air balloon.

The 1878 Paris Exposition, along with the customary exhibitions of paintings and sculpture (including some of Sarah's, which annoyed her colleagues for a start) and the pavilions of all the different countries, featured a large number of sideshows. These included a captive hot-air balloon owned by a M. Giffard, to whom Sarah, one day when she was walking around the exhibition with Prince Napoléon, remarked how much she would enjoy a ride. No sooner said than done: M. Giffard said he would be delighted to give her a ride, but she would have to wait a week, as this would be a big responsibility and he would have to get everything in order. 'Plon-Plon' wanted to come as well, but he was fat and clumsy, and although he was renowned for his wit he annoyed Sarah on account of his frequent disparaging references to the deposed Emperor, of whom she had been such a fervent supporter. The final complement consisted of Sarah, Clairin, and a young balloonist called Godard.

Sarah had forbidden Giffard to breathe a word of her plans, because her family would be terrified and would stop her going; nevertheless, word did get about, although not soon enough for the press to hear of it before the launch. Shortly after the balloon had ascended, Comte Robert de Montesquiou, who was then one of Sarah's great friends (he was even said to have gone to bed with her, despite being homosexual, with the unfortunate result that he was afflicted with uncontrollable vomiting for a week afterwards[7]) happened to meet Perrin on the Pont des Saints-Pères. 'Look!' he said, pointing upwards. 'There's your star running off!'

'Who's in there?' asked Perrin.

'Why, Sarah Bernhardt!' replied Montesquiou, who always took a malicious delight in making trouble.

Perrin turned purple with rage, ground his teeth and said, 'Another one of her tricks! But she'll pay for this one!'[8]

Sarah and her party found the voyage quite delightful. The balloon left the ground at half-past five in the afternoon, watched by a few friends (but not Sarah's family). Soon misty Paris was below them and they were above the clouds, bathed in sunshine. At six forty-five they had reached 2,330 metres and began to feel cold and hungry. They dined on *foie gras*, fresh bread, oranges and champagne, and climbed still higher, to 2,600 metres, by which time Sarah began to feel uncontrollably drowsy from a combination of cold, altitude and champagne. They decided to land, and pulled the rope which controlled their descent. Soon a forest came into view. Where could they be? 'We must come down at once,' said Godard. If they missed the plain they were liable to land in the dark in the forest of Ferrières, which would be extremely dangerous. The valve was opened, and the redoubtable Godard produced a trumpet, which he blew loudly. After a while they heard a whistle blow in reply, and, five hundred metres beneath them, saw a uniformed man shouting at them unintelligibly – presumably the station-master of a little station they could see. 'Where are we?' Godard shouted into his trumpet, but all they could hear was 'At en-en-en-ille!'

They let out more air and began to come down, but a gust of wind blew them towards the woods and they had to rise a little again. Finally they landed in a field, helped by a crowd of children who had been following their progress all the way from the station, and some men who had also come to help. They landed safely in a torrent of rain and climbed out into the muddy field. The young proprietor of a nearby château, who had also arrived, offered Sarah his umbrella, but she declined, saying, 'I'm so thin, Monsieur, that the raindrops just fall around me' – a witticism which was much appreciated. However, things did not seem so merry when it turned out that the station was an hour's drive distant along a muddy track; but as there was no vehicle available, and given the weather, that would be more like two hours walk for the lady. However, the young chatelain came to the rescue: it turned out he had a carriage, and could provide a cart for the balloon as well. So they drove to the station they had seen, which turned out to be called Emerainville, and waited for the ten o'clock train back to town. While they waited, the station-master kindly provided a meal of cheese, bread and cider. Sarah hated cheese and had never been able to bring herself to eat it, thinking it 'unpoetic', but now she was extremely hungry, and, urged on by Clairin, tried it and found it excellent.[9]

They arrived back late at night; and next morning came a letter from the Comédie-Française demanding Sarah's presence. Perrin hit the roof. He scolded her unmercifully for her insubordination and bad behaviour, and fined her a thousand francs for making a journey (in the balloon) without the authority of the Administration. Sarah burst out laughing, refused to pay the fine, declared that she had had enough, and offered her resignation, which she wrote out and sent off as soon as she got back home. However, things had not yet come to that pass. It was agreed that Perrin had overstepped himself, the fine was cancelled, and things went on as before, except that now Perrin and Sarah were not on speaking terms.

'My celebrity,' writes Sarah, 'annoyed my enemies and, I must admit, had become a bit much even for my friends. But at that time I enjoyed it all immensely. I didn't do anything especially to attract attention,' she adds disingenuously. 'It was simply that my thinness, my pallor, the way I dressed in my own particular style and ignored Fashion – all these things set me apart from the general run of people.'[10] All the distinguished visitors who arrived in Paris to see the Exposition came to visit Sarah and the Comédie-Française, where she was playing almost every night.

The big new production in 1879 was *Ruy Blas*, with Sarah and Mounet-Sully. Francisque Sarcey went into raptures over this performance. 'She sang, absolutely sang the lines with that musical voice, breathed them out like a sad melody which the wind draws from an Aeolian harp . . . She didn't bother with nuance: it was just one long caress of sound, which was unspeakably sweet and penetrating in its very monotony.'[11] It was the technique known as *mélopée*, a technique which, coarsened by fifteen years of overuse, would send Bernard Shaw into paroxysms of fury over the famous golden voice, but which here, at its tender birth, opened new theatrical perspectives.

Success, however, did not make Sarah more serious about her art. In the last act of *Ruy Blas*, the eponymous hero secretly kills himself while the Queen is lost in despair and fails to notice what he is doing. Mounet provided himself for this purpose with a little phial which was filled with coffee and water, and made much play of drinking this with great gurglings and bobbings of his adam's apple. This annoyed Sarah – 'how could I possibly not have heard all that noise? You'd have heard it from the next room!' She repeatedly asked Mounet to tone it down, and to make the whole thing shorter and more discreet, but he failed to do so. So one evening, at the end of her patience, while Mounet was gargling away, she clasped her hands, raised her eyes to heaven and cried in a piercing voice, 'Help! Help!' – and then fled into the wings, to the stupefaction of everyone there, who had not been expecting her so soon. Perrin, of course, was furious, but Sarah said simply, 'But, M. l'Administrateur, I thought my colleague was choking – I was frightened. So of course I called for help!'[12]

Whether Perrin liked it or not – and he did not – Sarah was now established in the public's eyes as that unheard-of phenomenon, the star of the Comédie-Française. While she was playing *Hernani*, she was replaced when she was unwell by the coming young actress Adeline Dudlay. The receipts fell the very next day. It was the first time this had ever happened at the Comédie, where the great attraction was supposed to be the ensemble. The committee was not happy; but short of ejecting Sarah – and they could hardly do that – no obvious remedy was available.

18

In 1879 the Comédie-Française decided to try a season in London. They had done this twice before: once many years earlier, when they had not met with much success, and once in 1871, when they had made enough money to save them from what looked like financial catastrophe after the events of the Commune. The London season was to be in the summer, when Paris houses were notoriously thin, and would be at the Gaiety Theatre, whose director was John Hollingshead.

A glance at the rules and regulations set out by the Administration of the Comédie regarding this tour is revealing. After looking through them the reader may wonder, not why Sarah made trouble as often as she did, but rather why the entire company did not throw up its collective hands and stage a rebellion: for they are couched in terms more applicable to a school party than to a group of the most talented and sophisticated men and women in France. Before the company left, Perrin (who was not at his best – his wife was seriously ill, and died a few days later) read everyone a lecture about what would happen on the trip. He made a particular point of insisting that, although the Comédie would be playing in London and in a strange theatre, it should behave exactly as if it were in its own home. The ordinary rules would not be modified, the usual practices would apply, and the company would be as if still in Paris. Perrin said he hoped everyone would try and get on with each other, and recommended to the members 'a

214

quality which, in his experience, [was] very precious when one [was] travelling: good humour'. Then he went on to more detailed instructions. Article 8 of the company's agreement with Hollingshead and his partner Mayer forbade any of the company to appear at any other theatre during the Comédie's stay in London. But the members should not merely consider themselves bound by the express terms of the contract, but by 'more delicate and high-minded considerations' regarding not just public but also private performances. This was a matter of some delicacy indeed: for both musicians and actors might expect to make a good proportion of their income from private engagements. In those days before gramophone records and cinemas, anyone wishing to enjoy a play or concert had either to attend a public performance or engage the artists to perform in private, with the natural result that actors and musicians were often invited to recite or play in the drawing-rooms of the wealthy. Marcel Proust, who chronicled so many such occasions in *A la Recherche du temps perdu*, at one point in his life made a habit of getting his favourite string quartet to come and perform weekly in his cork-lined bedroom; his friend Comte Robert de Montesquiou often engaged Sarah to perform at his sumptuous parties, as did many other rich aristocrats; and the habit was as widespread in London as in Paris. So, while it was not unreasonable to forbid members to allow their names to figure on any poster or newspaper announcement not pertaining to their engagement at the Gaiety, private parties were another matter. Clearly they could not be altogether forbidden. 'If,' said Perrin sternly, 'it is difficult for an artist to refuse because the invitation is personal as well as a mark of esteem for talent, the artist should confine himself to personal recitations. Group performances will not be tolerated.'[1] But did this include two-handed performances, where an actor and actress might perform a scene together? It was not as if the stay was going

215

to be very lucrative for the performers in other respects. Full members were to receive a per diem to cover all expenses of sixty francs for men, fifty francs for women; those who were not yet full members would get thirty-five francs if they were men, thirty francs if they were women. And authors' royalties were to be calculated at seven and a half per cent rather than the usual fifteen.

It may be imagined that all this led to a certain amount of grumbling. As for Sarah, she was outraged. After Perrin had given his speech, she sat quite silently, and he, disquieted by this uncharacteristic behaviour, took her to one side and asked her what she was hatching. It was, quite simply, that she would not consider going to London unless she was made a full member – *Sociétaire à part entière* – instead of a partial member, as she then was, for the duration of the trip. This was put to the committee, who rejected it; upon which Sarah announced that in that case she would not be going to London. The committee was reconvened, and Got, the doyen of the company, probably spoke for them all when he said, 'All right, then let her not come. She's just a damn nuisance!'[2] But things were not so simple. Hollingshead and his partner Mayer were less concerned with the Comédie's tradition than with its drawing-power, which of course was related to its star players. They now informed Perrin that if Coquelin, Mounet-Sully, Croizette or Sarah did not come, the contract was null and void and the trip was off.

Mayer, in despairing mood, came to see Sarah after this discussion, and she, horrified to see the harm she was doing the whole company by her selfish whims, rushed to Perrin to tell him she would back down and go under any conditions. The committee was in session once again; he told her he would be with her shortly; and when he arrived it was to say that Sarah and Croizette had both been given full membership, not just for the duration of the trip but in perpetuity.

Meanwhile Sarah had received a momentous visit. This was from a tall, silver-haired, steely-eyed Englishman who had more or less forced his way into her studio while she was in the middle of modelling and had refused to be turned away by the maid. However, it seemed that he had no wish to offend: he was very polite about the studio, the sculpture, the paintings . . . Finally Sarah asked him who he was and what he wanted. It turned out that his name was Edward Jarrett, he was an impresario, and what he wanted was to become Sarah's manager and to make her some money. Would she like to visit America? He could make her a great deal of money there. No, she replied, she would not: the very thought of going to America appalled her. Never! All right, he said; no need to get angry; how about making a bit on the side in London? Of course, she was always happy to do that; but how? By playing in drawing-rooms, said Jarrett; he could make her a fortune doing that. Sarah was not as yet sure whether she would be going to London; meanwhile she signed a contract with Jarrett in which all eventualities were catered for. Then the quarrel with Perrin was made up, the two embraced and were friends again, and Sarah forgot all about the contract.

But not for long. Five days later Perrin arrived at nine one evening, in the middle of a dinner-party, and held out a copy of the *Times* with a grim injunction to 'Read that!' And Sarah read an advertisement announcing that Mlle Sarah Bernhardt would be available to play in drawing-rooms, with one or two other artistes from the Comédie-Française, without scenery and in formats specially adapted for society parties: details on request from Jarrett, His Majesty's Theatre.

Cornered, Sarah explained what had happened and asked, not unreasonably, why she should not make a little money

217

for herself this way? 'It's not me, it's the committee,' Perrin prevaricated. 'That's rich!' cried Sarah, and called her secretary to find a note she had just received from Delaunay, who was himself a member of the committee, asking if she would play Musset's *La Nuit d'Octobre* with him at Lady Dudley's on June 5 – they were offered 5,000 francs just for the two of them . . .

For a few days the papers eagerly took up this new story of a rift in the Comédie featuring their favourite subject, until finally, on May 29, Perrin inserted an announcement in the *National* to the effect that all members of the Comédie, including Mlle Sarah Bernhardt, were perfectly free to use their free time in any way they wanted. Ironically, all the other members of the company took the opportunity to insert their own advertisements in the *Times*, and peace – just – reigned again.

The send-off from France to England was frenetic. Sarah, like most French citizens at that time, knew nothing of what England might be like, and was particularly nervous at the thought of the boat trip across the Channel. She had had a specially warm fur coat made to protect her against the cruelties of the early June ocean, and embarked amid a welter of sea-sick pills, compresses to hold against her diaphragm, silk paper to put down her back, and, at the last minute, a vast bladder-belt designed to save her should she fall into the sea. The arrival at Folkestone was equally spectacular. A crowd was awaiting her – Sarah describes it as consisting of 'thousands of people' – and a cry of '*Vive Sarah Bernhardt*' went up as she disembarked. The actor Norman Forbes-Robertson handed her a gardenia and his companion, the young Oscar Wilde, hearing someone remark 'They will soon be making you a carpet of flowers!' acted upon the suggestion and immediately cast his armful of lilies at her feet.[3]

However, anticlimax soon set in. The train from Folkestone to Victoria was an hour late; it arrived at nine o'clock in the evening to an empty platform. There was, it was true, a red carpet, which Sarah had assumed, after the welcome at Folkestone, must be for her – but it turned out that this was a leftover from the departure a short time before of the Prince and Princess of Wales *en route* for Paris; which meant, too, as Mayer soon confirmed, that the royal couple would not be in London to grace the Comédie's opening night. The weather was overcast, the streets of London were grey and dingy, crowded with people but lacking in animation compared with Paris, and when she got to the house she had rented for the next six weeks, 77 Chester Square, she could hardly bring herself to get out of the cab. But the door of the house was open, and she could see a lighted hallway filled with flowers in baskets, bunches, sprays . . . Descending, she asked her manservant if he had kept the cards. He had; here they all were on a tray. It turned out that most of the flowers had been sent from Paris the day before. Only one bunch was from London. It was an enormous bouquet and the card read 'Welcome! – Henry Irving.'[4]

It turned out that, on Jarrett's instructions, her entire first day was to be devoted to receiving journalists – a prospect which naturally appalled Sarah, who wanted to get them all over with at once by holding what would today be termed a press conference. But Jarrett would not allow this. They were to be received one by one, every single one of them, with Jarrett as interpreter. Each of them began with the same question: 'Well, mademoiselle, and what do you think of London?' Sarah found it hard to know what to say – her entire experience of London being confined as yet to Chester Square, 'a small dull green square with a black statue in the middle and an ugly church'.[5] The next day, however, she was surprised to learn how much she appreciated London's many and varied attractions. And in fact it was not long before she did; London became one of her favourite cities,

219

where she felt at home and was always sure of a warm welcome – though, she said, she could never get used to British sash windows, which can never be opened more than half, either the top or the bottom, or a little of either, unlike the French design, which can be flung wide without so much as a glazing bar to block the air and the sun. (Not that Sarah, with her overheated, carpeted, feathered, perfumed interiors, was much of a one for flinging the windows wide.)

By five o'clock the journalists had gone. The next caller was a friend from Paris, Hortense Damain, who knew a great many people in English society, and who informed Sarah that in half an hour the Duchess of – and Lady – would be coming to call, and that Lady Dudley would follow soon after.

Sarah had not known what to expect of London, and it is hard to imagine she could have anticipated what was to happen. She recounts her reception by English high society with a sort of stupefaction; and this is entirely understandable, because the relation of artists to society was so completely different in London from anything she had known in Paris.

In *The Tragic Muse* Henry James has his young heroine, Miriam Rooth, who is destined to become a great actress in London, say to a friend, as she contemplates the portrait of Rachel in the foyer of the Français, 'Doesn't such a woman as that receive – receive every one?'

To which her friend Peter Sherringham, the English diplomat, replies, 'Every one who goes to see her, no doubt.'

'And who goes?'

'Lots of men – clever men, eminent men.'

'Ah, what a charming life! Then doesn't she go out?'

'Not what we Philistines mean by that – not into society, never. She never enters a lady's drawing-room.'

'How strange, when one's as distinguished as that . . . Then where does she learn such manners?'

'She teaches manners, *à ses heures*; she doesn't need to learn them.'

'. . . But in London actresses go into society,' Miriam continued.

'Oh, in London *nous mêlons les genres*!'[6]

In fact it was not entirely unknown for actresses to rub elbows with duchesses in Paris. It had happened – once: at the comtesse de Castellane's. The reason for this was that Mme de Castellane was devoted to the theatre: it was in her private auditorium that Got had made his stage début. So she was happy to receive 'from all worlds – thirty-two quarters of nobility and thirty-two quarters of genius . . . It was charming; the faubourg Saint-Germain had the wit and the good grace to give a genuine welcome to actresses. Mlle Rachel and Mlle Brohan, among others, were the best of friends with duchesses there. But it needed the magic touch of Mme de Castellane to achieve that miracle.'[7]

Mme de Castellane, however, was no more, and the two worlds had kept apart ever since, each feeling much more comfortable that way. Dukes met actresses all right – everyone knew that – but such meetings took place within that other world where wives – much less duchesses – did not set foot, and where the talk was freer and the company much more amusing, not to say relaxed. It was true that in the 1880s there were salons in Paris – Mme Straus's was one, Mme Lemaire's another – where the Faubourg mingled with the artistic and literary world; but while this might include writers and painters, it did not extend to actors, much less actresses. If they came to the parties, it was in a professional capacity to provide the entertainment.

In England, however, on that very first day, Sarah, after receiving Lady Dudley and her friends, was whisked straight off to dinner with another great lady at Prince's Gate –

followed by recitations: but that evening, Sarah was not expected to recite herself. In her memoirs she records some impressions of the occasion – how well everybody spoke French, the unexpected excellence of the food, her surprise at seeing how the young girls at the dinner seemed genuinely to be enjoying themselves and not bothered with finding a suitable husband, which was very different from Paris; and how even very elderly ladies exposed their wrinkled necks in *grand décolleté*, which Sarah found disgusting but which her friend Hortense Damain explained was simply smart. Everything was wonderful, and when she got back to Chester Square and found some colleagues there who had just arrived off the boat-train, she bored and annoyed them (one can imagine it vividly) with her effusions about English hospitality.

Later, she remembered things slightly differently. 'I know now that they meant to be kind, but I didn't understand; it was so different – I thought they were all trying to insult me,' she said. 'As you know . . . in France and in most other countries, we artists – the Bohemians – live in a world of our own. No Society woman in Paris would think of asking me to her house except as an artist, and I should not ask her to mine. I thought – there must be some mistake.'

This being so, Sarah set about correcting the mistake; and whenever she attended an aristocratic party she took Maurice with her and had herself announced as 'Mademoiselle Sarah Bernhardt and her son'. 'Nobody minded – not a bit' – but, not surprisingly, 'they crowded round and stared. I felt that they did not care for my art – for my work – but only wanted to stare because I was very thin and horrible stories were told about me. I was miserable.'[8] Her misery was compounded by the misunderstandings which followed upon her own behaviour. If she was not a lady, then she could only be – the other thing. Sarah grumbled to Mrs Patrick Campbell, the celebrated and beautiful English

222

actress who was to be her partner in a notable attempt at international art, that 'on her first visit to England a supper was given in her honour; she was treated like a queen, and felt a queen. Her host, when seeing her to her carriage, "stole a kiss". She did not speak to him again for years. It was *abominable*, she said, *abominable*. It showed he had no respect for her.'[9]

If this was so – and in another version of these excursions into society Sarah concedes that, on account of her *outré* behaviour, some of her hosts were 'very upset – anywhere else, I should have made enemies'[10] – this was because, if they invited actresses into society, they expected the actresses to behave like ladies.

The relations between actresses and respectable society in London were on a quite different footing from those prevailing in Paris at this time. In Paris, relations between members of the respectable world and the *demi-monde* (including actresses) were an openly acknowledged fact of social life. Everyone knew where they stood and what they might (and might not) expect. In Britain, on the other hand, these things were swept under the carpet, and the pretence was made that they did not exist. But of course they *did* exist; and the absence, in London, of an acknowledged social device such as the *demi-monde*, so essentially Parisian in its sophisticated cynicism, meant that the whole question of relations between rich and respectable men and unrespectable ladies was a matter to be mentioned only in whispers. Naturally this resulted in the whole matter acquiring the *frisson* and fascination of forbidden fruit. One of the more bizarre aspects of Victorian society was its highly equivocal obsession with 'fallen women', memorably personified in the extraordinary activities of such figures as Mr Gladstone and the journalist W. T. Stead, who spent much of their lives ardently pursuing these ladies in the name of morality. (This fascination was shared by a good many progressive ladies as well – Octavia Hill and Olive Schreiner, to name but two.)

Actresses, of course, were not necessarily 'fallen women' in England, any more than they were necessarily courtesans in France. The theatre at this time was, rather, a world of its own, almost a separate 'caste', in which actors' children, born, as it were, in the wings, automatically went on the stage themselves and imbibed its free-and-easy mores with their mothers' milk. Ellen Terry was a member of one such acting family (which still entertains us: Sir John Gielgud is the son of her older sister Kate). Nelly Ternan, Charles Dickens' actress mistress, came from another. And – as the lives of both Nelly and Ellen demonstrate – actresses, if not necessarily promiscuous, were (like their colleagues across the Channel) more apt to enter into longstanding unmarried relationships than respectable ladies – to whom no respectable gentleman would anyway have dreamed of putting such a proposition. The difference was that, whereas in France such arrangements were an accepted part of life – everyone knew, for example, that the celebrated actress Marie Dorval was the mistress of the Romantic poet Alfred de Vigny – in England they were not: Dickens and his friends took infinite pains to make sure nobody should suspect his relations with Nelly Ternan, even though their association lasted twelve years; Ellen Terry hid herself away in the country during her relationship with the architect E. W. Godwin, and only returned to the stage and the public eye after it had ended.

Paradoxically, as one result of all this, there was not the unscaleable social wall between society and the stage in London that there was in Paris. Lillie Langtry, a society beauty, took to the boards when she was hard up – and was still received: something that would have been inconceivable in Paris. For the fact was that a fair number of these English duchesses had been actresses, and a great many

English actresses aspired to be duchesses. There could be no question of Nelly Ternan marrying Dickens, or Ellen Terry marrying Godwin, because these gentlemen were married already. But of course not all the gentlemen who saw and were smitten by actresses were married. Many of them were young and eligible; and, in the absence of a recognized and rigid social framework within which the inevitably resulting friendships might be conducted, there was no limit to what an actress might hope for. After all, a successful young actress was probably both more attractive and more intelligent than either the normal run of society girl or the normal run of tart; and if her pursuer was not already married – in which case she might or might not decide to sacrifice all for love – why should she not try for the best of all worlds? Naturally the young man's family would not approve. But then, since the young man was undoubtedly keeping the whole affair as secret as he possibly could, his family need know nothing about it until it was too late and the deed was done.

The result of this was a stream of marriages between young actresses and besotted scions of the British aristocracy which would have been unthinkable in the French *gratin* – a social circumstance whose blithe inappropriateness provided the scenario for many of the immortal works of P. G. Wodehouse. Cranstoun Metcalfe's *Peeresses of the Stage* (published in 1913) lists no less than thirty-one such alliances. 'What is there "to" musical comedy, as an American might say, that appeals so strongly to our nobility?' he wondered, and supplied the answer in the next sentence: 'Part of the answer is . . . that the average age of the bridegroom is about twenty-six years. It is a splendid age, at which, however, if one may be a man about town one is not necessarily a man of the world.'[11] These were just such young men as the Comte de Kératry and the Prince de Ligne, upon whom such ladies as Sarah's Aunt Rosine relied for her living, and who had taken such pleasure in the company of Sarah herself, but who (a circumstance of which Maurice was the living proof) would never have dreamed of marrying her.

The young British aristocrats, as it happened, would probably not have married her either: their marked preference, as Cranstoun Metcalfe pointed out, was for musical comedy over the 'legitimate' stage. But this did not prevent distinguished actresses hoping for the best. Mrs Pat herself was a notable example of this. Her memoirs (in great contrast to Sarah's) resound with dropped aristocratic names: no occasion is too small for an effusive mention of Lady This or Lord That. Bernard Shaw, a devotee of hers who was constantly trying – and usually failing – to persuade her to play his heroines, once reproached her for her lack of professional application to her art. 'I choose to be an amateur,' she replied; to which he retorted, 'You don't want to be an amateur. You want to be a lady.'[12] And Shaw, as usual, was right. If you wanted to be a lady, you could not be even an amateur, let alone a dedicated professional.

There was also another side to this coin – and this was that British actresses, at least on the legitimate stage, were supposed to behave like ladies. The doyen of the English stage at this time, Helena Faucit, was a lady who was received in the highest circles and who (conveniently forgetting her own youth as a hard-working professional) preferred strict propriety in her colleagues. The leading young actress was Ellen Terry, and the irregularities of her private life – after what was virtually a child marriage to the middle-aged painter G. F. Watts she left the stage to live with the architect E. W. Godwin, by whom she had two children; Henry Irving had only recently persuaded her to return to the theatre to partner him at the Lyceum – were more or less overlooked because she appeared so very wholesome and ladylike. But this very particular appeal undoubtedly restricted her range, even though without it she might have found acceptance more difficult. And although Terry was undoubtedly a great actress she never acquired an international reputation in the way that those hardened professionals Bernhardt and Duse succeeded in doing.

As yet, however, Sarah was neither dedicated nor really very professional: whims are no part of professionalism. That she did become so was due in no small measure to the fact that she thought of herself, first and foremost, as an actress with her own place in her own world: a place and a world with which she was very satisfied. It has been pointed out that in order to find any real parallel to Bernhardt on the English stage it is necessary to go back to Elizabeth Barry and the great days of the post-Restoration theatre.[13] Then, an English actress enjoyed a position vis-à-vis the world very comparable to that of French actresses of Sarah's day. Sarah had her own professional pride; she did not have to try to be a lady in order to be respected; the friendship and social approval of duchesses was a matter of no great moment to her; she was therefore able to devote all her energies to being an actress without worrying about what society would think.

The Comédie-Française opened in London on 2 June 1897 with Molière's *Le Misanthrope*, followed by *Les Précieuses ridicules*. That should have been enough for one evening. But things began as they were to go on. By popular request, it was announced that Mlle Sarah Bernhardt would give Act Two of *Phèdre* as an entr'acte. After her appearance the house went mad, as it was to do every time she showed herself on stage that London season.

If anything were needed to prove to Parisians that Sarah's reception in London had absolutely nothing to do with the

227

quality of her acting, that first performance sufficed. It was a fiasco, even as described by Sarah herself. She was once more paralysed by stage-fright; this evening, as before every important performance throughout her life, she shook and her throat was dry. 'Three times I rouged my cheeks and darkened my eyes, and three times I sponged the whole lot off again. I thought I looked terrible, ugly, thinner, shorter. I shut my eyes to listen to my voice. The exercise I use is "le bal", which I make deep by emphasizing the *a*: "le baaaal" or send up high by shortening the *a* and pushing on the *l*: "le balll". But that night I couldn't hit the note, neither high nor low ... Mlle Thénard, who was playing Oenone, my old nurse, said, "Calm down, all the English have gone to Paris, the house is full of Belgians" ... I said, "But you know how nervous I was in Brussels." "There wasn't any need," she replied coldly. "The house was full of English that day." It was time to go on ... The house burst into applause when I made my entry, and ... I said to myself "All right – you'll see: I'm going to give you everything I've got." But when I began, as I wasn't in control of myself, I pitched it too high. There was no coming down once I'd begun. I was off and nothing could stop me.' But, although she had begun badly, in Sarah's view her performance then improved: 'I begged Hippolyte for the love that was killing me, and my arms held out to Mounet-Sully were Phèdre's arms, twisted by cruel desire. The god was there that night [Sarah's term for the nights when she felt her performance was inspired]. And when the curtain fell, Mounet-Sully caught me as I fainted and carried me to my dressing-room.'[14]

Others, however, did not agree with her assessment. In the French classical theatre, in which Sarah had been schooled and of which the Comédie-Française was the highest manifestation, there were very definite rules appertaining to the use of the voice. The upper register had brilliance and passion; power was in the lower register;

natural tone, in the middle. Overuse of the top notes –
'more heard than heeded' according to Sarah's old teacher
Samson[15] – would lead to strain and tuneless shrieking, just
as overuse of the low tones led to monotony. As Sarah's
voice was light and silvery, its note easily strained, to begin
this scene – a scene which becomes steadily more emotional
and powerful – on too high a pitch was little short of
disastrous, and certainly a terrible strain. It was little wonder
that she fainted at the end.

Naturally all this was quite obvious to such French critics
as Francisque Sarcey, who was in London to report on the
Comédie's season. 'Her voice had to begin from there and
could only rise as the feelings she had to express grew
stronger and more pathetic; she couldn't help shouting,
began to gabble, and was lost.' But to Sarcey's astonishment,
the fact that this had been a fiasco had no effect on Sarah's
reception in London, as it most certainly would have done
in Paris. Indeed, that very lack of control which most
condemned her in French eyes seemed particularly to appeal
to the British. The *Times* remarked upon 'a self-abandon-
ment that took no measure of her strength. She seemed like
a leaf whirled away by the torrent of her passion. And when
at last the storm seemed to shatter her being, and she sank
inert and insensible into the arms of Oenone, the house
seemed rather to be relieving its pent-up feelings in its
tumult of applause than offering a tribute to the frail, fair
creature.'[16] Could this flood of praise, Sarcey wondered,
really last for forty days and forty nights (the Comédie's
season was to last from 2 June to 12 July)? 'What will they
say when she's really good?'[17]

This was not to be revealed, for it seems clear that during
this season Sarah was rarely at her best. In *L'Etrangère* one
evening she simply forgot most of a long speech in which
various crucial details of the plot are unravelled ('The reason
I sent for you here, Madame,' she said to the astonished

Croizette, 'is that I wished to tell you why I have acted as I have. I have thought it over and have decided *not* to tell you today.'[18]) while on various other occasions she was so exhausted by the exigencies of her offstage life (which included overseeing an exhibition of her paintings and sculptures, many of which were most advantageously sold, acquiring a menagerie of exotic animals which were kept in the garden of 77 Chester Square, to her neighbours' horror, and of course infinite numbers of social engagements and drawing-room recitations) that she either played very perfunctorily or else missed performances altogether at the shortest possible notice. But did all this disillusion her devoted public? It did not. When she was not playing, receipts fell; the average receipt for the season was 10,000 francs, but this rose to 13,350 francs on the evenings when Sarah was appearing. What was even worse as far as her colleagues and the representatives of the Paris press were concerned, other members of the company, notably Sophie Croizette, who were playing superbly, were by contrast quite unappreciated. Sarcey plaintively recorded this injustice. '[Croizette] was looking wonderful,' he wrote. 'She was playing at her very best, as she rarely plays in Paris. But in spite of all this they didn't like her . . . The next evening she was playing the duchesse de Septmonts in *L'Etrangère*; she brought to the part that bewitching seductiveness with which we are all familiar, and she failed to fascinate . . . I can't understand it . . . I can only think that the English are incapable of worshipping two goddesses at the same time, and they've given themselves heart and soul to Mlle Sarah Bernhardt.' He added, 'As for *her*, it is impossible to convey an idea of the adoration she arouses. It is plain madness . . . Everybody wants to know the smallest details of her life. Photographs simply disappear . . .'[19]

Was there anything that could explain this apparently irrational preference? As far as Croizette was concerned, several critics pointed out that, despite her piquant combination of black eyes and blonde hair, which Parisians found so charming, she was too fat for the English taste ('the amplitude of her person', as Henry James put it, 'has reached a point at which, in the parts of young girls, illusion tends to vanish'[20]). She also appeared rather too assertive. Tom Taylor, the theatre critic of the *Times*, considered that, apart from her 'amplitude', 'a certain roughness in the lower tones of [Croizette's] voice, . . . a certain air of assured self-dependence and power to stand alone, have much to do, we are convinced, with the coldness which so puzzles M. Sarcey.' This was of course paradoxical, since (as we have seen) Croizette was much more conventional, malleable and reliant on powerful protection than Sarah. (Though Taylor may have been right in detecting that Croizette had more underlying confidence in herself: Reynaldo Hahn recounts an incident retailed by Sarah in which she and Croizette went to the Variétés and witnessed a skit on the pair of them, who were just then appearing together in *Le Sphinx*. Croizette thought it was very funny, but Sarah walked out in a huff.[21]) But all that matters on stage is the impression one gives; and, said Taylor, in the absence of great genius (which he did not attribute to Sarah), 'the British public asks, first and above all things, to be interested in the woman who presents herself before it as an actress. For this purpose, the specially feminine elements of grace, fragility, physical delicacy, a slender figure, a sweet voice, whatever most suggest purity, tenderness, even weakness, and the need of protection – all the points, in short, that most distinguish woman from man are of paramount effect . . . [These] characteristics . . . meet . . . in Sarah Bernhardt in a rare degree, united with a strangeness and originality which add to her womanly graces a piquancy of their own.' Taylor summed up Sarah's virtues as 'a wonderfully graceful figure, beautifully dressed, picturesque of pose, fair of face, loving

231

of look, feminine of gesture, sweet of voice – admirably fitted, in a word, for what she has chiefly to do [as Doña Sol] which is to receive the full rush of the love of three men.'[22]

Such an enconium, though honest, hardly says much for the sophistication of London taste. And clearly there was more to it than that. Critics and audiences for the next quarter century were to affirm that Sarah was possessed of a particular magical charisma accorded to very few, which was either beyond Tom Taylor's powers of analysis, or which she had not acquired in 1879 (though the nature of her successes before then, in Paris as well as London, would indicate that she had begun to acquire it at the Odéon and that it never left her thereafter.) Whether that was separable from her abilities as an actress – a separation which both Sarcey and Tom Taylor were trying to make in these criticisms – is another matter. Ellen Terry, for one, did not think it was. 'I never thought Croizette – a superb animal – a "patch" on Sarah, who was at this time as thin as a harrow,' she remarks in her memoirs.[23] Elsewhere, she enlarges on this: 'She was as transparent as an azalea, only more so; like a cloud, only not so thick. Smoke from a burning paper describes her more nearly. She was hollow-eyed, thin, almost consumptive. Her body was not the prison of its soul, but its shadow.' She seemed 'more a symbol, an ideal, an epitome than a woman. It is this quality that makes her so easy in such lofty parts as Phèdre . . . [It is] this extraordinary decorative and symbolic quality of Sarah's which [makes] her transcend all personal and individual feeling on the stage. No one plays a love scene better, but it is a *picture* of love that she gives, a strange exotic picture rather than a suggestion of the ordinary human passion as felt by ordinary human people.'[24] Later Sarah was to select plays which depended on these symbolic, hieratic qualities; but the power of suggestion described by Ellen Terry, combined with her particular style and beauty, would go far to account for her overwhelming effect on her audiences, as well as the impossibility of explaining it in terms of the French classical tradition.

Of course, when London audiences thought of Paris and the French theatre, it was not the classical tradition that sprang first to their minds. In Paris audiences had a choice of the traditional repertoire available at the Comédie and the Odéon and the gamut of modern plays, in which such authors at Feuillet, Dumas *fils* and Sardou represented the top of the pyramid, generally known as 'boulevard' theatre. In London, the choice at this time was much poorer. You could either go to see Henry Irving and Ellen Terry at the Lyceum playing Irving's very particular versions of Shakespeare, or else take your choice of plays which were very often no more than watered-down translations and imitations of Paris boulevard successes. Censorship saw to the watering-down, and the watering-down saw off the play. One such was a version of *La Dame aux camélias* known as *Heartsease*, in which Marguerite's profession was (according to Henry James) 'enveloped in the most bewildering and mystifying pruderies of illusion'.[25] Of another adaptation, entitled *Peril* and taken from Sardou's *Les Intimes*, James remarked that 'the usual feat has been attempted – to extirpate "impropriety" and at the same time to save interest. In the extraordinary manipulation and readjustment of French immoralities which goes on in the interest of Anglo-Saxon virtue, I have never known this feat to succeed. Propriety may have been saved . . . but interest has certainly been lost . . . M Sardou's perfectly improper but thoroughly homogeneous comedy has been flattened and vulgarized . . . and the play, from being a serious comedy, with a flavor of the tragic, has become an elaborate farce, salted with a few coarse grains of gravity.'[26] And acting in these pale shadows was, as we have seen, a generation of actresses much taken up with avoiding vulgarity. Even the American Ibsenite Elizabeth Robins was upbraided for this by Shaw, who told her, 'You'd be a much better actress if you were less taken up with being a lady'; something which preoccupied her because (she explained) the profession of actress was still, even in the 1890s, 'liable to be confused with the oldest profession'.[27] This confusion, of course, also existed in Paris, but there actresses, living unabashed in their own world, were able to take it in their stride. One was a professional and one had received a professional training: one's private life was one's own concern. Henry James allowed that Ellen Terry was 'intelligent and vivacious . . . singularly delicate and lady-like' and 'in a certain measure, interesting'. But he also thought that she was 'simply *not* an actress . . . essentially amateurish'.[28] That was perhaps unfair to Ellen Terry; but that was the impression of a critic whose theatrical formation had been essentially French. It is interesting to note in this context that the only English actress of whom Sarah thought highly was Marie Lloyd the music-hall star (not to be confused with the French Marie Lloyd who had won first prize at the Conservatoire), whom she thought a theatrical genius.[29] And of course, Marie Lloyd, like the rest of the music hall, was the antithesis of ladylike.

What was more – as the role of Phèdre herself so amply demonstrated – Bernhardt was the product of a theatrical tradition whose most exalted and classical female roles, those in Racine's plays, were frankly sexual in a way their English, Shakespearean equivalents (especially in bowdlerized Victorian versions) were not. Rosalind, Juliet, Beatrice, Katharine, are wonderful roles: but they were written to be played by boys and young men, while Phèdre, Monime, Andromaque and the rest of Racine's female roles were written for actresses the author knew well, even intimately.[30]

Paris, then, was for British playgoers the home, not only of all that was new in the theatre, but also of all that was sexy and immoral – a sexiness and immorality of course immensely increased in effect because only hinted at in those shadows of Paris which reached the London stage. And Sarah, whose extraordinary sexiness on stage – in the eyes even of *French* critics – was a matter of record, and whose stormy reputation had preceded her to London, was the embodiment of all this forbidden exoticism.

Thus, when Sarah Bernhardt stepped onstage at the Gaiety, she represented for her rapt audience everything they hoped the French theatre would be and that their own theatre definitely was not. But, more than that, her personal style was also accessible to a British or American audience in a way that the more usual style of the Comédie-Française was not. We have seen that part of her peculiar originality lay in combining an acting style more usually associated with the boulevard than with the classical repertoire of the national theatres. But in London, where the niceties of the French classical style were apt to be overlooked, this was easily accepted. At the Lyceum, Henry Irving rendered Shakespearean tragedy in the style of boulevard melodrama, and was lionized, not criticized, on that account. When Sarah put into Phèdre everything that was in her – as she alone of her contemporaries did – this simply seemed normal and comprehensible to English audiences, who were not distanced from this interpretation as they might have been from a more strictly classical one.[31] Her operatic style recalled the palmy days of English theatre, the days of Mrs Siddons and Edmund Kean, before it was embalmed in the mediocrity of the mid-century and finally revolutionized by the school of Ibsenite naturalism so energetically propounded by the man who was to be Bernhardt's greatest denigrator, Bernard Shaw.

19

Not surprisingly, Sarah's behaviour in London, especially when coupled with her disproportionate personal success, led to a good deal of bad feeling both within the company and also in Paris. As usual she was accused of courting publicity for its own sake, and as usual this was certainly true. Her behaviour in this respect continued the manic merry-go-round which in Paris had climaxed in the balloon trip. In London, when she exhibited her sculptures and paintings in a Piccadilly gallery, she sent out a hundred invitations, beginning with the Prince and Princess of Wales and including Mr Gladstone (who conversed with her about the moral lessons to be drawn from *Phèdre*). Twelve hundred people came; almost everything was sold, including one group entitled *After the Storm* which brought four hundred pounds. With this money, and taking advantage of three evenings when she was not playing, she made an unauthorized trip to Liverpool, where she had been told there was a menagerie with animals for sale: she wanted to buy some lion cubs. It turned out that none were in stock, only full-grown specimens which even Sarah had regretfully to conclude were too big for the back garden. (Later, in Paris, she did acquire a lion cub which she kept in a cage in her salon; it had to be removed after a short while, however, on account of the offensive smell.) Undeterred, she returned to London with a leopard cub, an alsatian and six chameleons, a present from the proprietor of the menagerie. These joined the three dogs, the monkey and the parrot already in residence. When everyone got back to Chester Square nobody dared let the leopard out of its cage. Sarah had the cage taken out into the garden and personally opened the door, whereupon the leopard, overcome with the joys of liberty, leapt upon the terrified dogs, while the parrot squawked and the monkey rattled the bars of his cage. Furious heads appeared at all the neighbouring windows, and Sarah and those members of the 'little court' currently in attendance – Louise Abbéma, the painters de Nittis and Gustave Doré, a musician called Georges Deschamps, Georges Clairin who sketched the scene – all doubled up in helpless laughter. Of course the story was soon in the papers, and Got, who was in charge of the Comédie in the absence of Perrin, summoned Sarah to scold her about bringing the company into disrepute by her behaviour. She invited him to the scene of the crime, let loose the leopard once more, and soon had Got laughing too.

However, it was clear that things could not go on in this way. All this extraneous activity took its toll. On 21 June Sarah was due to play a matinée of *L'Etrangère* and *Hernani* in the evening; but at the last moment she sent a note to say she was not well and would have to drop out of the matinée at least. The panic-stricken company gathered itself together as best it could and sent Coquelin out front to announce that Sarah was indisposed and that *Tartuffe* would be given instead, but the public, unimpressed, left the theatre and demanded its money back. Receipts that day fell to 2,215 francs for the matinée and the evening performance was cancelled. The Earl of Belgravia wrote to the *Times* in a rage to complain that the audience, which included the Duchess of Edinburgh and Prince Leopold (and himself) had not been told the news until 'carriages had been dismissed on a wet afternoon'.[1] He demanded assurances that on the next occasion when Sarah was scheduled to appear both in the matinée and the evening performance, she would not cancel again, since he had booked seats in the stalls. She did not: four days later, *L'Etrangère* in matinée made 11,710 francs, and *Hernani*, played in the evening, 13,730.

Not unnaturally, everyone – including the Paris press – was outraged at this cavalier behaviour. Sarah's excuses – how she had told Mayer at eleven that morning that she would be unable to play that day, how until then she had been hoping to do so, but that a violent spasm in which she coughed blood had put paid to those hopes – cut little ice. The papers in France retailed lurid stories – how, if you paid a shilling, you could see Sarah dressed as a man, how she smoked large cigars, how she took her maid to grand parties to act as her 'feed', how she fenced in her garden dressed in Pierrot costume, how she was taking boxing lessons and had broken two of her teacher's teeth . . . [2] Scathing attacks were made upon her which inevitably began to have their effect even in London, hitherto so adoring, but where critics now began to attack her performances for their narrow range, which lacked variety, since all parts were played upon the same plaintive and pathetic note. 'She still needs a great deal of labour and study before she can rein in her passion, wind it to her will and compel it to obey her, instead of obeying it,' wrote the *Times* severely. '. . . Rachel did not shrink from devoting months on months of strenuous preparation to a part.'[3] Finally Sarah felt obliged to reply. She telegraphed at length to Albert Wolff at the *Figaro* disclaiming the stories – somewhat disingenuously: 'I give you my word that I never dress as a man here in London! I haven't even brought my sculpting outfit . . . I've only been once to my little exhibition, just once, when I sent out a few private invitations for the opening . . . You know that I'm one of the least well-paid of the *sociétaires* at the Comédie-Française. I think I'm entitled to make up the difference a bit. I'm exhibiting ten pictures and eight sculptures, that's true. But since I brought them in order to sell them, I must at least show them . . . If Parisians are tired of reading all these stupid things and want to give me a bad time when I come back, I don't want anyone to do anything silly on my account and I'll resign from the Comédie-Française. And if the London public is tired of all this fuss and wants to turn nasty when it's been so kind, then let the Comédie send me home, to spare itself the humiliation of seeing one of its members hissed and booed . . .'4

This reply had its desired effect. There was a lot of comment, generally coming down on Sarah's side, although the consensus was that she had behaved like a spoilt child. Perrin sent an affectionate letter from Paris, begging her not to resign. All her friends rallied round. Croizette threw her arms round her and told her how glad she was Sarah was not resigning; Mounet read her little sermons on art and integrity; Delaunay gave her a solemn lecture on the bad form of writing to the newspapers off her own bat as she had done, when she should have gone through the Comédie's organization; Coquelin congratulated her on abandoning her mad idea of resignation, as 'when one is lucky enough to have the honour of being at the Comédie-Française, one should stay there for the rest of one's career'; Febvre, another actor, advised her to stay put – 'you've got your living when you get old'; and Got said, 'Do you know what resigning like that is called? – Desertion!'

The best advice came from Madeleine Brohan, one of the Comédie's great artists, and a good and respected friend of Sarah's. She said, 'You poor darling, there's nothing to be done; you're an original whether you want it or not, nature's given you that crazy head of hair, you're too thin, you've got a musical instrument in your throat, it all sets you apart: it's a crime of *lèse-banalité*! That's the physical part. Then you can't hide what you're thinking, you're incapable of compromise, you won't put up with hypocrisy – and that's *lèse-société*. That's the long and short of it. So it's quite inevitable that you'll arouse jealousy, hurt people's feelings and get yourself disliked. If you let these attacks worry you then you're lost, because you won't have the strength to fight. If that happens I advise you to flatten down your hair, put on some weight and spoil your voice a bit, and then you won't worry anyone. But if you want to stay yourself, well then, darling, better get ready to climb that little pedestal of calumnies, rumours, adulations, flatteries, lies and truths. And when you're on top, hold on tight and cement your position by talent, hard work and good nature. Everyone will try and kick you off. But you'll stay there if you want to, and I hope you will, Sarah darling, because you really want so much to be famous. Personally I can't imagine why, all I've ever wanted is peace and quiet.'[5]

Brohan's little homily gave Sarah a moment of worry. Brohan was so beautiful with her sad eyes, the pure lines of her face, her tired smile ... Could she be right? Was resignation, peace and quiet the best way? Questioned, Brohan confessed that she was fed up with the theatre, she had had so many struggles within it; that the very thought of her marriage still appalled her; that motherhood had brought her nothing but worries, and love had broken her heart and worn out her body. Relieved, Sarah concluded that her own way was best after all. Brohan only wanted peace and quiet to recover from the wounds inflicted by a life she had already lived. And Sarah still felt – rightly – that she had all her life before her. Later, people would marvel at her apparent agelessness, at her ability still to play young lovers when she was in her sixties. Perhaps one of the reasons for this was that she really did take longer to age than other people. Now in her mid-thirties, she not only looked ten years younger than her age, but behaved that way as well. At a time when many women feel they are on the threshold of middle age Sarah, the mother of a sixteen-year-old son, conducted herself like the impossible young girl she could still appear to be.

So the resignation threat was withdrawn – 'Nothing but a bit of a joke!' said the Comédie's official chronicler, Georges d'Heylli. 'Mlle Sarah Bernhardt's departure would have been a sad day for the Comédie-Française ... but an even sadder day for herself.'[6]

The Comédie-Française, which had set off for London in such high spirits, returned much subdued; those who had been misunderstood were saddened, those who had failed to please were furious. Sarah had hardly been home an hour when Perrin was announced. He began by reproaching her gently regarding her excesses and the way she abused – and so publicly – her uncertain health, and as usual she defended herself. Was it her fault if she was too thin, if she had too much hair ...? If she tried to put on weight and shaved her head, everyone would say that she was courting publicity! 'But my dear child,' said Perrin, 'there are people who are neither fat nor thin, neither shaven nor hairy, and who reply yes and no.'[7] Sarah had to admit that it was so, but that she would never be like those enviable souls. But this discussion, interesting though it might be, was not the purpose of Perrin's visit. The next big date on the Comédie's calendar was the ceremony which would mark their return to their old home. He had come to advise Sarah that it might be better if she did not appear, as he had reason to think that a claque might be organized against her. She had occasioned, rightly or wrongly, a lot of bad feeling.

Sarah heard him out in silence, which discomfited him. Then she declined to abide by his suggestion. There was nothing she liked more than a fight. Besides, she knew all about the claque: she had already received three anonymous letters to that effect. She held one out for Perrin to

241

read: 'My poor skeleton, you'd do better to keep your nasty Jewish nose out of the Ceremony the day after tomorrow. I'm afraid it would just be a target for all the apples that are being baked with that in mind in Paris just now. Better tell the papers you've been coughing blood, and stay in bed to think about the consequences of too much publicity. – A Subscriber.'[8]

Perrin handed it back in disgust. The two others, Sarah assured him, were even nastier. There could be no question about her missing the Ceremony. 'Right!' agreed Perrin. 'We rehearse tomorrow.'

The artists came on to the stage in pairs, each holding a palm or a crown to honour the bust of Molière. When it came to Sarah's turn she entered alone and stood looking straight out at the audience, daring them to make good their threats. For a moment there was a strained silence. Then the house broke into a tumult of applause – a tribute to the courage of their sometime favourite who had won them back to her side. It was a great triumph. It was also the first of many such strained moments. The Parisian public always felt very ambivalent about Sarah. She was their discovery, they had created her, and when she did not show proper gratitude – by behaving badly, by going away and then expecting to be received back as though nothing had happened – they always had to be wooed until, invariably, they received her back into their bosom: until the next time. (Sarah remarks on the delight of her fellow actresses on this occasion, much more wholehearted than that of the actors. In her experience there was far less jealousy between women in the profession than between the sexes, where actors were always only too happy to do an actress a bad turn.)

So Sarah and the Comédie were reconciled. But it could never last. The real incompatibilities were too great, and it was not as if the marriage had been very enthusiastically contracted in the first place – on either side. The break came in April the next year, 1880. Sarah had not been well, and was feeling increasingly unhappy. The company was to put on *L'Aventurière*, a very mediocre piece by Augier, in which Sarah was to play the title role. She hated the play; she had not been well and considered herself under-rehearsed. Nevertheless, Perrin insisted that she should appear. She did so, with bad grace, and was duly slated. As Sarcey had had occasion to remark before, 'Sarah Bernhardt is so richly gifted an artist that she is able to do anything she wants. She had decided she was going to be bad and bad she was, beyond our worst expectations.'[9] The first night was on April 17; on April 18, after reading her dreadful notices, she sent in her resignation to Perrin. 'I didn't want to appear,' she wrote, 'but you absolutely insisted. I foresaw what would happen. It did – but even worse than I feared ... This is my first failure at the Comédie, and it will be my last. I warned you on the day of the dress rehearsal, but you took no notice. I am keeping my word. When you receive this letter I shall have left Paris. Please take this as notice of my immediate resignation. Yours faithfully, Sarah Bernhardt.'[10] Copies of this letter were sent to the papers, to make sure that this time it would be final.

If Sarah had expected the Comédie and the press to beg her to stay on yet again, her expectations were confounded. 'Is it the Comédie-Française's fault if one of its members would rather be a phenomenon than an artist?' demanded Sarcey. 'And is that news to Parisians? ... Mademoiselle Bernhardt has resigned and is leaving us. It is a pity, of course, but more so for her than anyone else. The Comédie-Française will lose a charming actress and will have to drop, for the time being, some plays which are hardly performable without her. But the number of these plays is small, for her art, divine instrument though it is, has not many notes. Her absence is to be regretted, but we shall get over it, and someone else will come up . . . Actors come and actors go. Remember the old proverb: the abbey does not collapse for want of a single monk.'[11]

20

In taking this step, Sarah could be tolerably sure that she was courting neither penury nor uncertainty. Sure enough, three days later Jarrett appeared once more with a contract for an American tour. The terms were generous: five thousand francs per performance plus half any takings in excess of fifteen thousand francs, plus a thousand francs a week for hotel expenses, and a special Pullman train for the inevitable travelling with a bedroom for Sarah, a salon with a piano, four beds for her personal staff, and two cooks. Jarrett would take ten per cent. There would also be a hundred thousand francs on signature to cover the expenses of preparing for the tour. This time Sarah signed at once: all she wanted was to get out of Paris. The Comédie had started a lawsuit against her, claiming three hundred thousand francs damages for breach of contract. 'I hardly gave it a thought,' she says.[1]

The American tour was scheduled for the autumn; it was now May. To fill the gap and work up a repertoire, Sarah decided to assemble a company which she would first take to Brussels and London, where she hoped to capitalize on the reputation she had made the previous summer. The plays she would take on tour included some of her greatest successes from the Comédie – *Hernani*, *Phèdre*, *Le Sphinx*, *L'Etrangère* – plus four new plays: Scribe and Legouvé's *Adrienne Lecouvreur*, Meilhac and Halévy's *Frou-Frou*, and two by Dumas *fils*: *La Princesse Georges* and *La Dame aux camélias*. *La Dame*, after her first incarnations as Mlle Doche and Aimée Desclée, had languished; the Comédie had tried a revival, but without success. According to Pierre Berton, who was a member of this original troupe of Sarah's, this was because Dumas' original version was almost unplayable. Sarah had suggested substantial alterations prior to the Comédie's unsuccessful revival, but these had been angrily rejected by Dumas, and failure had ensued. Now, when Dumas heard about Sarah's new company, he got in touch with Sarah and 'begged' her to play it including the amendments she had suggested.[2] (Or maybe he merely swallowed the bitter pill in the interests of having his play revived. Thirteen years later, in 1893, Sarah persuaded him to attend a revival of what was now her most frequently-acted role, and he was not at all happy to see, when the curtain rose, a great many characters onstage who had never featured in his play. Sarah had found that the opening supper did not have enough guests, and had added guests of her own: for example, she had given one of the originals a natural son, who joked with his father – and so on. When, in the interval, Dumas visited her in her dressing-room, she threw herself into his arms and murmured, in that golden voice, 'Are you happy, maître?' To which he replied, 'It's very good,' but added in a low voice, 'but it's another play.'[3]) At any rate, with or without Dumas' approval, *La Dame* became the cornerstone of her repertoire – a role it also played for Eleonora Duse, who was, as we shall see, as utterly different from Sarah as it is possible to imagine. They differed here, too: although Duse, like Sarah, regularly reduced audiences to tears with her interpretation of Marguerite Gautier, she grew to loathe the part and the play; acting it became a kind of purgatory for her, while Sarah always revelled in it.

This summer tour was an enormous success – not only in the eyes of the audience, but of the critics as well. It seems clear that in this summer of 1880, Sarah Bernhardt was at her apogee: her talent had matured, and her beauty was at its height. The French critics, who had been unanimously vitriolic regarding her antics surrounding the break with the Comédie, nevertheless followed her to Brussels and London, perhaps because summer is a dead season in the Paris theatre, perhaps because their curiosity (and that of their readers) compelled them to do so. To their astonishment, and, it is clear, somewhat to their chagrin, Sarah, whom they had dismissed as being no real loss to the national company, and for whom they had predicted a gloomy future without it, rose to unprecedented heights. Auguste Vitu, who had thundered, 'Let her go abroad with her monotonous voice and morbid whims,' wrote of her performance as Adrienne Lecouvreur (with which she opened in London): 'The sincerity of my admiration cannot be doubted when I confess that in the fifth act Sarah Bernhardt rose to a height of dramatic power, to a force of expression, which could not be surpassed. She played the long and cruel scene in which the poisoned Adrienne struggles against death in her fearful agony, not only with immense talent, but with an artistic science which up to the present she has never revealed.' (*Adrienne Lecouvreur* remained perhaps the most famous, certainly the most harrowing, of Sarah's many set-piece death scenes – scenes in which she died so variously, convincingly and ingeniously. It was, of course, a subject to which she had always given long and detailed thought.) And of her *Frou-Frou*, which came next, Sarcey, who had dismissed her with the phrase, 'There comes a time when naughty children must be sent to bed,' concluded: 'I don't think that in the theatre emotion has ever reached so poignant a pitch. There are in the art of the stage these exceptional moments when artists are transported out of themselves, beyond themselves, and do better than their best, in obedience to the dictates of some familiar spirit or *daimon* such as Corneille used to say whispered rhymes into his ears.'[4] This success in *Frou-Frou* had been particularly important to Sarah: everyone had been exceedingly nervous, not knowing how this possibly rather scandalous play would be received, and it had been rehearsed until all hours. Afterwards Sarcey said to her, 'Well, that was an evening which would reopen the doors of the Comédie-Française to you, if you wanted.'

To which she replied, 'Don't let's talk any more about that.'

'What a pity!' What a pity!' he concluded.[5]

That, too, was the opinion – arrived at, we may be sure, with equal reluctance – of the Comédie itself. Perrin had shown how little he had forgiven Sarah by, at the last minute, preventing Coquelin from coming over to partner her during this London season. But now, notwithstanding Sarah's reiterations to Sarcey that nothing would induce her to reconsider her position, Got was dispatched as an ambassador to try and induce her to rejoin after her American tour.

It was an extraordinary tribute to the blinding quality of Sarah's brilliance, but there was never any chance that Got would succeed. Sarah herself commented that Got was the wrong man to send. If it had been Worms, his frank affection might have persuaded her; if it had been Delaunay, she might have found it hard to resist the all-pervasive charm and grace with which he presented his absolutely unconvincing case. But Got had neither affection nor charm. Rather, he was genuinely convinced that the Comédie must be the acme of any sane actor's aspirations. It was an ensemble – the quality of its ensembles was the hallmark of the best French theatre, and the Comédie stood at the peak of this tradition. But 'this doesn't prevent those artists who are born geniuses from developing their personality to its highest degree. The teaching at the Conservatoire supports the weak without holding back the strong.'[6] Convinced as he was of this – that if Sarah wanted to shine, she could shine nowhere so brightly as at the Comédie – he informed her how lucky she was to be able to re-enter the company on her return from America, when she would undoubtedly be worn out. The advantage would be all hers.

But this was not how Sarah saw it. For now, as only once before in her life – when she was running her hospital in 1870 – she was tasting the sweets of freedom and control, and she found that they suited her as nothing else did. It was the beginning of a sea-change in her character so extreme that, reading about the indomitable, tireless Sarah of later years, it is almost impossible to believe that this is the same person as the capricious, unreliable young star who set her colleagues by the ears at the Comédie-Française. Miraculously she found that her health improved; she was more relaxed, less nervous. 'Resting upon laurels gained by myself alone, I slept better,' was how she put it; and sleeping better, she ate better, and so got stronger. And if being in charge of her own fate made her feel less tense, conversely the chanciness of her new way of life – the prospect of being suddenly left without money, of the continuous, unyielding treadmill she would have to face running her own troupe, the endless tours no matter how tired or ill she might be, the constant knowledge that, if she was in control, the price she paid was that she could rely on nobody to look after her if things went wrong – all this worried her not at all. It was true that this way of life had destroyed more than one famous actress. Marie Dorval had been no less celebrated in her time than Sarah, and had ended her life tired, ageing, ill, and touring, relentlessly touring, for only so could she make enough money to support her husband, her daughter, herself – and she made less and less . . . This was all Got could see in prospect for Sarah. But that was never Sarah's way of looking at things. To a friend who once asked her the name of her banker she replied, 'I haven't any money. When I've got it, I spend it; when I haven't any more, I earn some.'[7] She had that complete self-confidence and that ability to live entirely in the present which are the two essentials of the happy freelance. There was never a chance that, having escaped, Sarah would ever again bind herself in slavery to someone else's ensemble.

Some, but by no means all, of the outstanding actors of the period chose Sarah's way. Duse, Bernhardt, Henry Irving, ran their own companies, but Ellen Terry and Coquelin, who were equally brilliant, chose to appear under other people's aegis. The latter were the embodiment of Got's ideal – actors of genius who nevertheless benefitted from and complemented the ensemble: sublime interpreters of the great classics. The former, however, relied for their appeal on the dominance of their own characters, and could and often did carry the most mediocre supporting cast, the most indifferent material, to great heights. Indeed, the paradoxical thing about them is that they seemed often to achieve their greatest and most sublime effects in mediocre vehicles. Maurice Baring, who often saw Irving act, makes the point that he 'distorted, travestied and sometimes butchered Shakespeare to make a Lyceum holiday', and that 'his successes were more popular and more artistically satisfactory when the occasions, instead of being Shakespeare, were plays like *The Bells* or Wills' *Charles I*, or *The Lyons Mail*, when it did not matter what he did with the play, when the play without him was nothing, just so much material, practically a scenario of which his personality made a masterpiece – the masterpiece being his performance'.[8] Similarly with Duse. She was a sublime interpreter of Ibsen; but, that apart, her great successes were with the stock 'warhorse' repertory popularized by Sarah, which she hated but transformed, while she never succeeded with the plays Gabrielle D'Annunzio wrote for her, and flopped in Shake-

250

speare's *Antony and Cleopatra*. As for Sarah, she and only she could play the absurd vehicles created for her by Sardou and Edmond Rostand. They were grandiose, they were sometimes ridiculous and often sentimental and melodramatic, but in Sarah's hands they were moving and magnificent. 'The best,' she liked to say, 'is the enemy of the good.'

In 1880 most of this was still in the future. But from the outset Sarah was quite sure of her style. Some things she would *never* do. William Graham Robertson, a famous scenic artist of the time, describes one of Ellen Terry's most wonderful stage effects – as 'Fair Rosamund': 'She looked her loveliest, especially in the rich gown of her first entrance, a wonderful, Rossettian effect of dim gold and glowing colour veiled in black, her masses of bright hair in a net of gold and golden hearts embroidered on her robe.' The effect, however, was not what it seemed: 'The foundation was an old pink gown, worn with stage service and reprieved for the occasion from the rag-bag. The mysterious veiling was the coarsest and cheapest black net, the glory of hair through golden meshes was a bag of gold tinsel stuffed with crumpled paper, and the broidered hearts were cut out of gold paper and gummed on. The whole costume would have been dear at ten shillings.'[9] By contrast, Sarah's first act, as soon as the American contract was signed, was to go out and spend a fortune on elaborate clothes. She ordered twenty-five outfits at Laferrière, who was then her couturier; from Baron she ordered six costumes for *Adrienne Lecouvreur* and four for *Hernani*, while her *Phèdre* costume, which alone cost four thousand francs, was made by a young stage designer called Lepaul. In all, these thirty-six costumes cost sixty-one thousand francs – three times the highest yearly salary Sarah had yet earned.

However, it was soon clear that it would not be hard to recoup these expenses. The average London taking was nine thousand francs, and a short tour of the French provinces organized for her on her return by her old friend Duquesnel brought in another fifty thousand.

Then it was time to set off for America. It was the beginning of a voyage which was to go on, almost uninterrupted, for the next forty years.

21

International touring, in the way it was practised by Sarah, was a recent phenomenon. Of course, actors had toured from time immemorial. But the limits of their territories had been set by the distance it was possible to travel in a day or a week, which until the nineteenth century had been dictated by how far a horse and cart, or an actor, might walk in the time. The coming of the steam engine had changed all that. It had opened up the seas and the American west; and it had opened up the further reaches of Europe and the Americas to anyone who cared to visit them. In 1855 Rachel visited Russia, and the following year, America, inspiring Emile de Girardin to comment that 'a great artist no longer belongs to his native country; he belongs to the civilized universe'. She was contributing, 'perhaps without suspecting it herself, to the fulfilment of true progress. Unknowingly she creates universality, unity, that is to say, civilization.'[1] The traffic was not all one way. In 1889, for instance, Buffalo Bill brought his circus, complete with rodeo and redskins, to Paris. But at this point, before moving pictures turned things so decisively around, Europe was generally the sender, America the recipient, of cultural events. Travelling players in the American backwoods gave scenes from Shakespeare – as an added attraction, Mark Twain makes his, in *Huckleberry Finn*, pretend they are British. New York welcomed, with varying degrees of warmth, William Macready, who was driven out by the anti-British Opera House riot in 1849; Rachel and the Italian

Adelaide Ristori, who played there against each other in 1855 – Ristori with considerably more success than Rachel; and now, Sarah.

In Sarah's account, the setting up of the American contract was, as we have seen, very straightforward. Jarrett, once he had agreed the deal, telegraphed to Henry Abbey, the leading American producer, who arrived in France thirteen days later and finalized the contract. But according to the ubiquitous Marie Colombier, things were slightly more complicated than that. Colombier was involved because Jeanne Bernhardt, Sarah's sister, who was to be one of the company, was taken ill, and Colombier was engaged to take her place until she should be better. The resourceful Marie augmented her income by sending back progress reports on the tour to the French papers, and these were later collected into a book. These reports, in Colombier's racy, catty style, definitely constitute a worm's eye view of what went on; and it was probably the resentment arising from what Marie considered the unworthy treatment meted out to her at this time, when the troupe, even old friends such as Colombier, lived so squalidly compared to the star and her entourage (not to mention a difference over money at the end), which led to the infamous *Sarah Barnum* book, published a few years later.

In this version Sarah, while she is still with the Comédie, signs a contract with Jarrett in which she agrees that, for three years, any theatrical enterprise she undertakes outside France should be arranged through him. (Even Sarah's own account is unclear as to when Jarrett first appeared: at one point it is just before the Comédie's London season, at another a year earlier, in 1878, which agrees with what Colombier says.) Sarah then dismisses this from her mind. A year late, during that first London season, Mayer, her director, proposes an American tour, to which she agrees, and signs another contract. Belatedly she thinks of Jarrett, but Mayer dismisses this – 'I'll fix it up with him.' Jarrett, however, takes the matter to court, and the court upholds him. A little later, Abbey presents himself in Paris, offers tempting prospects, and Sarah signs a third contract. 'But what about Mayer?' 'Bah! I'll do a European tour for him as compensation.' Mayer accepts this. Then comes the break with the Comédie. Sarah telegraphs Abbey, who sends his agent Schwab to Paris. In a month, a troupe is organized and rehearsing; they play in London, Belgium and France. In eight days they will leave for New York. Suddenly, like the demon king, Jarrett appears on the scene. 'So you made up your mind at last? Quite right! I think we shall do very well.' Sarah bows gracefully to the inevitable, and puts her affairs in his hands. And when they arrive in New York, the astonished Schwab finds that Jarrett is organizing everything.[2] Colombier's version, written immediately after the events in question, has the ring of chaotic truth to it. Sarah was perfectly capable of signing three contracts at once and leaving everyone else to sort out the mess. As for Jarrett, his behaviour as described seems equally characteristic.

Jarrett was a formidable operator. From 1880 until his death in 1886 he organized all Sarah's tours, and was, during this turbulent period, a centre of stability in her life. He was, when Sarah first met him, in his late sixties, tall, with 'the face of King Agamemnon, crowned with beautiful silver hair, the most beautiful hair I ever saw in a man. His eyes were so pale a blue that, when he was angry, they lost all colour and he looked blind. In repose he had a very handsome face, but when he laughed, his upper lip creased in a ferocious snort, revealing his teeth, and the corners of his mouth seemed to be pulled upwards by his pointed ears, which moved, as if on the alert for some prey. . . .'[3] And indeed, if his stories were to be believed, Jarrett could be a dangerous man. 'I've made my way with the help of two weapons, honesty and a revolver,' he would say. He had

255

found that honesty was the most effective weapon when it came to dealing with crooks, because they had never met it and often didn't believe it could exist. As for the revolver, he would point to a deep scar under one eye and recount how he had acquired it during a dispute over a contract for Jenny Lind, the celebrated singer. Jarrett had supposedly said, 'Look hard at this eye, sir – it can read in your thoughts everything that you're not saying.'

'Then it's a bad reader,' returned the other, 'it didn't see this!' – and he whipped out a revolver and aimed at the eye in question.

'Sir,' said Jarrett, 'this is the way to shoot if you really want to close it,' and he shot the man between *his* eyes, at which he dropped dead.[4]

The Sarah Bernhardt company set out, needless to say, in a blaze of publicity, on the whole resentful rather than well-wishing. 'Nestor' summed up the popular view in Paris. 'When this expedition is finished, let's hope she doesn't start another one. She owes her talent to Paris, for it is a talent not without its little peculiarities, and only Paris would appreciate it . . .'[5] The voyage was to take place on the *Amérique*, a boat which had acquired a bad reputation when the captain, trying out a new pumping system, had inadvertently filled the hold with water and had to abandon ship – he had worked the pumps the wrong way round. Now, needing the good publicity which would accumulate around so celebrated a voyager, the company offered Sarah a cheap passage which she happily accepted. Only Angélo (her current lover and leading man) de Silva and Marie Colombier, then still a particular friend, travelled with her on the *Amérique*. The rest of the company went ahead in the *Wieland*, in less sumptuous style. There was a fond parting from Maurice, who was to live meanwhile with Julie's brother Edouard Kerbernhardt and numerous family (is it possible that Sarah's devotion to her son was increased by the undoubted fact that she never actually spent very much time with him?) During the voyage Sarah inadvertently prevented Mrs Abraham Lincoln from jumping overboard and assisted at the birth of a baby, whose godmother she became, to a steerage passenger. Otherwise it was uneventful and they arrived in New York on 27 October to find that an early frost had iced up the Hudson so that a passage had to be broken for them – an eventuality which naturally delighted Sarah, the more so as she was very superstitious and an arrival in bright sunshine would have been a bad omen for her opening night.

'I strongly suspect,' wrote Henry James of Sarah at this time, 'that she will find a triumphant career in the Western world. She is too American not to succeed in America. The people who have brought to the highest development the arts and graces of publicity will recognize a kindred spirit in a figure so admirably adapted for conspicuity.'[6] Certainly no actress who refused to meet the press would help her career in America, as Eleonora Duse was to prove thirteen years later, when she issued a statement (much to the fury of her impresarios) that she had come 'not to speak but to act', and was coolly received.[7] Nevertheless, not even Sarah could cope with the reception awaiting her in New York.

By the time the Bernhardt troupe arrived in New York, there can hardly have been an inhabitant of the entire United States who was unaware of the impending event, nor of the scandalous nature of the star herself. Not only had Jarrett been assiduous in his advance publicity, but all the details he had *not* supplied, chiefly relating to the scandalous and indiscriminate nature of Sarah's love-life, were filling the press and giving rise to a spawn of scurrilous pamphlets. One such entitled 'The Loves of Sarah Bernhardt' recounted how she had seduced all the crowned heads of Europe including the Pope. Another stated 'on incontestable authority' that she had given birth to four illegitimate sons, one by a hairdresser, one by the Emperor Louis-Napoléon, one by the Tsar of Russia and one by a man condemned to the guillotine for murdering his father. Neither story was entirely fanciful – rumour had it that Sarah and the Prince of Wales were very good friends, and rumour was probably right. She certainly did have one illegitimate son. And she knew and liked the anarchist Vaillant, and had herself specially called so that she should not miss his execution. Thus do great oaks from tiny acorns spring.

One natural result of all this, in the stronghold of raucous morality that was one aspect of America, was a wave of writings, meetings and sermons protesting that such a harbinger of vice should not be allowed to sully American theatres, and discussing how best to defend virtuous Americans from her example. Another was a jostling mass of journalists and other interested parties poised, in the freezing New York morning, to leap into boats and race to set eyes on the phenomenon, question her, examine her clothes, her entourage, her deportment – in a word, to *interview* her. A launch containing Henry Abbey, her impresario, some members of the company and a great many journalists was first to reach the *Amérique*. As it approached a tricolour was raised and a band played the 'Marseillaise'. As soon as a gang-plank was in place, everyone rushed on board. Sarah, appalled, locked herself in her cabin and refused to come out. The Transatlantic Steamship Line's agent ordered a champagne breakfast for all the visitors while they waited. Jarrett, who did not sympathize with this sudden horror of publicity, went and knocked on her door and told her to get ready at once to meet the press. Later, when Sarah, horrified at some of the things that were being written about her, wanted to protest and sue for libel, he was not sympathetic either. 'Mademoiselle, we must not discourage publicity!'' was his only reaction to that. As for escaping the reception committee whose only desire was to welcome her in style – he would not hear of it. She gave in, came out, leant on his arm and allowed herself to be led to the lounge where the journalists were waiting. As she stepped over the threshold, the band burst once again into the 'Marseillaise' and the French consul spoke some words of welcome. After that, the journalists were free to attack their prey.

She was, they agreed, a vision. 'Mlle Bernhardt,' reported the *New York Times*, 'glided into the main salon as lightly and as rapidly as a leaf borne along by the wind. It was the opinion of all present that no pen-picture of the "divine Sarah" has done her justice. The apparition was not gaunt, nor did it have red hair . . . but was somewhat ethereal, yet womanly. A perfect head, set almost defiantly on a slim and delicate neck, is crowned by a wealth of silken hair with a tint of burnished gold . . . A faultless nose of the best Hebrew type reveals in its delicate chiseling the aesthetic artist and her race . . . Mlle Bernhardt was enveloped in an unusually long sealskin ulster with a robe . . . of olive-green cashmere . . . A heavy silk boa was loosely wound around the trage-dienne's neck.'⁸ Sarah also wore long gloves and a great many gold and jewelled bangles. The *New York Times* considered this a refreshingly simple and unelaborate toilet.

For an hour, under the relentless gaze of Jarrett, Sarah shook hands and tried to repeat unpronounceable names. Soon she ceased to take any of this in, or indeed to think of anything except how much she would have liked to remove her rings, since all this hand-shaking was beginning to be literally agonizing. All she could do was smile mechanically and keep on shaking. 'Finally,' she recounts, 'I decided to faint. I gestured, as one who would but can no more . . . I opened my mouth, shut my eyes, and let myself collapse gently into Jarrett's arms.'⁹ Immediately another kind of pandemonium broke out, as everyone hastened to advise on the best thing to do. When suggestions began to be made to the effect that her corset should be loosened (she didn't wear one) and her dress undone, Sarah began to be nervous; when a doctor arrived with a bottle of ether, she judged it was time to come to. Jarrett took pity on her and told the journalists that, for the moment, enough was enough. They would have to come and find Mlle Bernhardt at the Albemarle Hotel, where she was staying. As they left, Sarah noticed that each of the journalists had a private word with Jarrett. When they had all gone, he explained that they had all been asking for personal interviews, which he had granted, at ten-minute intervals, starting in an hour's time. Meeting Sarah's recalcitrant gaze he only said, 'Oh, yes! It's absolutely necessary.'

Sarah, however, was adamant. First of all she intended to have a nap, on her own. As soon as she arrived at the hotel and had been shown to her apartment she rushed to the bedroom, locked and bolted all the doors; against the only one without a lock she pushed a heavy piece of furniture. Then she lay down on the carpet and went to sleep. As she drifted off she could hear the angry voices of the reporters and Jarrett crossly trying to cope with them on the other side of the door. When she woke an hour later they were still there – more than a hundred of them now, Mme Guérard and her maid Félicie assured her. Quickly she told them to get out a white dress, then go and fetch Jarrett, who, surprised to see her fresh and smiling, postponed the scolding he had prepared. Then she entered the salon which had been readied for her.

To her astonishment, it had been arranged to recall, as far as was possible, her Paris house. There were busts of Racine, Molière and Victor Hugo, big sofas, lots of cushions, and a great many potted palms – all courtesy of Mr Knoedler who kept a famous art gallery. Sarah was overwhelmed by this gesture, and delightedly made his acquaintance. She was presented to some other visitors, who gradually faded away. But the press relentlesssly stayed on. They asked her what was her favourite role ('None of your business!'), what she ate when she got up ('Oatmeal!' said Jarrett), what she ate during the day ('Mussels!' said Sarah), what was her religion . . . 'Will it be like this at every town we visit?' Sarah wanted to know. Jarrett was able to reassure her. This was it. What she said now would be telegraphed the length and breadth of the States, just like all the calumnies which had preceded her arrival.

At the end of the ordeal Sarah took a deep breath. 'I really don't believe,' she said, 'that there can be a single person in the whole world, since reporting was invented, who has suffered more from it than I did on that first tour. But only death is fatal,' she concluded philosophically.

22

It was thus quite clear to everyone, from the raucous beginning, that America was indeed a different world; and the longer they stayed, the more evident this became.

After the baptism by interview, Sarah and the troupe had two days to rest before going down to Booth's Theatre, where they were to open.

Arriving at the stage door after lunch on what was to be the first day of rehearsals, Sarah saw an animated crowd waiting for her. It was clear they were neither artists nor reporters; there were no women, only men who seemed to be there on business, in dirty work clothes. As her carriage drew up there was a cry of 'There she is!' and they crowded into the theatre after her.

At the top of the stairs waited Jarrett, Abbey (whom Sarah always called Monsieur l'Abbé, much to his embarrassment), some reporters and some friends. Sarah was astonished to see Abbey, who was normally frigid and haughty, give a polite greeting to the leader of the unseemly mob behind her. They raised their hats to each other, and then Abbey led them onto the stage, where Sarah's forty-two trunks stood in serried ranks. Each of the ruffians placed himself between two trunks and then, at a given signal, raised the lids. Meanwhile Jarrett had explained what was happening. This was the customs examination. A recent change in the law meant that theatrical costumes and scenery imported for use by individual actors were liable for duty. Another word was given: and, as one, the grubby mob plunged their hands into Sarah's precious and fragile laces and embroideries. Sarah, wrapped to the ears in chinchillas, watched in agony; her maid was in tears. Rapidly, she decided what must be done. Félicie was to take out each dress herself and show it to the men before laying it gently down where it would not get spoilt. Meanwhile more visitors had arrived: two ungainly ladies who, it turned out, were the dressmakers brought in by the customs to assess the value of the outfits. They, too, plunged in with eager oohs and aahs, avid to know how everything was cut and how much it had cost. This went on until half-past five, when the men offered to repack the trunks. Even more horrified than before at this prospect, Sarah declined and sent out for five hundred metres of blue tarlatan, to keep the dust off her dresses, shoes, gloves, coats, hats ... She was finally taken away to see the not-yet-completed Brooklyn Bridge, a less unattractive aspect of this bizarre land.

For another two days the customs examination continued, while Sarah raged and fretted. Finally it was done. It was Thursday 4 November: the company was due to open on Monday evening. The news (according to her memoirs) was that Sarah could not have her trunks until she paid twenty-eight thousand francs duty. In cold fact the sum was less dramatic. Her wardrobe had turned out to be less extensive than the customs had anticipated (what can they possibly have had in mind?) and everything she had worn at least once was admitted duty-free, so that the final sum was estimated at a fraction of what they had feared. The sum was lodged, and the trunks released.

The opening performance was *Adrienne Lecouvreur*. It was a glorious success. Afterwards, a lady was heard to remark, 'I'm *disappointed* to have been disappointed. I hoped she wouldn't be so good. I would never have believed a person could act so well as that!'[1] When she got back to her hotel after the performance, the persistent crowd forced Sarah to appear on the balcony outside her room (Abbey had chosen her particular suite in hopes of just this eventuality). The temperature was minus twelve, but Sarah was warmed by the affection of this crowd which she had been warned was generally cold in temperament, and which had been regaled with so many unpleasant and defamatory stories about her. When she came back in and shut the window she said, 'I'm happy, very happy!'

'Do you know, madame,' said a New Yorker, 'that even the emperor Don Pedro of Brazil didn't get a better reception?'

Marie Colombier couldn't prevent herself replying, 'Yes, but he was only an emperor!'[2]

Not all New Yorkers were as enthusiastic as this. New York high society, for whom exclusiveness was all, definitely excluded Sarah. It was a very recent creation – it had been born only in 1872, when Ward McAllister had created the twenty-five Patriarchs who governed the invitations to the Patriarchs' Balls. He had set out his principles quite clearly: 'We knew . . . that the whole secret of the success of these Patriarch Balls lay in . . . making it extremely difficult to obtain an invitation to them, and to make such invitations of great value.'[3]) In Chicago the principle of exclusiveness was taken even more literally. Mrs Potter Palmer, the city's social arbiter, kept people out in the simplest possible way: there were no handles on the outside of her doors, so that admission might only be obtained at the discretion of those within.) And although, in the fast-moving New World, not so very many years need lapse between exclusion and acceptance – 'Where were the Vanderbilts, socially, even five years ago? The Astors had just fifteen years the social start,' commented *Town Topics* in 1877 – no one who wanted to be accepted would receive a person as doubtful in every respect as 'the Bernhardt', as she was universally known. The rich New Yorker James Stebbens, known in Paris as 'le tableaumane', had given a party in the Champs Elysées and was greatly honoured when Sarah consented to perform at it. But in New York, when she went to see him, he would not allow her into his house. 'But, monsieur,' she protested, 'in Paris I only came to your house because you came ten times to beg me to play *Le Passant* in your salon. And now that I'm in America you won't receive me?'

'Ah, mademoiselle,' replied Stebbens, 'we are not in Paris any more: we're in New York!' Apparently Sarah's social reputation in that city had been irreparably sullied by an early dinner at Delmonico's with, among others, the notorious James Gordon Bennett, the owner of the *New York Tribune* and a playboy of ill social repute . . .[4] When her art exhibition opened – she had brought with her twenty-four sculptures and paintings, and announced that she intended to complete a portrait of Marie Colombier while she was in America – there was an unnerving hour when it seemed as though nobody was going to attend it. The invitations for the private view were for seven; by seven forty-five, when Sarah herself arrived accompanied by Jarrett and Colombier, hardly anyone was there. Then at eight the rush began, and by the time Sarah left at ten the place was packed and it was hardly possible to breathe.

These complex social aspects of the reputedly egalitarian United States could hardly have been anticipated. It was a strange new world indeed. In fact America at this period was a closed book to most Europeans – to all those, that is to say, who did not take it into their heads to emigrate there. The European view of America was generally formed by travellers' tales of adventures in the New World – books such as Frances Trollope's *Domestic Manners of the Americans* – an early contribution to the genre, published in 1839 – or Paul Bourget's *Outre-Mer*, published in 1895. It was a time when virtually all the social traffic was in the other direction, a traffic which found its chroniclers in Henry James and Edith Wharton and whose frequent aim was the alliance of American wealth with resonant European titles. The antics of Ward McAllister and his friends were specifically dedicated to the aping of that layer of European society into which the daughters of Patriarchs might hope to marry.

Certainly the fact that so much American culture was European in origin was of no small importance to the success of ventures such as Sarah's. A large proportion of the audience would already be familiar with the plays she was presenting, and this meant that people would be more likely to understand what was going on, even in French. But this was not to say that America did not have its own heroes, some of whom were known throughout Europe. There was one American in particular who had captured the European imagination – had, indeed, captured the imagination of the entire civilized world – and that was Thomas Edison. The Wizard of Menlo Park, the inventor of the gramophone, the electric light, and (so he claimed) the telephone was truly a fabulous figure – much more so than earlier wizards, because his magic was not buried in myth but was real and available to all. It must have seemed at times that there was nothing that was beyond him. So it was hardly surprising that Sarah, the goddess of the old world, decided she must pay a visit to Edison, the wizard of the new.

Perhaps she decided on this off her own bat; or possibly she was following a sort of script. For just before her departure, on 4 September 1880, the *Gaulois*, of which her devoted friend Arthur Meyer was the editor, began to publish a strange novel called *L'Eve nouvelle* (later to be retitled *L'Eve future*) by Villiers de l'Isle Adam. The central character of this fantasy is Thomas Edison, who in his sorcerer's den of a laboratory in Menlo Park, creates, for the benefit of one Lord Ewald, an Andreid – an artificial woman, the eponymous future Eve – in the image of a celebrated actress, Miss Alicia Clary, whom Ewald loves to distraction but in vain. And this Andreid, whose name is Hadaly, is kept – for one cannot say she lives – in a sumptuous coffin, whence she arises when she is summoned. Was Sarah, then, on that freezing night when she and her company entrained for Menlo Park after their last New York performance, re-enacting in some way this fantasy whose central female characters clearly owe so much to herself? It would perhaps be strange if she were *not*.

At any rate, off they all went, though not without a good deal of commotion first – for the next day they were due to arrive in Boston and everything had to be shifted on to the special train which was to carry Sarah and her company all round the United States and Canada.

The afternoon's show was *La Dame aux camélias* – known to Americans in translation as *Camille*. By now Sarah had become the rage of New York. It had taken her twenty-five minutes to push through the crowd of rubbernecks and souvenir-seekers which stood between her carriage and the stage door before the performance, including a woman armed with large scissors whose aim was to secure a lock of Sarah's hair but who only succeeded in clipping the end of one of the feathers on her hat. There were seventeen calls after Act Three, twenty-nine at the end. The play had finished an hour late, due to all the applause and diversions. Then Jarrett arrived with the information that more than five thousand people were waiting for Sarah outside the theatre. What could be done? It seemed as though she was destined never to leave. Jarrett suggested that her sister Jeanne, who had by now joined the company (much to Marie Colombier's disgust, since Marie now had to relinquish most of her roles), should put on Sarah's coat and boa and leave by the stage door while Sarah slipped out the front way. Finally, at nine o'clock, the company was able to board the train and set off for Menlo Park.

Menlo Park, in New Jersey, is not very far from New York. Nevertheless the train journey took five hours, as Sarah's train was always being forced into sidings to let other trains pass, or having to wait at signals. Finally, at two in the morning, they arrived at Menlo Park station. Two carriages were waiting for them. It was snowing heavily. Only the dim light of a single carriage lamp illuminated the station, for orders had been given to turn off the electric lights (with which Menlo Park was naturally provided). Behind the light cabriolet with the lantern was another carriage, larger and without a lamp. Sarah, Jeanne, Jarrett and Abbey got into the first, the rest piled into the second, and they set off through freezing snow.

Sarah dozed, buried in her furs as the carriages jolted through the snow. Then, suddenly, she was wakened with a start by a shout of 'Hip, hip, hurrah!' and, as if by magic, all the countryside was lit up. They had arrived.

Inevitably, at that hour, in that company, nobody knew quite what to do with themselves. Mrs Edison presented Sarah with a bunch of flowers; then Sarah tried to guess which of the four men standing before her was Edison himself. 'One of them blushed slightly, and there was such an anguish of embarrassment in his blue eyes that I knew it must be him,' she recalled.[5] Marie Colombier told her readers what happened next: 'Sarah looks at him in silence for half a minute. Edison blushes. Doña Sol holds out her hand. A *shake-hand*, during which she pays the man of genius a careful compliment. Unfortunately, Edison hasn't understood a word . . . Sarah begs Jarrett to help out. Solemnly he translates: "The great joy of Mme Sarah Bernhardt at meeting a man of such genius etc etc." Edison bows, his face now purple. He tells Sarah, through her agent, that he will demonstrate some of his machines for her.'[6] As the demonstration progressed, however – the electric light, the telephone, the phonograph – everyone

268

relaxed, and by the end, Edison was enjoying himself so much that he insisted on playing the whole of 'John Brown's Body' on the phonograph, as recorded on the spot by two of his aides.

The company left Menlo Park amazed, and seized by helpless giggles.

The company's introduction to America by way of New York had been a feverish one; and the same mad pace was to be kept up for the following seven months, during which time they ranged from Montreal to New Orleans. Travel has always been the legendary American activity, and this was the age of the railroad, when the railway kings vied with each other to produce the most luxurious travelling hotels it was possible to imagine. Sarah's Pullman was one of these. Her private car consisted of a saloon, with plush, furbelows and flowers just like the house in the avenue de Villiers, panelled, carpeted, and with an upright piano. She had a bedroom, there were sleeping compartments for her personal staff and members of her family, a bathroom and an observation platform. The car occupied by Jarrett and Abbey was very similar. There were also two cooks specified by the contract, who prepared her food. The rest of the company, however, (apart from the leading man, Angélo, who was Sarah's current lover, and so naturally spent his off-duty time with her: the leading man on her tours usually doubled as her lover) did not travel in such style. They were given two Pullman cars in which to live, and when the company stayed two days in the same place, the train was often shunted into a siding and was used as an hotel. 'The artists grumble all the time about the way in which they are completely abandoned, without guides or directions, in the middle of a strange country, never two days in the same place,' reported Marie Colombier, who, we may be sure,

269

contributed her share to the grumbles. 'We live on pre-
serves, sandwiches and tins of sardines . . . When we are
lucky enough to find that rooms have been reserved for us
in an hotel, it is usually impossible to get a meal, as dinner-
time is long past: which doesn't prevent us being charged
the fantastic prices which have been agreed between the
agent and the hotelkeeper.'[7] When special favours were
wanted, the lot of the company was wont suddenly to
improve. One day they were snowed up outside Chicago,
where they were due to play a matinée. Sarah, mindful of
her lost receipts, sent out conserves, turkey, partridges,
coffee, to the troops at the back of the train. They finally
arrived at two-thirty, rushed to the theatre, unpacked the
costumes and at half-past three were ready to perform to a
packed house.

The timetable was hectic. Evening performances usually
began at eight and ended at eleven; then, as often as not, it
was time to start out for the next destination, travelling
from midnight until morning, or sometimes until midday.
As soon as the company arrived, they went straight to the
theatre to rehearse for the evening's performance – lighting,
scenery, props, all had to be set up. Inevitably, there were
some disasters. One night in the deep south the space on
stage was very limited, and the table bearing the supper for
one of the scenes in *La Dame aux camélias* would not fit
through the doorway. The audience roared encouragement,
a young black boy jumped on stage to help: finally, the table
was manoeuvred into place via the chimney. Not long after,
a sudden gust of wind blew over one of the flats. These were
made of paper, and the artists found themselves sitting with
their heads protruding through their erstwhile walls.

Under such circumstances, obviously, the performance
deteriorated into farce. And at other times, too, farce crept
in, though the audience did not always realize it. Since the
company performed in French, and since, outside the large

270

cities, few if any members of the audience were likely to speak French, they were hardly to know if liberties were taken with the text. Even in large cities, although the audience might pretend to understand, it is doubtful whether very many did so. It was noticeable that when Sarah played in Montreal, to French-speaking audiences, there was much more, and more appreciative, reaction while the play was going on, not to speak of the absence of the rustling pages of a thousand cribs. 'All the other critics understand the language perfectly,' complained Max Beerbohm in London − apropos, as it happened, of Duse: but exactly the same point might have been made about Bernhardt − 'else they would not be able to tell us unanimously that [her] technique is beyond reproach. The technique of acting lies in the nice relation of the mime's voice, gesture and facial expression to the words by him or her spoken. Obviously, if those words are for you so much gibberish, you cannot pass any judgment on the mime's technique.'[8] More than once, Sarah capitalized on the opportunities this afforded her. The Italian playwright Giuseppe Giacosa, who spent a fortnight touring with the Bernhardt troupe some years later, recorded an instance where the hall in which the company was performing was booked for another engagement at eleven, so that the play would have to end at ten or soon after. It was impossible to start early as the audience would not yet have arrived: an hour must therefore be cut from the text. Everybody was distressed at this brutal prospect, but finally Sarah, accepting the inevitable, set to work with a will 'in the same way that a woman, seeing her house attacked by robbers, might set fire to the beams herself so that the horror of destruction is less drawn out'. The play in question was *La Tosca* by Sardou, from which Giacosa wrote the libretto for Puccini's opera. 'I can't tell you the mess they made of poor old Tosca . . . When we got to the famous torture scene, where Tosca rages and screams at the cries and groans of her Mario, Bernhardt, struggling and twisting like one possessed, instead of the anguished words of the text, began to reel off the names of the characters of the drama . . . I had to rush off so as not to burst out laughing, but the public, delighted and moved, applauded fit to bring the roof down.'[9] On other occasions, Sarah took advantage of the audience's lack of familiarity with the language to relieve her feelings if she felt they were insufficiently appreciative. In Youngstown, Ohio, she roundly scolded the populace who had not packed the Grand Opera House to see her perform *La Dame aux camélias*. She told them Youngstown people were stupid and utterly lacking in appreciation – criticism which was received with wild applause as it was interpolated in a touching love-scene with Armand of which, clearly, nobody understood a word.[10] (It was not unknown for Bernhardt to play similar tricks even in Paris. Once during a performance of Hamlet she was heard to declaim: 'Would I had met my dearest foe in heaven, I know the names of those ignoble persons who have left the skylight open so I shall catch cold, Ere I had ever seen that day, Horatio!' And in one of the first-act tirades of *Phèdre* she spoke one day for quite a long time about how the lighting should be done, and no one so much as coughed.[11]) And when she did not make her own interpolations in the script, she often gabbled. She had always been fond of a technique known as *déblayage*, in which she would race through a lengthy speech in a monotone, with no regard for nuances, in order to put the maximum emphasis upon a specific verse. It was a technique deplored by Sarcey, but one to which she stuck, using it even more often and more extremely when she was touring. Her delivery when she was abroad was often too fast even for Frenchmen to follow; it may be questioned whether foreigners were able to do so. This technique had two advantages from Sarah's point of view. One was that of obvious dramatic effect; the other was that it got through the evening quicker. On one occasion, when she was in a particular hurry, she raced through *La Dame* at such speed that a member of her company dared to remonstrate. 'Careful or I'll die straight away!' was her reply.

Yet these tricks did not appear to dismay her audiences. They adored her: she was fêted wherever she went. And, clearly, for American (or South American, or German, or Russian, or British, or Italian) audiences, the niceties of language could hardly constitute the most important part of the evening's experience. Generally a rough crib was provided with which they were able to follow the action. Sarah's attraction, however, lay elsewhere.

But where? That is, of course, the question; and it is one to which there are several responses, some simple, some less so. The simplest, perhaps, is the charm of the spectacle she presented. As Henry James put it, 'Madame Sarah Bernhardt was helped to relieve the burden of the French tongue to the promiscuous public by being able to add to her extraordinary cleverness her singular beauty, and then to add ever so many wonderful dresses and draperies to that.'[12] Undoubtedly she was quite right to splash out on wonderful fabrics and embroideries, as she always did. If nothing else, it was always worth going to see Sarah Bernhardt for the sake of the spectacle – no mean attraction in the further reaches of the Americas.

Undoubtedly, too, we encounter here the knotty problem of what may be termed 'star quality' – in other words charisma, the power of holding an audience almost regardless of what is said or done.

What constitutes this quality? Nothing could be harder to define – though we all know when we are in its presence. Greta Garbo and Marilyn Monroe had it; John Kennedy had it. Sarah undoubtedly had it. We want to know everything about its possessors; we hang upon their words; we wish nothing better than to meet them; we would take any opportunity to see them.

The impact of star quality may of course be enhanced by well-handled publicity. As Henry James had pointed out, Sarah, even in the early days of her career, had been eagerly aware of this, and Jarrett, in orchestrating her American tour, found in her a (usually) more than willing collaborator. But hype alone was not enough of an explanation for the effects produced by Sarah. Nor were acting ability, good looks, the famous golden voice. All these things contributed to Sarah's stardom, but none of them explained it.

Part of the explanation may lie in the fact that Sarah desperately needed the constant acclaim, the exaggerated adulation, that are part of stardom – and whose obverse side is what most people would experience as a pitiless lack of privacy. They might see this as the price that must be paid for stardom: if you want the one, you must suffer the other. But for Sarah, so desperate for attention and so unwilling to risk a moment's avoidable isolation, this was perhaps more of an attraction than a penance; and perhaps this is an essential feature of the star mentality – for would anyone who did not actually welcome constant exposure be prepared to endure it even in order to be a star? Greta Garbo, forever wanting 'to be alone', had had enough by her mid-thirties and retired (though, as we shall see, there might have been other reasons for that). The psychologist Alice Miller talks about the effects of a childhood in which the child has been forced to ignore its own needs in order to accommodate the demands of a parent who may herself have had an unsatisfactory childhood, and who now puts her own needs before those of her child – very much the situation of Sarah and her sisters in Julie's household. One of the results of this may be an insatiable need for 'the drug of grandiosity', which must be taken continuously in order to push back the depression, emptiness and self-

alienation which may result from such a childhood: 'It is
. . . impossible for the grandiose person to cut the tragic
link between admiration and love . . . He seeks insatiably
for admiration, of which he never gets enough because
admiration is not the same thing as love.'[13] And in fact a
deprived and loveless childhood, with its resulting craving
for the compensating love and attention of the whole
world, is a clichéd precursor of 'stardom' and star
quality.

However, in Sarah's case, if we accept the hypothesis of
her multiplicity, this craving was complicated and intensified
by the trauma which gave rise to the disorder. For if the
desperate desire to be admired provided that single-minded
impetus to stardom which was so evident and extraordinary
to observers such as Henry James and Edmond Got, the
therapeutic need to give rein to her alternate selves in the
shape of the characters she played on stage meant that there
were no walls between Sarah and her stage personae – and
none, therefore, between her and her audience. A great
many of those instances where her fellow professionals try
to define the extraordinary capacity she possessed to attract
and hold the attention have to do with a blurring of the
edges of her own personality, as though she were inviting
her audience to share her very inmost self. 'Even in scenes
where she is depicting other passions than love, she is not
afraid to deploy, if I may put it this way, everything that is
most intimate and secret in her feminine self,' wrote Jules
Lemaître.[14] But this irresistible invitation to complete intimacy was, in an almost paradoxical way, combined with a
capacity to transcend the boundaries of whatever character
she happened to be playing. Ellen Terry talks about Sarah's
'capacity to transcend all personal and individual feeling on
the stage'. As a result, even in the most objectively ludicrous
situations, she carried complete conviction. Marguerite
Moréno, who acted with her some years later, noticed how

275

'she carried her listeners into the unreal world where she was so much at ease and where the most extraordinary occurrences were no more surprising than they would have been in a dream'.[15] Indeed, as I have suggested, it is possible that in many ways Sarah was more at home in this unreal world – where she was able to explore otherwise forbidden aspects of herself – than in the real world, where she often functioned so uneasily.

For some Americans, of course, the attraction of Sarah was as a symbol, a reminder of all they had left behind. Some *émigré* Frenchmen living out West, in Wyoming, learned that Sarah was to pass through a nearby station the following week. They planned to hold up the train, rush into her car, carry her off, put her in a buggy and gallop off with her at full speed. 'No doubt our illustrious guest would struggle. She would have hysterics.' Anyone who knew Sarah could have assured him that this was most unlikely – she would probably have enjoyed herself enormously! ... But once at the ranch, we should make amends by our respect. We should obtain our pardon and would live over again a few days of France, getting her to recite for us the finest passages in her repertory.' The plan was thought out: they even had a rehearsal with an earlier train, which they held up by galloping alongside the locomotive, their rifles on their knees, until the engineer stopped the train. All went well; they galloped off firing into the air, and set out to wait for the Sarah Bernhardt special, due at Green River at eleven fifty-two. One of their number was to board the train at the preceding station and would have his handkerchief at the door of the car containing Sarah. But nothing came of all this: the train did not arrive until midnight, and they saw their comrade get down, with no handkerchief in sight. 'Sarah Bernhardt

276

had passed through the town an hour earlier, by the Salt Lake City express.'[16]

The poignancy of that story lies in the fact that Sarah never knew anything about it. But about her welcome in Montreal she could be in no doubt whatever. Here, in the capital of Quebec, from French-Canadians marooned in a sea of Anglophone culture, Sarah received a welcome that overwhelmed even her.

They arrived at eleven at night: everything was covered in snow, the temperature was minus twenty-two. Just outside the station the train stopped, then began to crawl along so slowly it hardly seemed to be moving at all. A low noise began to be heard, which grew louder and louder, until it could be distinguished as music, and suddenly, with a cry of 'Vive la France!' from the enormous crowd gathered there, a band burst into the 'Marseillaise', Sarah stepped on to the platform flanked by Abbey and Jarrett, and an immense bouquet was thrust into her arms. Sniffing the flowers, she felt her face gently scratched by the petals, which had frozen solid. She, too, began to feel she would freeze solid, but everyone had to wait while a young man recited a long ode to Sarah by the French-Canadian poet Louis Fréchette – *'Salut donc, ô Sarah! salut, ô doña Sol! Lorsque ton pied mignon vient fouler notre sol, Te montrer de l'indifférence Serait à notre sang nous-mêmes faire affront, Car l'étoile qui luit la plus belle à ton front C'est encore celle de la France!'* 'He read very well, it is true,' recalled Sarah, but it was all too much – the crowds, the noise, the unprecedented cold. She took refuge, as so often, in a faint, coming to conveniently in her room at the Hotel Windsor. Later, her sister Jeanne told her that she had been saved, just as the crowd seemed about to crush her entirely, by an enormous man who had caught her as she fell and carried her to the hotel. Next morning the unknown saviour came to call – a singularly beautiful man, Sarah noted, but there was something worrying about him. Not long after she discovered what it was, for hot on his heels came the police: he was wanted for a murder in New Orleans, and four months later was hanged, to Sarah's fascinated horror.

Various exploits restored her gaiety: the anathema upon her and all her immoral works pronounced by the bishop of Montreal, which ensured capacity audiences and enormous receipts for all four of the company's performances in Montreal; a visit to the Iroquois Indians, organized by Fréchette, on which she was accompanied by Jeanne, Jarrett, and Angélo – 'For I always felt quite safe by his side, so calm and brave, and as strong as Hercules: the only thing he lacked to make him quite perfect was talent, but he didn't have any, and never had.'[17] And, above all, the enthusiasm of the students, who packed the theatre as soon as the door opened, sang while they were waiting, and rigged up arrangements of pulleys to send bouquets and doves over the heads of the crowd during curtain-calls, the bouquets to fall at Sarah's feet, the doves to fly around in freedom. Finally, at the end of the last performance, the orchestra played the 'Marseillaise' – (followed, at a signal from the Marquess of Lorne, the Governor-General, who stood throughout the French anthem, by 'God Save the Queen'). It was a tribute to France, personified by Sarah.

23

Bernhardt's first American tour, then, was a resounding success, both artistically and financially. By the time it ended, the magazine *Judge* estimated that America's loss ('We shall miss the tearing terror of Sarah Bernhardt. We shall miss her smile of love and her expression of trust and confidence. We shall regret the absence of that thin countenance on whose surface appeared more of the counterfeited soul than anybody has succeeded in picturing. We shall miss that magnificently cultured voice, those secluded eyes, those conspicuous teeth, that serpentine twist of the body.') would nevertheless be Sarah's gain, to the tune of about half a million dollars clear profit. In fact, after paying her agent's percentages, salaries and other expenses, the final figure was less than half that – $194,000, to be precise (about 500,000 francs): still a fair sum. The *Gazette Anecdotique* estimated that her average earnings per performance in the United States were 20,000 francs, compared with 5,000 francs for the average Comédie-Française performance in Paris.[1] This money was, then and always throughout her career, paid in gold coins which were carried around by Mme Guérard in a battered chamois-leather bag. Sarah insisted on this: the payment had to be in twenty-dollar gold pieces: she would never accept a cheque (she never had a bank account), and the payment had to be made at the end of the first act. This insistence on cash was regarded as just another of Bernhardt's quaint whims, to be honoured and grumbled about. In fact, for one whose financial situation was as precarious as Sarah's so often was, it made a great deal of sense. Her extravagant habits (and Maurice's) ensured that her footsteps were constantly dogged by impatient creditors. She was always having to sell jewels, horses, furniture, in order to pay her debts. But even in such circumstances a person must live, and a bank account is more easily distrained upon than a discreet bag which just happens to be stuffed full of gold coins.

In later years, when both the chamois bag and Mme Guérard had faded away, the current money was carried by her private secretary Pitou in an elegant flat leather box especially made for this purpose, which contained eight copper tubes each holding fifty of these gold pieces; when the box was full, the money would be changed, or stored in a strong-room. One rainy evening in San Francisco Pitou, who was trying to open a window of the automobile in which he and Sarah were riding, opened a door by mistake. The leather box fell out and flew open, the caps came off the tubes, and thousands of dollars in gold coins were scattered along the steeply inclined, slushy street in the pouring rain, to be rescued eventually by Sarah's leading man and her resident doctor while she and Pitou quarrelled about whose fault the accident had been.

By the time that incident took place Sarah was, and had been for many years, one of the legendary institutions of the theatrical world. But in 1881 this was far from being the case. The tour had been a success, but there was nothing settled about that, nor about Sarah. Everything about touring this extraordinary country in this bizarre way was as new to her as to all the other members of her troupe. And as for herself, the linchpin upon which the whole enterprise depended – she, too, was far from being a settled entity. She had discovered the only way of life which would suit her – or, to put it another way, the only one she could tolerate. She had to run her own show, and would do so for the rest of her life. Eventually this would change her from the spoiled, unreliable troublemaker she had undoubtedly been at the Comédie-Française into a trouper who was always ready to work harder and more unremittingly than anyone of her enormous acquaintance – although she always remained a creature of outrageous whim. But the transition was not effected all at once. For a few years after her departure from the Comédie, it was clear that, although the major problem – that of having to work for somebody else, thus not being in control of her own life – had been solved, Sarah was still by no means a stable character.

This nervous uncertainty hovers in the background of her account of this first tour, emerging to take concrete shape in some hysterical incidents over which hangs, like a pall, the old fascination with death.

Some of these brushes with death were not of her own making. One such took place in Chicago – or rather, on the way out of that city – and was a result of the extraordinary, overblown publicity which was the hallmark of the whole of this tour.

Such were the lengths to which the publicists went that even Sarah, with her delight in self-advertisement, was appalled by some of them. For example, there was the case of Henry Smith and his whale. Mr Smith had first emerged when she arrived at Boston from New York (finding, incidentally, none of the stuffy and self-conscious social rejection in Boston that she had encountered in New York: the Beacon Hill ladies were delighted to welcome her to their homes).

Henry Smith ran a cod-fishing fleet, and one of his boats had recently towed ashore a whale. The arrival of the cetacean coinciding with that of the actress, Mr Smith took the chance to make the headlines by persuading her to clamber aboard the (now dead) whale and gingerly extract a piece of bone. After this Sarah could not get away fast enough, but escaping Mr Smith was not so easy. Next day all the Boston papers carried a large drawing of Sarah and her bone, captioned 'How Sarah Bernhardt gets the whalebone for her corsets'. And the matter did not end there. Mr Smith, seeing he was on to a good thing, put his whale into a tent and charged twenty-five cents admission to view 'the gigantic whale killed by Sarah Bernhardt to furnish bones for her corsets which are made exclusively by Mme Lily Noah of New York'.[2] This show was advertised by a horse-drawn carriage sporting a large billboard and a megaphone, which dogged Sarah not only through Boston but also through her next tour stops at New Haven, Hartford and Springfield, at each of which towns Mr Smith, bearing a large bouquet, was waiting to greet the increasingly furious actress. (The whale was by now imperfectly preserved with several tons of salt.) Even in Chicago she could not escape Henry Smith. There, in the station waiting-room, he stood to greet her on her arrival, decked out in furs with a diamond ring on every finger, the customary bouquet in his hand. Sarah threw the bouquet back in his face: she was in such a rage that she hardly knew what she was doing or saying. But Smith could not get enough of it. It was all publicity, lovely publicity, and more visitors for his whale.

Sarah, in spite of this, greatly enjoyed Chicago, impressed by its vitality and the determination of all its inhabitants to *get somewhere* – qualities with which she could deeply empathize. But Henry Smith and his whale were not the only awkward pieces of publicity to meet her there. Another was provided by one of the city's leading jewellers, who filled his window with what he declared were 'Sarah Bernhardt's jewels' (some were; most were not) – a display which naturally drew gawping crowds and excessive valuations. As a result of this, the 'Bernhardt Special', when it left Chicago bound for St Louis, was held up by a gang of thieves after those jewels. But the hold-up (like that other attempted hold-up in Wyoming) went wrong. The plan had been for one of the gang to mark out Sarah's coach, ride underneath it, uncouple it, and then the gang would make off with the jewels at their leisure. In case this did not work, a fail-safe was organized: a derailment, to take place a little further along the line. Unfortunately for the gang, the coach was not decoupled, nor was the right train derailed, since a freight train which they had not been expecting was travelling the same line a little way ahead of Sarah's. So that, as things turned out, no one was hurt (though they might have been), and by the time Bernhardt's train halted behind the freight train, enough men were at hand to overpower the gang even without the aid of Sarah, who, priding herself on her shooting ability, had brought out her revolver and loaded it – though not very fast, as its holster was too tight to allow for a quick draw. But in spite of the fact that no great harm was done, the leader of the gang, a young man of twenty-five, was arrested and hanged a few days later: the second time during this tour that Sarah had encountered a man who was shortly after executed.

This set Sarah, in her memoirs, thinking about executions she had witnessed: for in spite of the fact that she was appalled by the death penalty, she was drawn to them, and with her professional eye for the detail of a death scene, recalled the dramatic essentials of each in a way that would have delighted Edmond de Goncourt. She had seen a man hanged in London – 'the most hideous . . . of all deaths'[3] – and recalled that he had seemed taller than the other people there, his thoughts loftier than theirs – 'perhaps because he was nearer than we were to the supreme mystery' – and that, the moment before they covered his face with the hood, he smiled. Then she had witnessed a man garrotted in Madrid, whose assertion of innocence, ringing and convincing, was translated for her by the English ambassador, who was with her at the time. The two others were both

guillotinings in the Place de la Roquette in Paris. One was a
medical student who had killed an old woman, in Sarah's
view because he was unbalanced from overwork, 'more
mad than bad'; 'a superior being . . . I can see him now,
pale, staring into space. His eyes were so sad, poor boy!'⁴
The other was Louis Vaillant the anarchist, who had visited
her in her dressing-room when she was playing Musset's
Lorenzaccio. He had told her that his politics were different
from the Florentine's, for where Lorenzaccio had killed only
the tyrant, his aim was to kill tyranny. Then a few days
later, he threw a bomb into the Chamber of Deputies, which
killed nobody but for which he was sentenced to death.
Sarah asked to be told when he was to be executed. That
night, after the theatre, she went to the corner of the rue de
la Roquette – she had not been able to get a permit to enter
the prison itself. In the streets everyone was singing and
dancing, for it was *dimanche gras*, the Sunday before Lent.
Sarah sat on a first-floor balcony and waited. 'The hours
passed slowly . . . I could hear only those strange noises
which, when the dawn came, revealed the scaffold all set
up. A man came and put out the street lights . . . The crowd
arrived slowly, huddled together. The streets were barred
. . . Then suddenly the Paris guards, doubled in case of some
anarchist disturbance, surrounded the scaffold. On a signal
they drew their sabres, the prison door opened. Vaillant
appeared, pale, energetic, brave. He cried *'Vive l'anarchie!'* in
a strong voice. There was not a word of response. They
seized him and threw him on to the block. The blade fell
with a thud . . . In a second the scaffold was demolished,
the ground swept, the barriers removed; and the crowd
rushed in to see if they could spot a drop of blood.'⁵ It is
hard to imagine that any of the plays she presented had a
denouement more dramatic, or better observed.

Those were other people's deaths. But several times on
this tour Sarah came within an inch of her own. She was

still unable to resist the urge to push things just too far; and now that there was no longer the hierarchy of the Comédie-Française to push against, she chose the even more exciting course of playing with her own life.

The first of these episodes occurred in Montreal. The last performance there, *Hernani*, took place on Christmas Day, ending with a triumphant farewell in which Sarah's sleigh was unharnessed from its horses and pulled by devoted students through a huge crowd round the city. Next morning at seven she and Jeanne set out with Jarrett to make a trip along the St Lawrence river. The river was of course frozen, and Sarah stopped the carriage to go and try the ice. Jeanne said 'Why don't we try that big floe which looks as if it's going to crack?' No sooner said than done: there they both were on the ice-floe, doing their best to make it break away from the bank. All of a sudden a terrified shout from Jarrett indicated that they had succeeded. They were adrift on the river. They both sat on the ice-floe and giggled. But the giggles soon stopped, because it became clear that it would not be easy to get off. The ice-floe floated back and forth, jolted by the current and other blocks of ice. People came, attracted by Jarrett's shouts, and tried to throw ropes and hooks, but it was impossible to get near enough, because the ice at the sides of the river was too fragile to hold a man safely. The women's lives on this occasion were saved because their floe got itself wedged between two large icebergs, solid enough for a man to climb on, and quickly, before it could break away in the current again, these were scaled and a harpoon lodged in the ice-floe. Then a ladder was leaned between the bergs, and Sarah and Jeanne climbed to safety. By the time they reached the bank Jarrett was waiting for them in the carriage. He was white, not with fright but with rage; if Sarah had died that would have been the end of the tour, and he stood to lose a fortune. All he said was, 'If you had died, Madame, that would have been most dishonest, because it would have meant you broke your contract by a wilful act.'[6]

On the next occasion Sarah's behaviour was even more irresponsible, for this time she endangered not only her own life but that of the whole troupe. From Chicago they had gone to Cincinnati, and were now on the train to New Orleans, their next stop. Suddenly the train came to a halt. There was a knock on Sarah's door, and in came Jarrett and Abbey. Shutting the door carefully behind them, they explained that, because of incessant rain during the past fortnight, the waters had risen so high in the bay of St Louis that the pontoon bridge which had to carry the train had become dangerous: at any moment it might be washed away. If they crossed the bridge they would be in New Orleans in a couple of hours; if they turned back, the journey would take another three or four days. They had the driver with them; he thought he could still get across and was prepared to take the risk; only, he was newly married, and would only attempt the crossing if Sarah would pay him five hundred dollars, which he would send at once to Mobile, the town where his wife and his father lived. Sarah, naturally, latched happily on to this proposition. What was a little risk compared with the prospect of three or four more days locked in the eternal snows? 'Pay him the money and let's go!' she cried. 'It was only at the moment of departure,' she writes, 'that I realized that I was risking the lives of thirty-two people, and without their consent. But by then it was too late.'[7] In fact it is hard to believe that she ever gave this a thought at the time. Sitting in the observation car she and Jeanne watched the bridge sway like a hammock as the train rushed across. When they were halfway over it sank so deep that Jeanne clutched Sarah's arm and murmured, 'We're drowning – that's it!' But the driver, desperate, forced an extra burst of speed out of his engine. The train lurched on to the bank; behind them a

286

column of spray rose far into the air as the bridge collapsed. It was eight days before any more trains could pass that way. That sight finally brought home to her the risk she had taken. For a long time afterwards, Sarah writes, she was troubled by terrible guilt whenever one of the troupe spoke to her about their family, and how glad they would be to get home and see their loved ones again.

All this, however, could not stop her playing yet more dangerous games. This time the setting was the Niagara Falls, where the company was enjoying a day out. It was deep winter, and although the great mass of water in the falls themselves never froze, they were surrounded by fantastic icicles. On the Canadian side, steps had been cut in the ice so that it was possible to go under the very falls themselves. The company descended, kitted out in all-enveloping waterproofs and fur-lined hobnailed boots. Over them hung a fantastic ice cupola. To their right, Sarah could see an ice formation which looked just like a rhinoceros about to enter the water. She decided that she would like nothing so much as to climb on its back. 'It's impossible!' said a friend, thus deciding her. If it was impossible, then of course she had to do it.

'Oh! impossible! Nothing's impossible. One's just got to risk it!' she reports herself as replying. But between her and the rhinoceros was a crevasse. Sarah pointed out that it was no more than a metre wide; but a painter who was with the party said that it was very deep. Sarah said, 'My dog's just died. I'll bet you a new dog that I can do it!' And she did – just; but once there, she found that the rhinoceros was very slippery. Far from standing upright, it was all she could do to lie down on his back and hang on to a bump of ice on top of his head; and from there, she declared, she would not budge: unless someone came to help her, she could never bring herself to cross back to the other side of the crevasse. Jeanne had hysterics; Mme Guérard was terrified; Abbey

287

begged her to try, Jarrett begged her to try – all in vain. The painter made sketches of the scene. Finally Angélo bravely jumped the crevasse, demanded an axe and a plank, and constructed a makeshift bridge. Sarah slid down the rhinoceros's flanks and slowly, heel to toe, not daring to look down, crossed the plank. Once again she had cheated death. But these days, if she pushed things a little too far, she not only stood to lose her life, but – as Jarrett had pointed out so succinctly – a great many other people would lose their livelihoods.

The tour was nearing its end. After Buffalo, near Niagara, the company played Rochester, Utica, Syracuse, Albany, Troy, Worcester, Providence, Newark, then down to Washington and back to New York, where the last matinée was *La Princesse Georges* and the last evening performance – naturally – *La Dame aux camélias*. Then, amid thunderous applause, Sarah left New York and returned to France on the *Amérique*, the same ship on which she had arrived and which had brought her such good luck. The pattern of her life was set. From now on she would be truly a citizen of the world – at home in whatever country she was booked to perform.

24

Sarah refers to this tour as her *'grand voyage'*, even though it lasted only seven months, while all her subsequent tours lasted between eleven and sixteen months. But a journey always seems longest the first time one makes it, and, far from any kind of routine having yet been established, her life was as much of a muddle, as formless and unpredictable, as it had ever been, and was to continue in ever-increasing chaos for the next several years.

The return to Le Havre (on 1 May 1881) was a triumph in itself. First of all there was the joyful reunion with old friends and relatives – above all, and most especially, Maurice, who was growing up into a handsome and profligate young man with a particular taste for gambling. When Sarah first caught sight of him on the launch which was bringing him out to meet her, she was overcome with joy and excitement, waving, shouting and gesturing, laughing and crying. There was also Clairin, Abbéma and the rest of the 'little court'. Then there was the special delegation of Havrais fishermen, who welcomed her back with a bouquet of flowers 'grown on the sweet soil of France', to say nothing of hundreds of tricolour-bedecked small boats which crowded out into the harbour to greet her. When they landed the troupe was asked if they would stay for a day to put on a special benefit for the wives and children of fishermen lost at sea. Sarah happily agreed, though not all the troupe were so pleased – particularly not Marie Colombier, who now re-encountered the mountain of debts she had left behind her in the persons of a posse of bailiffs waiting for her on the quay and preparing to distrain her luggage. Sarah, however, was too busy to take any notice of her plight.

But it was as if this, the last echo of the triumph she had so recently enjoyed, were designed only to point up the gulf separating the rest of the world from Paris. Elsewhere she had enjoyed – and was always to enjoy – treatment that was really quite unprecedented for one who was not royalty. The Tsar of Russia, the Queen of England, Napoleon at the height of his glory, might have experienced the kind of adulation she had everywhere met with; the stars of the screen and the recording studio would do so in the future. But Bernhardt was the first of this new breed, the royalty of popular culture; and in her lifetime her position as a kind of ex-officio queen, which had first manifested itself during the 1879 London season and which was strengthened with every subsequent foreign engagement, remained quite unique.

However, this new phenomenon did not arouse universal enthusiasm. The doyens of the higher intellect found it as hard then as they do now to accept that enormous popularity may be consonant with great art, and this was particularly true in Bernhardt's own home town. Paris liked to think that it had its own standards in these things; and, especially when it came to great acting, it knew what those standards were and where they were best embodied. As Got had rather smugly written when the Comédie-Française was in London two years (was it really only two years?) before, the English theatre relied on talent and instinct and sometimes, in this way, happened naturally upon effects which would have cost the French much more labour in terms of conscious application. But (he thought) the French reliance on tradition and training made for a much higher overall standard.[1] Sarah, however, had turned her back on all this, and therefore the Parisians were inclined to turn their back upon her. To begin with, they wouldn't even believe the tour had been a success – having heard about it at first hand only through Marie Colombier's catty despatches, which record more debacles than triumphs. And, more seriously, it became clear that she was not going to get an engagement in Paris. People simply did not want to know she was back. Before her departure, after her return from the happy provincial tour organized by Duquesnel, Victorien Sardou, Paris's most successful playwright, had promised her his next play and Raymond Deslandes, the director of the Vaudeville, had said he would stage it. Now, however, they showed no sign of remembering these promises. Meanwhile Maurice and the rest of her household were leading the same expensive life as before. She went over to London for three weeks and was received with the usual rapture; but Paris cold-shouldered her.

Clearly desperate measures were called for. Sarah saw her opportunity in the grand gala which was scheduled to take place at the Opéra on July 14 to celebrate, not only the storming of the Bastille, but also the tenth anniversary of the departure of the Prussians. Meyerbeer's *Robert le Diable* was to be presented, after which Mounet-Sully would read a patriotic poem and, as a finale, Mlle Agar – Sarah's old partner from *Le Passant* – would lead the audience in the 'Marseillaise'.

At the time of *Le Passant*, it will be remembered, Agar, then in her thirties, had been in love with François Coppée, the young author of the piece. Now, twelve years later, she was tenderly attached to a captain in the cavalry, then *en poste* at Tours. Sarah arranged with Agar's old maid Hortense, who was also an old ally of hers, for Agar to receive a message on the afternoon of the fourteenth to the effect that her handsome captain had suffered a bad fall from his horse and was asking for her. There was of course no question in Agar's mind as to what she should do: before the hour was out she was on the train to Tours, while Hortense was charged with notifying the direction of the Opéra in time for them to find a replacement. Naturally Hortense did nothing of the sort, with the result that, at the appointed moment, everyone at the Opéra was thunderstruck to see, not Agar, but Sarah, waiting in the wings, decked out in the cap of Liberty and white dress with tricolour sash, ready to declaim the 'Marseillaise'. By then it was of course too late to do anything; Mounet had finished his recitation; and Sarah stepped out before the President of the Republic, Gambetta, that Republic's first hero, and the entire Parisian social and theatrical world.

At her appearance – as on that other occasion, after her return from the first London season – there was a moment's silence. Then the music started: and by the end, as on that other day, Sarah's audacity, allied to all her other charms and talents, had once again brought Paris under her spell. The house roared: the ice was broken. It was not long before Sardou and Deslandes were round at her house offering her the new play – *Fédora*.

Writing plays had made Sardou a rich man; but his success was definitely as a man of the theatre rather than a literary genius – he was, as one wag put it, 'a mere set of fingers with the theatre at the tips of them'.[2] His association with Sarah, for whom he wrote seven plays, beginning with *Fédora* and ending with *La Sorcière*, was undoubtedly one of the great theatrical partnerships of history. 'Sardou,' wrote Maurice Baring, who was a great fan of both his and Sarah's, 'was the first person to guess what undiscovered provinces were yet to be annexed to [Sarah's] kingdom, and he set about to write plays for her.'[3] We shall have more to say about the pros and cons of 'Sardoodledom', as Bernard Shaw – no fan of either Sardou or Sarah – immortally christened it. But whatever their merits or demerits, it was clear that Sarah and Sardou were made for each other. It was a symbiosis. Maguerite Moréno described the rehearsals of *La Sorcière*, which opened in 1903: 'You couldn't tell who had written the piece and who was playing it. Suddenly there was Sardou, wearing his eternal black velvet beret, his white scarf knotted round his neck, standing on a table, gazing at the ceiling and miming the scene of the *auto de fé* while Sarah, sitting opposite him, spoke the lines; two minutes later it would be Sarah perched on the same table, miming the text while Sardou spoke it.'[4] Of *Fédora* Maurice Baring commented (apropos Eleonora Duse, who failed in it) that 'it was made like a tight-fitting garment for Sarah Bernhardt, and we have never seen another artist who could wear it'.[5]

On this particular afternoon in the July of 1881 Sardou read the play while Sarah and Deslandes listened, and Sarah at once recognized the possibilities of what was being offered her. The play was (like almost all Sardou's plays) a melodrama. It was about Russian nihilists, who were then much in fashion (later appearing in works as diverse as Conrad's *The Secret Agent* and E. Nesbit's *The Railway Children*). The central character was a Russian princess, Fédora, whose husband is brought back dead from a house where he has been keeping an amorous rendezvous; but no one knows about the affair, and the death is attributed to a nihilist, Ipanoff. Fédora decides to revenge herself for her husband's death, meets Ipanoff in Paris, makes him fall in love with her, but then (of course) falls in love with him herself. Just as her carefully-laid plans are coming to fruition, and he is being arrested and hauled off to Siberia, she discovers that her husband was unfaithful to her and Ipanoff never had anything to do with his death. Fédora then kills herself — the death scene which was rapidly becoming *de rigueur* in all Sarah's performances.

When the reading was finished, Deslandes set out his terms. He was offering 1,000 francs per performance and a guarantee of 100 performances – an enormous offer: Sarah's salary at the Comédie had been 20,000 francs a year. But now she had her revenge for the slights she had suffered a few weeks earlier. She told Deslandes that she knew that when the Vaudeville was sold out, which it would be, it grossed 7,500 francs per performance: she therefore wanted 1,500 francs per performance plus twenty-five per cent of net profits. This set Deslandes back on his heels; but both he and Sardou knew that nobody else could play Fédora; finally he gave in, and asked when she could start rehearsals. Ah, sighed Sarah, not until 1882: she had agreed with Jarrett to do a European tour starting in October; she would be away for six months.

25

Sarah's European tour of 1881–2 was, at least to begin with, the kind of hysterical success that was by now nothing out of the ordinary for her. The only sour note came from displays of anti-Semitism in southern Russia, where she was hissed in Kiev and stoned in Odessa on account of her ancestry. The company arrived in Odessa the day after a pogrom, and there was another pogrom the day after they left on the pretext that 'Sarah the Jewess plundered the people'.[1] But Sarah could deal with that: she simply moved on somewhere else. What set this tour apart was something she could not deal with: the bizarre infatuation which led to her marriage on 4 April 1882, in London (whither they had rushed for the purpose from Nice, where the company was currently performing), to Jacques Damala.

Who introduced Sarah to Damala? Her granddaughter Lysiane, who presumably had it from Sarah, says that he was an aspiring actor recommended to her by Sardou, who came to see her just as she was about to set off. However, Sardou resolutely refused Sarah's request that his protégé (if Damala was such) should play Ipanoff in *Fédora* when they returned to Paris. Another possibility is that he was an acquaintance of Jeanne's. At any rate, the acquaintance was made.

Damala was twenty-six in 1881 (Sarah was then thirty-seven), the handsome son of a rich and prominent Greek family (his first name was really Aristides), who had been educated in France. According to one version of events, he was destined for a diplomatic career, and was about to depart for St Petersburg when he first came to see Sarah. A less likely version, but one put about at the time, is that Sarah had made him her leading man immediately she met him in Paris. What is certain is that when Sarah's troupe arrived in St Petersburg, which was not until January, she began an all-consuming affair with him, whose brazenness outraged the protocol-ridden reaches of Russian court circles and infuriated the troupe's leading man, Philippe Garnier, an excellent actor who had now replaced Angélo as Sarah's current lover. Garnier left for Paris, pleading ill-health; the tour went on; Damala resigned his post and took over Garnier's role in *Frou-Frou* and Angélo's – that of Armand Duval – in *La Dame aux camélias*.

The story of Sarah and Damala is, on the face of it, banal enough. Sarah was used to making it clear when she wanted to go to bed with someone, and as a general rule the man in question was only too pleased to comply with her request. To this rule Damala was the exception. He was not particularly interested in Sarah – on the contrary, he was always flirting with other women. This drove her to such distraction that she evidently decided marriage was the only answer. Presumably, for the cynical Damala, the material advantages of being M. Sarah Bernhardt were not negligible – what had he to lose? The Naples newspapers recorded that when Bernhardt left that city just before her marriage her luggage filled two immense vans, and comprised hundreds of boxes of all sizes (including a long one which gave rise to the story that she was carrying her coffin about on tour with her) – a solid selection of assets in which a husband might hope to participate: and these were only the things she took on tour with her.

Sarah was a Roman Catholic; Damala was Greek Orthodox; in England, such details would make no difficulties. Hence the dash to London and the ceremony there, at St

Andrew's Church, Wells Street, where Damala gallantly gave his age as thirty-five, only two years younger than his wife rather than the factually correct but more embarrassing eleven. The wedding was witnessed by two of Damala's friends, Sarah's manager Mayer and another of her friends. Afterwards they all had dinner together, then went off to the station, where the Prince of Wales came in person to congratulate the bride before her departure (or so she said). Then they rushed back to Nice. They left London on Wednesday night; on Thursday morning they were in Paris, where the *Figaro* caught them at the Gare du Nord and snatched an interview. The flying marriage she had just gone through, she declared, was just the kind of proceeding that suited her. She did not feel a bit the worse for her journeys. 'Well, and what effect did my marriage produce in Paris?' she asked.

'Nobody would believe the story,' returned the journalist.

'I have not time to get married like other people,' affirmed Sarah. 'If I had to go through the ordinary formalities I should have been obliged to wait three weeks or a month, and I should never have been married at all.'[2] That would certainly have saved a lot of trouble and unhappiness all round; but unfortunately, the deed was done. It had been kept secret from everyone except Maurice, whom she had informed only just before she left Naples (he had presumably joined her for part of this tour) instructing him to make the facts known only after he and the rest of the company were at sea en route for Nice. The whole thing was conducted and recounted in breathless haste, a sort of culmination to the increasingly hysterical fandango Sarah had been engaged upon ever since she had first landed in London nearly three years earlier. The wild adulation she had since received from all countries and societies, the continual touring, the non-stop high-pitched round had led to an increasing sense of detachment from anything resembling

297

normality. Of this unreal life, the marriage was at once a symptom and a product.

In Nice, where Sarah had unavoidably missed several performances, Jarrett fined her twenty-five thousand francs for breach of contract. Then the tour resumed, but almost at once, things started to go wrong. Playing in Genoa two or three days after she had resumed the tour as Madame Damala, she was hissed in *La Dame aux camélias* ('Her company,' recorded one critic, 'is so bad as to be of no help to her – rather the contrary'[3]) – at which she had a fit of hysterics on the stage and vomited blood so copiously 'as to frighten everybody before and behind the footlights and to bring down the house in enthusiastic support of an artist "who so identified herself with the part as to have a real haemorrhage of the lungs"'.[4] This unscripted drama led to an unprecedented run on the ticket-office next day; but, that evening, she coughed blood once more, and the citizens of Genoa began to think this might be a trick. Indeed it was – the time-honoured trick of bursting a bladder of red fluid held in the mouth. The house exploded in fury. The jinx which was to attend Sarah as long as the marriage lasted had begun its work.

This episode in Genoa cannot but bring to mind those countless other occasions when Sarah got herself out of some awkward circumstance by collapsing and, in her weakened and emotional state, coughing blood. This, since it is a symptom of the last stages of tuberculosis, invariably brought her, not the wrath she generally deserved in whatever sticky situation had brought on the attack, but a flood of sympathy and concern. The question that never resolved itself – and it was often asked – was how Sarah, while being apparently terminally ill for so long, still managed to conduct the riotous life she did, and live on to a ripe old age? The Genoa episode may hold the answer to the question. It is hard to believe that this was the first or only time she used the bladder trick – it had simply never been spotted before. She was certainly pushing her luck using the same trick in the same place two nights in succession – another result, perhaps, of over-confidence resulting from too much uncritical applause. The question was – how ill had Sarah *ever* been? Certainly she was thin – a symptom of tuberculosis, but in her case the result of anorexia, which undoubtedly induces a thoroughly unhealthy look. More than once in her memoirs she tells how doctors 'gave her only a few months to live' – and were repeatedly confounded. She may well have had a weak chest. She was undoubtedly an excellent actress. It would hardly have been beyond her powers to cough convincingly, bring her handkerchief (containing a bladder?) up to her lips, and bring it away stained with red. At any rate, the blood always seemed to appear suspiciously pat on cue.

Needless to say, marriage did not alter Damala, and Sarah, instead of enjoying married bliss, found herself, all too predictably, confronting the ravages of jealousy once more. Why had she married him? Speculation was rife. 'I am acquainted,' wrote one commentator, 'with many personal friends of Sarah Bernhardt and some acquaintances of Aristides Damala. Among them all I have not found two who anticipate that the happy couple will long dwell together in unity.' One opinion was that 'she married Damala to have the official right to be jealous'. One thing was obvious: infatuation had, for the moment, overridden reason. If proof were needed, one had only to recall that she had committed the grave imprudence of marrying without a financial contract – something Girardin, had he been alive, would never have countenanced. This meant that Damala was entitled to any money she earned – and he had already run through one fortune, the one left him by his father, which he had spent principally on a pretty singer. 'M. Damala is liked by his old chums, one of whom assures me he has some fine instincts,' concluded this commentator doubtfully.[5] If this was true, it has to be said that these instincts were never in evidence where his wife was concerned.

Clearly infatuation and jealousy had something to do with it. That overwhelming desire to be loved, sought-after and admired which formed such an important part of the bond between herself and her public – the 'beloved monster' whose approval was everything to her – meant that she would always most strongly desire those who witheld themselves: the Paris public; and now, Damala. And maybe there was, at first, something more than infatuation on Sarah's part. Perhaps the secret lay in that observation of Marie Colombier's that she was always looking for the man who could arouse her sexually; and perhaps Damala – unfortunately for both of them – was that man. But why *marriage*? It was not as if, like a reluctant virgin, he could not go to bed with her under any other circumstances.

Perhaps part of the answer lies in the extremely banal fact that Sarah was fast approaching the dread milestone of her fortieth birthday – a time by which a woman might feel she had better be married if she is going to marry at all. Sarah was not alone among her contemporaries in being bitten by the marriage bug this year. 1882 also saw the marriage of her classmate and old friend and colleague Sophie Croizette, who married none other than Jacques Stern the banker, by whom she already had two children. Evidently he was a man fatally attracted to actresses.

Another answer is conceivably provided by the extremely conventional views Sarah held on marriage – she in whose family life marriage had never played any part whatever. An old friend – the same to whom she confessed, '*J'ai été une des plus grandes amoureuses de mon temps*' – recorded that 'infidelity in husbands and wives shocked her; once married it was a sacred duty to hold fast to the bargain was her dictum'.[6] Perhaps, feeling this herself, and knowing that her own previous promiscuity had no bearing on her views about marriage, she thought that Damala would feel the same. That would have been naive, but when it comes to wishful thinking, many of us are naive.

It certainly seems improbable that there was ever any real emotional attachment between Sarah and Damala. For one thing it would have been entirely one-sided, and deep feelings do not generally flourish in a void. For another, her whole upbringing had, as we have seen, made that kind of involvement virtually impossible. Indeed, everyone is agreed that there was only one man whom Sarah ever really loved, and that was her son Maurice.

Obviously there is a particular pleasure for all women in the company of their grown-up sons. But between Sarah and Maurice there was something more than that. It is clear that Maurice, from a very early age, fulfilled the social function of Sarah's ideal husband. As soon as she possibly could she began to treat him as an adult. 'When he was twelve, Maurice was already quite a "man about town," preferring adult companionship and evincing precocious likes and dislikes. When he was fifteen, Sarah settled a large sum on him and before he was twenty his income from her was sixty thousand francs annually. She always told her friends that she did not mind what he did with the money, so long as he dressed himself properly,' wrote Thérèse Berton, and there is no reason to disbelieve her.[7] Suze Rueff describes him as 'tall and fair, with a small head which he carried high, lively blue eyes and clean-cut features . . . an aristocrat to his finger-tips'.[8] Of course, as far as Maurice was concerned, he *was* an aristocrat – was he not the son of the Prince de Ligne? There was a story that, when the lad was seventeen, the prince, won over by Maurice's hereditary charm and by his resemblance to himself, offered to recognize him and give him his name, but that Maurice announced that he preferred to remain Bernhardt. Certainly it is the kind of story that would have appealed both to Maurice and to his mother. However, as the same Prince de Ligne had so brutally implied seventeen years earlier, it was hard to be certain about Maurice's paternity. But by now, whatever the bald truth might have been, the Ligne ancestry was all part of that delightful tissue of fabulation amid which, as everyone agreed who knew him, Maurice, like his mother, preferred to live. As Maurice Rostand, the son of one of Sarah's devoted playwrights and himself an unqualified admirer of hers, put it: 'In that theatrical milieu to which he always seemed to condescend, he retained a sort of aristocratic grace, a *ligne* – if I may presume to put it that way! – which was full of style; it wasn't very hard to imagine that one of his ancestors, born in Brussels, had been celebrated for his wit, whose remains Maurice had inherited.'[9]

For Sarah, who had had to face such harsh realities from her earliest childhood, the great priority had been to make sure that Maurice should never have to face such realities. And he never did. 'Brought up in a world of make-believe, in princely luxury, his tastes were fastidious,' writes Suze Rueff. 'He was extravagant and a gambler, which generally led to the conclusion that Maurice alone was responsible for Sarah's never-ending financial difficulties. There is no doubt that he largely contributed to them . . . It is disconcerting to look back and realize that he never made an attempt to stand on his own feet, to relieve his mother of at least part of the responsibility for his family and himself.' But Rueff discounts the notion that, without Maurice's constant drain on her resources, Sarah would have been able to put money aside for her old age and retire gracefully. 'I for one am inclined to believe that her artistic manifestations would have been equally costly, her furs and fancies and general train of life still more luxurious, and all would have been as it was.'[10] Meanwhile Maurice, as he grew up, was inclined to behave with that excessive courtliness and correctness with which people sometimes compensate for a somewhat dubious background, and which marks out pretend aristocrats from the real, much more relaxed, thing. His education had been that of many French bourgeois boys. He had had a tutor to begin with, and then spent his adolescence largely in boarding-schools and with crammers. He was an excellent swordsman, and was constantly (beginning, as we have seen, at the age of sixteen) challenging people to duels over what he saw as slurs on his mother's character: his daughter's biography of Sarah is peppered with references to these duels.

It may be imagined that not least among the problems Sarah faced when she returned to Paris in May 1882 as Mme Jacques Damala, was Maurice's disgust. He was now eighteen, and did not relish the idea of sharing either his mother's affections or her finances with a usurper. Clearly she would have to find something for him to do. There was also the other, far more troublesome problem of her husband. Damala was now taking his place as leading man opposite his wife. Not surprisingly, the critics thought far more highly of Sarah than of him. After a benefit performance of *La Dame* in Paris, at which everyone was agog both to see Sarah's Marguerite – for, amazingly, she had never yet performed this play in Paris, although she had taken it all over the world – and to see 'Monsieur Bernhardt' in action, a critic concluded that 'with a great deal of work he might perhaps make a passable actor. Certainly he has with him a great teacher whose coaching should be most profitable.'[11] And when they took the production for a short season to London, Damala was hardly noticed at all. Instead, reported Francisque Sarcey, 'Nothing can give an idea of the craze that Sarah Bernhardt is exciting. It's a mania. In the theatre when she is about to appear, a tremor runs through the audience; she appears and an 'Ah!' of admiration and astonishment escapes from every throat . . . Wherever you go, it is her they are discussing.'[12]

But in fact this English season was not altogether a happy one. After playing in London Sarah took the company up to Lancashire and Yorkshire, where she found the Wakes Week crowds less than sympathetic to what she had to offer. In Blackpool she was booked to appear in the huge Winter Gardens on 28 August. Damala inspected the stage in the morning and made no complaint; in the evening, Sarah left her hotel showing no sign of illness. But when she saw the Winter Gardens, she at once developed a sore throat. 'I thought I was to play in a theatre and not in a hall containing fifteen thousand persons and open to all winds,' she complained. The crowd first of all complained that they could not hear, and then when they could hear, that they couldn't understand a word – the performance was in French! Sarah, furious, walked off. The manager, appalled at the prospect of having to refund so many customers, begged her to continue: if people couldn't hear, they would be happy to see the famous Bernhardt mime her way through the play. 'I am an artist, not an exhibition,' was Sarah's indignant retort. She said it served the manager right for making her perform in such a place instead of a normal theatre, where he would have taken less money, but where it would have been possible to perform.[13] A doctor visited her that evening, and found her sitting up in bed complaining of a weak chest and sore throat, but he could find no symptoms. After he left, she got up and went down to supper. Damala somewhat disloyally told the manager that Sarah often did this kind of thing, and had to pay large fines for it. However, it seemed that no lessons were learned. The fiasco was repeated in Bradford only ten days later, where the management arranged for Bernhardt to play *Adrienne Lecouvreur* in the vast St George's Hall, holding fourteen thousand people. She struggled, uncomprehended and unappreciated, through the first act, received with respect but in dead silence, and not surprisingly, could face no more. By the time the second act was rung up she had disappeared, slipping out through the back door, whence she made it safely back to her hotel. Another actress took over the leading part, but the audience gradually dispersed, fortunately without taking out their frustration on the furniture.[14] By now Sarah had had enough of England. She was booked to play *Adrienne Lecouvreur* in Sheffield on 1 September, but sent a telegram to the lessee to the effect that she had been ordered by her doctor to discontinue her tour – she was, once again, coughing blood. Notwithstanding this debility she was on her way back to Paris by September 4.

All this attention – welcome or otherwise – directed so exclusively upon his wife did nothing for Damala's self-importance, and his fury was increased when Sardou categorically refused to hear of him taking the part of Ipanoff in *Fédora*, which was about to go into rehearsal. (The part went to Pierre Berton.) He fell back upon his usual consolations: sulks, women and – in increasing quantities, so that it now became noticeable where before he had been able to conceal the habit – morphine.

Sarah hit upon a solution to the problems of both Maurice and Damala. She took the lease of the Ambigu, one of the big boulevard theatres, in Maurice's name. Maurice was to be the manager, and also direct the plays that would be put on there. However, as he was still only seventeen – legally a minor – Sarah would be personally responsible for any losses he incurred. The first of Maurice's plays was to be *Les Mères ennemies* by Catulle Mendès, a relatively unknown dramatist, in which Damala would take the lead. This opened in the middle of November, 1882, and, surprisingly considering the inexperience of both director and leading man, it did very well.

Then, on December 12, came the opening of *Fédora*. Such was the public's curiosity both to see the new Sardou and to see what eighteen months of highly publicized travels had done for Bernhardt, that the house was sold out for the first twenty-five performances before the curtain rose. But, when it did rise, Sarah found that curiosity was not the same thing as warmth. As usual whenever she first returned to Paris, and in the usual sharp contrast to the tumultuous reception she was accorded everywhere else in the world, her entry was marked, not by explosions of enthusiasm, but by a reserve bordering on frigidity. This – which she had not been expecting – threw her off-balance, and made her terribly nervous for the whole of the first act – her normal first-night stage-fright which was amplified and transmitted to the rest of the cast, so that hardly anyone was audible. But such was Sardou's skill in the piling of detail upon pregnant detail that gradually the audience was caught up in the plot, and by the end of Act Two Sarah had relaxed and it was clear that the evening was going to be a triumph. 'Only one word: Sarah, *la grande* Sarah,' concluded Francisque Sarcey. But he also noted that, although one could only admire her with all one's heart – 'so passionate, so vibrant' – the poetic ideal of earlier days had vanished. Sardou had taken care to cut up the dialogue so that Sarah had no chance to perform her *mélopée*, that golden sing-song in which she specialized, and whose disappearance Sarcey much regretted.[15] He did not consider that the outbursts of tigerish passion which were to become another of Sarah's specialities, and which first appeared in this play, were any substitute artistically; and indeed, did not think highly of the play itself, summing it up as a sensational paragraph (*'un fait divers'*) cut up into slices by an extremely skilful hand and the dialogue executed with wonderful brio. Sub-

306

sequent performances of *Fédora* by other actresses showed that he was quite right: no one but Sarah, for whom and around whom it had been carefully built, could make it work. But other critics had no such reservations. 'The electric, chimerical woman has again conquered Paris,' wrote Jules Lemaître. '. . . Mme Sarah Bernhardt always seems like a very strange person returning from far away; she gives me the feeling of the exotic, and I thank her for reminding me that the world is wide, and that it cannot be contained in the shadow of our steeple, and that man is a multiple being, and capable of everything.'[16]

Damala did not welcome his wife's success, which so far eclipsed his own. Indeed, he was so outraged by it that, a few days after *Fédora*'s opening, after having made himself as unpleasant as he knew how, he announced that he was leaving the stage and joining the Foreign Legion. 'France, which treats my wife as a spoiled child, will, I hope, have room for me under the shadow of her flag,' he announced touchingly.[17] With his going *Les Mères ennemies* folded, and Maurice was left nursing gigantic losses at the Ambigu. Sarah tried to cover them by selling her jewellery, but the proceeds of the sale were disappointing. The jewels – which included a pearl collar presented by the Queen of Italy, a gold and sapphire bracelet from the Duke of Aosta, three dragon brooches from a Russian princess, two presents from the Prince of Wales (a gold serpent bracelet set with diamonds and rubies and an Indian bandeau scattered with emeralds, rubies and pearls) and a wrought gold comb with '*Quand-même*' worked in it given by Girardin in acknowledgment of Sarah's portrait bust of him – had been estimated to fetch 500,000 francs; in the event, only 175,000 were raised. Meanwhile she had to deal not only with Maurice's losses but also with a fine of 45,000 francs incurred by Damala on his sudden departure, to say nothing of the balance – still unpaid – of the fine she herself had incurred when she left the Comédie-Française. On top of this she had begun suing the *Indépendance Française* for insinuating that her marriage was in difficulties, had decided not to pursue the suit, and so had lost by default.

Now began for Sarah a period of great difficulty. The years 1883–1885 mark a low point in her life. Despite her enormous achievements in the short time since she had left the Comédie, in which she had shown that she was a star of the world stage, in which she had begun the partnership with Sardou which was to be one of the most fruitful in her career (to say nothing of his) – she gives the impression of thrashing about in panic. One catastrophe after another overtook her.

After Damala left, another play had to be found for the Ambigu. Sarah decided upon *La Glu* by the swashbuckling young poet Jean Richepin. This was put on with a very strong cast including Mlle Agar (who bore no grudges for the trick Sarah had played on her on the fourteenth of July) and the young Réjane. But in spite of good notices it closed after fifty performances, and Sarah was obliged to give up the Ambigu, on which, largely owing to Maurice's misman-agement, she had lost about 450,000 francs. Even her extremely large income from *Fédora*, added to the disap-pointing proceeds of the jewel sale, were not enough to pay her creditors. It was rumoured that she had been paid 100,000 francs to write her memoirs, which were promised for that October (1883). But they did not appear. This, it was asserted, was because of a quarrel between Sarah and her publisher, Dérembourg, who would not agree to let her name all her lovers in low and high places, as she insisted upon doing. Since no agreement could be reached on this point, Sarah was trying to buy her manuscript back. In fact it seems probable that this was the precise opposite of the truth. That the memoirs, or part of them, undoubtedly did exist we know because scenes from them were quoted — scenes approximating very closely to equivalent episodes in the memoirs that finally did appear in 1907, twenty-four years later. But, as we have already noted, the salient fact about *those* memoirs is the complete absence of any reference in them to Sarah's love-life. So that the more likely scenario is that it was Dérembourg who wanted the spicy episodes which would sell the book, and Sarah who refused to provide them. The fact that the book was to be called *Ma vie au théâtre* makes this even more probable, excluding as it does life *outside* the theatre.

So, to try and raise the necessary money, she closed *Fédora*, even though it was still playing to full houses, and took it on a whirlwind tour of European cities where the receipts might be even larger. Richepin accompanied her on this tour, during which he consoled her for the departure of Damala; she also commissioned a new play from him, which she would put on in Paris. Brussels, Copenhagen, and ten delirious days in London restored her self-esteem and, to some extent, her coffers.

But her troubles were not at an end. When she got back to Paris, she found that Damala was lolling about the house — which, as he rightly pointed out, was his house as much as hers. He had in fact returned to Paris just before she left for London — and not alone. He was acccompanied by an Arab, one Rahem ben Khral, whom he had supposedly captured during a Foreign Legion raid. The presence in Paris of Damala and his Arab had become known to a journalist hostile to Sarah, who had concealed the news. Just before the curtain was due to rise on the last performance of *Fédora* the journalist presented himself at the Vaudeville with Damala and Rahem in tow, demanding an interview. He assumed, probably rightly, that no actress in the world would be able to get through a performance after an unexpected interview with a husband she had hoped never to see again, flanked on one side by a Bedouin, and on the other by a sneering journalist. Unfortunately for the trio they were met in the foyer not by Sarah but by Sardou, who flatly refused to allow them anywhere near Sarah's dressing-room until after the performance. Damala knew that, by then, the effect would be wasted, so they bided their time and pounced just before a charity performance of Richepin's dismal *Pierrot assassin* billed for the following Saturday. It was agreed that both the play and Sarah were very bad; but rumour had it that she had taken one look at Rahem, cooed, 'What a beauty!' and taken him off with her to Brussels.[18] Now, however, she was back; and a miserable time ensued, in which Damala passed his time between morphine and other women and sneered at Sarah, who had leased the Porte-Saint-Martin (again in Maurice's name) for a season of *Frou-frou* and *La Dame aux camélias*, those reliable money-spinners. At length Sarah could bear it no longer, threw Damala's drug supply down the drain and arranged for him to take a cure in a sanatorium.

Sardou now approached her with a new play, *Théodora*; but Sarah could not accept this as she was committed to Richepin, who had come up with the promised play, *Nana-Sahib*, and who, now Damala had departed once more, was reinstated as Sarah's lover. This extremely bad piece was also very expensive to put on. What was more, the leading man fell ill after a week, and his place was taken by Richepin, who had always wanted to try his hand at acting but (as it turned out) should not have done so. Business was bad; and, to rub salt into the wound, Damala, temporarily cured, was now playing at the Gymnase in a piece by Georges Ohnet, *Le Maître des forges*, in which he scored a telling success as a rich, uncouth ironmaster who turns out to have a heart of gold. On afternoons when Sarah was playing and he was not, he enjoyed coming to the empty Porte-Saint-Martin to scoff; after one of these exhibitions

Richepin, a large, manly, sporting fellow, could not resist beating him up.

On the day before *Nana-Sahib* opened in December, 1883, Paris was regaled by a terrific scandal. Marie Colombier had taken her revenge for all the slights, real or imagined, that she had suffered at Sarah's hands (though principally for the fact that Sarah was successful while she was not) by publishing an unimaginably scabrous work entitled *Les Mémoires de Sarah Barnum*. She had got the idea when Sarah had announced that she was writing her memoirs. Clever Marie saw how she could both capitalize on and spoil the effect of these by publishing her own version: if Sarah would not provide the public with the scandalous details they craved, Marie would oblige.

This extraordinarily unpleasant book, based under the thinnest of veils upon Sarah's life and family, gains its effect from the fact that Colombier really does know her subject and writes with distinct verve and enjoyment. But it is entirely the product of hatred and jealousy, filthy, vicious, malicious and anti-Semitic. The technique is the most damaging possible. Real people and situations from Sarah's life are taken and then distorted so that, for all the reader knows, they *might* be true. Régine, for example, (called Reine by Colombier, and presented as the daughter of Julie's friend Régis, which may well have been the case) is portrayed as a maltreated innocent, hated by all her family including Sarah.

It was not that she was an angel. Brought up in the same way as her sisters, as prematurely corrupted as them, little Reine was marked out only by her happy character and her innate loyalty. She was always neglected and often ill-treated . . . A precocious resignation pointed up her grace, paled her complexion, and filled her eyes with tender tears. But when she began to grow up, when she became a woman and yet still remained a child, and excited the

311

jealous anger of her sister [Jeanne], her life was a
martyrdom which Sarah never bothered to notice . . . Living
at this time in the rue d'Italie [rue de Rome] but not in the
luxury she still dreams of . . . the tragedienne is still the
same fantastical creature, egotistic, arrogant and cold. More
desperate than ever to be noticed, she seeks notoriety with
the same perseverance that she devotes to finding a man
capable of arousing her sensually . . . She is coldly corrupt,
habitually vicious, contrary by preference, greedy by
instinct, prone to spoil things through laziness and a desire
to cover her tracks, envious by temperament; but she is an
artist, and, loving nobody, she adores her work. She is
fundamentally artificial, crazy but aware, very aware; her
most outstanding characteristic is a happy scepticism. She
doesn't give a damn about anything . . . But, of all the
unpleasant feelings women are prone to, jealousy is most
deeply rooted in her. She is jealous of her colleagues,
jealous of her sisters . . . [Sarah now meets an exotic
Peruvian millionaire nicknamed Scarface] Scarface saw
Reine at Barnum's place and immediately wanted to make
her his mistress. She was only fourteen or fifteen at this
time, and, although deeply corrupted by the examples that
had surrounded her all her life, she was nevertheless still a
good and loving girl. . . The Spanish-American dreamed of
being this child's first lover, and, desiring her more every
day, he had no hesitation in proposing an odious bargain.
He would buy her virginity for forty thousand francs. Sarah
was mad with jealousy. Forty thousand francs for that child!
She could happily have strangled Lope, who, given a choice
between the famous actress and the child, chose the child.

Determined to prevent this, Sarah throws Reine into the
arms of a brutal and sadistic society scoundrel who rapes
her and then abandons her onto the streets, where in her
innocence she fails to make a living.[19]

Such was the revolting stuff which filled Marie Colombier's book. It reflected more on the author than the subject,
but the public were not interested in such niceties. Colombier clearly knew Sarah well, and her book was even

provided with a respectable preface by a young writer called Pierre Bonnétain, who was well known as a journalist (and who had just published a pornographic fantasy called *Charlot s'amuse*).

Obviously the best thing would have been to ignore the book and wait for the fuss to die down. And in fact Sarah did not react when first it was published, perhaps preferring to pretend she knew nothing about it. But some kind person sent her a copy, making sure she could no longer ignore it; she flew off the handle; and – to the delight of the press – trouble naturally ensued. First there was a duel – not, as Colombier liked to point out, involving Sarah's husband, who had declined to act on her behalf, but between Bonnétain and Octave Mirbeau, a fiery journalist (later a successful playwright) with a strong line in indignation. Then, on the day this duel was to take place (Mirbeau scratched Bonnétain's hand and was declared the winner) Colombier received a visit, in her apartment in the rue de Thann, from Maurice, accompanied by his cousin and another friend. Maurice demanded that Colombier name anyone who would fight him on her behalf; but Colombier just laughed at him and told him to go back to school. He was leaving in outrage when in burst Richepin, followed by Sarah wielding a riding-whip.

There are two versions of what happened next – Sarah's and Colombier's. According to Sarah, she whipped Colombier all round the apartment, smashing furniture and ornaments in the course of the chase, until finally, shrieking in pain and terror, Colombier made her escape down the back stairs, by which time the apartment and everything in it had been broken to pieces and Marie's face was brutally scarred. According to Marie, however, (in a justificatory description she gave later of the affair) Sarah enjoyed no such satisfaction: 'Neither her dagger, not her horsewhip, nor the cutlass of M. Richepin touched me. Concealed behind a curtain I

313

witnessed all that passed.' The immediate effect of all this was, naturally, to give a vast boost to the sales of *Sarah Barnum*, such that Colombier (who had long been better known for her performances in bed than on the boards) was soon able to replace her smashed furniture. By January 1884, it was in its eighteenth edition and still printing. Sarah's friends were appalled; her enemies, triumphant. Colombier impudently declared that Sarah was wrong in supposing herself to be the imaginary heroine alluded to in the book, and added that, before it appeared, since she was advised that she might be accused of painting Bernhardt, she had sent her a letter and afterwards met her and Maurice, and neither of them had complained.

Félicien Champsaur, who had recently published *Dinah Samuel*, his own semi-pornographic and anti-Semitic novel about a Jewish actress, remarked that 'she has exposed herself too much in public to have any more private life. The risk of using publicity for self-aggrandisement is that it will get out of hand and kill you.'[20] Sarah's apparent success, on her own terms, had been a bitter pill for many people to swallow: now they revelled in what appeared to be her come-uppance. Sarah foolishly wrote, or commissioned, a reply – *La Vie de Marie Pigeonnier* – which could hardly match the original in bile, but certainly gave the affair added life just when it might have died down. On 26 May 1884, Colombier was sentenced to three months' imprisonment and a fine – but that was little consolation to Sarah.

In the midst of all this – just when, as she might have said, her daughter was fulfilling all her worst expectations – Julie Bernhardt died. Sarah described this event to her granddaughter in typically unreal and romantic terms. 'She was discovered one morning lying on her yellow sofa, dressed in a pretty négligé, with her head on a lace pillow. Her beautiful hands held a small tray-cloth which she had been embroidering. She was smiling, a coquette even in death. And I was so upset that I fell ill.'[21] All her life Sarah's one real desire had been to please her mother so that she would love her. Now it was too late.

But there was no time to be ill. Money was short once more. Once again *La Dame aux camélias* was rolled out to save the day, and once more she obliged. Then Damala, who had been carrying on with an *ingénue* in Sarah's troupe, ran away with the girl, and, from Monte Carlo, sent a bill for eighty thousand francs gambling debts. Once more Sarah paid up. Then, when he returned with the girl, Sarah definitively threw him out, separated from him (while they remained legally unestranged he was entitled to take any money she earned), and thankfully saw him off to South America, where he had an engagement. 'His departure saved me,' she told Lysiane. 'It was as though I had been exorcized.' It must have been shortly after this that she ran into the young English stage-designer Graham Robertson; he found her poring over patterns of chintz and brocade, trying to decide what would be best to hang in her bedroom.

'"I like white for a bedroom," said I.

'"White," said Sarah, in tones of deep amazement.

"*White*?"

'"Well, why not?" I asked.

'"White!" repeated Sarah, who seemed unable to get over the suggestion. "Why, it would be ridiculous. People would *laugh*. They would find it absurd."

'"I didn't know the chintz had to be allegorical," I said. "What would be the proper thing, then?"

'"I was thinking of this pattern of violets," said Sarah, who had of course made up her mind before asking advice. "Or this with the bunches of lilac – "

'"But," I began, "I don't see why lilac – "

'"It's mauve," said Sarah. "Mauve and violet are half mourning, and if a woman of my age is not a widow she ought to be"'[22]

315

But despite this feeling of liberation, Sarah was not yet by any means out of what she herself described as the 'tunnel'. Her next theatrical venture, *Macbeth*, in a laughable translation by Richepin, was a disaster. It was a miserable failure in Paris and London alike, although in Paris (but not London) the sleep-walking scene made something of a sensation. Virtually the only person who liked it was Oscar Wilde, then in Paris on honeymoon. He thought *Macbeth* Sarah's finest creation – Sarah's, because 'Shakespeare is only one of the parties. The second is the artiste through whose mind it passes ... There is no one like Sarah Bernhardt.'[24] Wilde even liked Richepin's prose version of the play. But no one else did; and this marked the end, for the moment, of Sarah's relationship with Richepin.

This, it appeared, was more his idea than hers, and in July she retired to her villa at Ste Adresse where she received a succession of journalists and poured out the woes of her innermost heart, at the same time complaining bitterly about the way the press pried into her private life. She told them about how Maurice had known nothing of the true nature of her relations with Richepin, and how, now everything had come out, she could no longer face him; how she had booked a passage with the intention of fleeing to America; how she had sent orders to Paris to have her house and furniture sold so that nothing should remain to remind her of her lost love (Richepin); how she had urged Maurice to leave at once for Chile; how, in eighteen months' time, when she had fulfilled all her engagements in Paris, she herself would disappear, 'and one day, from far, very far away, the news will come that she who was Sarah Bernhardt is dead.'[25] The whole thing was a mess, not least for Richepin's wife and family, who also found themselves targets for scandal-hungry journalists. Sarah's thoughts, when not focused on blessed oblivion in South America, turned to other suitably dramatic exits. She complained during a rehearsal of *Frou-Frou* of how weary and tiresome her life had become. Dumas *fils*, who happened to be there, remarked that in that case she was very hard to please: no woman since Catherine the Great had been adulated, obeyed and adored as she was. 'Yes,' replied Sarah, 'that's all very well. But what about the end? The thing is to find a good ending, a dramatic and soul-stirring denouement. Suppose Rochefort had been killed by a musket-ball at the moment of his escape! What an admirable death! I should like to end like that! Gambetta ended well, too – it was dramatic and mysterious. Tell me, how do you think I shall end?'[26]

But once again, salvation reappeared in the guise of Sardou, whose next offering, *Théodora*, Sarah was at last free to take up. She spent a happy time at Ravenna drinking in the mosaics and the atmosphere which had produced that monstrous empress. (Both Sarah and Sardou were always very keen on accurate historical detail, though in Théodora's case Sardou gingered up the rather undramatic reality of the lady's death from cancer in the interests of good theatre: a move upon whose defence and justification he was later to spend much time and paper.) *Théodora* finally opened on 26 December 1884, and was a huge and immediate hit. 'What a first night that was!' Sarah recalled. 'The public was cold, even hostile. But after the first act, I felt that its heart was beating in time with mine. I wanted to dominate the house and to persuade it that nothing mattered except Art. After the second act the curtain rose to cries of "*Vive* Sarah!" Then I whispered to Angélo: "They're coming back!" Angélo understood and pressed my hand. Yes, the public was coming back to me.'[27] She loved *Théodora*. 'It is my favourite play,' she said a few years later, 'superb, simply superb, though it's the most terribly difficult character to play I have ever known.'[28] She much preferred it to *Fédora*, feeling that

317

the role of Loris Ipanoff was stupid, and that no one could feel any sympathy for him.

Once again she had forced herself back into the heart of that Parisian public which was always so eager to disown her. It was clear that *Théodora*, like *Fédora*, could have run for ever. For if there were not many who would have agreed with Sarah about the supremacy of Art in this particular venture, there was undoubtedly drama (or melodrama), spectacle, and the satisfaction of watching a theatrical tour de force on the part of both Sardou and Bernhardt. But, once again, Sarah failed to make the most of her opportunity.

In May 1885, Victor Hugo died. He was given a State funeral. Naturally, Sarah joined the cortège; and when, after a while, the other participants realized who she was, one by one they fell back until, by the end, Doña Sol was walking, alone, behind the poet's family, recognized by all as his greatest interpreter. A vogue for Hugo now ensued; and Philippe Garnier, who was Sarah's leading man and, once again, her lover, suggested that they revive *Marion Delorme*. This, Hugo's last play, had never been successful; and when, after two hundred nights, *Théodora* was taken off and replaced by the Hugo piece, it was unsuccessful once again, running for a fortnight before collapsing. Garnier now persuaded Sarah to let him fulfil one of his theatrical dreams and play Hamlet to her Ophelia. She agreed, but it was a disaster. Garnier was hissed off the stage: the production folded. Once more Sarah had allowed infatuation to spoil judgment. Pierre Berton wrote to Sardou suggesting that they revive *Fédora*, but Sardou replied, 'Why would Sarah play *Fédora* in which Garnier has no role? . . . It's Garnier who runs everything in that madhouse of which Duquesnel fancies he's the director – but he's more of a *pensionnaire* than he knows.'[28]

This time Sarah was seriously broke. Her creditors would take no more excuses. Much against her will the dire prophecies of the previous summer were fulfilled, and the house in the avenue de Villiers was put up for sale with its contents. The sale, once again, was a failure. Derisory prices were paid for even the best pieces: the Pleyel grand piano, which had cost eight thousand francs, went for five hundred; a huge Chinese vase from the Imperial palace in Peking fetched only eight hundred francs. Not that Sarah herself was quite reduced to penury: in French law, creditors were forbidden to seize more of her salary than she could 'reasonably do without', so that she was still able to live in relative luxury in a furnished apartment.

She did not languish there long. The previous summer Maurice Grau, Jarrett's American partner, had announced that he had been able to engage Bernhardt for a world tour on terms that he declined to disclose: 'Well, really, it would be quite useless for me to make them known, as nobody would believe what I said!'[29] The tour this time would begin in South America (was this why Sarah had had Chile on the brain? Or maybe it had been suggested to her because Julie's brother, her uncle Edouard Kerbernhardt, had recently emigrated to Valparaiso.) She would fulfil an engagement in Lisbon, and sail thence directly to Rio. Then the itinerary would take her to São Paulo, Buenos Aires, Montevideo, Santiago, Valparaiso and Lima; thence to San Francisco and those towns of the western United States which she had not yet visited. She would go on to Mexico and Havana, and, in the spring of 1887, return to New York and so onwards all around the United States. Maurice, far from travelling to Chile miserably by himself, would go there in the company of his mother — travel indeed, as those who watched the progress remarked, 'like a Prince of the blood royal . . . to all intents and purposes the glass of fashion and the mould of form for all the young dandies of Peru and Brazil'.[31]

Sarah's impact upon South America may be imagined from the fact that in more than one place – the theatre at Iquique in the north of Chile, the opera house at Manaos in Brazil – posters advertising her visit are still displayed in the foyer as treasured possessions. It is hard to exaggerate the difficulties involved in transporting herself, her company, her scenery and costumes, to such places, where the only communication with the outside world was by means of steamships. Fitzcarraldo, in his famous journey, was contemplating only one leg of Sarah's tour. And who, in some of these remote mining towns, can have constituted her audience? A large proportion of the population in such places didn't even speak Spanish or Portuguese, let alone French. Even in Buenos Aires, that most European of Latin-American cities, one politician advised another, who was searching vainly for someone to give him French lessons so that he might appreciate *la divine*: 'You go to look at Sarah, not to listen to her. It's no use trying to understand what the words mean. It's what she looks like, the attitudes she strikes, that say it all. They're pure eloquence!'[32] A month before Sarah's arrival, Buenos Aires talked of nothing else. A presidential candidate was advised to drop everything in order to make sure he got to town in time to see her . . .

Could anyone live up to such expectations? Sarah's first night in Buenos Aires – she opened with *Fédora* on 17 July 1885 – was a disappointment. She was nervous – the usual stage-fright – and left the audience cold, while they found Garnier quite without attraction. But as the repertoire progressed through *Phèdre, La Dame, Frou-frou, Adrienne Lecouvreur* and the rest, their enthusiasm grew until the entire town talked and thought only of Sarah, and manufacturers of everything from hats to biscuits racked their brains for some way in which to incorporate Sarah into a selling-line for their product. By the time she left Buenos Aires six weeks later she had grossed nearly a million francs, and the whole thing had begun to get on some people's nerves. A certain relief was expressed by more than one person as she embarked for Montevideo, her next port of call; a leading critic commented crossly that he had never seen 'such histrionic vanity combined with such extravagance'.[33]

After Montevideo she steamed round Cape Horn to Chile, where she landed at Lota, a southern coal-mining town where she was welcomed by the mine owner (had he rounded up his miners to fill the house?). Then it was on up to Valparaiso, where Julie's brother Edouard Kerbernhardt now owned an hotel, and where Sarah had eight cousins; and thence to Santiago, where the famous poet Rubén Darío wrote an ode in her honour. Chileans wondered whether she was surprised at her eager reception in their country, and remarked that she probably didn't know that everything French was currently the rage in Santiago, from furniture to clothes to popular novels. She almost certainly was unaware of this; what on the contrary she was only too aware of was a certain coldness on the part of Chilean society, which was very proper, and which certainly did not open its doors to actresses – and especially not actresses who performed in plays like *Frou-frou* and *La Dame aux camélias*. When, after journeying via Lima, Rio, Mexico and Panama, she arrived at New York and was asked what she thought of South America, she replied that she adored Buenos Aires, Rio and Mexico, but detested Chile, even though she had family there. To which *El Mercurio* of Santiago retorted, 'What's Chile done to her? What happened to her while she was in our country? Absolutely nothing, except that we gave her all the praise she merited, and sometimes more. On the contrary, Chile was perhaps the only place which left her in peace without subjecting her to ridiculous excesses.'[34] That presumably, was just the trouble.

While she was on this tour, several things happened which were to have important consequences for Sarah. The first of these was the death of Jarrett, who had a heart attack in Montevideo. Maurice Grau came out and took his place, but he had been a good friend to Sarah, and she missed him sadly. The second was an injury to her right knee which she sustained when she slipped and fell on board ship during the voyage home. This refused to heal, and the ship's doctor could only recommend a treatment called *pointes de feu*, then much in vogue, which involved the application of slivers of burning wood to the affected part. When she got back to Le Havre, her own doctor there recommended the same thing. But the injury remained with her, and her knee was to give her more and more trouble for the rest of her life until, in 1915, the only thing that could be done was to amputate her leg.

The third thing was that, finally, she seemed to have emerged from the tunnel. She came back once again a rich woman, and bought herself a new Paris house at 56, boulevard Péreire (not very far from her old house at the avenue de Villiers), where she was to stay for the rest of her life; and a country estate at Belle-Isle, off Quiberon, in her beloved Brittany, where she would spend every summer when she was not on tour until she sold it the year before her death in 1922.

In 1887 Maurice got married. His bride was a Polish princess, Terka Jablonowska: a proof, if one were needed, that Sarah had produced, even in adverse circumstances, an excellent approximation to the real social thing.

Terka was a sweet, quiet girl who, even at her wedding, was eclipsed by her mother-in-law. 'We were barely seated,' recalled one guest, 'when a murmur swept the church: "*Voici Sarah*!" A slender figure scarcely more tangible than a column of smoke was floating up the aisle. A cloak of grey velvet opened over a skirt of soft pink faille. The white,

17. *left* With Lillie Langtry in New York. Sarah is pinching Lillie to make her laugh

18. *below left* Sarah in one of the gorgeous costumes with which she assumed her characters: Théodora

19. *below* Eleanora Duse looking typically introspective and intense

Sarah in *travesti*, early 1900s

20. As L'Aiglon

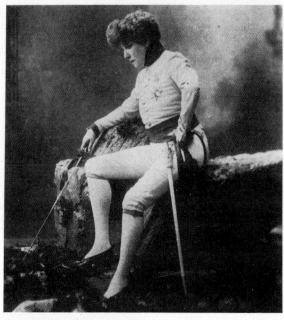

21. *Pelléas et Mélisande* with Mrs Patrick Campbell

"GREAT ATTRACTION!"

Now that Madame Bernhardt has made so conspicuous a success as *Hamlet*, why should not she and our Leading Tragedian join forces when she comes to London? Sir Henry's *Ophelia* would be sure to attract more than passing notice.

PUNCH   May 31, 1899.

22. Three views
of Sarah as Hamlet

23. Sarah outside her circus tent in Dallas, Texas
24. With Constant Coquelin
25. Sarah approaching sixty: as young and beautiful as ever

26. Return from America, 1911: Sarah is met by her granddaughter Lysiane (*left*), Eddie Gross, her other granddaughter Simone Gross (*right*)

27. 'The Muse of the Railroads': Sarah in her special train carriage

28. Belle-Isle: (*left to right*) Geoffroy, Suzanne Seylor, Reynaldo Hahn, Sarah, Mme Grau, Georges Clairin

29. Sarah and Maurice

30. Lou Tellegen as Hippolyte: he is wearing the jewelled belt

31. With Lou Tellegen in *Théodora*

32. Sarah as Daniel in 1921, aged seventy-seven

33. The funeral in Paris, 1923; the cortège is passing the Théâtre Sarah Bernhardt

heart-shaped face, blurred at the edges by the marabou of her coat, and the fluffy masses of her extraordinary blonde hair, were crowned by the misty tulle of her bonnet. Over her large white teeth, her reddened lips drew back in that smile of conscious fascination which is part of the daily toilette of every Frenchwoman.' *Truth* found this toilette 'very elegant, but carelessly so'. It thought that Sarah had hit 'just the right note' with it, but 'admired her pluck in coming forward as the mother of a bridegroom aged four-and-twenty'. Here *Truth* hit just the wrong note, for Sarah had never tried to conceal her grown-up son, and took nothing but pride in him; as for her age, there was never a sign to the very end of her long life that she let *that* worry her. That, indeed, was one of the aspects of Sarah which most set her apart from the ordinary run of women (and particularly the ordinary run of glamorous actresses): one of the many ways in which she did not conform to the stereotype. *Truth* went on to note, more percipiently, that 'pluck is the overweening element in Sarah's disposition, and, her talent aiding, it has kept her on the crests of waves ever since she started out on the sea of life'.[35] Once again she was indeed on the crest of a wave, financially at least. Her wedding-presents to Maurice and Terka had been a lavishly-furnished house to him and £4,000 worth of gifts to her. It seems improbable that Terka had had much to do with choosing the furniture in her new home.

Terka duly did her duty: before Sarah was forty-four she had been presented with her first grandchild and delighted in referring to herself as 'The youngest grandmother in France.' And, at just about the same time, Damala died. After his success in *Le Maître des forges* he had abandoned the theatre and sunk into a morphine haze, his condition growing more and more desperate until, finally, Sarah got to know of it. She rushed to where he was living in a squalid room in the rue d'Antin, where she found forty-eight grains of cocaine and fifteen grains of morphine. She had him taken back to her own house, where with constant nursing he seemed to be remarkably recovered. Then he collapsed, and died in hospital on 18 August 1889.

It is perhaps time to ask, once more, why Sarah had ever married him? And perhaps there is as much of a clue in the drug-sodden hopelessness of his end as in the swaggering pretence of their early acquaintance. For Sarah was no stranger to morphine addiction. On the contrary: she was acquainted with it only too closely in the persons of her sister Jeanne and Jeanne's daughter Saryta. And Sarah herself knew at first hand about the depression, weakness and misery which could lead a person into morphine addiction. It was, as we have noted, the obverse side of that grandiose posturing, that greed for work, that incessant clamouring for notice and admiration, which were the seeds of her own success, and which still sometimes threatened – as had happened at least three times on her first American tour – to push her over the brink, from mere posturing into more dangerous games. If Sarah had not behaved as she did, and as she was often reproached for doing, it seems reasonable to suppose that she might herself have drifted into the hopelessness that had done for Régine and was to do for both Jeanne and Saryta before very long. What had she, apart from her talent and her single-minded devotion to its exhibition, to differentiate her from them? Perhaps she sensed, in Damala, this family likeness; and perhaps it was this that made his handsome self so especially irresistible to her. With Damala, in his exasperating weakness, she could once again feel strong and indispensable, and thus, by comparison, bolster herself even more forcibly against a descent into those depths of which she was always only too painfully aware.

Gustave Flaubert (who was in a position to know) wrote to his mother: 'You can depict wine, love, women and glory

324

on the condition that you're not a drunkard, a lover, a husband, or a private in the ranks. If you participate actively in your life you don't see it clearly: you suffer from it or enjoy it too much. The artist, to my way of thinking, is a monstrosity, something outside nature. All the misfortunes Providence inflicts on him come from his stubbornness in denying that axiom.'[36] In this sense, Sarah was certainly a monstrosity, though not of the type depicted here by Flaubert. His problem was the reconciliation of active living with detached observation; hers, that of entering into what, for most people, is 'real' life with the same wholeheartedness that she applied to her stage characterizations. It was her inability to do this – and, conversely, her ability to give her whole self on stage – which made her such a spellbinding actress. But the same psychological peculiarity made it almost inconceivable that the marriage with Damala could have worked, even if so many cards had not anyway been stacked against it.

On the day after Sarah's marriage, the London *Times* had commented that 'Behind the Mlle Bernhardt whom the public know, is another personality of which they know nothing and can infer nothing with any particular certainty. It is occasionally good to remind ourselves that . . . all the actress is not in her parts . . . The abounding energy and intense vitality of the great actress seem to exhaust the possibilities of a single life, and leave us almost unable to comprehend the existence of a whole world of thought and emotion into which we have not been permitted to look . . . Whether married life will exercise upon her that subduing, not to say depressing influence which many of us have felt remains to be seen.'[37] The *Times* was right there – the influence of marriage on Sarah (and on the unfortunate Damala, too) was nothing if not depressing. But it was wrong in its first premise. The fact was that most of Sarah, emotionally, *was* in her parts; and, if it was difficult for her

325

public to imagine any room for private life outside them, the feat was just as difficult for her. This aspect of the actress as artist – and of Sarah in particular – had, as we have seen, proved particularly worrying to men such as the Goncourts who felt that a woman's role was primarily to be a loving, feeling being. Consider, in this light, her account of attending four executions, including that of Vaillant, a man she liked and respected. As Max Beerbohm put it, 'You, gentle reader, might not care to visit an execution – especially not that of a personal friend. But then, you see, you are not a great tragedian.'[38]

Where personal involvement – as opposed to what Beerbohm called 'emotion for emotion's sake', the study, rehearsal, and trying on for fit of emotion – where emotion truly engulfed her, as when she was distracted by her mother or Damala, her art suffered. So did her personal appearance, which was such an important element of the artistic effect she purveyed. Whether or not she was a great beauty, she was magically attractive; and the way in which she retained this capacity to captivate and enslave until she was well into middle age – almost approaching old age, indeed – became, as we shall see, one of the more extraordinary aspects of her career. There was only one moment when the paeans of praise lavished by the press on her apparent imperviousness to the effects of age faltered – and that was in 1886, just before the South American tour, when *Marion Delorme* had collapsed, she had sold her house, and Damala, who had robbed her of her magic touch, was still hovering in the shadows. The *Times* then wrote (of her appearance in *La Dame* in London): 'Time is not dealing kindly with Madame Sarah Bernhardt. The four or five years that she has spent in European tours and in playing melodrama at the Porte-Saint-Martin have told upon her voice, which no longer yields enchanting music, especially in passages where she attempts a sustained note of tenderness ... Moreover, she has begun to lose her abnormal thinness, and with it some of that wonderful *chatterie* which was her characteristic.'[39] She was then forty-two; it was the only moment when middle-age threatened to overwhelm her. By the time she returned from her tour, she had resumed her never-more-to-be-interrupted youth.

The only exception to this rule of emotional non-involvement was Maurice; but Maurice, who was literally her pride and joy, she had fashioned to her own design. She felt the same kind of pride in him, wrote Maurice Rostand, as some owners feel about a thoroughbred they own – 'and it was precisely a thoroughbred that Maurice brought to mind!' As for Sarah, 'she seemed to shine with malicious joy at having created a genuine gentleman of high degree, a role which she was quite incapable of playing herself'[40] – a role to which Maurice's marriage had added the final finishing touch. And if he was to some extent his mother's gigolo, 'who except fools and bourgeois could that possibly offend?'[41]

26

By the second half of the 1880s, two quite separate Sarahs were to be seen onstage at the Porte-Saint-Martin, or wherever else in the world she happened currently to be playing.

One of these was quite simply the most seductive incarnation of sexuality it was possible to imagine. 'She puts into her roles, not only her whole heart, soul and physical grace, but all her sexuality as well,' wrote Jules Lemaître after seeing her *Théodora*.[1] 'After the first words of her vibrant, lovely voice I felt that I had known her for years,' recorded Sigmund Freud, who went to see her play on every possible occasion during his visits to Paris (where he was studying with the great Charcot at the Salpêtrière: he might well have seen Sarah at Charcot's weekly open lectures, which she attended regularly, eager for the clues they might offer regarding human behaviour *in extremis*). '. . . Every inch of that little figure lives and bewitches . . . It is incredible what postures she can assume and how every limb and every joint acts with her. A curious being: I can imagine that she needn't be any different in life from on the stage.'[2] And if Freud at this time was young and susceptible, how much more susceptible was the even younger Pierre Louÿs: 'I'm going mad, I'm beside myself, I don't know what I'm doing, I can't think about anything else, I saw Sarah Bernhardt yesterday evening,' he recorded in his diary after seeing her Tosca, another of Sardou's made-to-measure creations. '. . . If only it were possible I could love her like a madman, oh,

328

Sarah! Sarah! My God, Sarah! you're as pretty and graceful as a seventeen-year-old. You are Sarah *la grande*. You're the only woman in the world. I understand now why people love actresses when they have the genius of Sarah. I can understand how one would do anything, leave everything, ruin oneself, kill oneself for a woman like that. But how can one compare Sarah with any other woman? . . . And this woman, this miracle of grace and suppleness, is an old woman of forty-four!'[3]

In one way this was nothing new. We have seen that Sarah's capacity to put unequivocal sexuality into her stage portrayals had always marked her out from other actresses. But this had been something that was in herself rather than in the plays. For, despite the Second Empire's reputation for licence and naughtiness, even plays such as *La Dame aux camélias* and *Adrienne Lecouvreur*, where the leading role was that of a courtesan, hinted at the heroine's excesses rather than depicting them onstage. Sarah's real innovation was that she played even Racine – notably *Phèdre* but also *Andromaque* – in a romantic, i.e. freely emotional, style. This, especially in the case of *Phèdre*, may seem no exceptional insight; but those who had seen Rachel play the same part remarked that, where Rachel brought out all the classic horror of the situation *and the character*, Sarah's interpretation, on the contrary, evoked pity and empathy with this victim of irresistible sexual desire (a sexuality she made explicit to the point of, at one moment, drawing her hands up the insides of her thighs). She managed to fill the character of Andromaque, too, with her own unique sexual power, even while emphasizing by her costume that here was a daughter deeply mourning her dead father.

But it was with the advent of Sardou that Sarah became, unequivocally, the Great Seductress. That – in those plays that Freud (who had seen *Théodora*) characterized as 'Dora and Feodora, . . . Thermidora, Ecuadora and Toreadora' –

was one of the aspects of her that Sardou set out to display, together with her gift for spectacle and attitude, her unrivalled stage presence, her capacity for conveying passion and suspending disbelief, and all the rest of the bag of tricks he could so brilliantly assemble, she so brilliantly present. The result of their joint efforts was the stunningly seductive figure whose effects are described with such touching ardour by the young Pierre Louÿs (then a precocious schoolboy of eighteen).

But Sarah was not *simply* seductive. There was about her (especially when acting Sardou's femmes fatales) an aura of sin which, in those decadent times, only added to the attraction.

> I would taste her in all her
> agonies, have her to spare not,
> Sin deep as she has sinned . . .
> To be, for a moment, the man of all men to her,
> All the world, for one measureless moment complete;
> To possess, be possessed! To be mockery then to her,
> Then to die at her feet.
>
> Arthur Symons [4]

Symons writes of Sarah's acting 'awakening the senses and sending the intelligence to sleep'.[5] Whatever she appeared in, and despite all absurdities, Sarah imposed herself in a highly disturbing way. No wonder poor Alice James, confined with her imagination and the latest journals to her sick-room in Leamington Spa, wrote: 'How revolting Sarah Bernhardt acting in a Passion Play! She is a moral abscess, festering with vanity.'[6] (Alice would perhaps have felt vindicated by the bathos of the actual event. Sarah had persuaded Edmond Haraucourt to write a Passion Play for her in 1890; since scoring a notable success as Joan of Arc she had become enamoured of religious subjects. Despite the condemnation of the Church, the event was fixed for

Good Friday night, not at a theatre – all theatres were closed on that evening – but in a reading as part of a larger entertainment at the Cirque d'Hiver. Philippe Garnier was to read the part of Jesus, Brémond, that of Judas, and Sarah, the parts of the Virgin, Mary Magdalen and Martha, not to speak of the women's chorus. Not surprisingly, the audience found it difficult to make out quite what was going on, and people began to leave. Then a wag in the gallery shouted '*Mousic*' in an imitation of the famous clown Auguste at the Hippodrome, and pandemonium broke loose. Cheers and hisses drowned the voices of the artists. Sarah burst into tears; Garnier and Brémond were pale and silent. Sarah got up to leave the stage, but cheers and shouts of '*Non! Non!*' held her back. Haraucourt leapt onto the stage, seized Sarah's hands, shook the actors' hands, and implored those who wanted to leave to do so and allow the rest to listen in peace. Then the actors read to the end of the first act and gave up.)

The shameless, irresistible vamp was one of the Sarahs of this period. But there was another. And this was a Sarah who, despite, or even because of, the full houses of adoring fans eager to experience her in the latest Sardou, was widely considered to be in decline, a sorry shadow of the actress she had been ten years earlier. By the end of the 1880s it was generally agreed by the critics that the demands of touring in countries where no one understood French, combined with the incessant pressure to make a lot of money in popular vehicles, had wreaked havoc both with her judgment and with that original and poetic genius which she had possessed. The low point was generally agreed to be *Léna*, a feeble adaptation by Pierre Berton of a worthless English novel, of which the only good thing that could be said was that at the end Sarah died quite beautifully. Writing about this, Jules Lemaître, who was one of her greatest supporters, meditated on the fiasco. What could be the state

331

of mind of this amazing woman, he wondered, after the extraordinary life which had been hers for the past ten years? All over the world she had been received with the overwhelming pomp and majesty which even kings could no longer expect, let alone the princes of the intellect. 'She must have believed, sometimes, that she could do anything she wanted. The absence of anyone who might gainsay her, the servility that surrounds her, the universal acclamation, the pretence of the stage which finally becomes her reality, the consciousness that she is unique in the world – might not all that lead to what one might call a *neronian* state of mind, in which the conditions of ordinary life are forgotten, where everything is subjected to sterile caprice?'[7] Even in London, her adoring home from home, critical voices were raised. A. B. Walkley remarked, in the summer of 1889, on her need – of which she herself must have been only too aware – for 'a larger, saner, more varied repertory. But she will never get that repertory so long as she goes wandering from pole to pole, with a new piece, specially constructed for her by M. Sardou, in her pocket.'[8]

Was it possible that she would be able to recover her artistic reputation? – or that it still meant anything to this woman who was so famous that peasants stopped her train in a remote corner of Scandinavia and would only let it pass when she had dressed herself, come to the window, and thrown them smiles and flowers, whose name was known even to an obscure ferryman in Bessarabia so that, picking it up in the midst of a conversation which was going on in French, he pricked up his ears, smiled, and repeated 'Sarah Bernhardt! Sarah Bernhardt!'[9]

For another year Sarah pursued an undistinguished course at the Porte-Saint-Martin, putting on an inferior Sardou – *Cléopatre* – and a patriotic drama about Joan of Arc. Then she gave up her lease, packed her bags, and in 1891 set off on a gigantic tour of Australia which lasted sixteen months. In 1892, after a London season, she toured Scandinavia, Austria and Romania; she then went on to South America, where she played Rio, Buenos Aires and Montevideo (but not Santiago). She returned with her coffers replenished and her loins girded, ready for another assault on Paris. She bought a small, rather dilapidated theatre, the Renaissance, refurbished it so that it became the most modern and comfortable theatre in Paris, and began a new season.

And the new Sarah was a triumph. Everyone admitted it, and it extended to every aspect of her art. She was willing to put on new works whose interest was not just spectacular but intellectual: a delicate and charming play by Lemaître, *Les Rois*, was one of her first productions at the Renaissance. (In fact this play nearly did not get put on. The Austrian ambassador objected to it because he thought the main scene was too strongly suggestive of the death of the Austrian Crown Prince Rudolph, and protested to the government against the production of a play evidently based on the Mayerling tragedy. Bernhardt and Lemaître were instructed that the offending scene must be modified: they retorted that this would be impossible. It looked for a time as though the play would be interdicted. But in fact it went ahead and was a great success.) She presented a realist drama, *Magda*, by the German playwright Sudermann, which was to remain one of the staples of her repertoire (and also of Duse's). As for her old favourites, it was generally acknowledged that her *Phèdre*, also mounted in 1893, stood on a level with anything she had ever done. She had given *Phèdre* once in Paris the previous year, on her way to London, and those who had seen her had raved about her performance. Francisque Sarcey, who had not, confessed that he had been sceptical – he who remembered her in the same part at the Comédie-Française 'in all the splendour of her youth and glory'. Then, he recalled, her performance had been admirable in parts, although she had been a long way from complete mastery of the role. It was hard to believe that she could have gained this mastery in the course of running round the world. But – he had been wrong. 'It's strange, unheard-of, inexplicable – but true: Mme Sarah Bernhardt is younger, more striking, and, let's say it, more beautiful than she has ever been – a dramatic beauty which makes one shiver with admiration, as when one sees a beautiful statue . . . The tears started from my eyes [Sarcey was well-known for his penchant for tears.] It is impossible to imagine . . . the intensity of despair about her whole person, and the divine poetry that envelopes her like a luminous fog.'[10]

From now on, Sarah was no longer an ordinary (though amazingly successful and publicized) actress over whom men might swoon, and whose powers and repertoire might (at least in her home town) be compared, favourably or unfavourably, with other actresses. In her seemingly eternal youthfulness, in her energies, in her apparently inexhaustible capacities – Sarah had become a Phenomenon.

27

Sarah entered into this, perhaps the most extraordinary of her apotheoses, at the age of forty-nine; and for almost the next twenty years she was to maintain herself as a phenomenon, outside age, outside sex, outside anything that most people might conceive of as real life. How was it done?

It was, first of all, the result of an almost superhuman vitality and capacity for work. Gone now were the days when the temperamental diva tormented the management with her unreliability and her tendency to cough blood when overstrained. Sarah was transformed in this respect not, as we have seen, when she first formed her own company, but rather when she leased her own theatres and became the management herself. In the Porte-Saint-Martin she had installed her old friend Duquesnel as manager; in the Renaissance, she (aided, in his way, by Maurice) was in charge. There was no aspect of a production, from the costumes to the health of the scene-shifters, that did not concern her. Edmond Rostand, who was to become her personifying playwright in this incarnation as Victorien Sardou had been in the last, described her day in a famous passage that may contain some exaggeration – but not much:

A brougham stops at a door; a woman, enveloped in furs, jumps out, threads her way with a smile through the crowd attracted by the jingling of the bell on the harness, and mounts a winding stair; plunges into a room crowded with

flowers and heated like a hothouse; throws her little
beribboned handbag with its apparently inexhaustible
contents into one corner, and her bewinged hat into
another; takes off her furs and instantaneously dwindles
into a mere scabbard of white silk; rushes on to a dimly-lit
stage and immediately puts life into a whole crowd of
listless, yawning, loitering folk; dashes backwards and
forwards, inspiring everyone with her own feverish energy;
goes into the prompter's box, arranges her scenes, points
out the proper gesture and intonation, rises up in wrath and
insists on everything being done over again; shouts with
fury; sits down, smiles, drinks tea and begins to rehearse
her own part; draws tears from case-hardened actors who
thrust their enraptured heads out of the wings to watch her;
returns to her room, where the designers are waiting,
demolishes their plans and reconstructs them; collapses,
wipes her brow with a lace handkerchief and thinks of
fainting; suddenly rushes up to the fifth floor, invades the
premises of the astonished costumier, rummages in the
wardrobes, makes up a costume, pleats and adjusts it;
returns to her room and teaches the figurantes how to dress
their hair; has a piece read to her while she makes
bouquets; listens to hundreds of letters, weeps over some
tale of misfortune, and opens the inexhaustible little
chinking handbag; confers with an English perruquier;
returns to the stage to superintend the lighting of a scene,
objurgates the lamps and reduces the electrician to a state of
temporary insanity; sees a super who has blundered the day
before, remembers it, and overwhelms him with her
indignation; returns to her room for dinner; sits down at
table, splendidly pale with fatigue; ruminates her plans; eats
with peals of Bohemian laughter; has no time to finish;
dresses for the evening performance while the manager
reports from the other side of a curtain; acts with all her
heart and soul; discusses business between the acts; remains
at the theatre after the performance, and makes
arrangements until three o'clock in the morning; does not
make up her mind to go until she sees her staff respectfully
endeavouring to keep awake; gets into her carriage; huddles
herself into her furs and anticipates the delights of lying

down and resting; bursts out laughing on remembering that
someone is waiting to read her a five-act play; returns
home, listens to the piece, becomes excited, weeps, accepts
it, finds she cannot sleep, and takes advantage of the
opportunity to study a part![1]

Account after account confirms Sarah's extraordinary
energy. Like many very successful people she could do
without much sleep, and also had the useful ability to take
a catnap anywhere, at any time, and awake refreshed after
ten minutes or an hour. And of course she did not act 'with
all her heart and soul' every evening. As Oscar Wilde
pointed out, 'Sarah never really *acts* more than twice a
week, if so often'[2] and it was only relatively rarely that, in
her own words, '*le Dieu était là*'. But this is perhaps hardly
surprising.

So much for the engine. But of course, that was what the
public did *not* see. As to what they did see – that was most
skilfully and curiously packaged.

Jules Lemaître, in one of his more rhapsodic moments,
had wished that Sarah should 'one fine evening, die on
stage, suddenly, in the midst of a great tragic cry, for old age
would be too hard a thing for you'.[3] However, at the
moment when age might have been expected to start its
depredations, Sarah stepped, if one may put it this way,
outside age.

The difficulties of overcoming this obstacle for an artist
whose physical glamour forms such an important part of
her reputation, may perhaps be grasped if we look at the
ways in which other actresses with comparable reputations
as epitomes of sex and beauty dealt with the same situation.
Greta Garbo side-stepped the problems of ageing by retiring
in her thirties, so that the image we have of her is always
that of a young and beautiful woman. Marilyn Monroe,
another of this select company, solved the problem in

337

another way – by committing suicide at a comparable moment, before having to face up to the onset of decay. Elizabeth Taylor subsided into fat and alcoholism. Sarah did none of these things. She could never have afforded to retire even if she had wanted to. As for committing suicide – by now the only thing that would have driven her to it was, perhaps, retirement. Her whole professional life was a statement of her decision to survive: to give it up would have been a declaration of ultimate despair. What she did manage to do was to preserve, for an extraordinary span of years, the image of herself as she had been at her apogee. The nature of what we should today call her image, so dependent upon her reputation for glamorous seductiveness, meant that for Sarah there could be no graceful descent into character roles – even if any worth playing had existed. This tour de force resulted, as we shall see, in her coming to seem not so much old as dated, rather as it is possible to tell a woman's age by the style of her make-up – generally, the style which was prevalent in her youth.

Sarah's 'phenomenal' stage dates, it will be noticed, from about the time of the menopause. And from this time on it is noticeable that the tone of the paeans of praise which continued to be lavished upon her person becomes less directly sexual and more poetical. Maurice Baring, for example, evokes a series of tableaux: 'La Princesse Lointaine crowned with lilies, sumptuous and sad, like one of Swinburne's early poems; . . . la Samaritaine evok[ing] the spices, the fire, and the vehemence of the Song of Solomon; . . . Gismonda, with chrysanthemums in her hair, amidst the jewelled glow of the Middle Ages, against the background of the Acropolis; . . . Izéil incarnating the soul and dream of India.' Without all these, 'you eliminate one of the sources of inspiration of modern art'.[4] Edmond de Goncourt describes her 'in her idol's outfit, with that indefinable seductiveness of an antique magician'.[5] Not that, even now,

338

the seductiveness was always so indefinable. Of *Izéil*, which she played in 1894 when she was fifty, one critic wrote: 'In the third act, Sarah Bernhardt wears a costume which clings to her figure so that she seems to be naked. She struggles against a rapist and her terror is translated into a gesture of the whole body.'[6] But the new plays which were being written for her at this period by the young poet-playwright Edmond Rostand – *La Princesse lointaine, La Samaritaine* – brought out this timeless, poetical quality, just as Sardou had emphasized the vamp in the period immediately preceding. 'Sarah isn't an actress any more,' quipped Jules Renard in his journal. 'What she is is more like the song of the trees, the sound of an instrument. It's perfect and one is used to it.'[7] Max Beerbohm contrasts Sarah with Réjane, who 'excels in virtue of seeming so essentially a mortal woman', while Sarah 'might be, aptly enough, called "Goddess," inasmuch as she is quite unlike any other woman. Her voice and her face, her reposes and her unrest, her expressions of love and hatred ... none of them ever recalls to you anything else of the kind. Generically feminine and specifically Parisian though she is, she has always a kind of lurid supernaturalness.'[8]

She could not only manipulate age: she could manipulate sex. For one of the most extraordinary aspects of this stage of her career is the frequency with which she played young men. At a time when her playing was becoming, in a sense, less innovatory, this startling fact stands out: that almost all her most notable roles were of this type. Rostand's Aiglon, Musset's Lorenzaccio, Maeterlinck's Pelléas, Hamlet – these were the parts which gained her the critics' attention, though not always their approval, at this period. Just as she had begun her career playing *travesti* – most notably in *Le Passant* – so as she got older she returned to her preference for playing boys. And the extraordinary thing was that, if the critics are to be believed, she carried conviction in the parts. At best – as the photo of her as Hamlet shows – she really looked like a boy. It is almost impossible to imagine that this is a woman fifty-two years old. By then, the extreme thinness of her younger days had disappeared; even so, the figure, the stance, are definitely boyish – paradoxically, more so than when, still in her twenties, she had played her first successful *travesti* part as Zanetto in *Le Passant*. Then, 'her disguise was at once revealed, and her acting occasioned the peculiar amusement which arises from the detection of a woman wearing the costume of a man and displaying in it a laughable degree of awkwardness and embarrassment. In her later parts, on the contrary, [she] conveys the most dignified and noble impression of being in reality the man whom she impersonates. Her ease is extraordinary. For a long time before appearing as Lorenzaccio or Hamlet she accustomed herself to her costume by wearing it in her own house, thus adapting to it her gestures and familiar movements.'[9]

These *travesti* parts held both advantages and disadvantages for Sarah. The main advantage (other than the obvious fact that far more good parts are written for men than women, and especially middle-aged women) was that a woman playing a man, because she has a lighter frame and voice, invariably seems like a very young man. As Elizabeth Robins, herself a fine actress, remarked apropos Sarah's Hamlet (in which she saw many fine points, although she did not think it was subtle enough to be called a great interpretation of the role), there is a stage law 'by which, apparently, a woman, when she plays at being a man, may hope with some show of success to climb to the height of twenty years, and then stops short, suffering, it would seem, from arrested development'.[10] These effects, of simplicity and extreme youth, may have been more intentional than Robins thought. Sarah's view of Hamlet was that 'his character is a perfectly simple one. He is brought face to face

340

with a duty, and he determines to carry it out. All his philosophizing and temporary hesitation does not alter the basis of his character. His resolution swerves, but immediately returns to the channel he has marked out for it. I know this view is quite heterodox, but I maintain it.' As to the view that Hamlet would have been at least thirty, she rejected this as well. In the play, she pointed out, he is still a student; his friends are older than him, and refer to him as 'Young Hamlet'.[11]

Both her *Hamlet* and her *Lorenzaccio* were generally received with enthusiasm by French critics, for whom they were part of a long tradition of cross-dressing by actresses (whereas in the English theatre, although a few actresses have played men's roles, the cross-dressing was traditionally, and particularly in Shakespeare's day, all in the other direction). They particularly welcomed Marcel Schwob's new translation of *Hamlet*, and Sarah's courage in staging Musset's *Lorenzaccio*, which had hitherto been considered unplayable. Colette, who was a friend of Schwob's, was persuaded by him to go and see this *Hamlet*, and was enchanted by it. 'I didn't go to see her act very often at that time, because I hadn't yet found out that, in Sarah's performances, there would be just a few moments which made all the rest of the evening worthwhile . . . In the "Get thee to a nunnery" scene between Hamlet and Ophelia, and the following violent and terrible dialogue between Hamlet and the Queen, Sarah's voice was low and intense, without any raging or arbitrary scansion. She did the same thing here and there in *Lorenzaccio* . . . At those moments she seemed to be the vessel of some unseen counsellor which could only have been her own genius.'[12]

Anglophones, however, gave these roles a more mixed reception. Some, such as Clement Scott and Maurice Baring, were wholly enthusiastic. For Scott, Sarah's Hamlet 'was imaginative, electrical and poetical . . . It all passed like a delightful dream.'[13] For Baring, Sarah's achievement was that 'whereas most Hamlets seem isolated from the rest of the players, as if they were reciting something apart from the play and speaking to the audience, this Hamlet spoke to the other persons of the play, shared their life, their extraordinary life ... This Hamlet was a Prince in Denmark ... there was real continuity.'[14] But Max Beerbohm was unimpressed. Entitling his notice 'Hamlet, Princess of Denmark', he confessed that 'I cannot, on my heart, take Sarah's Hamlet seriously. I cannot even imagine anyone capable of more than a hollow pretence of taking it seriously.' He sincerely hoped that Sarah would not set an example by which all actresses, as well as all actors, felt they must jump through this particular theatrical hoop; and concluded: 'Yes! the only compliment one can conscientiously pay her is that her Hamlet was, from first to last, *très grande dame*.'[15] As for her Aiglon some years later (she first played it in 1900 at the age of fifty-six), he commented that 'as L'Aiglon and other young men, she loses herself, but becomes no one else: she becomes merely a coruscating *thing*'.[16] Certainly the impression given by photographs of her in this role is fairly bizarre. And of her Lorenzaccio, William Archer wrote that 'if a youth with the grace of a tiger-cat and the genius of Edmund Kean should one day appear on the French stage, he will find a triumph awaiting him in *Lorenzaccio*. No young ladies need apply.'[17]

It was in *travesti*, however, and in London, that Sarah launched out into one of the more daring exploits of her career, in which she played Pelléas to Mrs Patrick Campbell's Mélisande in Maeterlinck's *Pelléas et Mélisande*. This was an extraordinary theatrical occasion, both because of the casting and because it was perhaps the only time in which Bernhardt ever tried a modern play of any literary or theatrical interest other than that which she herself injected into it. The production was a commercial success, doubtless

342

as much because it was a theatrical curiosity as for any other reason (although the notices were generally good except for a critic in Dublin who observed that 'Mrs Campbell played Mélisande, Madame Bernhardt Pelléas; they are both old enough to know better.'[18] On the other hand the Agate family, of whom May was to become Sarah's devoted pupil and James the leading drama critic of his day, all agreed that Sarah's Pelléas was the best thing she ever did, 'the butt and sea-mark of her utmost sail'.[19])

Sarah had seen Mrs Pat as Mélisande in an English production and been impressed; this led her to suggest the collaboration, which Mrs Pat took to be just a pretty compliment, but which, six years later, turned out to have been quite seriously meant. But there were problems. One was the difficulty of teaching Mrs Pat to speak the French correctly – for although the play is in prose, it is poetical prose, and the rhythm is important. 'How dared I?' was Mrs Pat's reflection later; but Sarah assured her that an English accent, so long as it was not too strong, would simply emphasize the other-worldliness of Mélisande. More of a difficulty was the fact that Mrs Pat – whose determined amateurishness was, as we have seen, the despair of Bernard Shaw – simply could not take the project entirely seriously. The differences in their approach are encapsulated in the story of how Mrs Pat, visiting Sarah in her dressing-room during a run of *Cleopatra*, noticed her painting her hands, 'staining her finger-tips and palms with the dusky red of henna. Mrs Campbell watched with some impatience; she had business to discuss and was in a hurry. "Why do you take so much trouble?" she said at last. "What you are doing will never show from the front. Nobody will see it."

' "I shall see it," replied Sarah . . . "I am doing it for myself. If I catch sight of my hand it will be the hand of Cleopatra. That will help me." '[20] Mrs Pat's lack of professional dedication sometimes drove Sarah to the brink of despair; but perhaps she did not take this production too seriously herself, for it was the occasion of one of her few recorded jokes on stage, when, in a moment of passion, she pressed a raw egg into Mrs Pat's hand.

It is perhaps interesting to note in this context that London would have been the occasion of her only other foray into serious experimental theatre, with Oscar Wilde's *Salomé*, which was written for her in French (the drafts were corrected by Marcel Schwob and Pierre Louÿs) and began rehearsals in June 1892. The production was designed by Graham Robertson; there was to be a violet sky, braziers of perfume in place of an orchestra; Salomé was to wear a golden robe with long fringes of gold, and her hair was to be blue. Sarah insisted that she would do the dance of the seven veils herself – as to how, 'Never you mind!' But the play was banned by the Lord Chancellor. It was finally put on in Paris by Lugné-Poë at the Théâtre de l'Oeuvre in 1896, when Wilde was in prison. Later, when he was short of money, he hoped for a while that Sarah would help him out by buying the play, but she never did.

However, phenomenon or goddess though she might be, Sarah in her working life was still moved entirely by practical considerations, and would undertake any necessary expedient. In 1905–6 a tour of America was arranged. Sarah was travelling under the management of the Shubert brothers, who were trying to break the monopoly of the Klaw-Erlanger syndicate, which dictated policy and performances in virtually all the legitimate theatres in the States. Sarah refused to agree to their terms, and as a result could get no theatres to accept her. Undeterred, she set out. Something like this had happened once before when she had been working with Jarrett, when theatre managers in the Midwest had refused to lease her their theatres because (they maintained) everybody from miles around made a day out in order to come in and see 'the Bernhardt', and spent all their money while they were about it, with the result that following American shows could get no audiences. Jarrett had got round that by arranging for Bernhardt's troupe to play in a circus tent. This time they did the same thing again – except that this time, Sarah had her own tent that travelled with her, Barnum and Bailey's largest circus tent, seating six thousand, which the Shuberts had hired. Nothing now could stop her appearing wherever she pleased. 'How glad – how fortunate – I am to be in the hands of such live, energetic managers!' she said.[21] She appeared in the tent in Chicago, Columbus, and some other cities; special trains had to be put on to transport the crowds who wanted to see Sarah. In Los Angeles she performed at Venice, in a pier built over the ocean. It was on this tour that Alice B. Toklas saw her perform *Phèdre* in the Greek amphitheatre at the University of California at Berkeley. She remembered the performance because it took place just after the great earthquake had destroyed much of San Francisco, including the Toklas house. She particularly remembered Phèdre's anguished cry as she leaves the stage at the end of the first act. 'Evidently Bernhardt had had no rehearsals, nor had she studied the large stage. Her arms outstretched, with her piercing cry she backed forever towards the curtained door. She prolonged the cry, the golden voice continued. The audience was breathless. Finally she reached the curtain and disappeared. I had seen her in many of her poignant roles but was never more moved than then.' After the performance the students, in the now hackneyed manner, unhitched Sarah's horses and prepared to pull her carriage themselves. Toklas got a good look at her. 'She fearlessly faced the California sun, her head thrown back with her famous radiant smile. I noticed, however, her visibly large teeth.'[22]

It was hard for this being, who spent so much of her time in a world apart, to descend thence into anything resembling a private life. The house in the boulevard Péreire, cluttered with mementoes, hangings, flowers and animals, so that it reminded one friend 'of the show-window in a second-hand furniture shop: priceless objects and rubbish, all mixed up in happy confusion',[1] and the equally cluttered dressing-room at the theatre, were simply two more settings within which the legendary creature might be encountered leading her legendary life. Visitors to the house, after unsettling encounters with animals – a parrot sharing a cage with a monkey which tormented it, but from which it could not bear to be parted, a puma on a chain unnervingly sniffing the guests before, to everyone's unspoken relief, it was led away, two enormous white dogs ensuring that everyone would be covered with white hairs – would be invited to sit down – but there were no chairs, only heaps of cushions and divans; later, taking Sarah in to dinner, Jules Renard, leaving her at the first chair, realized that he should have led her all the way to the throne set on a dais at the table's head, where she drank from a golden goblet.[2]

One result of this extraordinary life was that it was no longer easy for Sarah to make friends as an equal among equals. On her tours especially (she was generally known, now, as 'The Wanderer' and 'The Muse of the Railroads') she was absolutely isolated. It was almost inevitable that, after twenty-five years of constant gyration around that uncultured portion of the globe never visited and hardly dreamed of by metropolitan litterateurs, she should see herself, in relation to many of her audiences, almost as a being from another planet. During her 1905 tour of the Americas she had more than once to retract tactless comments which had outraged the nations under attack and threatened to close their theatres to her. It was reported that 'unless she denies that she once made a statement to the effect that Cubans are half-civilized negroes who wear evening suits, it may not be safe for her to visit Havana this season'.[3] She duly denied it, but the Cubans were (naturally enough) not entirely convinced. A little later, she was in trouble with the Canadians. She had been reported as saying they were behind the times, under the yoke of the clergy, and that 'it is idle to say they are French, as they are a mixture of English, Irish, French and Iroquois. They have no poets, no artists, no literature.' As a result of this, she and her company (including Edouard de Max, her leading man on this tour) were pelted with eggs after a performance at Quebec.[4]

But even at home in Paris she was isolated – a paradoxical situation, surrounded as she always was by crowds of adorers. Maurice Rostand wrote that 'there were two people in Sarah – an extremely virile one and an extremely feminine one, and she was the sum of the two joined together in a single body'. The conclusion he drew was that although this made her doubly the object of adoration – women adored her as Hamlet, men as Marguerite Gautier – it precluded any real emotional involvement. Rostand thought that in terms of real devotion, Sarah attracted women even more than men; he was thinking particularly of those women such as Mme Guérard and, later, the delightful actress Suzanne Seylor, who were happy to dedicate their whole lives to her. 'She has certainly been adored – but being adored is not the same thing as being loved.'

347

She was, in Rostand's view, 'above love – which is perhaps beautiful, but is also sad'.[5] Certainly one did not often surprise Sarah carried away by her feelings: what one saw more usually was a wonderful impersonation of someone carried away. She would fly into a rage with members of her staff in her dressing-room, but everyone knew that the rage was more for show than anything else and that the storm would soon pass, and most people simply enjoyed watching the performance. (In the same way her old admirer Pierre Loti, who was also a passionate play-actor and dresser-up, would fly into sudden rages. Robert de Montesquiou comments that both of them, 'like all despots, liked to get angry just so as to make themselves felt in a purely arbitrary way: one must just not take any notice, and the crisis passes'.[6]) Colette never forgot the sight of her taking a bow after a brilliant performance of some trivial role 'as if to say, "Yes, I know how to do this, too – what *don't* I know ..."' In the same way she liked to play at performing the ordinary chores of life: she would, with the greatest care and concentration, grill a pork chop on a gas-ring in her dressing-room.[7] But this didn't make her seem any more like an ordinary human being – it was simply Sarah acting the part of one.

Jacques Porel, the son of Réjane and Paul Porel, also remarks upon her isolated social position at this time: 'more than an empress, a sort of divinity ... Victor Hugo is the only person with whom she could be compared. She was so famous that relations with other people became difficult, resulting in a sort of holy but desolate solitude.' From this exalted position she nevertheless maintained close friendships with a few artistic families – the Porels, Lucien Guitry and his son Sacha, the Rostands and their son Maurice. Jacques remembered being taken to see her in her dressing-room:

'All right, my son, go on!'
There, among the lights reflected a thousand times by the

348

mirrors, twenty empresses, twenty queens, twenty
goddesses – Sarah – open-armed, an eternal smile on her
face, Sarah, in her celebrated attitude, was waiting for me.

It was like a sort of sprint into glory. I fell into her arms. I
couldn't see her eyes any more. My cheek met the
byzantine robe [Sarah, at this time, invariably wore long,
pale, waistless, sumptuous robes]. I plunged into the
pungent scent of the make-up of that era. And, for an
instant, I felt the sweet murmur of that famous voice in my
ear. I couldn't make it out, but already she was holding me
by the shoulders, shooting her inimitable smile at me.

'And how is your mother?'[8]

To children of her friends, such as little Jacques, she was a
sort of fairy grandmother. Maurice Rostand remembered
that, one Christmas, she gave him a blue and gold toy
theatre together with its company of actors, bearing the
legend *Théâtre Sarah Bernhardt*, complete even to the play-
bills, which were advertising *L'Escargot rouge*, a play in five
acts by M. Maurice Rostand. Sacha Guitry went 'to kiss
Madame Sarah' with his father every Sunday for ten years,
'in the same way as other children go to mass – piously'.
And every Christmas there was a party in her studio, with
an enormous tree in the middle, with a thousand candles,
and from whose branches hung fifty toys – 'for there were
at least fifty children there that day. Every toy was num-
bered, and when the moment came to give them out, Mme
Sarah held out to us a big velvet bag from which every child
picked a number – at random. But the randomness was
always so arranged that the most beautiful toy fell to the lot
of her son's little girl. Dressed like a storybook princess,
adored, pampered, Simone Bernhardt seemed to us somebody very precious, not quite like ourselves. It seemed quite
natural to us that her toy should be much nicer than ours,
and we even understood that we fifty other children were

only there to see her being happy, happier than any other child in the world.'[9]

Such was the enviable fate of being a child in Sarah's family – a fate so different from her own childhood which, in the persons of her grandchildren, she had finally exorcised. Not that she had done this by turning her back on those who might bring grimmer memories to mind: on the contrary, as everyone who knew her remarks, her doors were always open to any uncle, aunt or cousin. She was particularly close to her niece Saryta, Jeanne's daughter. Jeanne was now beyond help, a slave to morphine. She died in 1900, and poor Saryta followed her five years later. But while she was alive she was constantly in Sarah's company, and her aunt, as she had with Jeanne, did all she could to help her to a stage career – that career which had saved Sarah from Jeanne's and Saryta's fate – but with equally little result.

Perhaps the only member of Sarah's family in two minds about the advantages of belonging to it was Terka, Maurice's young wife. Marriage had not made him any less close to his mother, whom he still visited every day, and upon whom he still depended for his financial support. If more than one person remarked that he was a better son than he was a husband, this can hardly have surprised anyone. Terka, who died comparatively young, emerges as a somewhat subdued and melancholy figure. Reynaldo Hahn, the talented musician who was Marcel Proust's first great love, and who became a close friend of Sarah's at this time, remembered driving alone with Terka on Belle-Isle while she wryly discussed her husband and mother-in-law.

Only one thing ever came between Sarah and Maurice. It was the thing that divided all France during the second half of the nineties and the first few years of the new century: the Dreyfus case.

The Dreyfus case has always seemed inexplicable to foreigners. It all turned upon a scrap of paper, the infamous

350

bordereau, which seemed to be the text of a telegram sent by a French spy, working within the army, to his Prussian masters. It was found in a waste-paper basket in the German embassy by a cleaning-woman in the pay of French intelligence, and its handwriting was decided to be that of Captain Alfred Dreyfus, an Alsatian Jewish officer who would have had access to the information it contained. This handwriting identification was always very shaky, relying upon the conflicting evidence of three experts, two of whom denied that the paper was in Dreyfus's hand while the third affirmed that it certainly was. Nevertheless he was convicted at a court martial in 1894 and, after being officially degraded, was sent to the penal colony at Devil's Island in the French West Indies. After his conviction more and more evidence was unearthed indicating that Dreyfus was innocent, and pointing to a well-known gambler and mountebank called Esterhazy as the culprit, until in 1898, under great pressure (most notably from Emile Zola's famous pamphlet *J'Accuse*), the government was forced reluctantly to reopen the case. Almost incredibly, the new hearing once again found against Dreyfus. Nevertheless, some years later, after the suicide of one of the officers instrumental in incriminating him, an amnesty was declared and he was brought back from Devil's Island; and in 1906, twelve years after his degradation, he was finally reinstated as an officer in the army. Esterhazy was never convicted.

While all this was going on, it would be no exaggeration to say that the whole of France was split into dreyfusists and antidreyfusards. What the dreyfusists and most foreigners could not understand was how, in view of the shaky evidence upon which he was first convicted and the mountain of detail which emerged before the re-trial as to exactly who had framed him and how they had done it, anyone could possibly think Dreyfus was guilty and not recognize the horror of keeping an innocent man isolated in such a vile place as Devil's Island. But it soon became clear that

351

logic and the laws of evidence had little to do with the real case against Dreyfus, and less and less to do with it as time went on. What it was about was the violent polarization in society of which the Franco-Prussian war had been the catalyst. On the one hand this had led to the downfall of the Empire and the Catholic aristocracy (however mixed and diluted by new creations that might have become), and the triumph of the Republic and anti-clericalism. On the other hand there was an almost visceral need, not necessarily confined to Catholics and the upper classes, to believe in the integrity of the army, the only bulwark against a repetition of 1870. And allied to this was, naturally, a strong feeling of nationalism and xenophobia, which was again as rife among republicans as everyone else.

One result of all this was a rising tide, during the 1880s, of anti-Semitism. Sarah's own intimate circle of friends encountered this at close quarters. Many of her friends and acquaintances were, like herself, if not practising Jews, then of Jewish origin – there being a strongly Jewish element among intellectuals and writers. This, of course, was one of the very things that xenophobic nationalists objected to: for if the Revolution had declared that there was to be no differentiation between Catholic, Protestant and Jew but that all were simply French citizens (with the result that a great many Jews had come to live in France and particularly Paris), this way of thinking had not survived the Franco-Prussian war. Since then, Jews were increasingly seen as an alien nation, disproportionately powerful and influential, in France's midst. This was the gist of Edouard Drumont's infamous work *La France Juive*, published in 1886, which set out the horrible extent of Jewish wealth and influence.

One of the persons libelled by Drumont in this work was Sarah's old crony, one of the founder members of the *'petit cour'*, Arthur Meyer, editor of the *Gaulois*. Drumont had reprinted an old article describing him as a cardsharper; and as a result, Meyer challenged Drumont to a duel. Unfortunately, Meyer did not acquit himself well on this occasion. The duel was with swords in an old estate belonging to Baron Hirsch (as it happened, a Jew). Meyer parried the first encounter with his left hand, and, on the second encounter, grasped Drumont's sword while wounding him in the groin. Edmond de Goncourt (who was very anti-Semitic) described the aftermath. 'The whole boulevard outside the *Gaulois* offices was full of Jews, and every few minutes a brougham such as you see outside the church of Saint-Augustin when there is a society wedding discharged a sheeny on to the road. All the Dollfuses and Dreyfuses in creation were there, and Halévy and Koning and Ollendorff dragging Ohnet in his wake. Finally Meyer arrived and all the sheenies rushed up to him to congratulate him. "I don't deserve your compliments, gentlemen," he said. "I acquitted myself very badly in this affair . . . That man is a lion."'[10]

The result of the Dreyfus case eight years later was to harden nationalist and anti-Semitic attitudes still further. If one maintained that Dreyfus was innocent, one was *ipso facto* saying that a large proportion of the army general staff were lying conspirators. A great many people simply could not allow themselves to accept this. If one could not believe in the army, then the foundations of what many people saw as France's integrity were undermined. So, whatever the evidence, they resolutely did believe in the army and did not believe in Dreyfus and the dreyfusists who — in their eyes — were anyway mostly his co-religionists: another Jewish conspiracy. Proust has his *grande dame* Mme de Marsantes indicate the intense correctness of her brother the Prince de Guermantes at this time by saying, 'Naturally, he's as anti-Semitic as one could possibly be.' Her other brother, the duc de Guermantes, dismisses the dreyfusism of Swann, his Jewish society friend, by saying, 'It simply proves that they just have to support a member of their race, even if it's someone they don't know. It's a public danger.'

There were two classes of people who found themselves placed in a particular difficulty by this dilemma: those Jews who wanted to be accepted by high society; and those members of what we should today call the establishment who found that the force of the evidence was such that they simply could not go on believing in Dreyfus' guilt. The difficulty and reluctance with which these latter finally changed their position was a matter of astonishment to foreigners, who could see simply the dreadful facts. Sarah's old friend Georges Clairin was one of those reluctantly convinced. He believed so utterly in Dreyfus's guilt that he went to see him degraded at Rennes in 1894. But he became so utterly convinced of Dreyfus's innocence that, when he was finally reinstated in 1906, Clairin attended that ceremony as well. Arthur Meyer, on the other hand, deeply desired acceptance, and therefore became a vocal antidrey-fusard. He frequented ultra-nationalist salons, and in his memoirs published in 1911 he, almost unbelievably, wrote in support of his old enemy, the unspeakable Drumont, and deplored what he saw as excessive Jewish influence in public affairs. In the same way Marcel Proust, who was half-Jewish, although he was a supporter of Dreyfus at the time, made a point of remaining friendly with the anti-Semitic Léon Daudet, and gushingly dedicated *Le Côté de Guermantes* to him. And Catulle Mendès, the dissolute Parnassian poet and dramatist, son of a Bordeaux rabbi, became, like many people who wished to deny their Jewish ancestry, bitterly anti-Semitic. He liked to declaim, 'Name me just one Jew, just one, with any creative genius!'

'What about Spinoza?' said someone one day.

'Spinoza? Ha! I'm not sure whether his mother was Jewish, anyway!'[11]

Sarah herself – no more concerned than she had ever

been about being accepted by the right people – was a fervent dreyfusist, and one of those who encouraged Zola to write his pamphlet. (Sardou and her old champion Octave Mirbeau supported her in this; on the other hand Jules Lemaître was one of the founders of the ultra-nationalistic *Ligue de la Patrie Française*, in which he was joined by François Coppée.) But of course it was almost inevitable that Maurice should be of the opposite camp. How could it be otherwise? His entire upbringing had been designed to make him a gentleman of leisure. Too much capacity for moral courage, and how could he have remained his mother's pensioner, as both he and she wished? He had done his best to marry into good society – that society to which his lineage ought to have entitled him, if only he could have been sure of it. But of course he could not be sure of it; and the only lineage he *could* be sure of was as raffish as it could possibly be. It was therefore inconceivable that he should risk heterodox opinions, and he was as antidreyfusard as his mother was dreyfusist.

For a while the violent feelings aroused by all this came between even Sarah and Maurice, and he, Terka and little Simone went to live in the south of France for a year, during which they did not communicate with Sarah. After that the rift was healed – more or less; but even years later deep differences, and deep feelings, still persisted. Lysiane, who was not born until 1898 – she was named after a play Sarah performed that year – recounts a dramatic scene which took place at Sarah's in 1905, by which time most people had begun to lose interest in the case. It was a lunch in the boulevard Péreire:

I was seated in a high chair next to my grandmother, who was diluting the wine in my glass with water. Around the table sat a dozen people: my father, my mother (who was keeping an anxious eye on me), my sister, the Charpentiers,

355

the famous publishers, Madame Maurice Grau, Louise Abbéma, the comtesse de Najac [another of Sarah's devoted lady camp followers], Arthur Meyer, whose whiskers fascinated me, Georges Clairin, tall and dry, with his fine head and dark eyes, and my sister's godfather, Edouard Geoffroy, a stout, choleric gentleman . . .

The luncheon was proceeding gaily when suddenly the name of Dreyfus was mentioned, referring to the manager of one of the big Paris shops . . . who had just died in an accident. There was a moment of tension . . . Then Geoffroy muttered:

'It's a pity it wasn't the traitor.'

Georges Clairin told him to hold his tongue, and my grandmother exclaimed: 'We're not going to start that again!'

'My father told Clairin not to be rude to Geoffroy; my mother implored my father to be quiet . . . In short, it started all over again!

The butler no longer dared pass the dishes. Geoffroy accidentally knocked the salad all over Abbéma with his elbow. My sister began to giggle nervously. My grandmother poured me out another bumper of white wine, then, at a remark by my father (her son), she broke her plate in two. Her son (my father) took offence at this and got up and began to pull my mother away from the table by her hand. Then my grandmother broke my plate on Geoffroy's arm and Geoffroy became purple with fury. The Charpentiers got up and the whole party scattered with screams of rage.

I was left alone in the dining-room, perched on my high chair and drinking white wine until the moment when my mother came to fetch me, in tears. She was the only one who had expressed no opinion on the Dreyfus affair, and precisely because of that had just had a 'wigging'.[12]

The one place where Sarah did conduct a private life was at her retreat at Belle-Isle in Brittany. Here she had bought herself a seventeenth-century fort, a solid, square building, which she had transformed into a simple, charming country house with spectacular views over the sea. A little stone path led up through the entrance into the large mess-room which was used as a sitting and dining-room. 'Two sides looked out to sea, and the windows were draped with blue fishing-nets . . . At one end stood a large dining-table and chairs, at the other a huge divan covered with tiger and leopard-skins, and piled high with cushions of every colour, shape and size. In a corner was an upright piano. Adjoining was what had once been the captain's room, now Sarah's bedroom, and next to that was the kitchen. A steep, narrow staircase led to a few small bedrooms on the roof . . . A few low bungalows, white and green-shuttered like the fort, stood scattered in the grounds . . . In one lived her son and his family and they called it *"les cinq Parties du Monde"* because there were five rooms all in a row; the next one was occupied by her two old faithfuls, Georges Clairin, "Jojotte" . . . and Geoffroy, and yet another one standing somewhat apart was her studio.'[13]

Even in this remote fastness (to get there required, first, a long train journey with many changes, then several hours on board a steamer from Quiberon, and lastly a two-hour drive) Sarah was plagued by tourists who would come to view her estate from a nearby hill to see if they could glimpse her. Reluctantly, she was forced to build a high wall all along the road side of her property – it was protected on the other side by the sea and the rocky coast, so that at least she had no need to spoil the view in all directions. Later, an hotel – '*le manoir de Penhoët*' – was built on an adjoining plot by an enterprising gentleman, – 'Ah, if I only had a cannon, how I should enjoy blowing up that dreadful place!'[14] Finally she bought it, along with a good deal of the surrounding land, for the sake of privacy, and later, when she got older, she moved into it, since it was considerably more comfortable and commodious than the fort.

Sarah came to Belle-Isle every summer when she was in France, and here she could relax and receive friends young and old. The routine was energetic. She got up every morning at six, took a hunting rifle and shot a few sea-birds. Then, if the tide was right and the rocks were uncovered, she took a net to fish for pink shrimps. Then came a bathe – she much enjoyed feeling herself buffeted by the waves: Clairin, however, preferred to take his seaweed baths in the comfort of his tub. In what remained of the morning everyone would work – Sarah in her studio, visitors at whatever took their fancy. Then came lunch. The food was sumptuous, the fish freshly caught – fishing was one of the great pastimes at Belle-Isle – everything produced locally. Sarah still ate very little herself, and as she got older and suffered more from the pain in her leg and various stomach complaints, she was put on a mainly milk diet and ate even less, but she enjoyed ordering enormous and delicious meals for the company, of which they were expected to eat as much as they could hold. After lunch there was a siesta in the 'Sarahtorium', a sheltered clearing surrounded by tamarisks and amply supplied with chaises longues and large parasols, where lively conversation went on while Sarah lay back, covered her face with a veil, and occasionally murmured, '*Je dors, je dors.*' On one occasion she burst into peals of laughter, and explained that she had just realized (looking at Clairin and Geoffroy) 'that we three together are more than two hundred years old!' After a while she would declare that she was rested and the afternoon's activities would begin. Sarah enjoyed playing tennis; Geoffroy, who was terribly jealous of Clairin, insisted on carrying her racquet. Everyone knew she had to be allowed to win, but as her leg got worse, this became harder to arrange. There were walks with the dogs, horse-riding, shooting-expeditions – Sarah fancied herself as a shot, but everyone else became extremely nervous when she had a gun in her hand – boat trips to neighbouring islands, midnight fishing expeditions when everyone enjoyed watching the catch brought in, dripping with phosphorus, and sumptuous picnics when Emile, the major-domo, would be dispatched to set up tables and chairs and prepare a fire, to be joined by the company at the appropriate time. There were a lot of word-games and charades and courtly flirtation. Sometimes a hopeful author would arrive and read his play to Sarah; at other times she conducted long and detailed exchanges by telegram. Sarah's telegrams were legendary, often several pages long. During one such exchange, with Catulle Mendès regarding his play *La Vierge d'Avila*, one of his began '*Vous êtes puissante et câline*'; another was addressed to '*La grande faucheuse d'illusions*' (the great reaper of illusions).[15] In so far as she ever stopped acting, Sarah stopped acting at Belle-Isle. Or maybe, by now, she had stopped acting altogether. What, during the first half of her life, had been a constant trying-on of different roles had finally become an assumption of her greatest role, which was to be herself. 'What struck me most about her when I saw her in private life,' wrote Maurice Baring, who got to know her at this time and went more than once to Belle-Isle, 'was her radiant and ever-present common sense. There was no nonsense about her, no pose and no posturing. She was completely natural. She took herself as much for granted as being the greatest actress in the world, as Queen Victoria took for granted that she was Queen of England.'[16] Indeed, as far as the Belle-Islanders were concerned, Sarah was – in a sense – related to the Queen. Soon after Edward VII's coronation, his yacht anchored near the Pointe des Poulains on which the fort was situated, and Sarah came down in her victoria (an appropriate vehicle!) to meet her royal visitor, who landed surrounded by a bodyguard of sailors, kissed her hand, and joined his hostess in the victoria which conveyed them both sedately up to the fort. Everyone knew that the King had once, when he was Prince of Wales, been Sarah's lover, and gossip had it that this was Maurice's real father, which made Sarah's son Queen Victoria's grandson. The only thing wrong with this splendid theory was that, by the time Sarah first made the acquaintance of the Prince of Wales, Maurice was fifteen years old.

29

On 10 December 1896 two highly symbolic theatrical events took place in Paris. One was the *journée Sarah Bernhardt*, at which all Sarah's theatrical acquaintance gathered together to honour her at forty francs a head, beginning with a lunch for five hundred in the Grand Hotel and adjourning thence to the Renaissance, where they were entertained, first by scenes from *Phèdre* and Parodi's *Rome vaincue*, (an odd choice, some thought), then by sonnets to Sarah written by five poets. When this had finished, a large proportion of the company went on to Lugné-Poë's Théâtre Libre, where they witnessed a theatrical battle to rival the famous battle of *Hernani* sixty-six years earlier – the first night of Alfred Jarry's *Ubu Roi*. So that the same day, by a bizarre coincidence, saw both the crowning celebration of Sarah the theatrical phenomenon and the single event which, perhaps more clearly than any other, indicated that she was becoming a relic of the past. In a theatrical world which could countenance Jarry, there would be little place for Sarah.

In 1896, at the age of fifty-two, Sarah in no way gave the impression of having anything to do with the past, or indeed with normal ageing processes. Oscar Wilde described her as 'that "serpent of old Nile", older than the Pyramids'.[1] Arthur Symons, who had first met her the previous year, describes her as being 'then at the zenith of her fame and of her beauty ... Her fingers were covered with rings, her long and slender fingers; the nails were dyed with red

361

henna . . . She had the evil eyes of a Thessalian witch . . . There was in this tall and thin actress [Symons was not alone in making this mistake: in fact Sarah was not tall, but her proportions and presence made her seem so] such fire and passion as I have rarely seen in any woman, together with her luxuriousness, languor, indifference, haughtiness and hate.'[2]

Now, descending the spiral staircase into the Zodiac Room where the ceremony's celebrants awaited her, she seemed as little a mere mortal as ever she had. 'She seems to stand still while the staircase turns around her,' observed Jules Renard, to whom she appeared 'an image which gestures and has living eyes'. (The spiral staircase was a happy fixture: it might have been specially ordered by Sarah for the purpose of making a perfect entrance. She had always favoured a spiral line; the cut of her dresses, with their draped bodices and their skirts always tighter at the knees than the ankles, her manner of sitting and standing inside these dresses, whose train completed the effect, were as inseparably part of her as the abundant blonde coiffure, the famous smile.) Flanked by Sardou, one of the day's organizers – the others were Jules Lemaître, Coppée, Rostand and Catulle Mendès – and the influential critic Henry Bauër, she received the cheers of the guests. Then everyone turned their attention to the three menus, designed by two of Sarah's old friends, Abbéma and Chéret, and a new discovery, Alphonse Mucha. They ate:

Huîtres d'Ostend, beurre, anchois, radis, saucisson hors d'oeuvres

RELEVÉ
Truites saumonées froides, sauce verte

ENTRÉES
Cotelettes de Pré-salé aux pommes frites
Poulardes du Mans à la Sardou
Spoon au Georges Goulet

Faisans flanqués de Perdreau Truffés
Pâté de foie gras Grand Hotel
Salade à la Parisienne

ENTREMETS
Gâteaux Sarah
Glace
Bombe Tosca
Desserts
Compôtes de fruits, Patisseries

VINS
Sherry Golden, Chablis Montonne, Saint-Estèphe en carafes,
Chambertin 1884
Café Liqueurs

When they reached the dessert, Sardou rose to propose her health, to which Sarah replied, 'To all of you, my friends, from the bottom of a grateful heart I say Thank you! thank you!' And when more volleys of applause had finally died away she added, 'My heart, my whole heart, is yours!' This, the literal truth – for was not one of Sarah's great magnets the unveiled directness with which she offered the public her innermost self, which she could share with them as with no one person? – drew forth more applause and reduced some of the ladies to tears. Then everyone repaired, via a hundred carriages in procession, to the Renaissance, where, after *Phèdre*, in which she was not at her best, and the Parodi, in which, on the contrary, she was admirable although the piece was worthless, sonnets to Sarah (now seated in her Phèdre costume on a flower-strewn throne under a golden canopy, flanked by young actresses in white on cushions at her feet) were read by François Coppée, Edmond Haraucourt, Catulle Mendès, André Theuriet and Edmond Rostand. Rostand came last;

En ce temps sans beauté, seule encore tu nous restes
Sachant descendre, pâle, un grand escalier clair,
Ceindre un bandeau, porter un lys, brandir un fer,
Reine de l'attitude et Princesse des gestes.

En ce temps sans folie, ardente, tu protestes!
Tu dis des vers. Tu meurs d'amour. Ton vol se perd.
Tu tends des bras de rêve, et puis des bras de chair.
Et quand Phèdre paraît, nous sommes tous incestes.

Avide de souffrir, tu t'ajoutas des coeurs;
Nous avons vu couler – car ils coulent, tes pleurs! –
Toutes les larmes de nos âmes sur tes joues.
Mais aussi tu sais bien, Sarah, que quelquefois
Tu sens furtivement se poser, quand tu joues,
Les lèvres de Shakespeare aux bagues de tes doigts.

'What a success for Rostand . . . As great as if the sonnet had been in five acts!' observed Jules Renard.[3]

The day was rounded off with applause, flowers, tears, handshakes, and embraces. Maurice and Terka were both there, weeping (reconciled after the Dreyfus rift). 'Nobody really knows my mother. She's a good woman, a fine woman,' sobbed Maurice to Jules Renard, who repeated this to Sarah. Poincaré, who had recently lost office, was attacked regarding the eloquent failure of Government after Government to decorate Sarah with the Legion of Honour. 'If I regretted losing office at all, I couldn't do so more than I do at this moment,' he replied.[4]

It was the kind of occasion which was inevitably incestuous (perhaps not quite what Rostand had meant when penning his sonnet). But incestuous occasions are often the most enjoyable. Even Jules Renard – an observer who prided himself on his cynicism – found himself carried away: 'Sarah is an extraordinary "fisher of hearts", if one can put it that way. Maybe she is not talented, but, after her day, which belongs to all of us, where we love ourselves, where we worship ourselves, we feel renewed, bigger; and this state of overexcitement does us good, and if, next day, we are not talented ourselves, then we are nothing but cretins.'[5]

If one were required to imagine the theatrical opposite of the *journée Sarah Bernhardt*, the first night of *Ubu Roi* might well be what came to mind. Its author, Alfred Jarry, had for some time been helping Lugné-Poë, the genial director of the avant-garde Théâtre de l'Oeuvre, in a secretarial capacity. Diminutive, loud-mouthed and as deliberately outrageous as he could contrive, he had informed Lugné that he felt attracted to the theatre, and presented him with an incomplete draft of *Ubu Roi*, a sort of Hamlet for foul-mouthed automata brandishing lavatory-brush sceptres. At first Lugné could not imagine how it could be staged; but Jarry insisted, wheedled, inveigled Lugné into spending money on lay-figures to take part in the action . . . Finally Lugné agreed to present the piece, but not without many misgivings. His old friend and ally, the writer and journalist Rachilde, persuaded him to take the plunge. 'All the younger generation, and even some of the older, like a joke,' she wrote, 'and they're all waiting for this piece. What have you got to lose?'[6] Finally the music was written by Claude Terrasse, the scenery was prepared by Terrasse's brother-in-law Pierre Bonnard, helped by his friends Vuillard, Toulouse-Lautrec, Sérusier and Ranson, and on 10 December 1896 'le tout Paris' – a large proportion of those who had spent the earlier part of the day worshipping at Sarah's altar, plus a great many of the younger generation who most definitely had not – packed expectantly into the Théâtre de l'Oeuvre. Henry Bauër, who had long supported Lugné in his work and had encouraged him to persevere with Ubu, was there in his regular box, flanked by the life-size cut-out caricatures of Sarah which he always sat beside him on such occasions. The curtain rose to Père Ubu's opening cry of *Merdre!* – and pandemonium broke loose, not to die down until the end of that uproarious evening. Some were outraged; some enjoyed themselves hugely; many enjoyed themselves hugely by being outraged. The twenty-three-year-old Colette roared with laughter and cried 'Go on! Go on!' Jules Lemaître said, 'Surely it's a joke?' But, whatever people thought, they could not deny what had happened. As Catulle Mendès wrote, 'Someone, amidst the hullabaloo, shouted out: "You wouldn't understand Shakespeare any more than you do this!" He was right. Let's get this clear. I'm not saying that M. Jarry is Shakespeare, and if he has inherited anything from Aristophanes, it has become crude farce and dirty-minded sideshows. But, believe me, in spite of the idiocies of the plot and the mediocrities of the form, we have here a new kind of person, created by the brutal and extravagant imagination of a man who is almost a child. Père Ubu exists.'[7]

30

If the *journée Sarah Bernhardt* and the premiere of *Ubu Roi* had anything in common besides the date, it was that they showed how central a part the theatre played in the cultural and intellectual life of France at that time. In pragmatic, philistine England, theatrical events did not unleash passions or even a great deal of interest – a fact which Bernard Shaw, for one, never ceased to bewail. 'The theatre [in France] is a part of life,' wrote Henry James[1]; in Anglophone countries, by contrast, it was a cultural side-show. France, at this time, might not enjoy the political freedoms of England or America, but it was intellectually unconstrained. In the Anglophone countries, the situation – at any rate where the theatre was concerned – was the other way about. The Lord Chamberlain's office in England – which disapproved of Ibsen on the grounds that his women were all discontented with woman's traditional role as homemaker and mother – and the narrowly moralistic self-appointed censors of American fundamentalism precluded any real experimentation on the stages of the English-speaking world; and intellectual vitality and experiment are – and were – inseparable.

This sense of vital involvement perhaps partly accounts for the resentment Sarah's triumphant tours so repeatedly aroused in her home town. This was nothing new. Rachel had experienced exactly the same difficulty. Paris was the theatrical capital of the world, and if Sarah or Rachel were unwise enough to prefer other venues, then they could not expect to be automatically welcomed whenever they decided to honour Paris with their presence once more. Each time, like a sulky girl, the city had to be courted and won all over again. But, whether the Parisians liked it or not – and the *journée Sarah Bernhardt* shows that in the end they accepted it and even enjoyed it – it had to be admitted that Sarah was a pivotal figure on the stage of her time. Naturally this meant that a great many playwrights aspired to have her present their plays. And the result of *that* was that Sarah's particular requirements had a considerable effect upon French theatrical writing during the last quarter of the nineteenth century. 'M. Rostand was romantic because Mme Sarah Bernhardt is so,' wrote Henry James. 'Interesting enough, if we had time, to trace the influence of a particular set of personal idiosyncrasies, the voice, the look, the step, the very *physique* of a performer, with all its signs, upon literature, and curious thereby to see once more how closely in France literature is still connected with life . . . So long . . . as *La Princesse lointaine* is read, the voice, face, motion, art of Mme. Sarah will be active and present. It is only a question, accordingly, of how long the play will be read . . . Happy Mme. Sarah! And happy M. Rostand too!'[2]

Edmond Rostand, of course, was only the latest in the not-so-very-long line of playwrights in whose plays Bernhardt had scored smashing successes, beginning with Coppée in *Le Passant*, and leading on through Victor Hugo, Racine, Dumas *fils*, Legouvé and Scribe (with *Adrienne Lecouvreur*, which Sarah herself later rewrote), Meilhac and Halévy (with *Frou-Frou*) and Sardou. And it is not difficult, looking through this list and considering the roles involved, to work out what Sarah's requirements were. These were almost all what have been termed 'operatic' roles.[3] In almost all of them conflict and spectacle, on a grand rather than an intimate scale, are central to the dramatic effect. Four of

368

these authors – Racine, Coppée, Hugo and Rostand – wrote in verse, so that the plot could be seen as representing the libretto, the verse, the music. Sarah described her great partner in the Hugo plays, Mounet-Sully, as 'a great lyric performer, a singer'.[4] Arthur Symons observed that *L'Aiglon* 'was composed like a piece of music, to be played by one performer, Sarah Bernhardt ... One seemed to see the expression marks: *piano, pianissimo, allargando*, and just when the *tempo rubato* comes in.'[5] Two of Sarah's greatest successes – *La Dame aux camélias* and *La Tosca* – were of course turned into highly successful operas.

This quasi-operatic, grand style – which was what came most readily to Sarah – perhaps goes some way to explain her success in countries where the audience did not understand French. Her exaggerated use of *mélopée* might also be seen as part of this; as we have seen, critics such as Bernard Shaw hated it, finding it meaningless and annoying, but it may well have added a certain melodic and stylistic interest if you didn't understand the words. And, combined as this grand style was with an ability to evoke extreme intimacy, pathos and tenderness, it was exceedingly effective. But of course not all plays are best approached in this way; and as the nineteenth century progressed, it might be said that less and less of the most interesting were suited to Sarah's style.

In her earlier days, her approach to Racine was (as we have seen) genuinely innovative, while much of the existing repertory – Hugo, Dumas *fils*, *Frou-Frou*, *Adrienne Lecouvreur* – suited her admirably. These plays, in addition to being fairly simple and melodramatic in conception, were also excellent star vehicles. An actress such as Sarah could enhance, and be enhanced by, their strengths, while diverting attention from their weaknesses – absurdities of plotting and characterization, extreme improbability and psychological crudity. They needed a diva to carry them, and in Sarah that was what they got. But as time went on, divas were less in demand. The really innovative theatrical writers of the 1880s and 90s – Ibsen, Chekhov – were interested not in grand types, but in intimate detail and the intricacies of psychology, in their individual characters and the particular problems faced by these individuals. They – and, in a quite different way, Jarry – were trying out new approaches to the theatre; and they were much more interested in the integrity of their plays, and what they were trying to do in those plays, than in the demands of a particular actor or actress. Indeed, what Jarry, with his stylized characters and their monotonously chanted obscenities, was saying was that actors, as far as the writer was concerned, were nothing but puppets or puppet-substitutes.

The writers of this new generation, not surprisingly, were hostile to Sarah, who represented the antithesis of what they were trying to achieve. 'Every year,' wrote Shaw, a devoted Ibsenist who also had his own experimental approach to the theatre, 'Madame Bernhardt comes to us with a new play, in which she kills somebody with any weapon from a hairpin to a hatchet; intones a great deal of dialogue as a sample of what is called the "golden voice", to the great delight of our curates, who all produce more or less golden voices by exactly the same trick; goes through her well-known feat of tearing a passion to tatters at the end of the second or fourth act, according to the length of the piece; serves out a certain ration of the celebrated smile; and between whiles gets through any ordinary acting that may be necessary in a thoroughly businesslike and competent fashion. This routine constitutes a permanent exhibition.'[6]

That was written in 1897, when this view of Sarah was nothing very new. But as early as 1881 – when she had only just left the Comédie-Française – the young Anton Chekhov, seeing her in Moscow, had come to very similar conclusions. 'We are far from worshipping Sarah Bernhardt as a talent,' he wrote. '. . . She has none of the spark that alone is capable of moving us to bitter tears or ecstasy. Every sigh Sarah sighs, every tear she sheds, every antemortem convulsion she makes, every bit of her acting is nothing more than an impeccably and intelligently learned lesson. A lesson, reader, and nothing more! As a very clever lady, who knows what works and what doesn't, a lady of the most grandiose taste, a lady deeply read in the human heart and whatever you please, she very deftly performs all those stunts that, every so often, at fate's behest, occur in the human soul.'[7] Chekhov's antipathy to Sarah can partly be seen as the climax of a century in which conflict had raged in the Russian theatre between native impulses and foreign imports – Chekhov, a russophile, compares Sarah, to her disadvantage, with the Russian actress Fyodotova. But it is clear that he also found her acting style deeply antipathetic in a personal capacity – something that no one who knows his plays can find surprising. His compatriot Turgenev found her no more sympathetic.

As for Ibsen, we do not know what he thought about Sarah; but we do know what she thought about Ibsen. In an interview with an English paper in 1894 she said, 'Ah! you in England are quite devoted to the northern dramatist, are you not? It is delightful to be popular on your side of the water . . . for you all take things so intensely seriously. What do I think of Ibsen? I admire his Titanesque power, but I grieve at his obscurity and the cruelty we cannot but observe in his conception of life. When obscure, he is kind; when clear, cruel. Look at *A Doll's House* (a play, by the way, in which I should have acted over here had it not been that Réjane is going to show you her Nora Helmer) – can you imagine a more bitter story? I absolutely deny that Ibsen has "invented" the psychological play. Look at *La Femme de Claude*: it was one of Dumas *fils*'s first comedies, yet it is intensely human and as absolutely unconventional as *Hedda*

Gabler.'[8] Sarah thought Ibsen was too *voulu*, which might be translated as over-contrived.

This comparison between Ibsen and Dumas *fils* was nothing new: it was even made by the Danish critic Georg Brandes, who described Ibsen as 'Dumas on Northern soil'.[9] But in fact the comparison is very misleading. Sarah's 'realistic' plays – Dumas' *La Femme de Claude* and Meilhac and Halévy's *Frou-Frou* – are not so much explorations of a particular personal dilemma, rooted in the psychological peculiarities of the characters, as expositions of a stock theme: in Dumas' case the just punishment of the adulterous wife, in Halévy's, that of the heartless flirt. In his preface to *La Femme de Claude*, written in 1873, Dumas makes it clear that his play is a sort of parable illustrating the lengths to which, in his view, a husband is morally entitled to go, given that the law does not allow him to divorce an adulterous wife. Claude kills his wife Césarine, and in Dumas' view, Jesus would heartily have approved his doing so. In *Frou-Frou* the central character is a flirt who endangers her marriage, sees her place with her husband and child being taken over by her virtuous sister, recognizes the error of her ways, gives up her frivolous life for good works, and in the last act contracts consumption and dies. Plays such as these could be seen as the very antithesis of *A Doll's House*. They are profoundly misogynistic, indicating in the crudest possible way that the woman who steps out of line must expect to be punished. In Ibsen's play there is no neat ending of the kind Sarah was used to – suicide, murder or reconciliation – but a feeling of hope, as Nora leaves the doll's house to explore the possibilities life may offer outside it. This is hardly the spirit in which Frou-frou leaves home or Marguerite Gautier accepts her just deserts at the hands of her lover's father. If Sarah really thought Ibsen and Dumas were comparable, then she was clearly unable to understand Ibsen and was right never to play him (she

372

made one disastrous attempt, never repeated, at *The Lady from the Sea*).

What did all this mean for the second half of Sarah's career? She had to find new plays for her repertoire; she was not in sympathy with the new writer-centred movement in the theatre. She had therefore to find playwrights who would be willing to supply her with vehicles – who saw their plays, not so much as ways of expressing themselves theatrically, but more as ways in which they could display their talents to advantage through the medium of Sarah Bernhardt. This was what Sardou did. It followed from this, almost inevitably, that he must be a playwright of the second rank – no very interesting playwright, by then, would have been willing to work that way, although some – such as Oscar Wilde with *Salomé* – might see Sarah as the perfect vehicle through which to express what they wanted to say at a particular moment: a very different matter. As we have seen, at least one critic, Maurice Baring, thought this was of no importance, and considered that both Sarah and Henry Irving – a very comparable figure – were best seen in indifferent vehicles which displayed their talents to the optimum effect. (However, it must be borne in mind that Baring considered Sardou a far better playwright than Ibsen, which may say something about his theatrical judgment.) J. T. Grein, the Dutchman who was responsible for presenting many of the Ibsen and early Shaw productions at his Independent Theatre in London during the nineties, thought Sardou 'execrable' but maintained that 'the public the world over would always prefer to see Bernhardt carrying the whole weight of a poor play, than seeing her in a less glamorous role in a good one.' But he also thought 'there was ... such a thing as a fine play with Sarah in a truly great part, which could only be classical drama, or some work by a poet of genius – of necessity a rarity.'[10]

Was Edmond Rostand such a poet? There were certainly some people who thought so. Rostand was a young man from Marseille who made an early name for himself with a verse play, *Les Romanesques*, which was performed at the Comédie-Française when he was only twenty-six. This attracted Sarah's attention, and he wrote *La Princesse lointaine* for her. She put it on in 1895 with a very strong cast – she played the princess, Mélissinde, and Lucien Guitry and Edouard de Max played the Prince of Aquitaine and his knight Bertrand who set out on a mission to find her, and, having found her, both fall in love with her. The play lost a lot of money, but Sarah was not deterred. She had found a new playwright precisely suited to the hazily supernatural-romantic image she wished to cultivate at this period.[11]

And Rostand? He had, in the view of Henry James, done two things: 'committed himself, up to the ears, in the sentimental-sublime, and . . . started handsomely the question of whether or no he were a poet. I may as well say at once that he has remained, to my sense, exactly as much a poet as *La Princesse lointaine* charmingly showed him, but he has not . . . become an inch more of one. The reason . . . is of the clearest: he could never become more of one and remain within the limits of his cosmic boom, remain what I have called portable, and above all *ex*portable. He is as much of one as is consistent with the boom, the latest, the next exhibition, the universal reporter, the special car, the orbit of Mme Sarah Bernhardt.'[12]

Whatever reservations others might have, Sarah and Rostand had no reservations at all about each other. In her classification of French poets, Sarah places Rostand (and Jean Richepin!) with Ronsard, Racine, Hugo, Lamartine and Musset as the greatest of French poets – a comparison which says more for her loyalty than for her powers of literary judgment.[13] They began – as Sarah had begun with Sardou – with a flirtation, but that soon ended (Rostand's wife

Rosemonde Gérard was talented, beautiful, and half Sarah's age) and they became firm friends. 'He naturally *sees*, as it were, romantic or fantastic, just as certain persons before certain objects see blue, yellow, or red,' wrote James; and this unique vision was exactly what Sarah required, just as she was the only actress capable of putting it on a stage. She was the diva once more, with her adoring court, and everyone was perfectly delighted with the situation. Nothing could have been more goddess-like than her conduct of rehearsals. 'Rehearsals were called every day at one-fifteen for one-thirty,' Sacha Guitry recalled (the play in question was *L'Aiglon*, which opened in 1900). 'At least, that was what the notice said – in fact only the extras were there on time. The actors with speaking parts arrived unhurriedly, one at a time, my father [Lucien Guitry] never got there before half past two, Edmond Rostand appeared at three, and at about ten to four Mme Sarah Bernhardt made her entry. Everyone got up and took their hats off, and everyone in turn came to kiss her hand. Since there were at least sixty people in the theatre, this took a good half-hour. Immediately after the hand-kissing Mme Sarah Bernhardt retired to her dressing-room to put on her costume . . . As soon as she was ready, the rehearsal began. But, at five o'clock, it was interrupted for 'Mme Sarah's cup of tea'. The entire company watched her drink her tea, patiently, tenderly, respectfully. Everything she did was extraordinary, but the people who worked with her found it absolutely natural that she should only do extraordinary things. – But that's why rehearsals for *L'Aiglon* took five or six months!'[14]

Rostand followed *La Princesse lointaine* with *La Samaritaine* and then *Cyrano de Bergerac*, which he wrote for Coquelin; and this in its turn was followed by *L'Aiglon*. '[*La Princesse lointaine*] surpasses its predecessor in brilliancy by the same stride by which *Cyrano* was in turn to surpass it, and by which – as a mere literary, or, if it be preferred, scenic wager

– *L'Aiglon* was to surpass *Cyrano*,' wrote Henry James,[15] who saw in Rostand the direct poetic descendant of Victor Hugo – albeit of only a small section of Victor Hugo.

After the success of *Cyrano* – which he wrote after Coquelin had begged him for 'a role for me' – Rostand wanted to do another play for Sarah, and his fancy lighted upon a subject he had often thought about: Napoleon's ill-fated young son the duc de Reichstadt, 'that white Hamlet who leads one ineffably to think of Shakespeare's black Hamlet'.[16] (Sarah was just then playing the black Hamlet.) *L'Aiglon* was begun in the spring of 1899 and finished by the autumn, during which time Rostand lived in a dream of Schoenbrunn, the castle in Austria where the Eaglet had lived out his short life. He thought about visiting the place while he was writing the play, but found no time to do so until it was finished: when he finally went there, he told his family that he had been living so entirely at Schoenbrunn in his imagination that he recognized it as a place he knew intimately.

L'Aiglon was the last big role Sarah created, and was one of the most keenly anticipated. During the rehearsals the theatre was filled with her old friends – Georges Clairin drawing caricatures of everyone, Catulle Mendès, Sardou. Sardou was very talkative, an unparalleled raconteur, and also very greedy. He would sit in one of the boxes with a big plate of cakes, and, while he was eating, so that no one should interrupt him, he would make the same gesture 'as a driver who wants to monopolize the road – he monopolized the silence'.[17]

Finally the rehearsals were at an end. The first night of *L'Aiglon* was 17 March 1900. By this time Sarah had moved out of the Renaissance, which was small and intimate and where the audience was too near the stage for her to be able any longer to sustain the illusion of youth, to the much bigger Théâtre des Nations, which she renamed the Théâtre

376

Sarah Bernhardt, where the stage was further from the auditorium, there was more scope for crowd scenes and where a larger audience could be accommodated, thus increasing receipts while overheads remained much the same.

The house was packed for the premiere of *L'Aiglon*. Rarely had one of Sarah's openings been more keenly anticipated. Firstly there was the sheer challenge which she had to meet in order to play the part at all – she was by now fifty-six years old and playing a boy barely past adolescence. Then the play itself, concerning an episode and a character so piercingly part and yet not part of France's history – the exiled son of the great Napoleon who is unable to follow in his father's footsteps – spoke to an audience still concerned with many of the same issues, in particular the role of the army, and of foreigners. The Dreyfus affair was still raging, and factions of nationalists and dreyfusards took their seats, each ready to find lines in the play which would uphold their cause.

'I never saw before or since an audience which was prepared to be hostile so suddenly and completely vanquished,' wrote Maurice Baring. '. . . The atmosphere was tense. Sarah had a tremendous reception. When she spoke the line which occurs in the first scene – *"Je n'aime pas beaucoup que la France soit neutre"* – there was a roar of applause, but this, one felt, was political rather than artistic enthusiasm. The first quiet dialogue between the Duke and his courtiers held the audience . . . and when the scene of the history lesson followed, when Napoleon II suddenly gives his schoolmaster, who has hitherto taught him history bowdlerized of any mention of his father, an account of the battle of Austerlitz, Sarah played with an increasing accelerando and crescendo and . . . carried them off with a pace and intensity which went through the theatre like an electric shock. People were crying everywhere in the audience . . .

The rest of the play from that moment until the end was a progression of cunningly administered thrills, which were deliriously received by a quivering audience.'[18]

It was a theatrical triumph to rival any of the triumphs of her early days, a tour de force in a role which no one else has ever been able to play. Denigrators there might be, but the Sarah Bernhardt show remained inexorably on the road.

The guiding principle of Sarah's theatre was that no theatrical experience could compare with that of witnessing a great star in a great role, the greatest star of all being Sarah.

Could the new theatre produce a star of its own? In a way that was a paradoxical demand. Sarah's audiences came to see Sarah – the play was a secondary consideration; and this was exactly what the new writers objected to. Writers such as Ibsen and Chekhov required the actors to lose themselves in the characters. So long as that happened, the play would speak for itself. Theirs, as much as the traditional Comédie-Française, was a theatre for ensemble playing. Nevertheless, it became clear as the 1880s progressed into the 1890s that there was indeed an actress who was a great star of the new approach to acting: Eleonora Duse. Just as the young Anton Chekhov had instinctively felt that Bernhardt's acting held nothing of interest for him, so he was wholeheartedly captivated by Duse when she visited Russia ten years later, in 1891. 'What a marvellous actress!' he wrote to his sister. 'Never before have I seen anything like it. I looked at this Duse and I felt sadness, . . . I realized why we are bored in the Russian theatre.'[1] Since they played much the same repertoire in the same places at the same time, the comparison was frequently made, and invidious conclusions drawn in favour of one or the other.

Duse was fifteen years younger than Bernhardt. She was brought up in great poverty, the daughter of travelling actors; her mother died when she was fifteen, and thereafter she had – not to begin work, for she had always worked in the theatre – but to take her place as an adult with adult responsibilities. She moved from theatre to theatre; in Naples she got pregnant; the child's father refused to marry her, but the baby died soon after birth. She was at this time with the Rossi company, which now moved to Turin. The company's leading lady left, and Duse, who was barely twenty, took on her roles. She married a fellow-actor and bore him a daughter, Enrichetta. While they were in Turin, Bernhardt passed through on one of her European tours, and Rossi offered her his theatre for four days. On Duse, she left an indelible impression: 'She came irradiated by her great aureole, her world-wide fame. And, as if by magic, the theatre was suddenly filled with movement and life, and began to glitter anew. To me it was as if with her approach all the old, ghostly shadows of tradition and of an enslaved art faded away to nothing. It was like an emancipation. She was there, she played, and triumphed, she took possession of us all, she went away . . . but like a great ship she left a wake behind her . . . and for a long time the atmosphere she had brought with her remained in the old theatre. *A woman had achieved all that*!'[2] Emboldened by this vision of what could be achieved, Duse herself played with a new authority, and her career began to take off. Soon she was acclaimed in Rome, and began to establish a European reputation. As so often happens, her marriage broke down on account of this change of circumstances – Duse was by now much more successful than her husband, who could not share in her pleasure at this new recognition and took no interest in her new friends among the Roman literary intelligentsia.

It is hard to imagine two actresses more different than Bernhardt and Duse. But they had one thing in common: they both possessed that ability to sustain intense concentration over a long period that is essential to the tragedian.

Ellen Terry recognized this, and recognized that she did not have it. 'Emotional parts just kill me,' she wrote. 'On the stage I can pass swiftly from one effort to another, but I cannot fix *one*, and dwell on it, with that superb concentration which seems to me the special attribute of the tragic actress. To sustain, with me, is to lose the impression that I have created, not to increase its intensity.'³ This lack of sustained concentration meant that Terry could never tackle the great tragic roles in which both Bernhardt and Duse revelled. But, this fundamental ability apart, their approaches to a part were very different – a difference which may be characterized by the differences in their personalities.

For if one wanted to conceive of a personality exactly the opposite of Sarah's, it would be Duse's. Withdrawn, intense and bookish where Sarah was publicity-seeking, pathologically gregarious, a glamorous butterfly – it is hard to imagine two more different women living such strictly comparable professional lives.

To begin with what, for almost all working women, is the first and hardest problem: that of motherhood and how it is to be combined with a career. This was, as we have seen, something that never appeared to worry Sarah. But it constantly tormented Duse. Sarah adored Maurice, spoiled him when she was with him and happily entrusted him to others when she was not with him – which, of course, was very often. And their relationship, untainted by guilt, turned out just as she hoped it would. By contrast, Duse felt intensely guilty about her relationship with Enrichetta, which was often a difficult one. 'The joys of motherhood!!!!' she wrote to her lover, the Milanese poet Arrigo Boito. 'Yes! some people love to sing about them . . . provided they've never actually been through it!'⁴ This guilt was accentuated by the fact that, after their separation, Duse's husband repeatedly tried to gain custody of Enrichetta – something Duse resisted strongly, while having to admit to herself that the relentless demands of the art to which she was dedicated – the constant touring, the lack of a home base – prevented her from being much of a mother to the girl. Enrichetta spent her youth moving from one boarding-school to another, and eventually settled in England, married a Cambridge don and fervently embraced the Catholic church. Duse's ambiguous feelings about motherhood were revealed in her first portrayals of Ibsen's Hedda Gabler, when she removed from the script all references to Hedda's possible pregnancy – revolting 'against the thought of possible motherhood just as Hedda did – [she] would not even allow the formal indications of it, as written by the author'.[5]

Motherhood was not the only area in which Duse, but not Sarah, went through tormented heart-searchings. Duse was capable of falling deeply and unhappily in love – notably with Boito and with the poet and self-styled genius Gabriele D'Annunzio – something quite outside Sarah's experience. She was frequently racked by jealousy: both men, at one time or another, made her very unhappy. Sarah had been unhappy once on account of Damala, but it seems clear that her feelings for him, and consequently the pain he was able to cause her, were on a quite different level from those experienced by the intense, and intensely miserable, Duse. 'It became a legend, her sorrow,' wrote Gordon Craig, the avant-garde theatrical designer whose work Duse loved and Sarah abominated, 'and this legend about Duse being a "poor woman" gathered force until all England was groaning "oh, the poor woman" . . . whenever she was mentioned – adding "That brute D'Annunzio!"'[6]

Then Duse never had any interest in material things. Her apartment in Venice was as bare as a student's, filled only with books and a few sticks of necessary furniture; while everywhere that Sarah went, she surrounded herself with enormous quantities of objects, one of her pleasures being the accumulation of more and more such objects. And not just objects – she also collected animals and people. Even after the most exhausting effort she avoided solitude. 'When she asked us to supper after a *première*,' wrote Robert de Montesquiou, 'something which had cost her months of effort and preparation, we used to have to send her off to rest, after she had entertained us, throughout the meal, with brilliant repartee, never anything rehearsed, always entirely spontaneous.'[7] (This spontaneity was perhaps especially wonderful to Montesquiou, whose slightest move was always minutely choreographed beforehand.) Such a programme would have been the sheerest torture for Duse. A friend described how 'at Monte Carlo we stayed at the Victoria, the dullest, if most aristocratic hotel in the place. But Duse has a taste for the dismal and the melancholy. She is very sad – the saddest woman I have ever known. She cannot even bear people's voices. After the strain of her performance she drives home quite alone, and sits down to her supper in solitude and silence.'[8]

In short, one was introspective and guilt-ridden, the other entirely lacking in either introspection or guilt; and the capacity for introspection was the *sine qua non* of the new approach to literature and the theatre. The great writers of this time, in whatever field – Freud, Proust, Chekhov, Ibsen – are all chroniclers of introspection. On the other hand it might be said that Sarah's whole life had been an elaborate exercise dedicated to the avoidance of introspection. She had not the slightest desire to confront the dark secrets of her soul. Indeed, we have seen that her life in the theatre was part of a stratagem by which she was enabled precisely to avoid such a confrontation.

Duse's technique was based upon this introspection. Luigi Pirandello, one of the young writers who saw in Duse all they hoped for in an actress, wrote that 'in her everything is internally very simple, bare, almost naked. Her technique is the quintessence of a pure, lived truth, a technique that moves from the internal outwards.'[9] In this way, she was able to achieve the kind of effect Bernhardt could never dream of. Bernard Shaw, for example, saw a production of Sudermann's *Magda*, in which Duse was the heroine realizing that the man she is about to meet is the lover who deserted her years ago, the father of her child. 'She began to blush; and in another moment she was conscious of it, and the blush was slowly spreading and deepening until, after a few vain efforts to avert her face or to obstruct his view of it without seeming to do so, she gave up and hid the blush in her hands . . . In the third act of *La Dame aux camélias*, where she produces a touching effect by throwing herself down, and presently rises with her face changed and flushed with weeping, the flush is secured by the preliminary plunge to a stooping attitude . . . but Magda's blush did not admit of that explanation; and I must confess to an intense professional curiosity as to whether it always comes spontaneously.'[10]

Duse, then, *became* the character she was playing – and on evenings when she was playing an unpleasant character, such as Césarine in Dumas' *La Femme de Claude*, she was pretty unpleasant all day herself. (Life was easier when the play was to be Goldoni's good-humoured comedy *La Locandiera*.[11]) But Sarah did not do this. For one thing, it was not in her training. The Conservatoire, where she had acquired the foundations of her acting skills, emphasized the perfection of a technique whereby, by an intellectual effort and the application of his craft, the actor was enabled to assume the character he was playing while never losing sight of the fact that he – the actor – was another person. As Coquelin, perhaps the greatest exponent of this style of acting, put it: 'Study the part, make yourself one with your character, but in doing this never set aside your own individuality . . . Whether your second self weeps or laughs, whether you become frenzied to madness or suffer the pains of death, it must always be under the watchful eye of your ever-impassive first self . . . If you identify yourself with your part to the point of asking yourself, as you look at the audience, "What are all those people doing here?" you have ceased to be an actor: you are a madman.'[12]

In her book *L'Art du Théâtre*, Sarah rejected this notion of duality. 'How,' she asked, 'can an actor expect . . . to convince others of his emotional sincerity if he is unable to convince even himself to the point of becoming the very character he is portraying?'[13] But although this was what she said, it was not what she did. Earlier in the same book, speaking of her numerous death-scenes, she wrote, 'Although in my various death-scenes I have made the passing acquaintance of real death, I still continue to live. It has sometimes taken me more than an hour to come to life again. My head has felt faint. My heart has almost stopped beating. I was scarcely able to catch my breath. I had nevertheless retained sufficient will-power to resume my own personality just as previously I had had to retain sufficient *sang-froid* in order to remember both my role and the mise en scène.'[14] And May Agate, who was her pupil, praises Bernhardt's ability to move an audience while remaining herself unmoved: 'She could simulate tears and conduct a conversation about something else . . . under her breath . . . The voice with which she was acting would tremble with emotion, the one she was using for her asides, caught only by the other actors, would be perfectly steady!'[15]

In fact, far from becoming all the different characters she was called upon to play, critics generally agreed that Sarah tended rather to impose her own personality upon them, so that the person one saw, in whatever guise, was that marvellously interesting person, Sarah Bernhardt. Sardou and Rostand wrote their plays with this in mind; but even with other plays, 'whatever Sarah does — whether she speaks or is silent, whether she gets up or sits down, whether

385

she walks or stands still – she is divine. She is, however, both the same on stage as she is at home and the same in her roles as she is in private life. She does not become either Doña Sol or Phèdre or Maria de Neubourg. Sarah she is and Sarah she remains. Who can criticize her for it? What could she do that would be more inventive? Is it not equally good to be Sarah, a masterpiece of the eternal feminine wrought by nature, as to be Phèdre, a perfect creation of poetry?'[16] Of course this too bears out the concept of the stage, at least during the first half of Sarah's career, being to some extent a therapy – a way in which her various selves could play out their roles: all of them being, however, a part of Sarah.

Given these differences, it follows that while Sarah's repertoire, founded as it was upon Hugo, Dumas *fils* and Sardou, was ideal for her, it would not at all suit an actress such as Duse. For while Sarah could impose her fascinating self upon the rather undeveloped female characters of this repertory, enjoying the opportunities they gave her for spectacle, stardom and technical mastery, there was nothing in them to awaken the interest of an intense intellectual like Duse. And indeed Duse hated them. 'There is nothing left for me (oh, what a life!) except an established name, bound hand and foot to the old bundle of works by Sardou and Dumas . . . I want to *scream* my refusal, because I know I am right in this.'[17] Nevertheless, these were the plays her public imposed upon her; and if Sarah made the cardboard characters of Dumas and Sardou interesting by turning them into aspects of her unfailingly interesting self, Duse did so in a different way. 'The poor women in the plays I have acted so got into my heart and mind that I had to think out the best way of making them understood by my audience, as if I were trying to comfort them . . . But in the end it is generally they who comfort me. How and why and when this inexplicable reciprocity of feeling between these women and myself began; that story would be far too wearisome

. . . But this I can say: though everybody else may distrust women I understand them perfectly. I do not bother whether they have lied, betrayed, sinned, once I feel that they have wept and suffered while lying and sinning and betraying, I stand by them, I stand for them.'[18]

It was inevitable that a kind of rivalry should spring up between these two. During the 1890s, almost every summer found them both in London – Sarah at Daly's Theatre or the Gaiety, Duse at Drury Lane or the Lyceum – dazzling the English. 'There are three ways of raving about an actress,' wrote Max Beerbohm apropos Duse. 'One way is to rave about her technique; another is to rave about her conception of the part she is playing; another to rave about her personality. Well! I am debarred from the first way by the simple fact that I know no more Italian than did poor Mrs Plornish. This disability is the more humiliating for me, in that I am, evidently, the only critic who labours under it.'[19] Max was a supporter of Sarah's, as was Maurice Baring; Shaw, an impassioned advocate of Duse, who both enchanted him as the epitome of what sublime acting could attain to, and who also provided him with a handy stick with which to belabour, in the person of Sarah, the kind of acting he couldn't stand. 'Madame Bernhardt has the charm of a jolly maturity, rather spoilt and petulant, perhaps, but always ready with a sunshine-through-the-clouds smile if only she is made much of. Her dresses and diamonds, if not exactly splendid, are at least splendacious; her figure, far too scantily upholstered in the old days, is at its best; and her complexion shows that she has not studied modern art in vain.' Shaw contrasted Sarah's highly-finished complexion with Duse's, innocent of make-up, and concluded that 'the truth is that in the art of being beautiful, Madame Bernhardt is a child beside [Duse]. The French artist's stock of attitudes and facial effects could be catalogued as easily as her stock of dramatic ideas: the counting would hardly go beyond the fingers of both hands. Duse produces the illusion of being infinite in variety of beautiful pose and motion. Every idea, every shade of thought and mood, expresses itself delicately but vividly to the eye.'[20]

In fact make-up was essential to Sarah's acting, as it was one of the ways in which she entered into a character – a fact which Shaw would doubtless have found highly symbolic of her superficiality in this respect. She devotes a whole chapter in her *L'Art du Théâtre* to the subject. Unlike Duse, Sarah did not spend the whole day thinking herself into the character she was to play in the evening (although she did like to spend an hour by herself at the theatre before a performance of *Phèdre*). Apart from anything else, her way of life would never have allowed it. 'Many times,' she writes, 'I have arrived at the theatre tired, in pain, and dejected. Then gradually, I have begun to assimilate the character I was to represent. In the process of applying facial make-up I have made the most insignificant changes, perceptible to me, but almost invisible to the audience. If the character in question was a passionate, ill-fated woman, I would draw my eyebrows slightly together; I would thin them toward the middle and cast the tips toward the temples in a downward sweep. I would eliminate the bow of my upper lip to produce a straight and inflexible line. My face would then take on a mysterious remoteness.'[21] The reader will remember how, to Mrs Patrick Campbell's astonishment, Sarah tinted the *inside* of her hands with henna when she was playing Cleopatra.

Sarah, of course, laboured under the disadvantage of being fifteen years older than Duse. But what the critics principally held against her during the 1890s was the mechanical way in which she seemed now to go through her paces; something that Duse's advent suddenly brought home to hitherto fervent admirers. William Archer thought that, age notwithstanding, 'the physical and vocal advantages are all on Sarah's side. But how has she used them? Without taste and without conscience. She has fashioned her genius into a money-making machine. She has got together a repertory of showy, violent and sanguinary parts, and played them eight times a week, till all true vitality and sincerity has been ground out of her acting . . . Not for ten years or more has she added a single new effect to her arsenal of airs and graces, tremors and tantrums . . . there is something unsatisfactory, something almost depressing, in the Sarah of today . . . To Eleonora Duse, on the other hand . . . I owe some of the very keenest delights that the theatre can possibly afford.'[22]

In cities such as London and Vienna both Sarah and Duse were, to a certain extent, on neutral ground. But, although Sarah had frequently played in Italy, Duse had resisted attempts to woo her to Paris. Much of her repertoire was originally French; she hesitated to play Dumas and Sardou, in Paris, in Italian, while the idea of playing there in Italian-accented French was even more unthinkable. The play-wrights themselves did not share these reservations – they urged her to come, though for many years to no avail. But finally, in 1897, the ice was broken. Duse allowed herself to be persuaded.

Duse's Paris season of 1897 was, from first to last, a kind of barely-concealed duel between the two great actresses and their respective styles of acting. It might be said that the first honours in the fight went to Sarah, but Duse finally emerged triumphant.

Hostilities began with an invitation from Sarah offering Duse the use of her theatre, the Renaissance, since she was planning to be in London for most of the time Duse would be in Paris. The French press let it be known that it was Sarah who had persuaded Duse to come, and that she was letting her have the theatre rent-free. Schurmann, Duse's manager, denied this. 'Sarah . . . never asked her to come to Paris,' he wrote. 'It was only after my star had indicated her willingness that I rented the Renaissance, which Sarah Bernhardt let me have on exorbitant terms.'[23] Whatever the circumstances, the move was an astute one on Sarah's part. It had become clear that Duse was going to come to Paris. If she came to Sarah's theatre then the season would to some extent be under Sarah's aegis and control, and so would Duse. Meanwhile the press praised Sarah's generosity.

The next question was, what plays should she perform? There was a large section of Duse's repertoire that did not overlap with Sarah's, including her Italian plays and Ibsen. On the other hand, her most popular and successful pieces – *La Dame aux camélias*, *Magda*, *La Femme de Claude* – were all frequently performed by Sarah. In the end she chose a mixture, including these three, plus *La Locandiera*, *Cavalleria rusticana* and one or two others. She had also hoped to bring something new of her very own – *La Città morta*, D'Annunzio's new play. But although they had been lovers, whenever Duse's busy schedule permitted, since 1894, D'Annunzio was feeling annoyed with her at this time, and, when the play was finished, he sent it off to – of all people – Bernhardt. As it happened, D'Annunzio was a very bad playwright; and as it happened, *La Città morta* was an expensive failure for Sarah: when she finally staged it in 1898, it was taken off after fourteen performances. This may have been on account of D'Annunzio's defects, or Sarah's, or both: she certainly did not dream of adapting her style to the demands of a new playwright. 'Sarah is very good, everything she does is very good, and certainly as far as the public is concerned she is the best; but for us, for me, for the man of the theatre I want to be, she is no longer interesting. She makes anything original seem banal,' wrote Jules Renard of this performance.[24]

Even then, long after the contest with Sarah had been played out and she knew she had won, Duse felt that this should have been her play. On the night of the Paris premiere in 1898, she and some friends repaired to Count Joseph Primoli's house to await news from Paris. Various telegrams arrived, describing how the first act had been well received, how by the end the play seemed to be a great success. Even Primoli, who was Sarah's friend as well as Duse's, was prepared to run down the Frenchwoman; but Duse would have none of it. Lying on a sofa with a hot water bottle on her stomach, she defended Sarah: 'She is the mistress of the public because first and foremost she is mistress of herself.' She described how even the most apparently artless of Sarah's gestures was thought out, accurately repeated every time. But, try as she might, it was clear she was suffering. Then she seemed to take a grip on herself and began a eulogy of D'Annunzio 'so noble, confident and heartfelt that, had he heard it from those pallid lips at that hour, the applause of Paris would have seemed vanity to him. It was only when she fell silent that I realized that, as she had spoken, she had taken, one by one, all the flowers from a nearby vase and ripped off the petals with her nails.'[25]

But as it happened, Duse did have a new D'Annunzio play to take to Paris: meeting him again not long after the invitation to the Renaissance had arrived, she assured him she would not go if he did not write a new play for her. 'It's madness!' he said, to which she replied, 'Then write me a madwoman's part!' By Easter of 1897 the play was finished. It was called *Sogno di un mattino di primavera*, and it was about a young girl, Isabella, who goes mad after her lover is stabbed while he is in bed with her. Duse had her new play after all. It was as unsuccessful for her as *La Città morta* was to be for Sarah.

The first meeting between the two goddesses was arranged by Montesquiou, who knew them both and of whom Duse had begged this kindness. 'They hugged each other so tightly,' he reported, 'that it was more like a head-on collision than an embrace.'[26] Sarah invited Duse to that night's performance. When she and Montesquiou arrived they found that the big centre box had been set aside for them, all decorated with orchids. Sarah was playing *La Samaritaine* by Rostand; the house was sparse and unenthusiastic. Duse (to Montesquiou's horror, since he had to follow suit) insisted on remaining standing throughout, possibly as a mark of respect, possibly to make sure she was as much the centre of attention as Sarah.

Sarah, having made sure the contest would take place in her own theatre, scored yet another point in these opening skirmishes. She persuaded Duse not to open, as she had originally planned, with *Magda*, in which Duse was generally accepted as being superior to Bernhardt. But *Magda* was a German play, and to open with a German play given in Italian . . .? Sarah persuaded Duse that *La Dame* would be a better choice, and, unaccountably, Duse went along with this. She was thus opening, in Sarah's theatre, with Sarah's most famous role.

The house on the first of June, 1897, was packed: not a single empty seat. There was an air of immense expectancy, for although Duse, who had arrived a few days earlier, had refused (as she always did) to speak to the press, her presence in Paris had nevertheless been widely reported. The house boasted the aristocracy of both stage and society, including Eugénie Doche, the very first Marguerite Gautier, now an old lady, who had been invited for this special occasion. In the central box sat Sarah, in a richly embroidered silk dress, a wreath of fresh roses on her abundant hair. She was, and evidently intended to remain, the centre of attention. She was bowing and smiling to the visitors who had flowed in an uninterrupted stream through her box ever since her arrival. Then, as the performance began, she assumed an air of absorption.

It was clear that Duse, who was dressed for her part with uncharacteristic care in a beautiful white gown, was intensely nervous. At the start of the first act she could scarcely be heard, though by the end of it she had recovered. (She cannot have been helped by finding that Sarah had closed her own luxurious dressing-room for the duration of Duse's lease, so that the visitor had to use a much less comfortable and convenient one, further from the stage.) In the first interval, Bernhardt's box was again besieged, and it was clear she was being very magnanimous. Certainly she had made a point of applauding, though generally at rather quiet moments when one would not normally think of doing so. Act Two went better, but Act Three was very tedious. In Act Four Duse's leading man, Andò, played brilliantly as Armand Duval; by Act Five Duse had recovered herself, but by then it was too late. 'If someone had triumphed, it was not Duse,' was the verdict of the house.[27]

The next play Duse put on was *Magda*. Her first performance had been on a Saturday: the second was a Monday, and in this play, she performed much better. Where the critics allowed themselves direct comparisons between her interpretation of the role and Bernhardt's, they generally conceded that Duse's was more convincing, if lower-key. Then she fell ill and had to cancel the next two performances. After this, Bernhardt announced that she and Duse were to appear on the same stage in a gala evening to raise subscriptions for a monument to Dumas, who had recently died. At first she tried to work the same trick on Duse as on the opening night – they would put on *La Dame aux camélias*, in which Duse would play Acts Two and Three, Sarah Acts Four and Five. But Duse knew as well as Sarah that the last acts of this play are the strongest, and insisted on playing, instead, the second act of *La Femme de Claude* – something

Sarah could hardly refuse. In this Duse triumphed, and was warmly thanked by Sardou, who was presiding over the evening. Then on came Sarah, reduced the house to tears, was called back four times, and threw herself into Sardou's arms before running to Duse, taking her by the hand, and leading her to the front of the stage to bow together before the bust of Dumas. It had been Bernhardt's evening; and, well satisfied, she left next day for her London engagement.

But she had underestimated her rival. Duse, possibly feeling relieved now that Sarah had left town, set about giving as many as she could of the plays in her repertory; and the more she gave, the greater the impression she made. But a signal was needed that would permit the public to recognize what it had before it. This appeared, in the form of an open letter in *Le Temps* addressed to Duse, and regretting that she was to leave Paris while so few of her fellow-artists had been able to see her. Her methods had opened up new horizons; their loss was considerable; would she not offer, before she left, an invitation matinée performance for them? This was signed 'Sganarelle' – the pen-name of Francisque Sarcey, who was still, as he had been before Sarah began her own career, the most powerful critic in Paris.

This was the turn of the tide. There were no more hesitations or insinuations. 'Before we knew her,' declared *Le Figaro*, 'we incarnated . . . dramatic genius in three women: Sarah Bernhardt, Bartet and Réjane. The first of these represented for us poetry, the second, charm, and the third, cleverness. We can henceforth add to this trinity a fourth muse – truth.'[28] D'Annunzio's play was put on to a packed and prestigious house on 15 June. Meanwhile, Duse was considering Sgnarelle's suggestion. She wrote to a friend: 'For my performance there will be no invitations! I cannot invite my fellow-artists to come and hear me and applaud me! It would be a bit ridiculous, wouldn't it? It is they who are inviting me: I put myself at their disposal. That is all I can do.'[29]

Duse's lease on the Renaissance ended on 1 July, and the special matinée was fixed for July 6. When her manager, Schurmann, asked for an extension on the usual terms Sarah replied at once, putting the theatre at her rival's disposal for free provided only that the invitations to the matinée should bear her name and Duse's side by side. Duse hesitated; Sarah then announced that the theatre needed renovations and would have to be closed at once. Finally Schurmann took the Porte-Saint-Martin, which was anyway larger; and when the press got wind of what had happened, there was further sympathy for Duse. Schurmann received fifteen thousand applications for tickets for the matinée: there were only fifteen hundred seats. A hundred were sold at exorbitant prices to pay the expenses: the rest were free.

Duse was to play *Cavalleria rusticana*, then the last act of *La Dame aux camélias* and the second act of *La Femme de Claude*. It was a unique occasion. There had never been such expectations, and never were expectations so triumphantly fulfilled. At the end Duse was given a standing ovation from the entire audience through ten curtain calls. People were in tears, handkerchiefs waved, flowers flew through the air; there were calls of '*Au revoir! Au revoir!*' Next morning, Duse was entertained to breakfast by the Comédie-Française in the Bois de Boulogne. Then she left.

Among theatrical people, Sarah's reputation was temporarily dimmed both by Duse's dazzling performances and by her own petty manoeuvres. She was annoyed by this. 'Last year was my apotheosis, and now only a few months later, they're all attacking me!' she grumbled. But she still remained the darling of the public; and, for public consumption, the two actresses were the best of friends. (Direct competition, however, was never resumed.) As to their private feelings: when, not very long afterwards, Sarah underwent a serious operation at the hands of her old friend Dr Pozzi (another of those who had his own private chalet at Belle-Isle) and when, among the mountain of letters from well-wishers, a telegram from Duse was announced, Sarah's first comment was '*La rosse!*' ('That cow!')

Pozzi burst out laughing: 'I can hardly say that to her, what am I to write?'

At which, in her sweetest voice, Sarah replied, 'Send her all my love.'[30]

32

La Città morta, which opened on 21 January 1898, was Sarah's last new play at the Renaissance. Exactly one year later she opened her new theatre, the Théâtre Sarah Bernhardt, with a revival of *La Tosca*. The old Théâtre des Nations had been sumptuously remodelled; Abbéma, Clairin and other friends had painted ten life-size murals of Sarah in her greatest roles in the foyer; and in place of a simple (or not-so-simple) dressing-room she had now a five-room suite near the stage, in which she soon formed a habit of throwing large Sunday dinner-parties.

It was this new setting which saw *L'Aiglon*, the greatest triumph of Sarah's later career, and one which she must have felt fully justified her move to these new, larger premises. For here was a play in which distance could only enhance the illusion that the fifty-six-year-old Sarah was a twenty-year-old boy – and a play, moreover, which was sold out from the beginning to the end of its run, so that the fact that the new house seated 1,700 against the Renaissance's 900 was a considerable advantage. It ran for 237 performances and grossed 2.5 million francs, an average of 11,300 per performance. As she had lost two million *francs d'or* during her proprietorship of the Renaissance, a success such as this was more than welcome. Sarah must have hoped that it heralded a new era in the management of her theatres. At the Renaissance, despite all the fine words of the *journée Sarah Bernhardt*, the only play to make a profit during Sarah's term of occupation was Maurice Donnay's

Les Amants, which was staged while she was away. But even if *L'Aiglon* were to prove the exception rather than the rule, she also hoped that the new theatre would prove less personally ruinous. At the Renaissance she, as the sole proprietor, had been personally responsible for all debts and losses, so that she was continually being sued for non-payment of debts and rent and frequently had to resort to selling her personal effects in order to pay. But the Théâtre des Nations was a municipal theatre owned by the city of Paris, and Sarah was only the lessee. She hoped, therefore, that the city might help offset any future losses.

That year of 1900, then, was a happy one. Edmond Rostand had fallen ill soon after the opening of *L'Aiglon* and had moved out to the country to convalesce; and every day Sarah would drive out to visit him, 'dressed in a cloud of muslin under her chinchilla coat . . . in a fairytale coach which looked as if it had been ordered at Cinderella's carriage-maker,'[1] carrying the bunch of violets which had been a prop in last night's last act, to tell him all about the previous evening's performance. She was accompanied on these visits by Suzanne Seylor, who had assumed the role of lady-in-waiting, and sometimes by her two granddaughters. On one occasion, to the delight of Rostand's two little boys, she poured a bottle of Heidsieck Monopole over her hair in order to prove to them that the curls in that improbable mane were all natural.[2] Then, in the autumn, although it was still playing to capacity houses, she prepared to take *L'Aiglon* on tour to America, where it opened on 26 November at the Garden Theatre just a month after Maude Adams first performed it in English at the Knickerbocker.

This was perhaps Sarah's most successful American tour. For one thing the attraction she was offering was not herself alone. This time she had persuaded her old friend and ally Constant Coquelin to accompany her. He had agreed to play Flambeau to her Aiglon, a small part, while she played

Roxane, an equally small part, to his Cyrano in *Cyrano de Bergerac*. The other plays were *La Tosca*, with Coquelin as Scarpia, *La Dame aux camélias*, (she had, in the mid-nineties, devised a new production dressed in authentic period style which had endowed the old warhorse with a miraculous new lease of life) in which he played Armand's father, and *Hamlet*, in which the second character after Hamlet, listed on the programme, was the First Gravedigger, played by Coquelin.[3] Above all, Sarah was by now both unimaginably famous and still acting at the peak of her powers, so that people flocked to see her wherever she went. 'Mme Bernhardt,' commented the critic William Winter of this tour, 'has attracted large audiences in many parts of the country, and has received from the press in general such adulation and advocacy as have seldom been awarded to even the authentic benefactors of human society.'[4] People all over the world, said Edmond Haraucourt, knew two names which constituted their entire acquaintance with France and French history: Napoleon and Sarah Bernhardt.[5]

However, even Sarah was human, and, as she approached her sixties, people naturally began to wonder how long the phenomenon could be maintained. For some while yet, it seemed. At the age of fifty, Edmond de Goncourt (meeting her in order to try and persuade her to play *La Faustin*, which eventually she declined to do) had observed with some astonishment the beauty of her complexion – 'not even any rice powder, and a rosebud colour on a skin extraordinarily fine, delicate and oddly transparent at the temples, under the network of little blue veins. Bauër says it's the complexion of her second youth.'[6] And by common acclaim her voice was as beautiful as ever. Yet all around her she could see signs of mortality. Duse, after her break with D'Annunzio, refused to act any more in Italy, grew weary of constantly touring in worthless vehicles, and with some relief sent her costumes for *Hedda Gabler* to Suzanne

Desprès, a young actress in Lugné-Poë's company, whom she saw as Hedda's new incarnation. She finally retired, worn out after several years of ill-health, in 1909 at the age of fifty; she had been wanting to do so since 1905. Graham Robertson, who had been Sarah's friend since she had first met him as a skinny youth at Robert de Montesquiou's, recounts that 'I remained the Little Boy . . . for many years after my locks were growing scanty and my slimness a mere memory. But at last came a day when, as we sat together in her dressing-room and Madame Sarah, attired as the boy in *L'Aiglon*, was, in high good humour, addressing me in affectionate diminutives, she suddenly looked keenly at me and paused. "But, Graham," she said slowly, "you're – why, you're old!" "Really old," repeated Sarah, taking me in as if for the first time . . . "Why don't you marry? You must marry at once . . . If you don't marry now, nobody will ever take you!"'[7]

She – who had so often in her youth been given only weeks or months to live – had never been especially robust, and now the bouts of ill-health became more frequent. In 1898 she underwent a serious abdominal operation. In 1905 a fall aggravated her old knee injury, and she was never to walk without pain again. There was a long tour of the Americas in 1905–6; in 1907 she fell ill again and had another operation the following year. And in 1908, her youth seemed once again miraculously restored. When she visited London that year Graham Robertson called on her with a friend, and saw her descending a staircase ahead of them. His friend refused to believe it – 'That is not Sarah Bernhardt – that is a young girl!' After that night's performance, of *Phèdre*, Robertson visited her, and Sarah, contemplating herself in a mirror, said, 'Yes, it's ridiculous. That is the word. I can hardly believe it yet. I feel that I have been summoned before *le bon Dieu* and he has said to me, "Well, Sarah Bernhardt, you have been a very good girl on the whole – you have made the most of your time – you shall have your youth back again." '8 The young D. H. Lawrence, seeing her in *La Dame aux camélias* that year, was so overcome by the play's climactic scene that he rushed from his seat and battered on the door of the theatre until an attendant let him out. He described the experience to a friend: 'Sarah Bernhardt was wonderful and terrible. She opened up the covered tragedy that works the grimaces of this wonderful dime show. Oh, to see her, and to hear her, a wild creature, a gazelle with a beautiful panther's fascination and fury, sobbing and sighing like a deer sobs, wounded to death, and all the time with the sheen of silk, the glitter of diamonds, the moving of men's handsomely-groomed figures about her! . . . She represents the primeval passion of woman, and she is fascinating to an extraordinary degree.'9 By then, young men such as Lawrence, exposed to Bernhardt for the first time, no doubt experienced the performance as much in their imaginations, where the mere sight of her represented a fantasy fulfilled, as in the flesh. That, as Marcel Proust described (in the account of the narrator's first visit to see La Berma in *Phèdre*) might as easily result in disappointment as dazzlement. Nothing is more difficult to fulfil than a cherished fantasy. And if an actress (or actor) is too celebrated, then for an over-excited, over-expectant young member of the audience, the performance cannot be experienced on any level corresponding to reality. Like the young Marcel, Colette, when as a girl she first saw Sarah, was too overcome to recognize that here was, perhaps, a great performance – 'I was hardly aware, as the performance went on, that what I was watching was a great actress. The movements of her train, a few cries, a lighting effect which accentuated the features of the famous face – only these physical traits remained in my memory, as if Sarah Bernhardt was not interpreting a

401

dramatic work but was there to sing, dance, or juggle with knives.'[10]

It was now almost forty years since Sarah had first enchanted Paris in *Le Passant*, and thirty since she had become internationally known. Now, as she approached old age with the verve of her apparently eternal youthfulness, she had become more than just an individual actress. She had become a symbol, or rather several symbols: for to different groups of people, Sarah symbolized different things.

To the young writers and actors grouped around Antoine's Théâtre Libre, who saw themselves as representing the newest of the new theatre, she represented everything they wished to overthrow. 'I firmly believe,' wrote Romain Rolland, one of this group, 'that the Romantic drama is one of the most dangerous enemies of the popular theatre that we are trying to establish in France ... One performer has exerted a definitive influence on the shaping as well as the success of this art. It is her name – the name of Sarah Bernhardt – which best sums up this Byzantinized, or Americanized, neo-romanticism: stiff and congealed, without youth or vigour, weighed down with ornaments, with jewels real or fake, bleak in its bluster, pallid in its outlook.'[11] Antoine himself liked to recount how, one day, he had inadvertently found himself attending a performance of Rostand's *Les Romanesques* – 'I found it so good that I left after the first act, in case I found myself liking the two others as much!'[12] But in general, Antoine – who by 1906 had, in the way of rebels, begun to be absorbed into the establishment, becoming that year director of the Odéon – had no hesitation in abominating Sarah and all her works. He and his friends particularly objected to her tenure of a municipal theatre. They felt that premises such as this should be made available to the kind of experimental theatre that could not rely on making a profit, and complained that Bernhardt, with her frequent absences abroad, her expensive seats, her predictable and outdated repertoire and presentation, was a most unsuitable tenant. As we have seen, resentment at Bernhardt's disregard for the Paris theatrical establishment, coupled with her frequent absences abroad, was never far beneath the surface; and when her lease came up for renewal in 1909, and she requested an extension, this flamed up into outright political opposition. After prolonged wrangling she had to promise to enliven her repertoire and give up foreign touring. In 1910, with the lease safely under her belt, she spent the summer in London, appearing at the Coliseum music-hall, where, between other turns, she gave extracts from her most famous parts – a descent in the world that was tempered for her by the fact that the music-hall paid very well, and for her friends by the fact that both Réjane and Jane Hading were appearing at the same time in similar circumstances at other music-halls. Then she set off for a twelve-month tour of the Americas.

The account of this tour left by Lou Tellegen, who abruptly (and to his own surprise as much as anyone else's) found himself cast as leading man for the occasion, shows that, despite her age, Sarah was still a potent purveyor of sexual glamour. And, for Tellegen at least, this glamour was still as much actual as symbolic.

Tellegen was a handsome hunk of Greek-Polish-Dutch ancestry who had had a brief career as an actor at the Odéon before taking off to lead an adventurer's life in Brazil. On his return to Paris in 1910 he found a message awaiting him from Maurice Bernhardt; and when he met Maurice, learned that Sarah, who was then playing at the Coliseum in London (doing her music-hall turn) wished to speak to him. Maurice gave him some money; and next day he crossed the Channel and went to see her at the Carlton Hotel, where she was staying.

Tellegen was completely overwhelmed by Sarah. His devotion to her began from the moment he set eyes on her – 'I had never met, nor have I to this day, another human being from whom personality emanated so richly as from this divine person', was the way he put it.[13] It lasted throughout the four years he spent working with her and remained with him for the rest of his life. That is perhaps not surprising. When he met her Sarah – then sixty-four – was still in her ageless stage, and charming better men than Lou Tellegen every day of her life. What is harder to explain is why she picked on *him* to be her leading man.

He himself had not the slightest suspicion that this was what she had in mind. He assumed that she wanted him to play small parts in her company, but that first meeting was entirely occupied by his recounting his adventures in Brazil, after which she disappeared and left him with Pitou, who wanted to know whether Tellegen knew the plays in Sarah's repertoire. Learning that he had not even an idea what plays there might be in that repertoire, Pitou seemed depressed. Then Sarah reappeared clutching a bunch of papers and began to talk about contracts, salaries, travel and routes, and explained that she had drawn up a contract whereby Tellegen was to be her leading man for the next four years. His previous standing as an actor may be gathered from the fact that his first reaction (he is disarmingly straightforward in his account!) was: 'Four years! Earning a salary for two hundred and eight consecutive weeks!' His second was to kiss her hand and stammer, 'Madame, I have no words to express my innermost gratitude!' But all Sarah said was, 'We leave for America in ten days. The plays and parts you'll have to learn will be given you at my theatre in

404

Paris, when you return tomorrow. We won't have any rehearsals before we leave. Study your parts. I'll see you again on the boat and we'll have ample time for rehearsals during the crossing.'[14] And she gave him one hundred guineas as an advance on his salary and disappeared. Tellegen then went on a two-day spree of drinking, gambling and other diversions. When he finally got to Paris and picked up his parts, he was appalled to find out that, before they sailed, he was supposed to have learned the parts of: Armand Duval in *La Dame aux camélias*, Jean Gaussin in Daudet's *Sapho*, Flambeau in *L'Aiglon*, the Duke of Bedford in *Jeanne d'Arc*, Justinian in *Théodora*, Loris Ipanoff in *Fédora*, Hippolyte in *Phèdre*, the Cardinal in *La Sorcière*, Scarpia in *La Tosca* and the Duca d'Este in *Lucrezia Borgia*.

It will be recalled that Sarah had renewed her lease on the Théâtre Sarah Bernhardt the previous year by agreeing that there would be no more foreign tours, so that the news of this one, following immediately on the London season, raised quite a storm in Paris. Tellegen was besieged by the press, all as amazed as he was by Sarah's new choice of leading man. It may be imagined that he learned very little of his voluminous new parts, and also that his arrival at the Gare St Lazare was not the occasion of a tumultuous welcome from the other members of the company. 'Even though I was to be Madame's leading man, I was a newcomer, and at that the youngest of them all, and nobody introduced me to anybody else ... They all stared at me, some giggled, some looked daggers at me, and others tried, grotesquely, to impress their theatrical superiority upon me at once. In other words,' concludes Tellegen, 'I was resented.'[15] That was almost certainly true; and equally certainly every single actor on that platform was asking himself and all his neighbours the question: Why him? It was, after all, not very long since she had been partnered by Lucien Guitry, Edouard de Max, the incomparable Coquelin.

The only possible answer to this question is that Tellegen was selected for his looks. He was an extremely beautiful young man (and later became a successful actor in Hollywood, performing soulfully in silent movies). Perhaps Sarah felt that, with her fading charms, she should present the female part of her audience, at least, with something to swoon over. But the more likely explanation must be that she was still something of a coquette. If she still entranced men in her sixties (as clearly she did) then this was because she enjoyed doing so, and still set out to do so. And if one is Sarah Bernhardt and one cannot act opposite Coquelin, then who – especially in America – is going to worry about the leading man? He might as well be handsome! It was not long before Tellegen was, in the great tradition of leading men, invited to take a room in Sarah's private car, where he shared her delicious meals (which she herself hardly touched), took her out shooting when the occasion arose (she was particularly fond of blackbirds, which she prepared herself), enjoyed various japes and escapades with which the tours were enlivened (such as when Sarah insisted on adopting a charming small pig which had taken her fancy and keeping it in her hotel room, or when she hid a valuable golden belt Tellegen had to wear as Hippolyte and enjoyed herself watching his panic when he thought he had lost it), and was generally overwhelmed by his extraordinary situation and by Sarah herself.

But if there was as yet no diminution in Sarah's ability to dazzle young men, her triumphant arrival in New York on the occasion of this tour provided proof, if it were needed, that, for women, she was a symbol of quite another kind. When she arrived, on 30 October 1910, she was met on the dock by the Joan of Arc Suffrage League (a play about Joan was part of her repertoire for this tour, in which, harking back to even earlier youth than was usual for her, she represented a girl of seventeen – and was, by all accounts, absolutely convincing). Sarah had graciously accepted honorary membership of the League in April, and greeted them warmly. Every suffragette carried a cane bearing a yellow pennant inscribed with the name of the League: another such pennant was embedded in a bunch of chrysanthemums which was presented to a delighted Sarah.

For women such as these suffragettes, Sarah of course represented something they all aspired to – independence, and acceptance by the world on her own terms. She – so aware of all aspects of her public self – was of course pleased by this, and happy to play up to it. In the advance programme for her 1896 tour of America she had done so unashamedly. In it she had expatiated at length on the cultural power of American women: 'Yes, I adore this country, in which woman reigns, and reigns so absolutely. She comes and goes. She orders, wills, exacts, instructs, spends money recklessly and gives no thanks. This shocks some people, but it only charms me.'[16] That season her most important new role had been Sudermann's Magda, who epitomizes the successful New Woman overcoming the dark forces of the old morality: in it, Magda, who has been made pregnant and then abandoned by a friend of her father, is thrown out of her home, goes on to make a successful career as an opera singer, returns as a celebrated figure, and turns down her old lover when he asks to marry her after all these years.

Sarah – whose history, after all, in some ways echoed Magda's – had always been very attractive to women. Maurice Rostand thought this was because there was a strong element of virility in her, so that the attraction was partly sexual. This may have been true to some extent. But to many women she must simply have symbolized, in her proud independence and unprecedented success, all they had felt a woman could never achieve. Sarah was a glittering, glamorous example of what could be done if one were talented and determined enough. Duse had felt this, and it had given her the courage to realize her own talent. But even for women who would never themselves set foot upon a stage, Sarah became a sort of totem. Suze Rueff recounts how, as a schoolgirl, escorted by her headmistress, she first went to have lunch with Sarah – and how, to her astonishment, her sober schoolteacher knelt and kissed the hem of Sarah's dress. 'After a performance of *Phèdre* or *La Dame aux camélias*, sometimes after *La Tosca*, I have seen great ladies kneel before her and kiss the hem of her gown, produce a small pair of scissors from their bag or pocket and, with great dexterity, snip a bit as a souvenir.'[17] There was an Englishwoman who used regularly to send superb Malmaison carnations, winter and summer, wherever Sarah might be; there was an elegant South American lady who, after seeing her in Rio de Janeiro in 1886, sent wonderful orchids until both of them were very old ladies.

Yet despite all this – despite the fact that her whole life had been a battle to live on her own terms, a feat which she had triumphantly achieved and the achievement of which had, as she was well aware, been the source of a great deal of resentment on the part of those who felt threatened by her either professionally (like the bureaucrats of the Comédie-Française) or sexually (like the Goncourts and all those other men who preferred their women passive and adoring) – despite this, Sarah was very far from being what her American sisters might have understood as a feminist. It had never occurred to her that a woman should not approach the world on terms of perfect equality with men. But this was a result of specific circumstances: the peculiarities of her upbringing, in which men were such peripheral figures, necessary financially but in no other way; and the fact that the theatre was the one milieu where men and women met on terms of complete equality. This state of affairs did not obtain elsewhere in society; but Sarah had no personal experience of that disadvantage because, when she moved outside theatrical circles, she was generally received like a visiting queen; and, when she was not so received, she could simply brush off the affront and, always in demand, move to choicer social pastures. If feminism implies a political commitment to better the lot of women in general, then Sarah was not a feminist (though Duse was).

It would have been more surprising if she *had* been a feminist. For not only were Sarah's intellectual energies not engaged with politics, but there was no movement in France to compare with the various suffragette and other movements concerned with the 'woman question' which were springing up at this time elsewhere in Europe and America.

This was partly because the women of the educated middle-classes, who generally got these movements going and gave them a theoretical basis – the Mrs Pankhursts, the Susan B. Anthonys – were extremely conservative in France at this time. It was not that their lot was a particularly satisfactory one. It was not until 1907 that a married Frenchwoman was allowed to keep full ownership and use of her wages; in the eyes of the law, she had no separate legal existence until 1938. And women did not receive the vote in France until 1944. Why not? In 1919 the chamber of deputies, like the British House of Commons, voted for full female suffrage, but this was decisively defeated by the Senate. One argument advanced against women voting was that, if all women were granted the vote, this would mean that prostitutes had it, too; another was that it would be indecent for men and women to mix freely in the polling booths. But the real fear was that women, who were more regular churchgoers than men, would vote for the clerical parties and so threaten the existence of the lay Republic.[17] The fact was that feminism, during the Revolution and then in the persons of the *jeunes filles modernes* who had taken their cue from George Sand and her liberated life of 'senti-

409

mental equality', had arisen early in France and had burnt itself out.

But there were also other reasons for this political indifference of women in France compared with their British or American counterparts. In England or America, feminism was just one aspect of a culture in which politics was a real focus for intellectual excitement. In Britain the most interesting writers of this period – Wells, Shaw, in his way D. H. Lawrence – were concerned with the design of the progressive millennium. In America politics impinged upon all aspects of life from religion to railroads: the essential thing about America, for many Americans, was that it *embodied* the millennium – or rather, as many millennia as there were Americans. The achievement of this ideal was the central national preoccupation. Compared with all this, the arts were a sideshow. But France had had its millennium – had just suffered almost a century of varied millennia – and millenarian enthusiasm was, understandably, at a low ebb. In France the arts were the vital focus of interest. Their central place in French culture was enshrined by institutions such as the Comédie-Française and the Académie Française. Where (Dreyfus apart) was the political excitement that could compete, in France at this time, with the intellectual and artistic ferment of the new developments in poetry, painting, music, the theatre? Anglophone writers – Oscar Wilde, James Joyce, Henry James – whose preoccupations were aesthetic and intellectual rather than political (although Wilde, at least, was also deeply concerned about political questions) gravitated to Paris, and so did the most interesting painters.

So that whereas women who were unable to participate in politics in Britain or America felt themselves excluded from a vitally interesting and important part of life, and devoted their energies to changing that state of affairs, the women who might have taken a similar lead in France – as

410

once they had joined the egalitarian communities designed by such millenarians as Saint-Simon and Fourier – now looked elsewhere for their liberation. True freedom, in France, lay in the arts. George Sand had shown that, within the free-and-easy circles of Bohemia, women need not be subjugated. When Colette left her husband Henry Gauthier-Villars in 1906, after eleven years of marriage during which he had appropriated her novels (publishing them under his own name), taken their proceeds (as he was legally entitled to do) and systematically humiliated her, she sought her freedom in the world of the theatre. The new epoch in her life was marked by a duet in mime at the Moulin-Rouge which she performed with her lesbian lover Missy (the daughter of the very duc de Morny who had so fortuitously directed Sarah into the theatre), and she spent the next several years touring as a mime in music-hall: a hard and often lonely life, but one which gave her freedom and self-respect, as she recounts in her novel *La Vagabonde*. Sarah had had the advantage (though many people might not have thought it such at the time) of being born into this dubious but exhilaratingly untrammelled milieu – or one very adjacent to it. Colette, seeing its advantages, propelled herself into it and did indeed find the fulfilment she was hoping for – although not without paying a certain price in terms of loneliness and uncertainty. But she never wavered in her conviction that the price was worth paying. Where, for a Beatrice Webb or a Charlotte Perkins Gilman, women's road to freedom lay in the achievement of political and social equality, for Colette, as for Sarah and George Sand, the road to freedom led through the arts, where only talent counted. In a not dissimilar way, Marie Curie, the only other contemporary Frenchwoman of comparable stature, had found her freedom through science – where talent was equally essential – and through a fortuitous widowhood which had forced her to become an independent operator.

But obviously such recourses were not available to everyone. Most people have not the capacities, intellectual or
psychological, of a Bernhardt, a Colette, a Marie Curie. And
if, like Sarah, one made good in the theatre, this did not
necessarily mean that one's material was purveying the
same message as one's life. If Sarah had really been a
feminist this might have worried her – as it worried Duse.
For in the theatre, one had, of course, to have plays. Colette
wrote her own scenarios, and created her own subtly
subversive characters. But much of the existing repertoire
was (as we have seen) deeply misogynist. The overt acceptance of the *demi-monde*'s existence – which resulted in an
undoubted freedom of operation for women within its
confines – implied an absolute absence of this freedom in
the world of the respectable woman, and above all in that
of the respectable young girl. And the theatre – in the work
of those playwrights who had flourished under the second
empire, and whose work was still widely performed, by
Sarah among others – did its bit in maintaining this state of
affairs. Edmond About explained that 'we want above all to
keep women faithful to their husbands. So we hope that
the girl will bring to the world an angelic provision of
ignorance which will be immune to all temptations.' When
Scribe was accused of having only stupid, timid, insignificant girls in his plays, Jules Lemaître defended him by
saying that these were realistic portraits, and that men had
a taste for young girls like these. 'The impossibility of
penetrating the secrets of the feminine soul at eighteen, the
sentiment of a sort of inviolable mystery, are part of the
idea we have of the young woman.'[18] And if she deviated
from this path, then Dumas *fils* was happy to portray her as
a lost soul who would inevitably be punished in some dire
way.

Nevertheless, even if Sarah spent a large part of her
time on stage portraying these unfortunate figments of a

chauvinist's imagination, her life showed that her philosophy was very far removed from theirs. At all significant moments she had *not* done what she was supposed to do. She was a happily unmarried mother. She had not behaved in the way public opinion had thought she should by remaining with the Comédie-Française or confining her operations principally to Paris. She had not submitted to authority in its publicly enshrined and respected manifestations. And she had flourished, one could truthfully say, as no independent woman had ever flourished before. Sarah was a living proof that the way forward for women was to make their own way regardless of men's prescriptions and recommendations.

In 1914 Sarah was at last awarded the Cross of the Legion of Honour. It was not a very exalted decoration, and she should have received it years before. Indeed, for years now the annual list (which appeared in the new year) of the new Chevaliers had been anxiously scanned by her friends, who had as regularly protested at her exclusion. It was not that women were not admitted. Some were – but these were always respectable public servants, teachers and administrators. And in fact Sarah might have been decorated years earlier if she had agreed to receive the honour in some respectable category such as professor at the Conservatoire (where she had lasted only one term) or director of the Théâtre Sarah Bernhardt. But she was not interested in that. She insisted that, if she was to be recognized, it should be for what she was – an actress. This demand had delayed her recognition for perhaps twenty years. For actresses, like Sarah, were not respectable; they did not embody the morality approved by the State; on the contrary, they represented an anarchic trend utterly at odds with the State's view of what a woman should be. But Sarah's pre-eminence was such that her non-recognition was becoming a scandal. In the end, it was the State which gave in. When

413

a committee gathered at the boulevard Péreire to discuss how the belated honour should be celebrated, its first move was to exclude all men from its deliberations. In the view of the Paris Press – which thus found itself, almost for the first time, unable to report the inmost workings of Sarah's private life – this was a revenge taken because men as a sex had opposed the cross being given to an actress. If Sarah's art was dated, she herself was the most modern of women, a living – and now honoured – proof that the way forward for her sex lay in grim determination and disrespectful independence.

She celebrated her decoration by giving two public lectures about her life and work, in which she presented a significantly sanitized version of her early days. For example, she declared that 'at the time of her débuts at the Comédie, she lived only for poetry, and if ever anyone could reproach her with the least vulgarity, it was because she liked to mix with the poets'. This was undoubtedly true – the only question was: how closely had she mixed with them, and with how many? In another notable revision of history, she declared that in her early days at the Comédie-Française, the other actors were jealous of her because she had been invited to recite at Princesse Mathilde's salon, and that she got tired of their self-importance and decided to leave for the Odéon. But such details might be forgiven a *chevalière* of the Legion of Honour. More interesting were some of her thoughts regarding her art. Gesture and attitude, she declared, were all-important in the theatre, and for this reason it was better to have long arms than short ones. Gesture should indicate thought, and should always *precede* the word it was supporting. And the eye, likewise, should precede the gesture. As for the actress's relation with the author – 'She is the repository of the author's thought who sometimes, sadly, finds herself misunderstood by those unsuccessful litterateurs who crowd into all the dress-rehearsals.'[20] So the newly-respectable Sarah wreaked a gentle revenge on all those self-satisfied gentlemen who, throughout her long career, had always shown themselves so happy to criticize her.

33

The general mobilization order preceding the declaration of war in 1914 found Sarah with her family at Belle-Isle. 'Let's go to Paris, children!' Lysiane reports her as saying. 'I don't want to stay shut up on this island.'

Terka was by now dead, and Simone was married with children of her own. On their return to Paris everybody, Maurice, Simone and her family and Lysiane, moved into the boulevard Péreire, and so did Suzanne Seylor. They were entertaining some old friends – Rostand, Dr Pozzi and some others – when a caller from the Ministry of War gave Sarah the news that her name was on a list of planned hostages which had been captured from the Germans. She was persuaded to move south, to Andernos near Arcachon; and it was here that she decided that the only way she could bear to go on living would be to have her bad leg amputated.

As the pain from Sarah's leg had got worse, her appearances on stage were naturally affected. Not that there was ever any question of her not appearing: far from it. Quite apart from anything else, Sarah could not afford to retire. But, increasingly, she played sitting down when that was possible, and, when it was not, helped herself across the stage by way of conveniently-placed items of furniture. By the time she left Paris, the pain had got so bad that she could barely walk. The story goes that, when Sarah and her party were ready to leave boulevard Péreire for the station, Emile, her old major-domo, reported that no ambulances were to be found, and nor were any taxis. Sarah immediately began to unpack again: she would remain in Paris. In the nick of time Maurice appeared with a taxi in tow. But, on the way to the station, driving down the Champs-Elysées for a last look at Paris, they were held up by a policeman to allow a military convoy to pass. First came the grey army trucks; and following them, one after another, all the taxis of Paris, which had been commandeered to carry troops to the front line on the Marne. They were stopped by an officer. Didn't they know all taxis were under Army command? Sarah and her party would have to get out. Then, suddenly, he recognized Sarah, sitting with her bad leg stretched in front of her, and saluted. 'I beg your pardon, madame. I did not know. Chauffeur, take Madame Sarah Bernhardt to the station and then come back to place yourself at our disposal.'[1]

Professor Pozzi, Sarah's doctor, put her leg in a plaster cast to see if that would help ease the pain. At the beginning of 1915 he came to Andernos to remove the cast and see if it had done any good. At first there was some relief, but after a week the pain came flooding back. Sarah was deeply depressed. She announced to her assembled family that they must choose. She could not put up with this any longer. Either she would have her leg cut off, or she would commit suicide. She would not listen to any reasoning: her mind was made up. The decision was made in favour of amputation.

It was not, however, easy to find a doctor who would perform the operation. For one thing, most of them were on active service; for another, Sarah was by now seventy and in frail health. Pozzi refused; so did Sarah's other regular doctor. Finally Major Denucé of the Bordeaux hospital agreed to perform the operation. Sarah bombarded all her friends with telegrams announcing that she was 'so happy – my leg is cut off tomorrow'. The operation took place on 22

417

February. It was successful. Denucé explained that he had thought it best to cut the leg off well above the knee, to avoid any danger of infection. However, after some days uraemia set in. Sarah fought it off, and by May she was well enough to return to her villa. When finally the wound was healed, she refused, after a few attempts, even to consider an artificial leg. If she only had one leg she could not walk, and that was all there was to it. She had a carrying-chair constructed of white wood and cane, and narrow enough to fit into a car or a lift, and this, during the remaining eight years of her life, was how she got about.

She wanted to show herself to the public as soon as possible, perhaps as much to regain her own confidence as for any other reason. Eugène Morand wrote a one-act play for her called *Les Cathédrales* in which Sarah took the part of Strasbourg, and this, after a successful performance in Paris, she resolved to perform for the troops at the front. She made a successful tour for the 'Army Theatre' in 1915, and another in 1916. The first time she was accompanied by Lysiane; the second, by a young sociétaire of the Comédie-Française, Béatrix Dussane.

'I had never met her before,' wrote Dussane. 'I went to the boulevard Péreire and, over the fire, in a white boudoir, I saw an extraordinary creature huddled in the depths of a low easy-chair; it consisted of thousands of folds of satin and lace surmounted by a reddish mop. It was an upsetting, rather depressing, sight . . . But . . . for two hours she held forth, ordered tea, enquired about travelling conditions, got carried away, excited, amused; seeing everything, understanding everything, hearing everything. And all the time she never stopped scintillating.'[2]

It is clear from this, as from many other descriptions of Sarah in her last years, that, stripped of the bodily grace which had adorned it, the force of her charm and intelligence emerged as strongly as ever – making perhaps even more of an impact because of its contrast with the now frail

418

and ancient-seeming envelope which was the physical Sarah. Old age, which she had held at bay for so long, had suddenly descended upon her with the amputation of her leg.

Now, with war enveloping her beloved France once again, the frail old woman called upon reserves of strength which no one would have suspected in her – just as the frail young girl had done forty-five years earlier in similar circumstances. Her first performance with Dussane was at Commercy:

We got out at Toul, the only civilian party on the train. The little chair reappeared; it was painted white and decorated with Louis XV scrolls; even the chair seemed to smile, and to wish to appear a whim and not a painful necessity . . . Less than an hour later the cars came to take us to the scene of our first performance: a huge open market square in Commercy. There was a stage, with footlights and a curtain, but the place reserved for Sarah had no floor but the beaten earth; the stage could only be reached by a ten-rung ladder and the place was full of draughts. Sarah installed herself in her makeshift dressing-room, and declared herself to be enchanted with everything . . . the curtain rose, disclosing for us in the gloom beyond the bright light of the footlights first the stretcher-bearer musicians, then the wounded, whose white bandages riveted our eyes, and finally the multitude of eager-eyed faces . . . There was a little applause, fairly warm but not unanimous and certainly not prolonged. Sarah felt a shudder go through her. This audience meant more to her than any audience at any big first night. I was there, quite close to her. I neglected my own part and I looked at her. I knew almost by heart what she was going to say. But she made me forget it. Everything seemed to vibrate and, in a rhythm that rose like a bugle-call, she sang of the martyrdom of Rheims and of Belgium. She conjured up all the glorious dead of our race and ranged them beside the men fighting France's battles at the moment; the rhythm of her speech rose in a constant crescendo. It carried us away with Sarah, and when, on the last cry of '*Aux Armes*!' the band broke into the 'Marseillaise', the three thousand French lads cheered us to the echo. This went on for three days; on a château terrace from which, in the distance, wrapped in mist but facing us, we could see the enemy positions at Woevre; in a hospital ward; in a ruined barn where the men even perched on the rafters.[3]

The next year, 1916, Sarah set off for her ninth and final tour of the United States. She was accompanied by her two faithful retainers, Emile and Pitou. Emile was by now becoming a rather inefficient major-domo, but when some friends gently suggested that the time had come for Sarah to find someone else she replied indignantly, 'Emile has been with me for forty-five years, and this is his home!' As for Pitou, her secretary, she treated him absurdly and abominably. When she was annoyed with him she threw whatever was to hand – ink, plates, food. She sent him on ludicrous errands: when Rostand finally settled at Cambo in the Basque country, Sarah, not trusting the post, would send Pitou with an urgent message for the playwright, instructing him to come right back without stopping – instructions which he may or may not have followed. But he remained devoted to her, and now it was Emile and Pitou who carried her, in her little white chair, on and off the boat and in and out of hotels and theatres. She travelled with twelve artistes, her impresario Connor (who had billed her, in the advance publicity, as 'the oldest woman in the world,' which infuriated her), her personal staff and fifty trunks. The tour was wildly successful. Sarah draped herself in the French flag, metaphorically and physically. She played *Les Cathédrales* and some other one-acters, including extracts from *La Dame aux camélias*, up and down America, urged her hosts to enter the war and save France, and made the fortune she needed. In the spring of 1917, after a performance at Saratoga, there was another attack of uraemia, and she nearly died, but was saved by an emergency operation and a blood transfusion. Maurice and his family waited anxiously in Paris for news. The doctor who had performed the operation had promised to telegraph them. On 6 April 1917, a telegram arrived. They tore it open feverishly. It read *Hurrah! Sarah Bernhardt*. On 6 April 1917, America entered the war.

That summer, Maurice, his new wife and Lysiane sailed over to join Sarah. Maurice and his wife returned to France after a month, but Lysiane stayed on with her grandmother, and together (accompanied, for a while, by a lion cub kindly donated by a circus, not to speak of a Pekinese and an Airedale) they travelled the States on the Sarah Bernhardt Special. Lysiane observed that the gipsy life of the train enchanted Sarah. 'When her morning toilette was finished [she] would have herself carried into the dining-drawing-room where she worked, rehearsed, wrote or bickered with Pitou; if we remained in a station she would receive journalists, tradesmen, casual visitors and friends until luncheon-time ... After the matinée performance she and I would go for a drive seeing the town, the Central Park [where Lysiane would walk the lion cub] and the surrounding country. The evening brought the second performance, hullabaloo, applause, autographs, hysterics and smiles. And lastly, at one in the morning, we went quietly to bed, lulled by the noise of the engines which we no longer heard, and rocked by the swaying of the train which we no longer felt.[4] In August they played Atlantic City, Mendel, New London, Stanford and Columbus. In September they returned to New York and the Savoy-Plaza Hotel for a fortnight (the lion cub had meanwhile been returned to the circus, because no hotel would accept him). Then they were off again to Chicago, taking in Salem, Hartville, Portland, Bridgeport, New Haven, Worcester, Springfield, Pittsfield, Albany, Port Huron, Saginaw, Flint, Lading, Battle Creek and Grand

Rapids. After Chicago they crossed Illinois and Wisconsin, Minnesota, Indiana and Ohio, Ottawa and Montreal. Then they went back to New York for Christmas, leaving on 14 February 1918 for Havana, and returning to the U.S.A via New Orleans, whence they travelled on up to Canada. In July they made Vancouver, where Sarah hired a boat in which she and Lysiane went fishing every morning. Then on down the coast to San Francisco and Oakland. In Los Angeles they took part in a parade to promote the American Government's newly issued Liberty Bonds, and an official, remembering that Sarah had been married to a Greek, had the escort to her carriage dressed in what he took to be Greek soldiers' uniforms. That, considering the facts about Damala, would have been bad enough, but the uniforms were actually Turkish – Turkey being, of course, on the other side in the war. Sarah, however, made no comment. Then they crossed the continent back to New York, via Denver, Kansas City and Cleveland. Between 22 August 1917 and 14 October 1918 (when the tour ended in Brooklyn) Lysiane reckoned that they had played in ninety-nine different towns. On the way back to Europe an American soldier insisted on being introduced to her. It turned out that he was the baby who had been born on board the *Amérique* on her first voyage over to the United States in 1880: Sarah's godson, the first time she had seen him since he was born.

They arrived back in Bordeaux on 11 November 1918, and on the wharf as they drew alongside, heard the cries announcing the Armistice.[5]

By the time Sarah returned from her final American tour the ranks of her old friends were sadly depleted. She had always planned to have herself buried on Belle-Isle, in a tomb she had designed herself and in a particularly inaccessible spot, which had prompted Georges Clairin to remark that she was clearly determined to go on being thoroughly troublesome to her friends even in death. But she was fated to outlive most of them. Edmond Rostand died in the flu epidemic of 1918, which meant that there would be no new play from him for Sarah to perform on her return home (he had planned two, one about Joan of Arc tentatively entitled *Les Cloches* or *Le Coeur*, another called *Le Théâtre*, where she would be called Gloriane but would really be playing herself). Dr Pozzi was assassinated by a lunatic the same year. Geoffroy and Clairin both died before Sarah. And not only were her old friends dying, but the artistic world in which she had grown up was very largely dead. In 1919 those movements which had been gathering steam in the pre-war avant-garde were suddenly perceived as the artistic mainstream. In the world of Proust, Picasso, and Pirandello, what place was there for Sarah, who represented everything they were reacting against?

One answer to this question lay, as it had always lain, in the classics. In 1920 she decided to play Racine's *Athalie*, a play written for the girls of Mme de Maintenon's school at St Cyr and rarely revived since. Sarah's first real success had been speaking the lines of the chorus at the Odéon. This time, of course, she would play the old Queen herself. 'It's a role I've been thinking about for a long time,' she told an interviewer. 'It was on my mind even when I was with the Comédie-Française, but M. Perrin wouldn't put it on. But I don't mind about that – I've got my own ideas about it which I wouldn't have been able to put into effect there. But Athalie is one of the few roles it's possible for me to play these days ... The Oriental sovereigns of antiquity almost always appeared before their subjects reclining on litters, or if they had to move about, on thrones which were carried by soldiers or slaves. So that's how I shall make my entry. But I shan't be immobile. I'm still capable of quite enough movement to present the Queen of Judah as Racine indicates she should be presented. But you mustn't expect great storms of epileptic fury or crude gestures. It's possible to make one's effect more subtly, and that's what I shall try to do.'[1] After *Athalie*, she was supposed to undertake another American tour, but Maurice was against it. If she didn't go, then she would open in October in *Daniel*, in which she would play a morphine addict.

Daniel was one of the plays which were being written for her at this time by a new generation of playwrights. For even now she was a magnet. Edmond Rostand and Sardou were dead and their plays outmoded. But young men flocked around her, trying to act with her, to write plays for her.

One of these was Louis Verneuil, a young playwright who, in 1921, married Lysiane and so became Sarah's grandson-in-law. *Daniel*, his offering, was an improbable farrago about a young man (he is supposed to be thirty) who is wasting away through drug abuse and has retired to enjoy his final days in neurotic seclusion while he reflects upon his past life. Sarah was to play the young man. The part of his older brother, aged forty, was at first alloted to an excellent actor named Abel Tarride, but when Sarah found out that he was really fifty-six, she (now seventy-five) insisted that he be replaced by somebody younger 'or he'll look like my father!'[2] The play was constructed especially for her: Daniel never has to move and only appears in two acts.

Sarah, says Verneuil, was eager to play *Daniel* both because she needed the money and because it was a real play, unlike *La Gloire*, which another young man, Maurice Rostand, son of Edmond, had written for her. Rostand, for his part, says that she described *Daniel* to *him* as '*une foutaise! une foutaise!*'[3] But, because she needed to keep on working and needed new material, she played them both, and also the offering of yet another young devotee. Sacha Guitry, who had attended her children's parties with Maurice Rostand, wrote her *Comment on écrit l'Histoire*, also in one act, and had yet another play prepared, *Un Sujet de roman*, which she was planning to do in 1923. This would have involved the entire Guitry family: Lucien and Sacha and Sacha's young wife, Yvonne Printemps, as well as Sarah. Sarah was particularly looking forward to working with the Guitrys. She told the English impresario Charles Cochran, who saw her at this time, that she thought Lucien was the sole survivor of the great actors of the past, and she was especially interested in the progress of Yvonne Printemps.[4] But on the night of the dress rehearsal of *Comment on écrit l'Histoire* she collapsed with another attack of uraemia, and although her first words on coming to were 'When do I go on?' she was destined never to go on the stage again. The play was eventually put on without her.

Sacha Guitry and Maurice Rostand were both talented writers; Louis Verneuil was not. What is clear is that Verneuil was more than half in love with Sarah: even in her seventies, she was still bewitching young men. He describes her as she was when he first read *Daniel* to her in the boulevard Pereire in words that are almost those of a lover — 'she welcomed me with a charming smile and held out

425

her white hand that was so charming, so expressive, with its curved nails and its movement still so incomparably graceful.'[5]

Verneuil describes how, after his marriage to Lysiane, they all went to Belle-Isle for the usual family summer in 1921. By now the old fort had been abandoned, and everyone lived in the Manoir de Penhoët, the graceless but comfortable hotel which Sarah had been forced to buy. There was the usual large mixed group: Maurice, Simone and her two children (who were then eight and ten), Jeanne de Gournay (who had lately replaced Suzanne Seylor as Sarah's lady-in-waiting), Dr Marot who was now Sarah's physician, Louise Abbéma, Lysiane and her friend Denise Hellmann, Jacqueline Bernhardt, a cousin, Maurice Perronet, who was her godson and the secretary of her theatre, Reynaldo Hahn, Marcel Boulenger, a writer, Victor Ullman, the manager of the theatre, his daughter, the actress Alice Dufrène, another cousin called Violaine. Everyone breakfasted together, then all went up to Sarah's room to say good-morning. After that Verneuil would say, 'Can I stay with you, Great?' ('Great' was what her granddaughters called her; she hated being called 'grand'mère'.) And, at least five times a week, he would spend the morning with her, gossiping, and listening while she told him all the old stories of her long life. There was to be only one more summer at Belle-Isle. The journey was getting too much for Sarah in her weakened state. She decided she would get a country place nearer to Paris, and in 1922, Belle-Isle was sold.

The American tour was by no means the last tour of all. There was a return to London in 1921, and then, in 1922, another European tour, in a large automobile Sarah had had specially constructed in order to accommodate her chair. (An early make of French automobile had been named the Sarah, but it faded into oblivion before its namesake.) But the automobile was involved in a crash and written off, the tour had to be completed using trains, and Sarah, exhausted, returned to the boulevard Pereire. Her last public performance was in Turin on 29 November 1922. The play was another of Louis Verneuil's pieces written especially for her, *Régine Arnaud*.

Some people saw her as dragging desperately around in order to earn money to support her family when they should by rights have been supporting her; others, as occupying her life in the only way she knew, with new productions, new places and new interests to pass the long days which, in old age as at any other time, still needed filling. To see Sarah perform at this time (and she was still always performing, on or off the stage) was, variously, either moving and enchanting as ever, or an appalling travesty. James Agate was still dazzled by her, and indignant with those who were not. He wrote: 'You have only to turn to the notices of her latest appearance in *Daniel* to realize the blindness of those who will not look beyond the flesh. "It is a matter of regret," writes one lusty fellow, "that this actress should be driven by circumstances to parade her infirmities before us." Follows a catalogue of departed bodily graces. "I will not bring my critical functions to bear upon the spectacle of an old lady with one leg portraying a paralytic," he concludes. I do not know [concluded Agate for his part] that I would condemn this blind soul to any darker circle than that of its own sightlessness.' For Agate, 'As the artist's physical powers have waned, so her intellectual faculties have ripened. Thirty years ago she had been content to play this foolish little Daniel with "her beauty, her grace, her flashing eye, her sinuous charm" – I quote from the catalogue of departed virtues – gathering him up to heaven at the end in her well-known cloud of fireworks.

427

Today . . . she is fanciful, wistful, wayward, endowing little things with an actor's interest, with something of the writer's preoccupation with style. I cannot imagine any more delightful grace-note than that of the little blue flames of the rum omelette which shall enliven her loneliness . . . What panting English tragédienne, in the full measure of bodily vigour, may compass the intimacy and interest of the Frenchwoman's lowest tone and slightest motion?' For James Agate, it is clear, this incarnation of Sarah in old age was preferable to that period when, 'once definitely on the rampage, candour compels me to admit, as it compelled Joe Gargery, that she was indeed a Buster. . . . Her acting is now an affair of the spirit, the victory of the incorruptible. For victory it is, victory over the fraying scabbard, victory in the dauntless survival of the soul of steel, the will to persist, *quand même*. One picture springs to the mind. It is the transfiguration of Lear: "I will do such things/What they are, yet I know not; but they shall be/The terrors of the earth." Substitute for terrors, wonders; then picture this valiant woman still wresting a last, late secret from her art.'[6]

Of course, there had always been two Sarahs – at least. Her old colleague Edouard de Max, who had been one of her leading men at the turn of the century, itemized 'the one you see from the front of the house and the one you see from the wings. The difficulty is that, from the wings, you sometimes see the same one as from the front of the house – the beautiful one. That's hard, because on those days you can't control yourself . . . when the curtain comes down you kiss her hands with tears in your eyes . . . As an actor, I knew Sarah the actress. I also knew, at the same theatre, a little girl who also happened to be called Sarah. Did I love or detest that impossible little girl? I don't know any more. It's so long ago, and I've got older. She, however, has not. She's still an impossible little girl, full of whims and tantrums. God, those tantrums!'[7]

So which, now, was the real Sarah — the aged cripple making an unbearable exhibition of herself on the stage which she used to grace, or James Agate's subtle charmer? Was she the vision glimpsed on her last visit to London in 1921, of whom an acquaintance wrote that 'as she lay back in the carriage, extravagantly pale, and with the lamp-black an inch thick under the eyes and on her eyelids, she looked lovelier than the fairest beauty of the season. She took you into a world where fresh senses were accorded. Did one love this woman? Yes, but as that passion may be conceived on some other planet. What one felt began with admiration and ended there. One desired her just as much and just as little as one desires Cleopatra or Helen of Troy.'[8] Or was she the 'very old woman' (she was in fact now seventy-seven) who met the eyes of another old acquaintance at this time. This Sarah 'lay on a huge bed. An elaborate *couvre-pied* hid the lower part of her figure, and I noticed that its folds fell flat on one side. Her blonde hair, streaked by dye, had all its old vitality; but in the crude light from the window her face was ghastly. Instantly, however, the famous smile stretched its double line of red across the large teeth, yellowed by time. Smears of ill-applied lipstick gave her mouth a sanguinary appearance and increased her resemblance to a tigress. Her hands, claw-like and ill-manicured, rested on the counterpane, and the lacy dressing-jacket was soiled and shabby. The impression was both tragic and sinister.'[9]

Colette, who met her this last December for the first time in her life when Sarah invited her to lunch, found her not in the least sinister. She had never yet had the opportunity of meeting Sarah: 'I went in a state of excitement, eager to meet, close to, this woman who was still on the stage in spite of age and amputation . . . I declined to wait downstairs among the cold, dusty souvenirs of past glories. I found her still defying powerlessness, age and illness. She was arranged in the dining-room as she might be arranged on a stage, on a throne which raised her a little higher than the rest of the guests, and her dark dress drowned her useless body and directed the attention towards that little head, so vivid, so imperious. She was no more than delicate skin and bone, a fleshless armature, energy reduced to its essential flame.'[10] But that flame was still very far from extinct. Sarah discussed a recent interpretation of *L'Aiglon* which she dismissed trenchantly: 'The poor thing isn't man enough to make you forget the *travesti*, nor woman enough to make you accept it.' Neither was she indifferent to the pleasures of the corporeal world. 'She kept smiling, with a gay, immaterial smile that reached her eyes, and her active little hands, imperious, expressive, were as luminous as her face ... "The coffee," I said, "is as good as the coffee one used to drink at Mendès' house . . ." The illustrious face lit up with youthful, malicious gaiety; "I've drunk Mendès' coffee, too. It was good. And Mendès talked about it a great deal. Perhaps mine only needs a little well-placed publicity?" . . . The delicate and withered hand offering the brimming cup, the flowery azure of the eyes, so young still in their network of fine lines, the questioning and mocking coquetry of the tilted head, and that indestructible desire to charm, to charm still, to charm right up to the gates of death itself.'[11]

Yes, there had always been many Sarahs; but perhaps the difference now was that, whereas previously she had been able to control the effect at will, to charm whomever she wished whenever she wanted, to transform herself effortlessly into the beauty that even her greatest admirers conceded she physically was not – now the effect no longer lay so much in her power as in the eyes of the beholder. As James Agate put it, 'To him who would contribute his quota of good-will this great lady's art is still the quintessence of loveliness.' As to whether it was advisable, or even possible, for an old woman of seventy-seven, with only one leg and suffering from uraemia, to get up on stage and impersonate

430

a young man of thirty – when had Sarah ever cared about what was advisable, or even possible? Had she not spent her whole life doing exactly what everyone assured her was inadvisable and impossible? It had been impossible to imagine that the stick-thin little girl would ever succeed as an actress. It had been an act of professional lunacy to walk out of the Comédie as an unsuccessful débutante. It had been inadvisable to behave so badly at the Gymnase and impossible to imagine she would ever get back on the stage; mad to leave the Odéon where she was so well-established, unwise to leave the Comédie a second time, unthinkable to behave as she did when on tour and to undertake the tours she did, impossible to imagine that she would re-establish her reputation as a serious actress, or that a woman in her fifties, even her sixties, could successfully play a young man – several young men . . . She had never cared what people thought, and now, at the extreme of age and celebrity – 'the oldest woman in the world' – she was not about to break the habit of a lifetime.

Nor was she about to stop working, if she could help it. A lifetime's ceaseless activity had not prepared her for an idle old age. Now, as much as at any other time, it was an imperative to find an activity to occupy herself – what else was she to do with her afternoons? If her physical condition prevented her from appearing on stage, there was nothing to stop her writing. So she became a novelist, publishing *Petite Idole* in instalments in the *Gaulois* – a sort of idealized and melodramatized reworking of some aspects of her youth as she might have liked them to be, a fantasy-fulfilment in which she gave the young girl, Espérance, who was in so many ways like the young Sarah, a happy, warm and respectable family complete with father, and in which, at the end, there was a duel to the death between a count and a duke each of whom was desperate to *marry* the heroine. She began, too, to put together a sort of manual of her art –

431

L'Art du Théâtre – which, more than anything else, was an omnium-gatherum of thoughts and anecdotes on the subject which had occupied her life for the past sixty years. 'Bring out that heap of stuff, darling,' she would say to her secretary, Mme Normand, whenever she had a spare half-hour, and, starting with a word or a phrase – memory, pronunciation – would embark on a stream of advice and stories, tenuously connected. Sarah had never been a great teacher. When her professorship at the Conservatoire ended after a term, she had for a while taken exclusive (and expensive) classes for girls at her theatre – rich Americans and *jeunes filles bourgeoises*, among whom were mingled a few more serious and usually non-paying pupils such as her English protégée May Agate. May's brother James once witnessed one of these classes: 'A rostrum, screened from the draughts, was erected in the place where the prompter's box usually appears. The pupils, nearly all young girls, though here and there an actress with a foot on a lower rung of the professional ladder, sat round the back of the stage in a semicircle . . . And then Sarah appeared. She wore that mantle known to every photographer in Europe, and to me recalling the misty breasts of sea-birds. She was supported by a devoted secretary and a woman friend, and her entry was not unlike that which she used for the third act of *Phèdre*. . . . I remember that some American Sadie or Mamie, glittering with diamonds, endeavoured to take Sarah by rhetorical storm, and was accorded a frigid "*Vous avez fait du progrès mademoiselle! Continuez!*" But to a plain and clever girl, who had obviously given time and thought to a long passage from Racine's *Bérénice*, Sarah gave her most earnest attention. She did nothing but scold, and to be scolded by Sarah was an indication that the pupil possessed within her at least the seeds of acting. [Perhaps she recalled her own student days, when Provost had done nothing but scold her.] The plain girl was succeeded by a little waif, who

432

was making a study of the distressed heroines of melodrama. "*Au secours*" she lisped, in a voice which could not have been heard beyond the first row of the stalls. In vain was she exhorted to more desperate effort, and at last her twitterings broke down in tears. "Won't you say it for me, Madame," she sobbed, "and then perhaps . . ." "My child," Sarah replied, "*regardez-moi donc* those workmen painting the ceiling. If I were to cry for help they would come rushing down on to the stage, and I pay them by the hour!"'[12] *L'Art du Théâtre* was perhaps written with that plain but talented student in mind.

Writing had the advantage that it did not require any sustained physical effort. And although the same could not be said of film, at least filming can be done in short bursts. Sarah had early on become an enthusiast for film. One of the plays she had put on with Lou Tellegen, *La Reine Elizabeth* (he played the earl of Essex), had turned out an expensive flop. But the money was recovered by its being made into a movie, the first full-length film of its kind – it ran to seven reels. And even this was not the first time Sarah had experienced the new medium. In 1908 she had filmed *La Tosca* with Lucien Guitry and Paul Mounet, but she had not liked the result, and had prevented the film's release. There had also been a film of *La Dame aux camélias*. (Unfortunately she never worked with any of the great early directors, although Abel Gance wrote a stage play for her which she would have put on, had not the First World War intervened.) These films were hardly cinematic master-pieces: they were made with one camera, which stood in the same spot throughout and photographed everything as from a seat in the front stalls. Nevertheless, *La Reine Elizabeth* was released worldwide, made a great deal of money, and brought Sarah other film offers. There was a film of *Adrienne Lecouvreur* in 1913, a wartime propaganda film scripted by Richepin called *Les Mères françaises* in 1916, a film of Tristan

Bernard's play *Jeanne Doré* in 1917. Films paid very well, although neither the critics (nor Sarah herself) thought much of her abilities as a screen actress.

For Sarah's seventy-eighth birthday, 22 October 1922, a special birthday lunch had been prepared. She was, Lysiane Bernhardt recalls, in a very bad mood that day, because it had become clear that the play she had been so hoping to do with the Guitrys, *Comment on écrit l'Histoire*, was not going to be possible. She was very ill, confined to bed on doctor's orders. However, she insisted upon going ahead with the lunch. She sat at the head of the table, eating nothing, speaking in a whisper; at the other end sat Maurice, who had for some time now been afflicted by Parkinson's disease, and who had to be helped to eat. Immediately after this sad meal Sarah announced that she was very tired, and was helped back to bed.

According to Lysiane, this was the day when a Mr Abrams from Hollywood arrived with a proposition to make a new film, *La Voyante*, with Sarah in the title role of the fortune-teller. Maurice had begged her to give up any more thought of work; but she insisted on seeing Mr Abrams, and, characteristically, found that the thought of a new piece made her feel much better (as did the pay, which was to be $300 a day). There were further inducements. Sarah would not have to tire herself travelling to and from the studio and waiting around in dressing-rooms. The studio would be set up in the boulevard Péreire.

Was the day on which all this took place perhaps Christmas rather than Sarah's birthday? It seems more probable. According to Louis Verneuil, Sarah's last perform-ance on tour, in his *Régine Arnaud*, took place on 29 November 1922, and Sarah then came back to Paris to start work on the Guitry play, only to fall ill with her fourth attack of uraemia on 23 December. But she was up again by 15 January, planning her new country home at Garches near Paris, and preparing the part of Corneille's *Rodogune* which she was thinking of adding to her repertoire for her classical matinées. In old age, classical grandeur and *gloire* perhaps came more naturally than the agonies of rejected love, and she had finally overcome her dislike of Corneille.

Shooting for *La Voyante* began in March, 1923. On March 15, Lysiane arrived to watch the filming. The main room in the boulevard Péreire had had all the furniture removed and was filled with the usual filming clutter. It was very hot under the arc lights. Sarah was thickly made-up for her part, and wearing dark glasses. She picked up her cards to shoot a scene; but, before it was finished, she collapsed, and had to be taken up to her room in her little chair. 'Make my apologies to Abrams,' she murmured to Lysiane.

'At first,' writes Lysiane, 'she was in despair at not being able to act in Sacha Guitry's play and having let Abrams down, but she soon resigned herself to accept her illness, and this resignation gradually became torpor. Then we knew that Sarah was going to die.'[13]

On March 20 it became clear that there was no more hope. The world's press set up camp opposite her house. Sarah knew they were there, and knew why. 'Are there any journalists down below?' she asked. 'The press has tormented me enough all my life. I can certainly plague it a little by making it kick its heels now.'

It did not have to wait long. Sarah died on March 26 at eight in the evening. Dr Marot opened a window and leaned out to make the announcement. 'Messieurs: Madame Sarah Bernhardt is dead.'[14]

Many people, including some inside the government, thought that Sarah should have had a state funeral, but as it happened too many ministers were absent for the Conseil to make a legal decison. So the city of Paris, her home town with which she had had such a stormy relationship over the years, took the initiative and announced that it would give her a municipal funeral. The details were organized by Louis Verneuil, as Maurice was too incapacitated by grief and illness. The coffin was carried in and out of the church – St François de Sales, where Maurice and both her granddaughters had married – by the *jeunes premiers* actors of the Paris theatre. As well as the hearse and the family carriages, five huge carriers were allowed for wreaths and flowers, but they were not enough. Great mounds of flowers and wreaths were heaped in front of the church, and the enormous crowds which lined the route from there to the cemetery of Père Lachaise carpeted the streets in front of the hearse with the flowers that they threw. All traffic was at a standstill. The procession took three hours to make the journey from the church to the cemetery. Nothing like it had been seen in Paris since the funeral of Sarah's friend Victor Hugo in 1885.

'Beside me,' remembered Maurice Rostand, 'walked old Arthur Meyer, who was very tough, and who had made an unshakable decision to live as long as he possibly could. He had a sort of black silk bonnet and from time to time he would put it on his pink head, criss-crossed with dyed hairs.'[15] Was he thinking of the time when he had invited the exquisite young Sarah to dinner so insistently that she could not refuse, and when, on his departure, she had crossly called him 'that old calf's head', he had stuck his face back round the door and retorted, 'And don't forget the parsley'?

Later that year, Louis Verneuil and Lysiane Bernhardt divorced. It had really been Sarah that Verneuil was marrying.

Her tombstone read, simply, BERNHARDT. Maurice Rostand wrote her epitaph:

> *Ci-gît Sarah*
> *qui survivra.*

436

35

It is hard to imagine anything further removed from the sad, deprived little girl who was Sarah in early childhood than the quasi-divinity inspiring awe-struck reverence of her last decades. It must have seemed to many a paradoxical situation: but the real paradox was that the celebrity was a direct result of the misery. For it seems clear that many of the factors which enabled Sarah to make such an unprecedented success of her life resulted from the psychological battering she had received in childhood, and the ways she devised, then and later, to deal with it.

That she was, as a child and young woman, deeply disturbed, seems incontestable. The appalling tantrums, the anorexia, the fascination with death and suicide, the compulsive attention-seeking, are all evidence of it. Of course, it is impossible at this distance to be sure of the exact nature of this disturbance. I have described my own hypothesis, which is that Sarah was a multiple personality, and my reasons for believing this; others may have other ideas. That she was, during the second half of her life, one of the most balanced and fulfilled of women, is equally not in doubt. Her life had cured her.

Naturally, she had her share of luck. Who can do without luck? In Sarah's case, there were two really important lucky chances: the fortuitous presence of the duc de Morny at the family conference which decided her career in the first place, and the fact that (after she had left the Gymnase, had Maurice and seemed to be embarking on a re-run of her mother's career) she turned up at the Porte-Saint-Martin at the very moment when the leading lady had just fallen ill – a chance which re-opened the doors of the theatre to her. But luck is what you make of it: and Sarah's life, more than most, was what she made it. '*Quand-même*' was no more than the literal truth. Sarah's life was a laborious construct which harnessed her weaknesses as well as her strengths, and turned those very weaknesses into strengths by dint of talent and determination pushed to the point of genius. The determination was no doubt constantly strengthened by an unremitting awareness of the fate which awaited her should she ever let up – a fate personified in the desperate and tragic lives of her two sisters. Jeanne and Régine, fading away in drugs, illness and wretchedness, were no more than the products which might have been expected of the emotional deprivation from which all Julie's children suffered. Sarah's iron refusal to succumb is proof in itself of the extraordinary strength of character which was to be the foundation of all her future success.

What, when one comes down to it, were the planks upon which Sarah built her life? There was, of course, the one piece of luck we have not yet mentioned: the talent without which she could never have made a career as an actress. Even that, if it is accepted that she was a multiple, was much enhanced by the psychological stratagem she used to cope with her traumatic childhood – although nothing but the sheerest accident of birth could have endowed her with the wonderful speaking voice which was her best known attribute. But there were other important features of her success, and they were constructed from material which might as easily have contributed to her destruction.

The first was an intense self-reliance, a self-confidence pushed to almost pathological extremes. And from what did this arise if not from the awareness, when she was a child, that there was absolutely no one she could rely on *except* herself? One after another everyone else failed her – her mother, who was hardly ever there, and who didn't love her or want her when she *was* there; her father, who was so emphatically absent – 'travelling in China – who knows why?' as she put it in the opening sentence of her memoirs – and who, when finally he did appear, disappeared again almost at once and died; her nurse, whom she trusted and whose husband probably raped her. In her sisters, this abandonment (which they in different degrees shared) led to despair and death. But Sarah rejected this primrose path early on – first perhaps when she refused to sell herself into a loveless marriage, finally when she tried (and signally failed) to act herself to death in a fit of pique (though death retained its fascination for many years). But if she was not to die she must believe in her capacity to save herself – and save herself in her own way: for if experience had taught her anything, it was that no one else could or would save her. Part of the attraction of the convent had doubtless been that it offered a tried and tested route to salvation – an honourable way out of this hard choice. Nuns, once they have made the great decision to become a nun, do not need – are indeed forbidden – to make any more such decisions: that is the essence of their life. Sarah, being an optimist, would not submit to despair: the veil, had she taken it, would have been her easy way out.

But having once taken her life into her own hands, she was not about to give responsibility for it to anyone else. And this – especially in the hierarchical and authoritarian context of the Comédie-Française – meant that she was virtually unemployable. Her decision, in 1880, to form her own company and set off on that tour that was to last, effectively, for the rest of her life, has the stamp of inevitability about it. At the time, however, there can have seemed nothing inevitable about it at all. It appeared, on the contrary, to be nothing more than yet another of Sarah's silly and ungovernable whims, the result of a fit of pique. That much is clear from the reactions of her colleagues, friends and enemies alike. None of them thought the gamble could come off; all of them thought that Sarah would be the only sufferer. And it is clear, too, that what most appalled them was the idea of being out on their own in the way that Sarah would be. That anyone should *choose* this course seemed to them inexplicable.

And yet this, too, given Sarah's background, was not such an unexpected choice. For if she was used to anything, it was being on her own. That had been her experience from her earliest days. Her mother provided her with a family, certainly – sisters and aunts to whom she clung – but it did not resemble the families most children grow up in. It was different both in the total absence of significant male figures and, more importantly, of adult love, directed towards either the children or other adults, and the security arising from that. It is clear from Sarah's account that Julie could scarcely cope with her own life, let alone take responsibility for the lives of her children.

For many people – perhaps for most – this would be a source of terror. It clearly was in Julie's case, and in the case of Sarah's sisters. But, once again, Sarah was able to turn a potential source of despair and destruction to good effect. Just as the prospect of relying on herself did not frighten her, so the thought of cutting loose and being on her own clearly stimulated and excited her. The fact that she lacked the slightest sense of the need to take financial precautions and think about the future with bank accounts and investments is an indication of this. Her reaction to never having known security was not to crave it, but to dismiss it: it meant nothing to her. She had her terrifying self-confidence instead. She had coped before and she would cope again. Once she had Maurice she had all the family she needed. Indeed her one excursion into what for most people constitutes a wider family life – with Damala, himself an emotional cripple of the type with which her family had made her only too familiar – had been a disaster she was quite unable to deal with. While it lasted it left her uncharacteristically floundering. She had never been tempted to try it before, and was never to do so again. She could not deal with being tied down, emotionally or contractually. What suited her was the nomadic life of the touring player – that lonely, rootless life which Duse, upon whom it was forced by financial and professional necessity, so detested. Duse craved (or said she craved) the emotional and physical anchorage of a loving man and a home. Sarah, happy in her deluxe railroad-car, saw no necessity for either.

Acting, into which she had been thrust so fortuitously, offered unique advantages as a way of life. It was a field – at that time the only professional field other than courtesanship – in which women could operate freely and without disadvantages. But it also provided both a therapeutic means of working out her emotional disturbances and a way of life which was able to satisfy the peculiar demands of her character – demands which might have seemed so intolerably antisocial in almost any other sphere and which would almost certainly have made a merely domestic life a disastrous impossibility for her. It seemed for a time as though the exigencies of her character – her anti-authoritarianism, her compulsion to push every situation just too far – had pushed her even outside the tolerant bounds of the theatre. Sarah (but nobody else) realized, consciously or otherwise, that the only solution was to play along with her impossible character rather than continually to fight against it; and her tough boldness, the other side of that irresponsibility which was Julie's only legacy to her, enabled her to make the leap where others might have quailed. It was an unlikely cocktail. It resulted, from the public's point of view, in that unique theatrical phenomenon which, for fifty years, was

441

Sarah Bernhardt. As for Sarah, the reward for her boldness and determination was – after the roller-coaster ride of her first forty years – a life of fulfilment and excitement few men – and hardly any women – have equalled. Sullied by few of life's usual regrets, it was a triumphant anti-morality such as the world has rarely seen. No wonder the preachers inveighed; no wonder the adoring public searched in vain for new adjectives. Sarah had discarded – or had never bothered to acquire – all the accoutrements with which the nineteenth century tried to load women down: a husband, sexual shame, respect for conventions and authority, the need for security ... and which dutiful wife and mother would not have changed places with her on the spot, given the chance? No wonder women adored her. In the sense that she was more, or less, than human – at any rate, quite clearly *other* – by the end it could truly be said that she was Divine.

Notes

Chapter 1

1 Sarah Bernhardt, *Ma double vie*, vol. 1, p. 3.
2 Jules Huret, *Sarah Bernhardt*, p. 5.
3 Maurice Rostand, *Sarah Bernhardt*.
4 Huret, *Sarah Bernhardt*, p. 5.
5 Letter to Benoit Jouvin quoted Ernest Pronier, *Sarah Bernhardt*, p. 25.
6 According to Pronier.
7 Louis Huart, *Physiologie de la grisette*, quoted Johannes Gros, *Alexandre Dumas et Marie Duplessis*, p. 98.
8 See Joanna Richardson, *The Courtesans*, p. 65.
9 Paul d'Ariste, quoted Richardson, *The Courtesans*, pp. 68–9.
10 See Pronier, pp. 25 ff.

Chapter 2

1 When the Comédie-Française visited Holland early in 1880 the Amsterdam Handelsblaad made inquiries which showed that Sarah had often visited her Dutch grandparents as a child: this is the likeliest period.
2 Bernhardt, *Ma double vie*, vol. 1, pp. 8–12.
3 Ibid. p. 14.
4 Colette, *Mes Apprentissages*.
5 Liane de Pougy, *Idylle saphique*, p. 15.
6 *Le Temps*, June 1881.
7 Bernhardt, *Ma double vie*, vol. 1, p. 45.

Chapter 3

1 Bernhardt, *Ma double vie*, vol. 1, p. 58.
2 Osgood Field, *Uncensored Recollections*, p. 15.
3 Arsène Houssaye, *Les Confessions*, vol. 1, p. 409.
4 Osgood Field, p. 73.
5 Cora Pearl, *Mémoires*, quoted Richardson, *The Courtesans*, p. 52.
6 Houssaye, *Les Confessions*, vol. 6, p. 45.
7 Goncourts, *Journal*, 25 September 1886.

8 Bernhardt, *Ma double vie*, vol. 1, p. 64.
9 Ibid. p. 65.
10 Quoted Linda Kelly, *The Young Romantics*, p. 115.
11 Léonide Leblanc's preface to *Les Femmes de Théâtre* by Alphonse Lemonnier, quoted Richardson, *The Courtesans*.
12 Ibid.
13 Bernhardt, *Ma double vie*, vol. 1, p. 58.
14 Ibid. p. 47.

Chapter 4

1 Quoted by Jules Claretie, *New York Times*, 25 February 1883
2 Lysiane Bernhardt, *Sarah Bernhardt*, p. 30.
3 Bernhardt, *Ma double vie*, vol. 1, p. 73.
4 Ibid. p. 77.
5 Ibid. pp. 82–9.

Chapter 5

1 Jules Lemaître, *Les Contemporains*, vol. 5 pp. 260–1.
2 Bernhardt, *L'Art du Théâtre*, p. 171.
3 Gerda Taranow, *Sarah Bernhardt: The Art Within the Legend*, p. 3.
4 Paul Porel, *Fils de Réjane*, p. 172.
5 Marie Colombier, *Les Mémoires de Sarah Barnum*, pp. 11–12.
6 Ibid. pp. 3–4.
7 Bernhardt, *Ma double vie*, vol. 1, p. 112.
8 According to Maurice Rostand.

Chapter 6

1 Bernhardt, *Ma double vie*, vol. 1, p. 118.
2 Edmond de Goncourt, *La Faustin*, pp. 143–4.
3 *Opinion nationale*, 12 September 1862, quoted Bernhardt, *Ma double vie*, vol. 1 pp. 132–3.
4 Huret, *Sarah Bernhardt*, p. 15.
5 May Agate, *Madame Sarah*, p. 31.
6 Bernhardt, *L'Art du Théâtre*, pp. 123–4.
7 Y. Blaze de Bury, 'Sarah Bernhardt', *Fortnightly Review*, July 1899.
8 Bernhardt, *Ma double vie*, vol. 1, p. 125.

Chapter 7

1 Bernhardt *Ma double vie*, vol. 1 pp. 99–100.
2 Henry James, *The Scenic Art*, p. 74.
3 Bernhardt, *Ma double vie*, vol. 1, pp. 133–4.
4 Ibid. p. 145.
5 Louis Verneuil, *La Vie merveilleuse de Sarah Bernhardt*, p. 56.
6 Lysiane Bernhardt, *Sarah Bernhardt*, pp. 63–4.

Chapter 8

1 Lysiane Bernhardt, op. cit. p. 24.
2 Ibid. p. 60.
3 Bernhardt, *Ma double vie*, vol. 1, p. 153.
4 Ibid. p. 156.

Chapter 9

1 Colombier, *Les Mémoires de Sarah Barnum*, p. 47.
2 *Marthe, passim*.
3 See my book *The New Women and the Old Men*.
4 Epigraph, Jan Marsh, *Jane and May Morris*.
5 Alice James to William James, 30 July 1891, quoted Leon Edel, 'Portrait of Alice James', introduction to his edition of her diary.
6 Colette, *La Naissance du jour*.
7 Alexandre Dumas *fils* to Marie Duplessis, quoted Gros, pp. 254–5.
8 Ibid. p. 256.
9 Bernhardt *Ma double vie*, vol. 1, p. 158.
10 Arthur Meyer, *Ce que je peux dire*, p. 10.
11 Bernhardt, *Ma double vie*, vol. 1, pp. 160–1.
12. Ibid.

Chapter 10

1 Félix Duquesnel, *Le Figaro*, 16 September 1894, quoted Pronier, pp. 157–8.
2 Bernhardt, *Ma double vie*, vol. 1 p. 164.
3 Ibid. p. 166.
4 Ibid. p. 168.
5 Ibid. p. 170.
6 Quoted Gay Manifold, *George Sand's Theatre Career*, pp. 103–4.
7 Bernhardt, *Ma double vie*, vol. 1, p. 180.
8 'Ignotus' in *Le Figaro*, 18 February 1868.
9 Goncourts, quoted Otis Skinner, *Madame Sarah*, p. 54.
10 Robert de Montesquiou, *Les Pas Effacés*, vol. 2, p. 174.
11 André Gill, *Vingt Ans de Paris*
12 Bernhardt, *Ma double vie*, vol. 1, p. 180.
13 Maurice Rostand, *Sarah Bernhardt*, p. 16.
14 Blaze de Bury, p. 114.
15 Bernhardt, *Ma double vie*, vol. 2, p. 37.
16 Nicholas Humphrey and Daniel C. Dennett, *Speaking for Ourselves: An Assessment of Multiple Personality Disorder*. This case history is in part a reconstruction, but is true to type (and life). I should like to express my thanks to Nick Humphrey for drawing my attention to this.
17 Sylvia Fraser, *My Father's House*, p. 12.

18 Ibid. pp. 65–6.
19 Ibid. p. 92.
20 Ibid. p. 86.
21 Colombier, *Les Mémoires de Sarah Barnum*, p. 35.
22 *New York Times*, 30 April 1883.
23 *Independent on Sunday*, 21 October 1990.
24 Jean Truffier, quoted by Pronier.
25 Bernhardt, *Ma double vie*, vol. 2, pp. 41–2.
26 Fraser, op. cit. p. 113.
27 Bernhardt, *Ma double vie*, vol. 2, pp. 38–9.

Chapter 11

1 Berton/Woon *Sarah Bernhardt As I Knew Her*, p. 120.
2 Bernhardt, *Ma double vie*, vol. 1, p. 179.
3 Juliette Adam, *Mes Illusions et nos souffrances pendant le Siège de Paris*, pp. 4–5.
4 Ibid. pp. 60–1.
5 Bernhardt, *Ma double vie*, vol. 1, p. 209.
6 Adam, pp. 61–2.
7 Colombier, *Les Mémoires de Sarah Barnum*, p. 156.
8 Goncourts, *Journal*, 7 Jan 1870.
9 Adam, p. 240.
10 Sardou, *Les Papiers de Victorien Sardou*, p. 317.
11 Eric C. Hansen, *Ludovic Halévy*, p. 136.

Chapter 12

1 Reynaldo Hahn, *La Grande Sarah*, p. 146.
2 Mme Octave Feuillet, *Souvenirs et Correspondances*, p. 231–2.

Chapter 13

1 Judith Gautier, quoted Richardson, *Judith Gautier*, p. 86.
2 Goncourts, *Journal*, 7 November 1870.
3 Ibid.
4 Bernhardt *Ma double vie*, vol. 2, p. 3.
5 Ibid. pp. 13–23.

Chapter 14

1 Henry James, *The Scenic Art*, p. 72.
2 Count Joseph Primoli, Journal 16 Dec 1893 – *Pages inédites* p. 52.
3 Bernhardt *Ma double vie*, vol. 2, p. 25.
4 Goncourts, *Journal*, 8 May 1865.
5 Quoted Huret, *Sarah Bernhardt*, p. 38.
6 Ibid. p. 38.
7 Henry James, *The Scenic Art*, p. 73.

8 Lemaître, *Les Contemporains*, vol. 5, p. 300.
9 Quoted Huret, op. cit. p. 38.
10 Bernhardt, *Ma double vie*, vol. 2, p. 31.
11 Quoted Huret, p. 41.

Chapter 15

1 Bernhardt *Ma double vie*, vol. 2, p. 31.
2 Francisque Sarcey, *Quarante Ans de Théâtre*, vol. 3, 24 July 1882.
3 Bernhardt, *Ma double vie*, vol. 2, p. 34.
4 Feuillet, op. cit. pp. 317–8.
5 Bernhardt, *Ma double vie*, vol. 2, p. 36.
6 Quoted Huret, p. 36.
7 Ibid.
8 Bernhardt, *Petite Idole*, p. 36.
9 Hahn, *La Grande Sarah*, p. 95.
10 Quoted Otis Skinner, *Madame Sarah*, p. 79
11 Hahn, p. 96.
12 Lemaître, *Les Contemporains*, vol. 5, pp. 205–6.
13 Tom Taylor, *The Times*, 3 June 1879.
14 Hahn, p. 96.
15 Sarcey, op. cit. pp. 131–2; ibid. 28 June 1886.
16 Ibid. 6 August 1877.

Chapter 16

1 Goncourts, *Journal*, 28 December 1877.
2 Suze Rueff, *I Knew Sarah Bernhardt*, p. 209.
3 James, *The Scenic Art*, p. 144–5.
4 Lysiane Bernhardt, *Sarah Bernhardt Ma Grand'mère*, p. 979.
5 Pierre Loti, *Journal intime 1878–1881*, 26 March 1880.
6 W. Graham Robertson, *Time Was*, quoted Bram Dijkstra, *Idols of Perversity*, p. 46.
7 For a longer discussion of this question see Bram Dijkstra's fascinating book *Idols of Perversity*, to which I am indebted for many of the ideas in this section.
8 Alice James, *The Diary of Alice James*, December 1889, p. 66.
9 Quoted Richardson, *The Courtesans*, p. 10.
10 Houssaye, *Les Confessions*, vol. vi, p. 29.
11 Field, *Uncensored Recollections*, p. 6.
12 Goncourts, *Journal*, 5 December 1891.
13 Ibid.
14 Ibid. 12 January 1860.
15 Quoted Winifred Stephens, *Madame Adam*, pp. 124–5.
16 Goncourts, *La Faustin*, p. 62.
17 Pronier, *Sarah Bernhardt*, p. 163.

18 Quoted Stephens, *Madame Adam*, pp. 97–8.
19 Arthur Meyer, *Ce que je peux dire*, pp. 89–91.
20 Primoli, Journal 13 Feb 1893, *Pages inédites* p. 30.

Chapter 17

1 Houssaye, *Les Confessions*, vol. II, p. 22.
2 James, *The Scenic Art*, p. 90.
3 *The Times*, 26 September 1876.
4 Bernhardt, *Ma double vie*, vol. 2, pp. 72–5.
5 Ibid. p. 76.
6 Loti, *Journal intime*, pp. 80–85, 28 May 1879.
7 According to Elisabeth de Clermont-Tonnerre, quoted G. Painter, *Marcel Proust*, vol. 1, p. 129.
8 Bernhardt, *Ma double vie*, vol. 2, p. 77.
9 Ibid. pp. 78–82. Sarah wrote a little book about this trip entitled *Dans les Nuages*.
10 Ibid. p. 83.
11 Sarcey, *Quarante ans de Théâtre*.
12 Marguerite Moréno, *Souvenirs de ma vie*, p. 146.

Chapter 18

1 d'Heylli, *La Comédie-Française à Londres*, p. lxii–lxiii.
2 Bernhardt, *Ma double vie*, vol. 2, p. 89.
3 Ada Leverson, 'The Last First Night', *New Criterion*, January 1926, quoted Richard Ellmann, *Oscar Wilde*, pp. 112–3.
4 Bernhardt, *Ma double vie*, vol. 2, p. 96–7.
5 Ibid.
6 Henry James, *The Tragic Muse*, p.249.
7 Houssaye, *Les Confessions*, vol. V, p. 325.
8 W. Graham Robertson, *Time Was*, p. 123.
9 Mrs Patrick Campbell, *My Life and some Letters*, p. 141.
10 Bernhardt, *Ma double vie*, vol. 2, p. 100.
11 Cranstoun Metcalfe, *Peeresses of the Stage*, p. 207.
12 Quoted Richard Findlater, *Bernhardt and the British Player Queens*, Salmon ed., p. 104.
13 Ibid.
14 Bernhardt, *Ma double vie*, vol. 2, pp. 99–100.
15 Quoted Taranow, *Sarah Bernhardt*, p. 14.
16 *The Times*, 3 June 1879.
17 Sarcey, in d'Heylli, *La Comédie-Française à Londres*, pp. 78–81.
18 Quoted J. C. Trewin, *Bernhardt on the London stage*, Salmon ed. p. 116.
19 Sarcey, in d'Heylli, *La Comédie-Française à Londres*, pp. 72–3.
20 James, *The Scenic Art*, p. 130.

21 Hahn, *La Grande Sarah*, p. 150.
22 Quoted Taranow, *Sarah Bernhardt*, pp. 112–3.
23 Ellen Terry, *The Story of my Life*, p. 67.
24 Ibid., quoted Findlater, p. 102.
25 Ibid. p. 97.
26 James, *The Scenic Art*, p. 108.
27 Quoted Findlater, p. 96.
28 James, *The Scenic Art*, pp. 109–10.
29 Quoted Findlater.
30 For further discussion of this see Findlater.

Chapter 19
1 *The Times*, 24 June 1879.
2 Maurice Rostand, *Sarah Bernhardt*.
3 *The Times*, 16 June 1879.
4 *Ma double vie*, vol. 2, 124–5.
5 Ibid. pp. 121–2.
6 d'Heylli, p. lxxix.
7 *Ma double vie*, vol. 2, p. 130.
8 Ibid. p. 131.
9 In fact he made this criticism regarding her Monime, one of Racine's *jeune princesse* parts.
10 *Ma double vie*, vol. 2, p. 139.
11 Sarcey, *Quarante Ans de Théâtre*, quoted James Agate, *Alarums and Excursions*, pp. 43–4.

Chapter 20
1 *Ma double vie*, vol. 2, p. 141.
2 Berton/Woon *Sarah Bernhardt As I Knew Her*, pp. 225–7.
3 Jules Renard, *Journal*, 16 December 1893.
4 Quoted Maurice Baring, *Sarah Bernhardt*, pp. 50–61.
5 Sarcey, *Quarante ans de théâtre*
6 Quoted in d'Heylli, *La Comédie-Française à Londres*, p. 155.
7 Edmond Haraucourt, quoted Pronier, p. 160.
8 Baring, *Sarah Bernhardt*, p. 69.
9 W. Graham Robertson, *Time Was*, p. 154.

Chapter 21
1 Quoted Knepler, *The Guided Stage*, p. 52.
2 Colombier, *Le Voyage de Sarah Bernhardt en Amérique*.
3 *Ma double vie*, vol. 2, p. 183.
4 Ibid. p. 184.
5 Colombier, *Le Voyage de Sarah Bernhart en Amérique*.
6 James, *The Scenic Art*, p. 129.

7 William Weaver, *Duse*, p. 98.
8 *New York Times*, 28 October, 1880.
9 *Ma double vie*, vol. 2, p. 180.

Chapter 22

1 Colombier, *Le Voyage de Sarah Bernhardt en Amérique*.
2 Ibid. p. 80.
3 Ward McAllister, *Society as I have Found It*, p. 160.
4 Arsène Houssaye, introduction to Colombier, *Le Voyage de Sarah Bernhardt en Amérique*.
5 *Ma double vie*, vol. 2, p. 199.
6 Colombier, *Le Voyage de Sarah Bernhardt en Amérique*.
7 Ibid. p. 226.
8 Quoted Weaver, *Duse*, p. 6.
9 Giacosa, *Impressioni d'America*, pp. 115 ff.
10 *New York Times*, 15 February 1906.
11 Moréno, *Souvenirs de ma vie*, p. 144.
12 Henry James, *The Scenic Art*, p. 199.
13 Alice Miller, *The Drama of the Gifted Child*.
14 Jules Lemaître, *Les Contemporains*, vol. 5.
15 Moréno, p. 144.
16 Paul Bourget, *Outre-mer*, pp. 240–242.
17 *Ma double vie*, vol. 2, p. 220.

Chapter 23

1 Quoted *New York Times*, 7 Feb 1881.
2 Quoted Skinner, p. 156.
3 *Ma double vie*, vol. 2, p. 241.
4 Ibid. p. 242.
5 Ibid. p. 244.
6 Ibid. pp. 223–4.
7 Ibid. p. 248.

Chapter 24

1 Quoted Sarcey, in d'Heylli, *La Comédie-Française à Londres*, p. 155.
2 Quoted Skinner, p. 181.
3 Baring, *Sarah Bernhardt*, p. 72.
4 Moréno, p. 138.
5 Baring, p. 82.

Chapter 25

1 *New York Times*, 19 December 1881.
2 *Figaro*, 6 April 1882.
3 *New York Times*, 9 April 1882.

4 Ibid.
5 *Truth*, 30 April 1882.
6 Rueff, p. 92.
7 Berton, p.224.
8 Rueff, p. 99.
9 Maurice Rostand, *Sarah Bernhardt*, pp. 28–9.
10 Rueff, pp. 99–100.
11 Quoted Skinner, p. 190.
12 Ibid. p. 191.
13 *New York Times* 11 September 1882.
14 *New York Times*, 22 Sept 1882.
15 Sarcey, *Quarante ans de théâtre*.
16 Quoted Skinner, pp. 193–4.
17 *New York Times*, 24 February 1883.
18 *New York Times*, 22 December 1883.
19 Colombier, *Les Mémoires de Sarah Barnum*, p. 90.
20 *Le Réveil*, quoted *Affaire Sarah Bernhardt/Marie Colombier, Pièces à Conviction*.
21 Lysiane Bernhardt, p. 162.
22 Graham Robertson, p. 121.
23 Richard Ellmann, *Oscar Wilde*, p. 236.
24 *New York Times*, 22 Nov 1884.
25 Ibid.
26 Lysiane Bernhardt, p. 163.
27 *New York Times*, 14 March 1887.
28 Quoted Skinner, p. 207.
29 *New York Times*, 30 August 1884.
30 *New York Times*, 30 August 1884.
31 'Sarah Bernhardt en Buenos Aires', *Atlàntida*, 29 November 1951.
32 Ibid.
33 'Sarah Bernhardt en actuaciòn en Chile', Theatre Museum of Santiago.
34 Elizabeth Finley Thomas, *Ladies, Lovers and Other People*, quoted Skinner, p. 216.
35 *Truth*, 19 January 1887.
36 Flaubert, *Letters 1830–57*, p. 132.
37 *The Times*, 5 April 1882.
38 Beerbohm, *Around Theatres*, 7 December 1901.
39 *The Times*, 30 April 1886.
40 Maurice Rostand *Sarah Bernhardt*, p. 95.
41 Ibid.

Chapter 26

1 Jules Lemaître, *Les Contemporains*, vol. 5.
2 Quoted Ernest Jones, *Sigmund Freud*, vol. 1, p. 194.

3 Quoted Theodore Zeldin, *France 1848–1945*, vol. 1, p. 355.
4 Quoted Findlater, 'Bernhardt and the British Player Queens',
   p. 108, in Salmon ed., *Sarah Bernhardt and the Theatre of her Time*.
5 Arthur Symons, 'Sarah Bernhardt' in *Plays, Acting and Music* quoted
   Taranow, p. 119.
6 Alice James, *The Diary of Alice James*, 9 March 1890.
7 Lemaître, *Les Contemporains*, vol. 5, 27 Dec 1889.
8 Quoted Baring, *The Puppet-Show of Memory*, p. 233.
9 Hahn, p. 65.
10 Sarcey, 21 November 1893.

Chapter 27

1 Edmond Rostand's preface to Jules Huret, *Sarah Bernhardt*.
2 Letter to Mrs Bernard Beere, December 1889.
3 Quoted Alice James, *The Diary of Alice James*, p. 26.
4 Baring, *The Puppet-Show of Memory*, p. 232.
5 Quoted Montesquiou, *Les Pas éffacés* vol. 2, p. 224.
6 Henri Fouquier, quoted Robert Horville 'Stage Techniques of Sarah
   Bernhardt', in Salmon, ed., *Sarah Bernhardt and the Theatre of her
   Time*.
7 Jules Renard, *Journal*, 1906.
8 Beerbohm, *Around Theatres*, p. 161.
9 Henri Fouquier, 'Bernhardt and Coquelin', *Harper's Monthly
   Magazine*, December 1900.
10 Elizabeth Robins, 'On seeing Mme Bernhardt's Hamlet', *North
   American Review*, December 1900.
11 Bernhardt, *L'Art du Théâtre*, p. 136.
12 Colette, *Paris-Soir*, 24 October 1938.
13 Clement Scott, *Some Notable 'Hamlets'*, p. 49.
14 Baring, *Sarah Bernhardt*, p. 136.
15 Beerbohm, pp. 34–7.
16 Ibid. p. 160.
17 William Archer, *Theatrical World of 1897*, p. 186.
18 Quoted Mrs Patrick Campbell, *My Life and Some Letters*, p. 138.
19 James Agate, 'Sarah Bernhardt: A Postscript', *Alarum and Excursions*,
   p. 55.
20 Graham Robertson, *Time Was*, p. 254.
21 *New York Times*, 14 December 1905.
22 Alice B. Toklas, *What is Remembered*, p. 20.

Chapter 28

1 Rueff, p. 122.
2 Renard, *Journal*, 1 January 1896.
3 *New York Times*, 19 October 1905.

4 *New York Times*, 7 December 1905.
5 Maurice Rostand, *Sarah Bernhardt*, p. 94.
6 Montesquiou, *Les Pas éffacés*, vol. 3, p. 44.
7 Colette, *Paris-Soir*, 24 October 1938.
8 Jacques Porel, *Fils de Réjane*, p. 174.
9 Sacha Guitry, *Souvenirs: Si j'ai bonne mémoire*
10 Goncourts, *Journal*, 25 April 1886.
11 Colette, *Mes Apprentissages*.
12 Lysiane Bernhardt, pp. 180–1.
13 Rueff, pp. 158–9.
14 Yvonne Lanco, *Belle-Isle-sur-Mer: Sarah Bernhardt – souvenirs*.
15 Baring, *The Puppet-Show of Memory*, p. 217.
16 Ibid. p. 218.

Chapter 29

1 Oscar Wilde to Leonard Smithers, 2 September 1900.
2 *London Mercury*, October 1923.
3 Jules Renard, *Journal*, 10 December 1896.
4 Huret, p. 171.
5 Renard, *Journal*, 10 December 1896.
6 Alfred Jarry, *Ubu*, p. 426.
7 Ibid. p. 430.

Chapter 30

1 James, *The Scenic Art*, p. 317.
2 Ibid. pp. 317–8.
3 By Taranow, p. 185 ff.
4 Hahn, p. 149.
5 Quoted Knepler, p. 228.
6 Shaw, *Our Theatres in the Nineties*, vol. 2, p. 175.
7 Laurence Senelick, 'Chekhov's Response to Sarah Bernhardt', in Salmon ed., p. 173.
8 *New York Times*, 14 July 1889 – correspondence with a friend printed in *Vienne Neue Freie Presse*.
9 Brandes, *Reminiscences of my Childhood and Youth*, p. 258.
10 Quoted John Stokes in Booth et al., *Bernhardt, Terry, Duse*, p. 45.
11 Quoted Rueff, p. 111.
12 James, *The Scenic Art*, pp. 316–7.
13 Bernhardt, *L'Art du Théâtre*, p. 143.
14 Guitry, pp. 153–4.
15 James, *The Scenic Art*, p. 312.
16 Rosemonde Gérard, *Edmond Rostand*, p. 57.
17 Ibid. p. 62.
18 Baring, *Sarah Bernhardt*, pp. 140–1.

Chapter 31

1 Quoted Weaver, p. 89.
2 Quoted Knepler, p. 183.
3 Ellen Terry, quoted Michael Booth, *Ellen Terry*, Booth et. al., p. 94.
4 Susan Bassnett, *Eleonora Duse*, Booth et al., p. 154.
5 Ibid.
6 Craig, *Life and Letters*, September 1928.
7 Montesquiou, *Les Pas éffacés*, vol. 3, p. 140.
8 Quoted Knepler, p. 248.
9 Bassnett in Booth et al. p. 125.
10 Shaw, *Our Theatre in the Nineties*, vol. 1 p. 154 (15 June 1895).
11 Knepler, p. 249.
12 Constant Coquelin, *Acting and Actors*, quoted Taranow, p. 235.
13 Quoted Taranow, p. 236.
14 Quoted Taranow p. 238.
15 May Agate, *Madame Sarah*, quoted Taranow, p. 238.
16 Jean-Jacques Weiss, *La Revue Bleue*, 29 Jan 1881, quoted Taranow, p. 243.
17 Quoted Bassnett, in Booth et al., p. 124.
18 Quoted Knepler, p. 194.
19 Beerbohm, *Around Theatres*, p. 80 (26 May 1900).
20 Shaw, *Our Theatre in the Nineties*, vol. 1, pp. 149–51 (15 June 1895).
21 Bernhardt, *L'Art du Théâtre*, quoted Taranow, p. 239.
22 Archer, *Theatrical World of 1895*, p. 205.
23 Quoted Knepler, p. 212.
24 Renard, *Journal*, 18 January 1896.
25 Ugo Ojetti, quoted Weaver, pp. 202–3.
26 Montesquiou, *Les Pas éffacés*, vol. 3, p. 142.
27 Victor Mapes, *Duse and the French*, p. 22.
28 Quoted Mapes, p. 47.
29 Weaver, p. 158.
30 Montesquiou, *Les Pas éffacés*, vol. 3, pp. 144–5.

Chapter 32

1 Gerard, pp. 67–8.
2 Maurice Rostand, *Mémoires d'un demi-siècle*, p. 52.
3 Knepler, p. 227.
4 Ibid. p. 228.
5 Ibid.
6 Goncourts, *Journal*, 10 October 1893.
7 Graham Robertson, p. 339.
8 Ibid.
9 Quoted Stokes, in Booth et al., p. 55.
10 Colette, *Paris-Soir*, 24 October 1938.

11 Rolland, *Théâtre du penple*, quoted Stokes, Booth et al., p. 29.
12 Jules Renard, *Journal*, 19 March 1907.
13 Lou Tellegen, *Women Have Been Kind*, p. 189.
14 Ibid. pp. 193–4.
15 Ibid. p. 202.
16 Quoted Knepler.
17 Rueff, p. 86.
18 See Zeldin, pp. 356–9.
19 Ibid. p. 355.
20 *Excelsior*, 25 January 1914.

Chapter 33

1 Lysiane Bernhardt, p. 210.
2 Béatrix Dussane, *Le Théâtre Illustré* (1923), quoted Lysiane Bernhardt, p. 213.
3 Ibid.
4 Lysiane Bernhardt, p. 218.
5 This account taken from Lysiane Bernhardt, pp. 218–22.

Chapter 34

1 *Comoedia*, 1 April 1920.
2 Quoted Skinner, p. 191.
3 Ibid.
4 Charles Cochran, quoted Richardson, *Sarah Bernhardt*, p. 179.
5 Verneuil, *La Vie merveilleuse de Sarah Bernhardt*, p. 19.
6 James Agate, *Alarums and Excursions*, p. 35.
7 Ibid.
8 Quoted Richardson, *Sarah Bernhardt*, pp. 178–9.
9 Elizabeth Finley Thomas quoted Skinner, p. 293.
10 Colette, *Paris-Soir*, 24 October 1938.
11 Colette, *Figaro Littéraire*, 23 March 1923.
12 James Agate, introduction to Bernhardt, *The Art of Theatre*, tr. Stenner.
13 Lysiane Bernhardt, p. 226.
14 Ibid. p. 228.
15 Maurice Rostand, *Sarah Bernhardt*.

Bibliography

Adam, Juliette: *Mes illusions et mes souffrances pendant le Siège de Paris* Paris, 1896.

Agate, James: *Alarums and Excursions*, London, 1922.

Agate, May: *Madame Sarah*, London, 1945.

Antoine, André: *Mes Souvenirs*, Paris, 1928.

Archer, William: *The Theatrical 'World' of 1893–7*, 5 vols. London, 1894–8.

Baring, Maurice: *Sarah Bernhardt*, London, 1933.

Baring, Maurice: *The Puppet-Show of Memory*, London, 1922.

Beerbohm, Max: *Around Theatres*, London 1924, reprinted 1953.

Bernhardt, Lysiane: *Sarah Bernhardt, My Grandmother*, London, 1949.

Bernhardt, Sarah: *Dans les Nuages: Impressions d'une Chaise*, Paris, 1878.

Bernhardt, Sarah: *Ma double vie*, vols. 1 and 2, Paris, 1907.

Bernhardt, Sarah: *L'Art du Théâtre*, Paris, 1923.

Bernhardt, Sarah: *The Art of the Theatre*, preface by James Agate, London, 1924.

Bernhardt, Sarah: *Petite Idole*, Paris, 1920.

Berton, Thérèse (as told to Basil Woon): *Sarah Bernhardt As I Knew Her*, London, 1923.

Booth et. al.: *Bernhardt, Terry, Duse: The Actress in her Time*, Cambridge, 1988.

Bourget, Paul: *Outre-Mer – Impressions of America*, London, 1895.

Bradbrook, M. C.: *Paris in the Bernhardt era: Collected Papers*, vol. 2, Sussex, 1982.

Brandes, Georg: *Reminiscences of my Childhood and Youth*, London,. 1906

Campbell, Mrs Patrick: *My Life and some Letters*, London, 1922.

Castelot, André: *Sarah Bernhardt*, Paris, 1961.

Champsaur, Félicien: *Dinah Samuel*, Paris, 1882.

Christiansen, Rupert: *Romantic Affinities: portraits from an age: 1780–1830*, London, 1988.

Colette: *Mes Apprentissages*, Paris, 1936.

Colette: *La Naissance du jour*, Paris, 1928.

Colombier, Marie: *Les Mémoires de Sarah Barnum*, Paris, 1883.
Colombier, Marie: *Le Voyage de Sarah Bernhardt en Amérique*, Paris, 1882.
Colombier, Marie: *Affaire Sarah Bernhardt – Marie Colombier – Pièces à Conviction*, Paris, 1884.
Dijkstra, Bram: *Idols of Perversity*, Oxford, 1986.
d'Heylli, Georges: *La Comédie-Française à Londres (1871–1879)*, Journal inedit de E. Got et F. Sarcey, Paris, 1880.
Dumas *fils*, Alexandre: *Théâtre complet*, avec préfaces inédits, Paris, 1868–95.
Ellmann, R.: *Oscar Wilde*, London, 1987.
Emboden, William: *Sarah Bernhardt*, London, 1974.
Feuillet, Mme Octave: *Souvenirs et Correspondances*, Paris, 1896.
Field, Osgood: *Uncensored Recollections*, London, 1923.
Flaubert, Gustave: *Letters, 1830–1857, 1857–1880*, translated and edited by Francis Steegmuller, London, 1979, 1980.
Fraser, Sylvia: *My Father's House*, New York, 1988.
Gaillet, Eugène, and Liébold: *La Vie de Marie Pigeonnier*, Paris, 1884.
Gautier, Judith: *Le Collier des jours: souvenirs de ma vie*, Paris, 1902.
Gautier, Judith: *Le Second Rang du collier*, Paris, 1903.
Gérard, Rosemonde: *Edmond Rostand*, Paris, 1935.
Giacosa, Giuseppe: *Impressioni d'America*, Milan, 1898.
Gill, André: *Vingt Ans de Paris*, Paris, 1883.
Goncourt, Edmond de: *La Faustin*, Edition definitive, Paris, 1962.
Goncourt, Edmond and Jules de: *Journal 1851–95*, vols 1–9, Paris, 1887–1896.
Gros, Johannès: *Alexandre Dumas et Marie Duplessis*, Paris, 1923.
Guitry, Sacha: *Souvenirs: Si j'ai bonne mémoire*, Paris, 1934.
Hahn, Reynaldo: *La Grande Sarah*, Paris, 1930.
Hansen, Eric C.: *Ludovic Halévy – A study of frivolity and fatalism in Nineteenth-century France*, Lanham, Maryland, 1987.
d'Hartoy, Maurice: *Dumas fils Inconnu*, Paris, 1966.
Houssaye, Arsène, *Les Confessions: Souvenirs d'un demi-siècle 1830–1880*, vols. 1–VI, reprinted Geneva, 1971.
Humphrey, Nick, and Daniel C. Dennett: *Speaking for Ourselves: An Assessment of Multiple Personality Disorder*, Raritan, New Brunswick, 1989.
Huret, Jules: *Sarah Bernhardt*, tr. G. A. Raper, London, 1899.
James, Alice: *The Diary of Alice James*, ed. Leon Edel, London, 1965.
James, Henry: *The Scenic Art*, New Brunswick, 1948.
James, Henry: *The Tragic Muse*, London, 1890.
Jarry, Alfred: *Ubu*, ed. Noel Arnaud, Paris, 1978.
Jones, Ernest: *Sigmund Freud*, 3 vols, London, 1953–58.
Kelly, Linda: *The Young Romantics: Paris 1827–37*, London, 1976.
Knepler, Henry: *The Gilded Stage*, London, 1968. .

Lanco, Yvonne: *Belle-Isle-Sur-Mer: Sarah Bernhardt – souvenirs*, Paris n.d.

Langtry, Lillie (Lady de Bathe): *The Days I Knew*, London, 1925.

Lemaître, Jules: *Les Contemporains*, Vols. 2, 3, 5, Paris, 1886, 1891, 1892.

Louÿs, Pierre: *Journal intime 1882–1891*, Paris, 1929.

Loti, Pierre: *Journal intime, 1878–81*, Paris, 1925.

Manifold, Gay, *George Sand's Theatre Career*, Ann Arbor, 1985.

Mapes, Victor: *Duse and the French*, New York, 1898.

Metcalfe, Cranstoun: *Peeresses of the Stage*, London, 1913.

Meyer, Arthur: *Ce que mes yeux ont vu*, Paris, 1911.

Meyer, Arthur: *Ce que je peux dire*, Paris, 1912.

Miller, Alice: *The Drama of the Gifted Child*, London, 1987.

Montesquiou, Comte Robert de: *Les Pas Effacés: Mémoires*, Paris, 1923.

Moréno, Marguerite: *Souvenirs de ma vie*, Paris, 1948.

Painter, G.: *Marcel Proust*, 2 vols. London, 1959–65.

Porel, Jacques: *Fils de Réjane*, Paris, 1951.

Pougy, Liane de: *My Blue Notebooks*, tr. Diana Athill, London, 1979.

Pougy, Liane de: *Idylle saphique, 1901*; new edition, Paris, 1979.

Primoli, Count Joseph, *Pages inédites*, Rome, 1959.

Pronier, Ernest: *Sarah Bernhardt*, Geneva, 1942.

Renard, Jules: *Journal 1887–1910*, Paris, 1925–27.

Richardson, Joanna: *Sarah Bernhardt*, London, 1959.

Richardson, Joanna: *Sarah Bernhardt and her World*, London, 1977.

Richardson, Joanna: *Théophile Gautier – his life and times*, London, 1958.

Richardson, Joanna: *La Vie Parisienne 1852–70*, London, 1971.

Richardson, Joanna: *The Courtesans: The demi-monde in nineteenth-century France*, London, 1967.

Robertson, W. Graham: *Time Was: Reminiscences*, London, 1931.

Rostand, Maurice: *Confession d'un demi-siècle*, Paris, 1948.

Rostand, Maurice: *Sarah Bernhardt*, Paris, 1950.

Rueff, Suze: *I Knew Sarah Bernhardt*, London, 1951.

Salmon, Eric, ed: *Bernhardt and the Theatre of her Time*, Canada, 1978.

Sarcey, Francisque: *Quarante ans de théâtre*, vols. 1–8, Paris, 1900–1902.

Sardou, Victorien: *Les Papiers de Victorien Sardou*, ed. G. Mouly, Paris, 1934.

Scott, Clement, *Some Notable 'Hamlets' of the Present Time*, London, 1900.

Shaw, G. B.: *Our Theatres in the Nineties*, 3 vols., London, 1948.

Skinner, Cornelia Otis: *Madame Sarah*, London, 1967.

Stephens, Winifred: *Madame Adam*, London, 1917.

Taranow, Gerda: *Sarah Bernhardt: The Art within the Legend*, Princeton, 1972.

Tellegen, Lou: *Women have been Kind*, London, 1932.

Terry, Ellen: *The Story of my Life*, London, 1908.

Toklas, Alice B., *What is Remembered*, London, 1963.

Verneuil, Louis: *Rideau à neuf heures*, Paris, 1946.

Verneuil, Louis: *La Vie merveilleuse de Sarah Bernhardt*, Montreal, 1942.

Weaver, William: *Duse: A Biography*, London, 1984.

Zeldin, Theodore: *France 1848–1945: Vol. 1: Ambition, love and politics*, Oxford, 1973.

Index